LEO DILLON

Rachel Fouché

French Power in Africa

To CARROLL CHIPMAN

who died shortly before this manuscript was completed
and who would have taken great pride in reading it as
well as pleasure in commenting on it – kindly pointing
out its faults, warmly encouraging me to improve it
and generally, as always, providing wise counsel.

French Power in Africa

JOHN CHIPMAN

Basil Blackwell

Copyright © John Chipman 1989

First published 1989

Basil Blackwell Ltd
108 Cowley Road, Oxford, OX4 1JF, UK

Basil Blackwell, Inc.
3 Cambridge Center
Cambridge, Massachusetts 02142, USA

British Library Cataloguing in Publication Data

A CIP catalogue record for this book is available from the British Library.

Library of Congress Cataloging in Publication Data

Chipman. John.
French Power in Africa / John Chipman.
    p.   cm.
Revision of the author's thesis (Ph.D.)–Balliol College. 1986.

Bibliography: p.
Includes index.
ISBN 0-631-16819-2
1. Africa–Foreign relations–France.   2. France–Foreign
relations–Africa   3. France–Colonies–Africa.   4. Economic
assistance, French–Africa.   5. Military assistance, French–Africa.
I. Title.
DT33.C48 1989
327.4406–dc20   89-7198
                                                                 CIP

Typeset in 10/12pt Stempel Garamond by Ponting–Green Publishing Services, London
Printed in Great Britain by Billing and Sons Ltd., Worcester

Contents

List of Tables

Preface

For the genesis of this book I owe much, as do many others, to the late Professor Hedley Bull, who in 1981 suggested that I begin to investigate the history of the relationship between France and Africa and the sources of current French policy towards Black Africa. I am grateful to him for his initial encouragement and general guidance. It was in good measure the kind faith he displayed towards my early work which provided me with the later incentives to complete this study. The International Institute for Strategic Studies (IISS) funded a trip of mine in 1984 to Senegal, Ivory Coast, Gabon, Togo, and the Central African Republic, during which I had numerous interviews and informal conversations with both French and African officials. While in Paris between 1985 and 1987 I conducted many other interviews with French policy makers and past government officials. Though relying mainly on printed documents and published sources, this book owes much to the perspectives and personal experiences of the many French and African officials who agreed to give me their impressions of the unique Franco–African relationship. On my return to the IISS in 1987 to take up the post of Assistant Director for Regional Security Studies I was much helped by the kindness of Dr Robert O'Neill, then Director of IISS, who allowed me to take some time away from my IISS duties to complete my D.Phil. thesis (Balliol College, Oxford, defended in 1988). From October 1987 to April 1988 François Heisbourg, the new Director of the IISS, and other members of the directing staff kindly tolerated my many days away from the IISS. Numerous individuals, many of whom would prefer to remain unnamed, commented on the early drafts of this work, and to them I am most grateful for the efforts they made to help clarify my argument. Nicoline van der Woerd, my assistant at the IISS, prepared the final manuscript for publication and helped compile the index. For these tiresome, but absolutely necessary labours, she deserves special thanks. Finally, none of this work would have been possible without the moral and other support of my father, Carroll Chipman, who died a few days before I finished the thesis on which this book is based, and to whom it is dedicated.

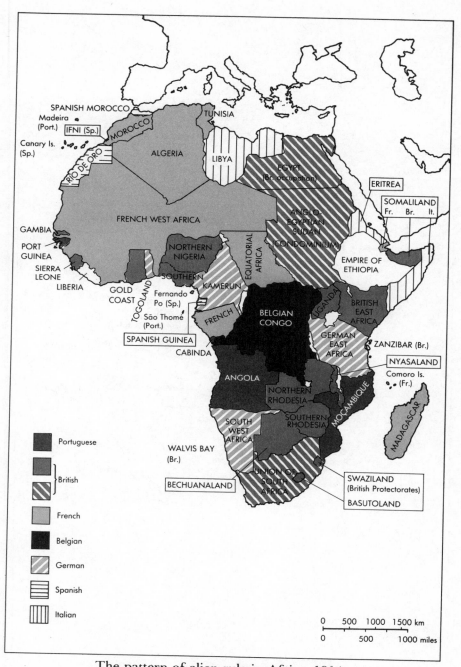

SPANISH MOROCCO
Madeira
(Port.)
IFNI (Sp.)
Canary Is.
(Sp.)
MOROCCO
RIO DE ORO
ALGERIA
TUNISIA
LIBYA
EGYPT
(Br. occupation)
ERITREA
SOMALILAND
Fr.   Br.   It.
ANGLO-
EGYPTIAN
SUDAN
(CONDOMINIUM)
FRENCH WEST AFRICA
EMPIRE OF
ETHIOPIA
GAMBIA
PORT
GUINEA
SIERRA
LEONE
LIBERIA
GOLD
COAST
NORTHERN
NIGERIA
SOUTHERN
TOGOLAND
KAMERUN
EQUATORIAL
AFRICA
Fernando
Po (Sp.)
São Thomé
(Port.)
FRENCH
SPANISH GUINEA
CABINDA
BELGIAN
CONGO
UGANDA
BRITISH
EAST
AFRICA
GERMAN
EAST
AFRICA
ZANZIBAR (Br.)
NYASALAND
Comoro Is.
(Fr.)
ANGOLA
NORTHERN
RHODESIA
SOUTHERN
RHODESIA
MOÇAMBIQUE
MADAGASCAR
SOUTH
WEST
AFRICA
WALVIS BAY
(Br.)
UNION OF
SOUTH
AFRICA
BECHUANALAND
SWAZILAND
(British Protectorates)
BASUTOLAND

Portuguese

British

French

Belgian

German

Spanish

Italian

0   500   1000 1500 km

0   500   1000 miles

The pattern of alien rule in Africa, 1914.

Source: *Africa South of the Sahara*, 18th edn. London: Europa Publications, 1988, p. 14

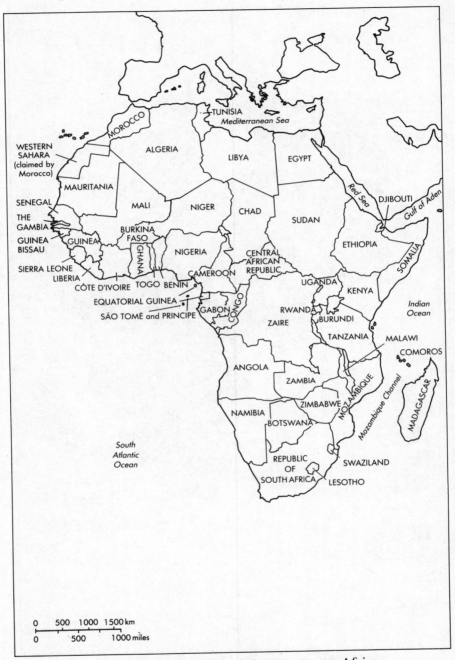

Outline Political Map of Contemporary Africa

Source: Africa South of the Sahara, 18th edn. London: Europa Publications, 1988, p. 288

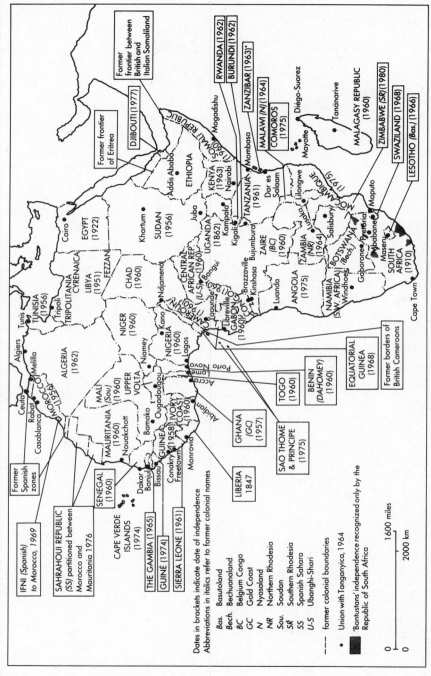

Political Africa, 1919–87

Source: J. D. Hargreaves, *Decolonization in Africa.* New York: Longman and New, 1988

Introduction

Africa arouses not only interest but passions in France. In the mid-nineteenth century French troops landed in Algiers because the dey had said nasty things to the French consul. In the late nineteenth century French political leaders attributed quite mystical importance to France's enlarging African Empire. Losing North Africa in the mid-twentieth century wrenched the nation apart. Hanging on to influence in independent francophone Africa is seen in the late twentieth century as a vital element of France's continued status in the international community. The French have had a long association with Africa, which dates back (in the case of Senegal) at least to the seventeenth century. Yet for over the last hundred years or so, the importance of Africa to France has been in the fact that France's political leadership has consistently used the nature of France's sway over parts of the continent to help define the power of France.

This book is an examination of French power in Africa. It argues that for successive French republics continued French influence in Africa has been an essential aim. Accomplishment of this aim has been linked to maintaining the strength of the state, to assuring some measure of success in implicit or explicit geopolitical struggles, and to improving the image of French power on the world stage. The fact of overseas influence, particularly in Africa, has helped to sustain the idea that the values of the French republic were universal. The maintenance of different degrees of influence in Africa and the French capacity to preserve independent and unique ties on that continent has helped to bolster claims to great-power status. The specific nature of French power in Africa, which is justified and presented as of benefit to the Africans, and as a reflection of basic values of the French state, in turn has helped French leaders preserve French prestige on the European continent and France's reputation as an important world power.

In the nineteenth century French leaders often argued that conquests and control overseas bolstered French power, but this sense of the importance of extra-metropolitan activity was especially strong in Africa. For most of the late nineteenth century and the first half of the twentieth century North Africa, geographically closest to France and also the place where Frenchmen settled with most ease, was the region of Africa which advocates of imperial strength felt contributed most to French power. Algeria, which was an integral part of France from 1848, and the protectorates of Tunisia (acquired by treaty in 1881) and Morocco (gained after negotiation with Germany in 1911) came to form a coherent geographical whole whose links with France were immensely important for those who wished to nurture the image of a 'Greater France'. Influence in North Africa was sought and cultivated with vigour and tenacity to give shape and substance to the idea that France was a European power with strengths on both sides of the Mediterranean. France's various possessions in Black Africa never had the same prestige as those in North Africa.

Dakar in Senegal and Brazzaville in the French Congo had some importance as the capitals of the two great areas which France controlled: *Afrique Occidentale Française* and *Afrique Equatoriale Française* but these areas held a relatively insignificant place in the hierarchy of France's imperial interests. Difficult and protracted battles were sometimes fought against powerful local warriors to acquire possessions in these areas, but there was still some truth in the austere judgement offered in 1934 by the *Cambridge Modern History* which noted that the French understood that: 'Organized travel and conquest were almost synonymous in three-quarters of Africa.'[1] Conquests in Black Africa were therefore made as much to add to the size of the Empire as to gain particular advantages, a fact cynically remarked upon by some French opponents of imperial expansion in the 1880s and 1890s. Supporters of colonialism effectively succeeded in entrenching the idea that French power and respect were distinctly related to France's degree of domination over others despite the intrinsic weakness of some of the objects of French military might and colonizing energies. Algeria would not suffice, Black Africa had also to interest France, or else others would move in and deprive France of an area in which to demonstrate the acceptability and hence the superiority of her culture and institutions.

As time went on, France's influence in Black Africa came to gain more importance. The contribution of Black Africa, in different ways, to the two world wars did raise the importance of this area in the eyes of many Frenchmen. After France lost her North African possessions, much of the ideology of France's African power which was attached to Algeria, Morocco and Tunisia, was transferred effectively to Black Africa. Since decolonization, France's continuing influence in the weakest part of the former Empire has been held up with pride by French leaders eager to claim that France is a power whose external strength – even in the admittedly impoverished regions of Black Africa – contributes substantially to French grandeur. This habit of mind is rooted in France's colonial past and appears even anachronistic to most contemporary observers. Yet the importance attached to these notions of externally derived power continues to exercise the adminstrative organs of the French state, and the passions of its political leadership. The early part of this book therefore focuses on the idea of overseas power (with special reference both to North Africa and Black Africa), the latter part on the management of France's power in Black Africa where French power is still strongly felt.

To understand the importance of Africa to France it is necessary to examine the ways in which the French themselves have defined the nature and sources of French power. These definitions have remained essentially constant, and have proved adaptable to changes in France's direct power in various regions. To appreciate how France sustains influence in Black Africa today, one must look at the form of French power on the African continent and the part the Africans have played in shaping the Franco–African relationship since the nineteenth century. French power in Africa can still be wielded largely because the African elites have collaborated in its maintenance. Finally, to grasp the use that France has made of proven successes in Africa, it is vital to see that the ideology of French world power generally and the images of French power in Africa specifically, have been inextricably linked and mutually reinforcing. A persistent myth espoused by French leaders, now implicitly accepted by the public, has been that Africa in both a material and psychological sense has served as a repository and source of French grandeur and strength.

Despite the claims of some of the more enthusiastic adventurers and colonial propagandists in the 'age of imperialism', African possessions did not contribute to French economic strength. North Africa did offer some markets for French goods, and raw materials were sometimes imported from there, but Black Africa was never an important trading area for France. North Africa may have been a buffer zone for French possessions in Black Africa, but it also needed military protection that risked drawing down forces needed for the defence of the French position in Europe. The most tangible contribution made to French power by the Africans was their participation in French war efforts, particularly in the First, but also in the Second World War, and it was this contribution which brought home to French public opinion the putative value of Empire. Still, the *intangible* contribution Africans have made to French power has always been thought at least as important by French leaders and publicists who developed an 'idea' of French power defended in international councils to protect and enhance French status. A capacity to exert political and military influence in

Africa has been maintained in order to give substance to an idea of power whose coherence the official Gallic mentality has often considered as important as the actual practice of power. Because, at various times, different regions of Africa have been controlled or affected by French political ambitions, this has made Africa important as a contributor to the imagery of French power. France maintains influence in Africa in order to prove she is still a major power; she is obliged to continue to appear relevant to African needs and aspirations so that her power can be maintained and perpetuated. This relationship now maintained with Black Africa is the last vestige of French imperial logic, and its deterioration would, in French official eyes, damage French prestige.

This book looks at the roots and nature of the idea that French power in Africa is an essential component of France's political strength and status because that idea persists and is part of the French political heritage that influences current policy. It then examines the scope and style of the post-colonial practice of power in Black Africa that French governments feel makes France a special actor in the contemporary international system, where influence without conquest commands respect.

Overseas Influence and the French State

The French Empire in Africa was constructed by adventurers and justified by propagandists. The acquisition of African colonies in the late nineteenth century was by and large an operation in which the state eventually acquiesced, but which was in no sense centrally directed. Only later did the idea of state and regime strength become associated with the possession and the maintenance of power overseas. Though the state did not initially push for colonial expansion, possessions were assembled on *behalf* of the French state and different regimes accepted responsibility for retaining the French position *outre-mer*. For this reason, external losses or shocks affected the whole of the French state rather than, as would be the case in Britain, political parties and their leaders.

Imperial control became closely wrapped up with the definition of French national identity; an assault on the structure of overseas possessions was an assault on the French state. While even during the Third and Fourth Republics the colonial cause was defended largely by individuals on the periphery of national life, external defeats affected the state, not merely the party in power. It was the Fourth Republic, not just a certain political grouping, that fell in 1958 owing to a perceived weakness in handling a colonial question.[2] After decolonization, the continuance of some residual influence in Black Africa was connected to a conception of French power and status. At the moment of colonization, the state was indifferent, even sometimes opposed, to imperial designs; in the post-imperial world, loss of influence overseas would be perceived as immediately affecting French status, prestige, and position in the international system.

This specific, eventually Gaullist, conception, that the most important role of the French state was the external defence of national independence persists and serves to condition the behaviour of the French state abroad. In the post-colonial era, the continuing overseas influence of France, particularly in Black Africa, has been supported by the fact that the new ex-colonial leadership *outre-mer* actively sought French assistance and even demanded that there be some continuity of French influence. But important as the evidence of some African desire for a French role may have been, the existence and further development of axioms and myths supporting this role was vital to sustain the legitimacy of the French presence. Certainly the long-standing *image* of France in Africa was held up by French leaders before French public opinion which, though previously uninterested in Empire, could nevertheless be engaged by the idea that the French national identity still deserved, and even needed, an African reflection.

This image was of a France whose standing in the world could be gauged by the number of people who looked to it for a cultural or political lead. De Gaulle's great criticism of the Armistice in 1940, had been that those who had negotiated it had misunderstood the 'immense forces' that France still maintained in the Empire.[3] References to Franco–African, Eurafrican and francophone 'unities' would later, as they had sometimes before, help perpetuate the myth that there was a natural logic to France's influence in Africa. In the days of Empire, as well as in the days since decolonization, that influence had economic costs, insofar as the importance of Africa as a market or as an irreplaceable source of raw materials was never as high as so often presumed. But these costs have always been thought worth incurring, because of the increased strength that a role in Africa could give to the state in France. The persistence with which French leaders have sought an individual role in Africa cannot be understood without reference to concepts of French power and the geopolitical circumstances in which that power was engaged.

After decolonization, the nature of the French relationship with its ex-colonies was structured to retain basic influence in those areas in which France formerly held imperial sway, while the presentation of that relationship was such as to emphasize France's basic affinity with the policies of independence pursued by the new countries. The importance of the presentational aspects of this relationship cannot be underestimated, for it is on the basis of the French argument that national policy is scaled to meet the essentials of African political and economic needs that French power can still be wielded effectively. France has succeeded in the post-colonial world in managing her relationships in Africa using the language of common partnership, co-operation and shared destiny. Though the days of Empire and of the French African Community are long past, France is still able, through the annual Franco–African summit meetings, to arrange her affairs with the African leadership on an apparently collective basis. While such meetings, and the relationships between France and Black African states in general, sometimes reveal the limitation of French power, they do so in ways which do not reflect adversely on the strength of the French political dream.

Part of that dream is to hold sway in Africa. France is still able to have her voice heard in African affairs. Her economic assistance is central to the development of Black African states, her military force vital for their defence. Decisions in many Black African states are still taken with the possible reaction of France in mind. France remains a point of reference for many of her ex-colonies in Africa, as a model, and as a link to the outside world. The respect with which France is still held in many parts of Black Africa allows French leaders to speak in almost imperial terms about the nature of extra-metropolitan power and the political benefits that accrue from this are thought to include the enhancement of France's image as a unique power in the contemporary international system. Often in French history, the claim that history has conferred on France a special world role has been matched by energetic attempts to make this claim appear realistic to France's friends and rivals. Sometimes, as for all powers, ambitious claims and the existence of demonstrable power have not perfectly co-existed. In the Fifth Republic, the desire for a continued place among the great powers, and the existence of the French lien on part of Africa have been linked, so that at least in this special respect, French political ambition has had some relationship with political reality.

Overseas Influence and Geopolitics

It is in this sense that France's post-imperial action in Africa is closely related, as in the days of Empire, to the geopolitical circumstances of the time. Often the French have asserted their importance in world affairs in absolute terms, without special reference to the relative powers of other states. Insisting on the uniqueness of French political traditions or culture, French leaders have often argued that France should command respect in international fora. But French leaders have equally tried to give substance to the abstraction of French power by ensuring that direct French influence could still be exerted overseas. The existence of overseas power has thus often been used rhetorically, but with considerable effect, to claim special status in Europe. Since the end of the Franco–Prussian war, perceptions of the French ability to act in world affairs have been dependent on the ability to wield successfully either continental or imperial power. In the nineteenth century, nationalist ideology itself was essentially divided between a European and a colonial variant.[4] The famous debate in the Chamber of Deputies in 1885 over the vote of credits for an expedition to Madagascar had seen the confrontation between these two principal visions of France – as a power oriented towards Europe, and as one having a special role *outre-mer*,[5] and by the time Charles de Gaulle had come to power in 1958 little, in this respect, had changed. The power of the French state in Europe was still seen by some as giving it regional power in Africa and the Mediterranean, by others as deriving from 'prestige' in the region in which French power, though challenged, was still accepted.

After the Second World War, French leaders claimed that France belonged to the councils of the great powers because it had an empire, and claimed, equally, to the peoples of the colonies, that it was their share of French grandeur, power, and 'independence' which gave them a special status. The importance that de Gaulle attached to francophone Black Africa after he came to power was unquestionably related to his ambitions in Europe. As a result, some have seen French foreign policy in the Fifth Republic as being determined by considerations of whether global or regional positions and responsibilities should be given preminence. One writer has suggested, for example, that while under de Gaulle the concepts of French grandeur and world-wide interests defined French policy in particular regions – that 'regionalism followed globalism', the Pompidou presidency saw a reversal of this axiom since global claims were based on the cultivation of a firm regional base so that 'globalism followed regionalism'.[6] While these sorts of generalizations hold some validity, they fail to explain how closely the concepts of local and world power are related, and how they have been seen by all leaders of the Fifth Republic as being dependent on each other. Questions of priority have not always been relevant.

The traditional debate in France on the importance of continental *vis-à-vis* imperial power, sometimes translated more broadly into a debate on the tensions between global and regional power, is one which for all states are seen as deriving from the nature of what we recently began to call 'geopolitics.' It is clearly inappropriate to consider global power and regional considerations as polar opposites since 'good regionalism is good geopolitics and bad regionalism is bad geopolitics.'[7] For one observer:

Geopolitics is, definitionally, the art and the process of managing global rivalry; and success, again definitionally, consists at a maximum of consolidating the strength and cohesion of the group of nations which form the core of one's power position, while preventing the other side from extending the area of its domination and clientele.[8]

While this definition was made in relation to a discussion of American power, it is equally relevant to an analysis of French foreign policy, given that its rhetoric, and at least some of its practice, has been devoted to sustaining a claim to great-power status. If this was to be successful, then the geopolitics of regionalism had to be well understood. To borrow again from the views of a former British ambassador to the US on American power:

Strength and toughness have their place, as does the ability discreetly to aid well disposed internal political forces in key countries whose geopolitical orientation hangs in the balance. All of these are necessary conditions; but none is a sufficient condition. A successful superpower must be able to display overt principles which are, in Kissinger's words, 'relevant to one of the great revolutions of our time', if it is to catch the regional tides that lead to geopolitical success.[9]

From 1960 onwards the French case for 'catching the regional tide' was based on France having understood the principal post-war revolution, and having revised the terms of the colonial pact. France had accepted the claims for independence from imperial masters (which the French government was making against the two superpower blocs), and struck a new bargain with the peoples of Africa who were still to a large extent sympathetic to the French position. For de Gaulle, as for subsequent French leaders, France's natural sphere of influence included Africa and the Middle East no less than Europe.[10] French leadership in all these areas, and arguably more so in Africa where its power could effect the most change, was intrinsic to the French geopolitical tradition, developed since 1870. Any global success had to be based on managing relations with Europe, Africa – and, to the extent that it impinged on the problems encountered in either of these two continents, the Middle East. The management of these various spheres of influence has been central to France's claim that it is a global power. The individualistic French foreign policy pursued in each of these areas can only be understood in the light of the evident French belief that France's singular approach to foreign policy helps to sustain French power. Certainly in Black Africa, where French economic, military and diplomatic weight can have a direct effect on the local situation, France has been keen to ensure that it remains the only *interlocuteur valable* of African states, since influence shared may be influence lost. The contemporary French desire for 'independent' approaches to both European and extra-European affairs has its intellectual roots in the imperial age. No other former great power has been so faithful to its attitudes of the past, no other so successful in transporting seemingly outdated images of power into the political discourse of the late twentieth century.

French colonial thinking had always emphasized the utility of the imperial adventure, on the grounds of the boost its success would give to French power on the European continent, and this argument persists. While some nineteenth-century nationalists argued that colonial activity was a strain on power (just as some today view development assistance as a waste), the supporters of imperialism were always able to rely on the argument (as do current proponents of France's extra-European policies), that power in Africa (less so in Asia) was vital if French status in Europe was to be maintained. Parallel to this line of thinking, to the effect that the creation of a France *outre-mer* was among the great missions France owed to history, (the idea of Jules Ferry in the 1880s, and of Charles de Gaulle in the 1960s) lay the idea (of Aristide Briand in the 1930s and Valéry Giscard d'Estaing in the 1970s) that peace both in Europe and Africa was only possible through the creation of a *Eurafrique*. Such a unity, these men thought, would protect the two continents both against the fissures caused by internal divisions, and those caused by outside interventions from great powers. In both cases the role of France was paramount, and the types of decisions taken by leaders of the Fifth Republic, as they have turned their minds to African problems, have been dependent on whether they thought that France should lead the countries of Black Africa, and convince them of the values inherent in sharing a glory that was exclusive to France, or that France should lead the countries of Europe in a rapprochement with all of Africa that would have meaning as much in economic, as in power political terms.

For those who, like Pompidou, saw the exercise of regional power and influence as dependent more on considerations of immediate expedience than on the need to create a permanent French or European sphere of influence, questions of African and regional power did not pose themselves so strictly, since the aim was more to create an *entente* with all, rather than a special relationship with traditional friends. For Pompidou, the hope of creating a sea of peace out of the Mediterranean was the basis of the myth that guided his foreign policy outside the continent, and visions of either a *France–Afrique*, or a *Eurafrique* were largely absent. Some of the practical tensions created by these myths, however, such as the decisions relating to whether a bilateral or multilateral aid policy to Africa was preferable, persisted, and gave evidence, if any was needed, that the problems of spheres of influence were not dead and could indeed be revived.

Overseas Influence and French Power

Certainly for all leaders of the Fifth Republic (as well as for those of the Fourth) the French imperial adventure had brought a number of rewards in the form of increased standing in the world community, with a number of responsibilities in the form of the need to ensure the wellbeing of those areas that had come under the imperial mantle. The geographic proximity of the African continent, and the history of the French experience there, meant that no president of the Fifth Republic could consider that French vital interests were not in some way engaged in Africa. While after 1960 or so, any action in Africa by Europeans as a group, or by France alone, would necessarily be attacked as 'neocolonialist', there was a sense in which a good deal of French activity in Black Africa was undertaken not only with compliance, but at the request of African leaders, so that French influence in the region came to be related both to the nature of French power as wielded by the French leaders, and to the definition given that power by African statesmen. That is, the claim of French global power being based in part on the fact of influence in Africa could be affected by the desire of Africans to move away from French control; and the attempt by various French governments to reimpose French influence in Africa, in different forms, grew out of an understanding that changing circumstances required different strategies. Privileged links could exist between equals, and French leaders have been careful to adopt the language of equality to ensure the preservation of influence in Africa. Early on it was understood that French power would be best served by adopting a stance towards the Africans that implicated them in a share of common power. In the creation of these relations the myths of 'France–Afrique' and 'Eurafrique' played an important role. French leaders have traditionally thought it insufficient merely to exert power, this power has had to issue from a design and be driven by an 'idea'.

In the postwar era, while the advent of nuclear weapons, and the position of the United States and the Soviet Union has created new measures of power, the French claim to having the ear of the Third World, of having been receptive to one of 'the greatest revolutions of our time', has come to form the basis of a new geopolitical strategy. The importance of overseas power was reasserted and helped to supply the rationale for a French claim of grandeur between the blocs. As the major continental European power, as the major outside power in Africa, France, the argument has gone, is in a unique position to stand as arbiter between the two continents. This perception that French influence in Africa and the 'privileged relations' France has with Africa are unique has been presented by French leaders as an important measure of French power.

Ever since the nineteenth century, French statesmen have intermittently referred to the vital boost that French power overseas could give to the French in Europe. These proclamations were naturally always related to specific domestic and international circumstances. They were not always profoundly felt by the French people. But by decolonization so much official political capital had been spent in promoting the idea that French power in Africa was an inherent and necessary feature of French power generally, that political leaders were forced to find new ways of maintaining French influence and prestige despite the juridical independence of ex-colonies in francophone Black Africa. The idea of French power in Africa could not be abandoned even if it had been directly challenged in rebellion. In the 1960s the idea was reshaped, and a new policy towards Black Africa was established which has perpetuated French regional power in Africa. This book shows that there is a close relationship between the presentational aspects of French power, the myths that have helped in the expression of influence overseas, the action that has ensued from the basic French decision to maintain a role in Africa and the form of current political, military, economic and diplomatic activity in Africa. It analyses how French leaders have used the language of power to achieve power in Africa, and how they have tailored that language to a perception of a link between influence in Africa and continental stature.

French Power and Africa: Methods and Sources of Analysis

Since this book attempts to explain the idea of French power in Africa and its current practice, the analysis is centred on the presentation of the concept and pursuit of the ends of power in Africa. It is neither a history of French imperialism nor an analysis of present French foreign policy towards African countries. Rather, it is an intellectual history of how Africa has figured in debates on French power, and an explanation of how French power in Africa is currently managed. As an intellectual history, it covers three broad themes: the idea of French power generally, the role of Africa and French colonies in the definition of that power, and the nature of the myths that served to create images of French power and influence in Africa. Analysis of these themes over the first three chapters of the book is intentionally not strictly chronological since the aim is to show that, at very different times, similar definitions of power were made, the same link with Africa drawn, and identical images called up by French leaders to explain France's African vocation. In these chapters, the book draws on some theoretical writing on the nature of power and international relations, primary sources such as the writings and speeches of politicians and colonial advocates, and secondary sources that have drawn attention to the ideological aspects of French power in explaining the history of the French imperial design.

In explaining the current strength of French power in Africa the book concentrates largely on Black Africa, since it is there that French power is exercised most effectively. The focus is on military power, because it is the links created by military co-operation and defence agreements that are most important in explaining the endurance of French influence in Africa. The scope of French economic activity in Africa is reviewed to show that though there is important activity, this is not central to the French economy and that the key feature of French economic influence in Africa remains the mere existence of the Franc Zone which links the economies of several African states to the stability of France's currency. French diplomatic power in Africa is analysed to prove the essential point that images still play a role in nurturing French links with African elites who see a need still to be co-opted into French political designs. In the chapters that cover these subjects reliance is placed on official government publications, specialized secondary source analyses of specific technical questions, and a good deal of interview material collected in France and numerous African countries.

he central chapter on decolonization attempts, not a history, but an analytical treatment of the link between the idea of French power in Africa and its post-imperial practice. It is through this chapter that the three main questions of the book are reflected: How did Africa gain its importance for French leaders concerned with the power of the French state? How was the idea of French power in Africa affected by the experience of decolonization? How is the present substance and scope of French power in Africa sustained by the French state? The sections that precede and follow this chapter seek directly to address these points. They show how France has been able, with enormous practical effect, to transform an ideology of overseas power into continuous influence in Africa even after having suffered defeats in particular areas. Though French power is now most relevant in the least developed part of her former Empire, Black Africa, France has proved herself capable of adapting her basic conception of overseas power to conform to the changing configurations of that power.

In pursuing these issues, I accept the view that at least in the French case a national ideology of power was the primary motivating force of the latter stage of imperialism. French explorers set out to conquer, and tried to give a certain symmetry to French overseas possessions. But in providing a rationale for these efforts, leaders in Paris referred to the need to expand in order to give shape to French power and in so doing gave expression and, by repetition, depth, to a basic ideology of French power. This ideology was summarized in the almost tautological notion that for France to be great it had to expand, and by expansion it gave proof of its greatness. Similarly, this book supports the argument that the capacity of imperialist states to co-opt native elites was a fundamental reason for the success of the imperial design. In the British case, emphasis came to be based on political structures – the Westminster model – in the French instance, the message was primarily cultural – the *mission civilisatrice* – which held out the promise of bringing together natives and Frenchmen into a common purpose. France's ability to carry this experience forward into the post-imperial age is unique and justifies the judgement of this book that the present form of Franco–African relations, based as it is on a specific idea and practice of national power, has become an important ordering principle of contemporary international relations.

1
The Nature of French Power and its African Dimension

It is perhaps because there was so little central direction to French overseas expansion in the nineteenth century that publicists and politicians were given to theorizing so openly about the need for overseas influence. The imperial adventure was initially just that, and the need to provide explanations to a perpetually sceptical public as to why money was being spent in the acquisition of territories overseas, gave an impetus to much general talk about the value of power attained, and then managed, in remote places. The ideology of overseas power which came to be established had its modern origins in the justifications first advanced in the 1830s and 1840s over the conquest of Algeria. It was in the late nineteenth century, however, when France undertook numerous campaigns abroad, that a whole body of ideas was advanced to give a coherent logic to the pursuit of overseas power. This ideology of power was often divorced from cold judgements about the actual effectiveness of its practice. A specific ability to gain a military victory, a particular economic gain, success in forcing local political change overseas: such considerations rarely entered into public debate. The effort was always to present Frenchmen with an image which could be made to satisfy national pride.

This ideology of overseas power, which helped to sustain political support for extra-metropolitan activity, applied to all areas of the world where the French were able to exert influence in a way which was seen to strengthen and embellish France's continental prestige. Yet a good many of the famous statements about the value to France of overseas influence were made in respect of Africa, geographically contiguous and in general easier to control than territories in the Middle East or Asia. When the process of decolonization left France only with some post-imperial sway in parts of Africa, an ideology of national extra-continental power, which during the imperial age had had a general application, became concentrated on those areas in Africa where France still had material and immediate influence.

The endurance of this ideology of overseas power, and its applicability even to French relations with African states many years after juridical independence was granted to them, is rooted in the abstract, almost poetic, yet demonstrably compelling notions that contributed to the ideology's formation. French power abroad was rarely explained, justified or analysed in terms of material control or military victories. It could therefore have a timeless quality which survived loss of control or defeat in battle. If twentieth-century international relations theorists have established elaborate definitions of the expression, content and effects of power in the international system, the politicians and propagandists of France who over the years have had to explain French power, have relied on images of France's 'vocation', 'prestige' and 'geographical position' to determine the causes, acceptability and effects of the use of French military, economic and diplomatic influence abroad. Naturally *material* expressions of power were necessary if the statements made about French power were to have any meaning, but over time the *presentational* aspects of French power, that is the ideology created to justify overseas adventurism and success, came, itself, to be part of French power. Thus, at least in its overseas expression, French national power could survive certain types of direct defeat so long as France was able to maintain the image of its enduring capacity to exert influence.

This chapter will sketch out the main themes of the ideology of French power in Africa. These themes will be revisited in ensuing chapters that expand on the idea of French power in Africa. Here, I merely intend to give an indication of how some of these themes have been expressed, by reference to both nineteenth-century and contemporary publicists and politicians concerned with French power. What emerges is a sense of French power which widens the normal definitions given by academic theorists, and which shows the specificity, for French leaders, of the overseas dimensions of that power. Central to this notion of power is the implicit belief that national greatness must be asserted and explained in cultural terms if it is to be absorbed as fact by those whom the state seeks to influence. The near irrefutability of a cultural claim to greatness in turn breeds its passive acceptance and, in the best of circumstances, results in the easy exertion of power and influence.

Raymond Aron has written that 'power is the capacity to make, do or destroy.'[1] But for the French, this power has rested not only on its content, but in the coherence of its form, in the ability to convince others that power existed. Even in the absence of great military or economic power, French leaders have insisted that French power – which was necessarily related to the political threat or use of force – had to be defined in the context of an ambition or the achievement of a design. As such, French power could be judged as much by the coherence of its expression as by proof of its existence. This striking French capacity to transform discussions about French international power into claims about its importance and reach, so strange to the Anglo-Saxon, nevertheless seemed to work, insofar as the objects of French power could be made to accept the greatness of France and adjust their own policies accordingly. This is why the advancement of an ideal vision of 'France' and of its extra-metropolitan reflection, is the first element in French power that should be examined.

Idealism and French Power

French nationalism and power has to be seen as both an ideal and a fact. Ever since one could speak of France as a nation, there have been those who have idealized France. As Théodore Zeldin has argued: 'These idealizers put forward theories as to what France ought to represent, and by force of repetition, these theories have been accepted as descriptions of what France in fact was.'[2] This idealizing tradition found its strongest expression in those who were concerned with French overseas power. Colonialists had to be 'idealizers' of France since it was their self-proclaimed duty to ensure that others accepted French overseas domination (both at home and in the areas that were colonized) on the grounds that domination would also mean the export of French values and traditions.

In the post-colonial age this ideal of France has also been upheld by those who have been concerned with French overseas influence. Its advocacy has been connected with the idea that France remains sensitive to the particular desires of countries in the developing world which were former European colonies. This is why it is now perhaps useful to think of France as a vanguard *status quo* power. She cannot change the international system, but she remains sensitive to the demands of others who, like France, want independence within the system. As a medium power fallen from the graces of great-power status but retaining some of its pretensions, French power takes complex forms. She is a state which to retain her position in the international community deploys a variety of techniques in her diplomatic and her general activity on the world stage. In the Fifth Republic the display of French power has sometimes taken negative forms through acts of 'exemption' and 'dissent', which have been meant to underscore French 'independence' as well as more positive attitudes (which have had the same purpose) of 'commitment' or 'direction' when she felt more secure. [3] France's activity towards the developing world has usually taken the latter form, a fact reflecting her still important, positive role.

The tensions observable in the methods and form of French power derive at least in part from the differences and contradictions in the French collective memory of recent and distant history. Defeats were followed by a *rénovation nationale* in part because it was possible to motivate Frenchmen on the basis of their memories of former greatness. French governments following the defeats of 1870 or 1940 rallied their peoples by reference to visions of what France had been or should be. Thus in analysing the form of French power and the special way it is exercised now, it is important to understand the role of these visions and ideals in French history. If, as Bertrand Russell commented, 'of the infinite desires of man, the chief are the desires for power and glory,'[4] a constant desire of the French state has been for power *through* glory, and therefore the presentational aspects of French power contribute greatly to its existence, its content and its style. Indeed the presentation of French power in times of crisis has been often dependent on the public manipulation of known ideal images of France.

In his *Essay on the Acceleration of History*, Daniel Halevy recalls the biblical idea that without vision people die, and argues that since the reign of Louis XIV, when French power was first 'personalized', the affairs of the French state have almost always been sacrificed to an ideal.[5] In France's darkest moments, an ideal vision of France has been presented by French leaders as still within the reach of the French state, and this ideal has been upheld in order to strengthen and rehabilitate national morale. Certainly this was the case after 1870 when defeat by the Germans moved Frenchmen to think of ways by which France could recover from her lost power. The philosopher Charles Renouvier believed that France's defeat was her own fault. She had forgotten the ideals of freedom and was backward in the pursuit of science. France needed a new ideal, he argued, based upon morality and reason. This ideal could be found, he thought, in the idea of civilization.[6] Whether through the influence of Renouvier or not, the idea of civilization became absorbed in the official doctrine of the French state, and affected the way the French defined their own power in international society. While evidence of an ability to control others or to impose conditions on their behaviour would always be necessary to prove that power had been wielded, the fact of French civilization was often put forward, during the nineteenth century, as itself evidence of the existence of power. If French civilization was influential, so was the French state. Sinand culture completely coincided in the French scheme of things, advances made by one translated into success for the other.

In a book on the civilization of France published in 1930, the German writer Curtius makes particular reference to this dimension of French power in noting that:

France has felt the need to sum up her national existence in the form of an idea. She felt she must have a picture, a formula, a word, in which she could be presented. This sense of a need for a presentation and conception of herself is an integral element in the French spirit. No other modern nation knows it in the same measure. England has never felt this need at all. In Germany it only appeared during the nineteenth century, but it expressed itself in the form of a problem not as a settled solution.[7]

This relative ability of the French to present a clear conception of the goals of the state, or more particularly of French foreign policy, must always be thought of as an element of French power. If, in general, power is defined by a state's ability to execute designs, in the French case power has also issued from an ability to give coherent and understandable expression to these designs. A foreign policy that is identifiable is at least one with which others must contend. The idea of 'civilization' – vague and indeterminate – was nevertheless made a rallying cry for those who wanted to expand French political power.

It was often argued that French civilization had to be exported if it was not to stagnate. The *mission civilisatrice* undertaken in Africa and the Orient to bolster French power in Europe was proof of that ambition to which only great powers could aspire. It was not good enough for the French to rest on their laurels. In the words of the great colonialist, Jules Ferry, *rayonner sans agir* (to radiate without acting), would be tantamount to abdication; it would mean that France would descend from a power of the first rank to one belonging to the third or fourth. In a famous speech of 1885 to which I will return later in this book Ferry argued that: 'nations, in the times in which we find ourselves are great only by the activity that they develop; it is not by the peaceful *rayonnement* of their institutions that they are great these days.'[8]

The corollary of this assessment, which Ferry drew expressly and which he felt justified the colonial enterprise, was that action overseas, if successful, would contribute to French standing in Europe.[9] The enhancement of France's reputation through the *mission civilisatrice* would make the exercise of power in Europe easier. The whole idea of French power, therefore, from the nineteenth century to the present, is wrapped up with the exportability of French ideas and institutions and the active cultivation of overseas appreciation for the values of the French state.

For this reason colonies, and particularly those in Africa, were essential to bolstering French power. Anyone who supported France's colonial position also uphf the *mission civilisatrice*. But acts of imperial conquest, either in Africa, the Middle or the Far East, were not immediately followed by the development of institutions which could quickly begin to civilize and to educate. The *mission civilisatrice* was not put into operation immediately on successful conquest. This was at least in part because the image of the French state as a civilizing power was, though vital, subordinate to the efforts made to regain France's status as a power of the first rank. Imperial conquest was a necessary condition precedent to the spread of a culture all French colonial leaders presumed to be universal, but it is evident that the declaration of the *mission civilisatrice* was in part a guise for the brute calculations of power politics. The importance of the *mission civilisatrice* lay precisely in the fact that it helped to achieve the primary aim of gaining more influence abroad. The establishment and then the defence of cultural interests *outre-mer* was a policy which would help find more adherents to the colonial cause. To the extent that the publicists pushing for a French policy *outre-mer* justified their case by invoking the concept of the *mission civilisatrice*, it gives an indication of how to define the sources of French power abroad as well as the meaning of such words as prestige, reputation and grandeur, so important to understand the presentational aspects of French power.

Prestige and French Power

The classic definition of prestige is E.H. Carr's: 'Prestige means the recognition of other people of your strength. Prestige, which some people scoff at, is enormously important: for if your strength is recognized, you can generally achieve your aims without having to use it.'[10] In his Rede lecture given at Cambridge in 1937, Harold Nicolson went further to point out that power and prestige are not synonymous since 'although you cannot acquire prestige without power, yet you cannot retain prestige without reputation. Moreover, a prestige which contains a high percentage of reputation is able to withstand a loss of power - whereas even a temporary decline in power will destroy a prestige which is devoid of reputation.'[11] It was important to point out, Nicolson felt, that the concept of reputation differed from state to state.

For the British, according to this conception, reputation was based on character and conduct, while for the French, reputation consisted of the military capacity of the French race and in their cultural achievements. The link between power and reputation, Nicolson argued, which together form prestige, on which all strong states rely to get their way, is particularly strong in the French mind. Again, in Nicolson's words: 'The French possess a very seventeenth-century sense of domination. They are vividly conscious of the importance of culture and of its vast exportable value. And they are fully aware that power without reputation is a most uncivilized thing.'[12] The colonial adventure can therefore be seen as an attempt by the French to add to their reputation so that French prestige or, to use the appropriate analogue to what Nicolson felt was a British concept, French grandeur, could legitimately be maintained. Yet success in military campaigns or particular gains through the export of French culture, though contributing to the strength of French prestige have not always been thought essential components of it. Statesmen have sometimes referred merely to the intellectual coherence of the values espoused by France as proof in itself of French prestige. Outsiders might contest the superficiality inherent in claims about France's 'universal values' but these have often been put forward by French leaders as sources of prestige and therefore power.

Thus the idea of French grandeur, which is essential to French power, is not based exclusively on the reputation of France derived from the success of her military campaigns, or the specific attractiveness of her civilization to others. Maurice Couve de Murville, President de Gaulle's long-serving minister of foreign affairs, insisted that Gaullist policy was based on universal principles as much as on specific accomplishments since

the spirit, the feeling, the genius of and, all in all, the soul of our country draws it towards the level of the universal. Over the centuries its vocation has been to witness, to inspire; and its action, its influence and its prestige have stemmed as much from this vocation as from its political or military undertakings, so that in the long run it cannot be measured by or equated with the victories and defeats or the glories and misfortunes which have beset its history. If there has grown up, according to the famous and now classic expression, a 'certain idea of France', it is indeed in this context that men have conceived it and in this form that it reappears with *éclat* whenever, following an eclipse or even a period of decadence, comes the renewal.[13]

In his biography of de Gaulle François Mauriac went even further to stress that 'grandeur ... must not be confused with material power or with technical success.' In his view greatness came from the fact that the French people have within them a 'principle', or a 'vocation'. De Gaulle's statements on French grandeur are in this sense classic examples of how ideas and images have been presented as both sources and proof of power. In his war memoirs, de Gaulle emphasized a theory of French intrinsic greatness:

All my life I have thought of France in a certain way. This is inspired by sentiment as much as by reason. The emotional side of me tends to imagine France, like the princess in the fairy stories of the Madonna in the frescoes, as dedicated to an exalted and exceptional destiny. Instinctively I have the feeling that Providence has created her either for complete successes or for exemplary misfortunes. If, in spite of this, mediocrity shows in her acts and deeds, it strikes me as an absurd anomaly, to be imputed to the faults of Frenchmen, not to the genius of the land. But the positive side of my mind also assures me that France is not really herself unless in the front rank; that only vast enterprises are capable of counterbalancing the ferments of dispersal which are inherent in her people; that our country, as it is, surrounded by the others, as they are, must aim high and hold itself straight, on pain of mortal danger. In short, to my mind, France cannot be France without greatness.[14]

These *idealized* elements of French power, which in the words of French leaders and thinkers helped to maintain French power even when the state had lost the material trappings of power, were always part of the imperial message. The logic of these ideas was, as a consequence, marvellously reinforcing, since the acceptance by overseas peoples of French ideas, institutions and civilization, even when this occurred as a result of the use of military power, could be held up as proof of the existence of French power based on 'universal principles'. The exportability of French civilization, however, also depended on France's unique *geographical position* which allowed and even impelled her towards civilizing missions overseas.

Geography and French Power

French grandeur, as presented to the outside world, has also derived simply from France's geographical position in the world. If one source of French power is reputation, which is based on accomplishments, another source is simply place, which is unchanging in the geographical sense, and which French leaders have used to justify certain acts, and to claim certain rights and duties of a political kind. Geographical determinism was certainly an element of the French justification for leading an expansionist policy overseas: Africa lay to the south of the French hexagon, and it was simply natural that French power should be extended there. More generally, the French have throughout the twentieth century, and especially in the Gaullist period, drawn attention to the balancing role France can play in the international system owing to its place on the map. Sometimes quite bald statements about the influence of geography on political destiny have been made to sustain the notion that France has a special mission in the international system. These quintessentially *geopolitical* ideas have remained relatively constant even as the international system has changed, and have become adapted where necessary to conform to changing political realities. The best early explanation of this sometimes extraordinary claim again comes from the German Curtius, writing in the 1930s:

To the French, the conception of being the central nation has an entirely different meaning from that it has to us Germans; when we regard ourselves as the nation which occupies the central position in Europe we mean by that that we are in the centre of two opposing forces. We mean therefore that we are related to all and that we occupy an all-reconciling position; for us therefore, the centre is a metaphysical category. To France it means, quite in the sense of the Ancient World something aesthetic and ethical: moderation and balance. In France the ideology of the central land is transmuted from the physical and climatic into the intellectual and political sphere. '*La Grandeur de la France*,' said Renan, '*est de renfermer des pôles opposés.*' (The grandeur of France is to bring together opposite poles)[15]

The idea that it was part of France's political destiny to bring together opposite poles was often extended to the economic and strategic spheres. Writers wishing to explain why France's power in Africa was a 'natural' political fact often referred to the inevitable complementarity between France and the African continent which gave France an important role to play in its development. Writing in the mid-1950s in the influential *Revue des Deux Mondes* a French officer argued that

It is an obvious geographic fact that ... Africa and Europe are economically complementary. There is no economic development possible for Africa alone, there is no chance of equipping, of economically improving, of industrializing, of raising the standard of living of African populations without the technical aid of technicians from European capitals.[16]

In the mid-1950s, few would have argued with the idea that the economic development of Africa could not proceed without European help. But it was symbolic of the history of French power in Africa and of its traditional justifications, that this argument proceeded from a statement stressing the geographical inevitability of the European role in Africa. The same author argued with even greater vigour the importance of geography and its political consequences when he spoke of military links:

North Africa ... constitutes with the European continent a single theatre of operations; it would therefore be illogical to create autonomous Tunisian or Moroccan armies with all that implies in terms of supplemental extra costs at a time when only great armies can dispose of modern armaments and when we tend more and more, for these same reasons, to integrate continental armies under single commands and administration.[17]

The idea that in the mid-1950s France could play this role in North Africa was clearly outdated, but it was an indicator of how strongly many felt that French and European power and security were intimately connected (and should therefore be bound) to the security of Africa. Four years later, in the same journal, the President of the Defence and Armed Forces Commission of the National Assembly made the case forcefully that French power depended on the link with Algeria, and he made this case virtually on the basis of geographical principles:

it is all our destiny and in any case our destiny as a great power that is in play. Because our ambition to figure among the Great Powers, that is among the nations invested with world responsibilities, could not be justified once we were relegated to the dimensions of our initial hexagon.

In this way our national salvation passes through Algeria.[18]

This was a clear statement of what was a basic principle for those who considered the question of French power. The more a state chooses only to ensure that it will keep control over domestic life, the more it begins to look like a small power. For a power to retain its important position in inter-national society, it must undertake a degree of activity which has implications for the lives of those living beyond its borders. Great powers must be able to assert a degree of exclusive power in a region of the world if they are to maintain their position and status. These, effectively, have been the tacit and sometimes explicit maxims of French power since the age of imperialism, and have been adapted to modern conditions.

Many of these political ideas that ensued from geographical imperatives can be found in the actions and statements of French leaders throughout the Fifth Republic. General de Gaulle's aim to create a Europe extending from the Atlantic to the Urals was born largely of a geographical understanding of what Europe was and where France was placed in Europe rather than from any special political concept of the forces that might make such a project possible. Similarly, President Mitterrand's first defence minister, Charles Hernu, gave a poetic explanation of the French role in the world which expresses the long-standing idea of France as a 'central power'. In a speech he gave at the *Institut des Hautes Etudes de Défense Nationale* Hernu once explained that:

The geographic and political situation of France places it at the centre point of the two great axes around which modern international relations are articulated – North–South relations on the one hand, East–West ones on the other. That is why the policy of the President of the Republic is established around these axes.[19]

French policy now, no less than at the time of colonial expansion, can thus be seen as deriving from the simplest of geographical propositions, which when translated into the language of politics allows French leaders to assume certain geopolitical stances, which by definition, no other state would have the power to maintain. The language used in expressing policy, the specificity of the French description of their place in the world, continues to be a vital element of French power, the most coherent shape of which was given by General de Gaulle in describing the 'certain idea of France' which animated his policy.

Prestige, Personality and Continental v. Overseas Power

The themes of prestige and geography that characterized the description of French power in the nineteenth and twentieth centuries were codified by General de Gaulle and virtually incarnated in the French Fifth Republic. Personality is recognized by most theorists as itself a source of power and General de Gaulle rose to power and then wielded it because of his capacity to convince others of his assertions. Power, it has been said, 'regularly passes to those who are able to assert the unknown with the greatest conviction,'[20] and de Gaulle did this with sufficient flair to rally others around him and around a special vision he had of France that corresponded to specific French concepts of power. He, too, attached great importance to the concept of prestige and argued that prestige cannot exist without a certain sense of mystery, since people have little reverence for what they know too well.[21]

In re-establishing the power of the French state, de Gaulle behaved in order to provide an *image* of power, and central to this presentation of France to the outside world was the vocabulary that defined the French place in the world. To assert French prestige eloquently there was a need to give it definition, but the words, if they were to carry weight, would have to retain an enigmatic quality about them. The ambitions of France both in Africa and in Europe were traditionally defined by words intended to magnify the idea of France and the practical policies that were to issue from these words were not always either inherent or clear.

In assuming the mantle of power in 1958, de Gaulle hoped he could re-elevate France to that position in world politics which he believed rightly belonged to France. De Gaulle's personal mission was to restore French grandeur after it had been whittled away by the experiences of Vichy and the Fourth Republic. In calling for a revival of French greatness, he was hoping in the first instance for a renewal of French national pride and consciousness, which could then be brought to bear on the international stage. If France was again to appear great in the eyes of others she must be seen to have inner strength.

It is worth noting, however, that in his famous romantic passage on the first page of his war memoirs, in which he conceives of France 'a certain way' and cannot 'imagine a France that is not great', de Gaulle subordinates domestic politics to foreign policy. Frenchmen are in the service of France, not the other way around.[22] Furthermore, only a grand design could unite a people whose instinct for individualism would otherwise have divisive effects. The display of French power on the world stage must therefore be seen as a method for consolidating national strength.

This relationship between international activity and domestic politics had also been present during the late nineteenth-century imperial adventure. Some would even draw the relationship very close, by arguing that colonization would help to cure many of France's social ills. Domestic problems could be solved by a policy of overseas settlement; even unattractive political options could be foreclosed. Ernest Renan argued that colonization was a political necessity of the first order as nations which refused to colonize were irrevocably condemned to socialism. But many in the nineteenth century, as new discoveries were made in Africa, questioned the validity of the imperial mission in the classic terms of power politics. The speech by Jules Ferry in 1885, to which reference has already been made, prompted Paul Déroulède to remark (in reference to Alsace-Lorraine): 'I have lost two sisters and you offer me twenty chamber maids.'[23] For some, losses in Europe, particularly Alsace-Lorraine, could not be compensated for by the acquisition of territories abroad. But, despite the general indifference of many to the act of colonial acquisition, once possessions became a fact of national life and colonial rule an administrative necessity, the need for justifications for expansion and maintenance of overseas power became self-evident. These justifications and the special vocabulary used in defence of French expansion moulded conceptions of French power. They also gave urgency to the need to translate abstract ideas of power into mechanisms for the competent management of that power. The onus of paying for and administering overseas territories, in turn, had to be shown to be useful for the enhancement of French global status.

That France had a special mission to initiate the colonial peoples into the responsibilities of modern political life became an easier rallying cry once it was obvious that there was a practical need to manage new territories efficiently.[24] This increased responsibility in the world – this mission – had to be presented as adding to French grandeur if it was to be acceptable to those who, invoking the main liberal tenets of republicanism or a priority for action in Europe, opposed colonial expansion. The elaboration of a colonial doctrine which in some of its aspects tested republican theses of liberty, freedom and equality, helped to consolidate domestic political opinion and establish colonialism as a national policy which could not be challenged except by the disloyal. This required of all political leaders a capacity to adapt parts of the colonial myth into the language of domestic politics. Associating the colonies to France gave France an opportunity to demonstrate the universality of her culture, but also eventually of her political principles. Once the idea was accepted that France and her colonies constituted an indivisible republic, rupture with the colonies would, by definition, be a 'domestic' problem; and this 'domestic' problem would, in turn, have an effect on France's international standing.

It was therefore inevitable that the test of de Gaulle's ability to reassert his own position of leadership within France and to regain for France its prestige and therefore its power on the international stage came with the problem of Algeria. To understand the nature of French power in the Fifth Republic it is important to understand that decolonization was not always a process by which France lost power, rather it was sometimes presented as a series of events that allowed France to assert influence and show its command of political change. Still, while decolonization in Black Africa resulted in a French capacity to exert power without juridical responsibility, the loss of Algeria, from the French perspective, could be presented in a positive light only with some difficulty. It is worth recalling here what Tocqueville wrote in October 1841 in a note entitled *Travail sur l'Algérie* :

I do not believe that France can seriously think of leaving Algeria. Such abandonment would be seen in the eyes of the world as the certain announcement of France's decadence. It would be much less inconvenient to have our force conquered there by a rival nation. A vigorous people in the middle of its expansion can be unlucky in war and lose its provinces... But if France withdrew from an enterprise where it had before her only the natural difficulties of the country and the small barbarous tribes that are there, she would appear in the eyes of the world to fold under her own impotence and succumb because of lack of heart. Any people that easily lets go of what it has taken and retreats peacefully from itself and within its own boundaries proclaims that the fine times of its history have passed. It enters visibly into the period of its decline. If ever France does abandon Algeria it is obvious that she can only do so at a time when she is seen to be undertaking great things in Europe and not at a time when she seems to be sinking to a secondary role and appears resigned to seeing the direction of European affairs pass into other hands.[25]

These strong sentiments guided Tocqueville's own assessments of French policy throughout his life. He believed that the African question was central to France's destiny and though he often criticized aspects of French administrative policy in Algeria and the manner in which certain bureaucratic practices were carried out there he felt deeply that it was necessary for

France to be present in Algeria. In 1847 he presented a long report to the Chamber of Deputies concerning a law on extra credits for Algeria. In large measure it denounced aspects of French policy and he insisted that one great problem was that the government of the day had no co-ordinated African policy. Yet it contained these phrases which for over a century encapsulated the essence of the French vision of Africa and particularly of Algeria:

The peaceful domination and the rapid colonization of Algeria are surely the two greatest interests that France has today in the world; they are large in themselves and by the direct and necessary relation they have with all the others. Our preponderance in Europe, the state of our finances, the life of a part of our citizens, our national honour are here engaged in the most formidable way.[26]

Just over a century after these words were spoken, in 1957, Francois Mitterrand wrote with reference to the problem of Algeria that 'without Africa there would be no history of France in the twenty-first century.'[27] If *Algérie Française* was such an important stake how could its loss not adversely affect French power? Part of the answer lies in the fact that, as Tocqueville predicted would have to be the case, the French were undertaking great things in Europe – the restructuring of Europe around a French-dominated Common Market and the creation of an independent nuclear deterrent were acts which would develop new symbols of French power. The loss of a few possessions in Africa or elsewhere would not be thought of as so significant when France was at the centre of the creation of a new political entity in Europe, and, at the same time, developing for herself the ultimate weapon which only truly great powers would possess. But more important than these 'acts in Europe' which served to compensate for lost power in Africa just as conquests in Africa had originally served to help boost power in Europe, was the way in which decolonization in Africa was presented to the world.

In his *Ancien Régime* Tocqueville referred to the essentially literary nature of French foreign policy and in the specific case of decolonization Raymond Aron once explained that the aesthetic instinct in the formation of foreign policy admirably served the aims of *realpolitik*. De Gaulle's great talent, Aron argued, was for transfiguration – an essentially poetic faculty.[28] As it happened, the loss of colonies in sub-Saharan Africa was managed so as to appear a victory. What would have been a tragedy for the Fourth Republic became a success for the Fifth. The reason was that de Gaulle was able to transform, to the benefit of France's own reputation in the world, the motives behind the need for decolonization. The great weakness of the Fourth Republic had been precisely that it did not know how to lose

Algeria. Under de Gaulle, the effective release of Algeria, and even more so of Black Africa, became a grand design. The handover of power to new leaders in the colonies was to serve French prestige. In the end it became an assertion of power, in the sense that it proved France could withstand the loss of formal control, while retaining indirect influence.

he manner of decolonization in sub-Saharan Africa was devised in order to enhance French power by increasing the esteem in which the state was held by those who benefited directly from independence. While, as all writers have noted, prestige is gained by the successful display of power, this need not be demonstrated merely by success in battle. Prestige can be both earned and later proven by the *refusal* to undertake or to exploit military campaigns. In his *Power Politics*, Martin Wight gives an example of this which can be compared to the French experience of decolonization in sub-Saharan Africa. Referring to the Napoleonic Wars when Britain captured all the French colonies and then returned most of them to France at the Vienna settlement Wight cites Castelreigh's justification of this apparently quite selfless act: 'I am sure our reputation on the Continent, as a feature of strength, power, and confidence, is of more real moment to us than an acquisition thus made.'[29] This, as Wight himself mentions, is a classic statement of the value of prestige. Likewise, in the case of French decolonization in the 1960s, the relinquishing of power showed that France was sensitive to the reaction of world public opinion to her policy, and that French interests would be better served by showing that she need not keep her colonies to keep her status. In fact, the skilful manipulation of the process by which the Black African ex-colonies achieved forms of self-government would strengthen French prestige and therefore power.

France was able to decolonize in sub-Saharan Africa because she was 'undertaking great things in Europe' and because the method of the retreat from Black Africa was such as to support French prestige. As important as these two factors was a third, that in the process of decolonization France was able to improve the presentation of her own special place in the international system and elaborate on the sources of her influence.

French Power, Africa, and Independence

In the postwar era French power has been based on French military capabilities as a nuclear power and the role in world politics at least formally assigned to France as a permanent member of the UN Security Council. French economic growth and the leading position of France in the European

Community have also been considered as essential elements of French global power. France's policy in Black Africa has been intertwined with a general world policy and its accompanying logic.

Thus, the two leitmotifs of French policy in the 1960s were independence and co-operation; the granting of independence to the ex-colonies in Black Africa made French claims for independence from the two superpower blocs appear as a logical element of a grand strategy. French prestige had certainly been eroded by the intensity of the battle to keep Algeria French. The immediate practical result of the Algerian war had been to increase France's dependency on the Western Alliance for defence of the home front. If prestige was enhanced by a policy of responsiveness to the demands of an emerging Third World, it was necessary still to ensure that France herself not fall under the dominion of others. The connection was quite clear in the French political mind even if it was rarely understood by others. Having given up her own formal imperial role by 1962, France had herself to make claims for a type of non-aligned status within the new international system, else her own power and influence in the world would only be defined as a function of the power of other states. Given the acknowledged strength of the two superpowers, French leaders wished to ensure that France's own measures of power would allow her still to conduct herself like a great power even though she was wielding the resources only of a medium power. Also, since French power had been defined by the attractiveness of French culture and its exportability, it would be difficult for France to allow her own power to be defined in American terms, or in the terms of the specific ambitions of other European partners. In practice, the words used in a decolonized world to explain French power drew on well-established notions and images of the French national identity.

Yet, over time, even as the language of independence became vital to the French political sense of self, it maintained an African accent. As politicians referred to the French place in the world, it was rare that allusion was not made to the strong links still maintained with Africa. These links did not constrain French policy, rather they gave it a purpose and proved that France still held a position of responsibility in the world. This sense of 'responsibility' remains essential to French descriptions of national power and the fact that the destiny of others can be affected by French policy and by France's reputation continues to be underscored by politicians. At the Franco–African summit meeting in Vittel in 1983, President Mitterrand raised all these various notions of French power in highlighting the importance of such conferences of heads of state. In the final press conference closing the summit he answered a question about the number of African leaders who had attended:

If we are numerous and in confidence, it is because we have common interests to defend. And if this serves the prestige of France, all the better from my point of view, since this serves also the prestige of African states who work with us and for whom we wish independence, not only from old colonial methods, but also from new ones, no doubt more insidious.[30]

In this essentially extemporaneous statement, the president of France gave expression to an enduring ideology of French power in Africa whose constituent elements had changed in substance but not necessarily in form after decolonization. The notions of prestige, independence, indivisible common purpose, and reputation are all implicitly or explicitly contained in this statement, which is effectively a justification of the lasting nature of French power in Africa and of its inherent logic. France is presented here as the protector of African states against the evils of an international system whose structure does not permit them properly to expand or to develop. In evoking the closeness of the Franco–African diplomatic relationship this comment underscores its quite peculiar characteristics which remain unique in world affairs. One writer has recently puzzled over the specificity of the French–African connection:

The problem of analyzing French–African relations is that the relations in question exist between actors who have more sovereignty than the mythology of the Francophone family implies, but also a stronger community of values and a more complex meshing of political processes than the conventions of international relations typically assure.[31]

The present form of these relations is due in large measure to the way in which France has been able to adapt positive images of her imperial power to the circumstances of a post-colonial order. The image of French power as presented by the French is carefully crafted to appeal to African sensitivities while also serving to maintain French power most efficiently in the international system as it is at present constructed. In order to understand how that power is wielded in Africa it is important to appreciate its essentially aesthetic nature. It is aesthetic partly because the French continue to point to their own culture and civilization as a source of power, and to the attractiveness of that culture and civilization to others as *proof* of influence. It is also aesthetic because the manner in which France's place in the world is described is as important as most of the other conventional measures of power, be they economic, military or demographic. In the description of that power, where notions of prestige and reputation hold an important place, the African connection is central. This is so because it is in Africa where France can still achieve the effects of power as it is conventionally deployed in international affairs: in Africa, France can still 'make, do or destroy'.

This classic form of power can be wielded in Africa by France in part because the exercise of positive influence and intervention is admitted by the objects of that power, the majority of francophone Black African states, as being in their interest. To the extent that French power in Africa depends on its acceptance by the Africans it is vulnerable to an African perception that there has been detrimental reliance by them on the terms of the post-colonial Franco–African contract. This means that France must give substance to the ideology of common partnership that governs her declaratory policy in Africa, and scale her activity in Africa to respond as much as she can to African needs *as expressed by the Africans*. The maintenance of French credibility in Africa depends on a continued ability to point to the difficulty the Africans would have in replacing France as their principal external provider of security and stability. It is often the impending prospect of being replaced, especially by the Americans, that forces France, from time to time, to readjust her policy so as to more completely conform to the declared requirements of African states. This may take the form of increased economic assistance, a particular act of military support, or a promise to defend specific African interests in relevant international fora.

France is willing to do this where possible precisely because of the importance of the African connection to her prestige and reputation. The consistent and public defence of Africa as a place where France belongs as a matter of course would make any apparent loss of influence in Africa especially damaging. As a repository of French prestige, francophone Africa would be more costly to lose than it is to maintain. The continuing investment of residual power that France has made in Africa owes its origins in part to the nature of French imperialism. Since its agents were, as Ronald Robinson has pointed out, 'soldiers, technicians and teachers rather than merchants and colonists: the exportable surplus of its standing army and efficient education, not those of its economy',[32] it is evident that the current ties to metropolitan France, despite the process of decolonization, should remain diverse, complex and therefore strong.

Particularly in North Africa, but also in West and Central Black Africa, France met initial resistance in the colonies by trying to draw them closer to the metropole.[33] The inherent economic weakness of the areas in Africa over which France held imperial sway may have been a symbol of weakness in the imperial age – France's Empire was one more of prestige than of interest – but this made it possible, at least in Black Africa, for France to offer its strength to the Africans confident that it would be accepted. French power in North Africa was largely lost as a result of the Algerian war. There are still 'privileged relations' between France and North Africa, but these have lost much of their lustre. It may well be that in the future France will again consider – for reasons of local power politics in the Mediterranean – that constructive policies towards North Africa will be essential for the maintenance of French regional power. But since decolonization, while France has pursued a carefully balanced policy towards the Maghreb, Black Africa is where France's military, economic and diplomatic policy is more consistently and effectively directed in order to service and give shape to the abstract ideas of French power.

The ideology of French power in Africa, initially devised largely (though not exclusively) with North Africa in mind, has been entirely transferred to Black Africa. The images, geographical truths, notions of prestige, theories of complementarity and ideas of partnership developed during the age of imperialism still have relevance to current Franco–African relations. The source and nature of current French power in Africa must therefore be seen against the background of the original imperial instinct, initially shared by few, but eventually a source of power for the state.

2
The Imperial Instinct

Though much of French activity overseas, both since decolonization and at the time of renewed imperial expansion in the nineteenth century, has been presented as part of a grand design, steps towards overseas expansion were often taken by accident. The French army was sent to Algeria in 1830 by Charles X three years after the dey of Algiers had struck the French consul (28 April 1827) with a fly whisk and had called him, among other things, a wicked rascal.[1] Hussein Dey had been angered by the fact that France had not paid a thirty-year-old debt, and Pierre Deval, as consul, could not provide him with a satisfactory explanation for why Charles X had not answered his letters. After considerable hesitation, Charles sent an expeditionary force to Algiers on 16 June 1830; the town fell on 5 July, prompting Bourmont, commander of the French troops to proclaim: 'Twenty days sufficed for the destruction of the state which for three centuries has tired Europe'. The eventual result of this military act to avenge national honour was the 'pacification' of Algeria and the declaration in 1848 by the Second Republic that Algeria was an integral part of France. Many wondered at the time of the Algerian conquest whether the effort was worth the price. Yet these concerns were pushed aside and soon it became part of the conventional wisdom that the defence of Algeria was tantamount to the defence of France.

All acquisitions made overseas were intended to enhance French prestige; for the opponents of expansion, the consequent need to maintain French positions often made prestige the enemy of reason and of economy. Expansionists who felt that French status in Europe could be best advanced by increasing the size of Greater France consistently clashed with those who believed that since power in Europe was the prize, Europe was where the competition had to be waged. The hyperactivity of French explorers, particularly in Africa, made the debate moot, and for the colonial propagandists, the fact that other European powers were engaged in overseas expansion meant that France could not be left behind.

While French expansion in the late nineteenth century took the French flag to many new parts of the globe, Africa was where much of the colonizing energy was spent and Africa was also where the sense of competition with other European powers was most persistently strong. It was therefore in Africa (both the North and sub-Saharan Black areas) that the French desired to obtain large areas of exclusive command. The strangest places became the object of European rivalry. One British analyst of the inter-war period gave a particularly elegant description of the problem:

Since 1900, Lake Chad has been the centre of a French dependency, vast but not so vast nor yet so exclusive as some Frenchmen designed, because a year or so later the English and German centres of gravity shifted somewhat from the Atlantic shores inland, and round this lake three empires met. In 1902, the Governors of British Nigeria and the German Cameroons established effective British and German rule on its west and south shores, and Lake Chad began to combine the physical eccentricities of Lob-Nor with the political interest of the Pamirs.[2]

For a section of the French state leadership the creation of large and coherent areas of control in Africa – along North Africa and throughout West and Central Africa – was an important political task. The geographical extension of France to the great continent that lay below would give the impression of a grand design efficiently turned into reality, even if it was often the whims of individual explorers that determined the designs presented by French politicians to a concerned domestic elite.

This chapter examines in further detail how the concept of French national power was deployed in defence of the new wave of imperial expansion that began in the 1880s. It was during this period that, often against the wishes of the central bureaucracy in Paris, soldiers overseas fought for their own ideas of national honour. It was then up to the colonialists and politicians at home to justify this activity, often retrospectively, as in the national interest. This took place despite continuing tensions between elements of the bureaucracies in Paris. But the development of an imperialist ideology by French public figures and the elaboration of colonial doctrines and propaganda that took place between 1880 and the First World War, led to the entrenchment of the idea that France's national destiny was wrapped up with overseas power.

The growth and strength of the imperial instinct in the France of the nineteenth century was largely dependent on the influence that colonial officers and adventurers could bring to bear on the political elite of the day. For the expansionist desires of a small group of individuals to be translated into a national mission in pursuit of state prestige, it was necessary for colonial propagandists to convince politicians that their individual aspirations could properly be turned into a collective, national design. The connection that was eventually made between colonial expansion and the growth or maintenance of state power became an accepted view of an increasingly large segment of the French political class. Yet it became a vivid popular perception only some time after the end of imperial expansion.

Historians are now relatively united in believing that the sense of Empire was never so strong in France as it was in England. Indeed, many French colonial propagandists lamented the fact that there was so little public understanding of the importance of overseas power. The Londoner had a sense of being at the centre of an empire whose unity and size was both taken for granted and understood; the Parisian felt at the centre of France, whose external dimensions were rarely taken into account or discussed outside political circles. The political elite who favoured expansion moved without public support, though often with the benefit of public indifference. The consciousness of Empire became greatest only at times of national crisis, and was most intense during the period of decolonization. The need for political leaders to educate the public about the value of Empire over time has led to one paradox: that state power now is still connected to the idea of overseas influence, and that the French public in the latter part of the twentieth century has a stronger appreciation of the virtues of extra-continental influence than did the average French citizen at the height of imperial expansion in the nineteenth century.

The public reflexes that therefore exist in France about the importance that extra-European influence has for continental stature have their origins in the elaboration of the imperial idea in the latter part of the nineteenth century. The young men who, decades after decolonization, perform their military service overseas as *coopérants*, teaching French in schools, helping to train African armed forces and improving local infrastructures do so conscious of a service they are rendering to the image of France both in the West and the developing world. In this sense they are effectively the inheritors of an ideology of overseas activity developed to explain the reasons for which France should make the effort to acquire further responsibilities *outre-mer*.

That ideology was based entirely on a conception of power politics. The language that accompanied its promotion was in the mid-nineteenth century part of the vocabulary only of a few ideologues; by the end of the Second World War it was part of the conventional wisdom of the whole nation. Anticolonialists in the 1880s would argue that colonies only served to engage France in wars, while wars only resulted in the loss of colonies.[3] By 1945 there was a general public perception that the Empire was a major source of French freedom and security. Such a change could only take place because of the ability of leading political figures to hold up the vision of France *outre-mer* as a basic condition of future French power. Those who supported the actions of independent French soldiers fighting indigenous leaders in Africa and elsewhere had to create a sense of purpose and design where there was initially only a sense of adventure and of experiment. Ordering the actions of French army officers into a coherent policy (though never an organized plan) for increased power on the world stage was one of the great accomplishments of French advocates of a new programme of expansion in the 1880s.

The French Bureaucracy, Armed Forces and Imperial Expansion

The work of civilian propagandists in the 1870s and 1880s was certainly helped by the vision that the existing colonial officer corps had of itself, and which made the case for further expansionism easier to justify. As Raoul Girardet has explained, the French colonial officer never thought of himself constrained by the traditional limits of his profession, rather he 'saw himself always as a fighter, but also as a tutor, a negotiator, an administrator, a builder. His mission, as he conceived of it, was to arbitrate and manage, to render justice and open roads, to create markets and new sources of riches.'[4] These economic motivations or duties of the officer sometimes affected the official justifications made to parliament or to individual politicians by those members of the elite who favoured colonial expansion, but they were rarely the true reasons why the colonial cause was enthusiastically advanced by its more prominent defenders. To the extent that economic arguments were put forward, the statesmen of the time, as Raymond Aron has argued, 'were exploiting an economic argument - frigid, passionless, but rationally acceptable to their contemporaries - in order to disguise their dreams of political grandeur.'[5]

While there were often intriguing economic arguments advanced both by pressure groups and colonial adventurers to make the expense of colonial acquisition seem appropriate (and some of these will be examined below), it was the larger political goal which eventually had the most attractiveness. The development of a commercial policy towards the colonies and the build-up of necessary ground and naval power to project overseas came about some time after the great period of colonial expansion, but the principal root justification of this expansion lay in the political ambition to create a Greater France. Yet France did not always have the appropriate instruments at hand for colonial exploitation and domination at the moment possessions were acquired. In fact what is interesting to note is that the creation of the mechanisms for overseas control did not always accompany, but rather often lagged very much behind, both the ideology that supported expansion and the fact of colonial acquisition itself. It was only after the late nineteenth-century colonial expansion became generally accepted by the political class as an essential part of French state activity that appropriate reforms were made in the armed forces to sustain influence overseas. Explorers conquered, politicians provided a rationale, and then, late in the day, commercial and military administrators created the means for France to take some practical steps towards overseas management. The gap between ambitions and capacities was certainly recognized by the less romantically inclined managers of France's destiny, who opposed expansion on the grounds that it used resources and tools that needed to be concentrated in Europe. It was, however, of less concern either to colonial propagandists or to soldiers in the field who often took advantage of government's ignorance to make undirected acquisitions and conquests abroad.

In order to appreciate the sense in which imperial desires were engraved on the hearts of certain members of the political class, and the degree to which these longings were strongly criticized by other members of the elite, it is important to grasp the mix of military, ideological and economic factors that affected public debate. All discussions on colonies were in the end debates about the elements that could contribute to state power and about the image of France in the world at large. But these geopolitical and aesthetic questions each played into more specific disputes about the type of armed forces France should maintain, the form of French political strength and the need to compete with other European states, as well as the nature of French commerce on the continent and *outre-mer*.

Despite the fact that many historians have argued that the majority of the French elite were won over to the imperial cause by the eventual creation of a colonial army – thus mitigating the need to use regular contingents in overseas expeditions – that claim does not stand up to scrutiny.[6] Even by the late 1890s that colonial army, the subject of so many parliamentary debates in the 1880s, was still only a paper force. When Paul Deschanel made his investiture speech at the Chamber of Deputies on 13 June 1898 he made a predictable remark about the way in which improvements in the armed forces had contributed to French strength. The army and the navy, he argued, were at once part of 'our security and our pride. Their strength gives to our diplomacy the means to defend our acquired results and to extend them.'[7] But in making this statement he was still referring implicitly to one army which would have the dual role of defending French interests both in Europe and abroad. A specific force for colonial warfare was not yet in existence; forces used abroad were merely drawn down from those needed for the defence of France in Europe.

The fact that French resources were so divided had always fed the anticolonialist cause, which insisted that France should not expand abroad using forces that were needed in the defence of the home front. When finally, in 1900, a law creating the colonial army was passed and put into effect, thus incorporating colonial forces such as the *tirailleurs sénégalais* into the French armed forces, General de Gallifet could remark both truthfully and ironically that 'France will now have two armies, one metropolitan army against Germany and one colonial army against England.'[8] It would still be some time before a proper system of administration was put in place to manage colonial possessions in West and Central Africa.

In any case, the argument that there was a need for a colonial army had coloured many of the debates on the utility of the new colonial adventure of the 1880s and a brief examination of these disputes helps to explain how difficult it was to centralize the imperial expansion that seemed to take place almost by accident. When, in the early 1880s, it was realized that the law of 1872 governing the armed forces was no longer appropriate for France's needs, and reforms were proposed both to the size and structure of the French army, the issue of colonial expansion entered immediately into the discussions. One of the principal concerns of those who were militating in favour of colonies was that adequate forces be put at the disposal of those conducting colonial expansion. The dispatch of young men performing military service abroad was judged ineffective, both because these were not appropriately trained for overseas struggles and because public opinion would naturally rise up against sending non-professional soldiers abroad. Though colonial expansion was to solicit nothing more grave than public indifference, there was still a perceived need to so structure the armed forces that those carrying out military service could be insulated from the difficulties of overseas tours of duty.

Equally, the fear that the prospects for efficient mobilization in the event of a European war would be significantly hampered if large elements of the armed forces were occupied abroad, gave added value to the argument that France needed a colonial army. In May 1885 the Chamber of Deputies thus considered a draft law creating a special force for the colonies. It provided for the attachment of the *troupes de marine* to the Ministry of War, the increase in numbers of the corps stationed in Africa and their complete separation from continental mobilization. Individuals assigned to this force would be volunteers paid an extra bonus to compensate for the difficulties of serving overseas. But, though in later electoral campaigns politicians would continue to call for a colonial army to take the burden of expansion off the shoulders of young soldiers, little advance was made. A further law was discussed in 1891, yet even by 1894, when Madagascar was conquered, no such army had been created, and the government of the day was roundly criticized for having committed troops needed for home defence to a costly imperial adventure. Yet no progress resulted on the creation of a colonial army until 1900 when the *Armée Coloniale* was finally constituted as an autonomous military formation under the Ministry of War.[9] While the *Armée d'Afrique*, created by the Orléans monarchy after France's 1830 landings in Algeria (composed of some white-European-only regiments and a number of both regular and irregular indigenous regiments) provided the units which garrisoned Algeria, Tunisia and Morocco, these units often had also a home defence role. Until 1900 when colonial troops were finally transferred to the responsibility of the War Ministry a complicated array of locally raised and metropolitan units had garrison responsibilities in France's expanding empire. During the long gestation period of the *Armée Coloniale*, French troops overseas had completed the conquest of West Africa and had strengthened the French position in numerous other areas with only minimal centralized organization. Most of Black Africa was conquered during the life of the Third Republic by the *troupes de marine* whose operations were barely supervised by the small colonial department of the Ministry for the Marine.[10]

The machinery and administration of external policy making in Paris had meanwhile been in a state of near anarchy.[12] The various ministries which could claim a *droit de regard* over colonial policy regularly had disagreements over questions of policy and often even undermined each other's actions or instructions. They were sometimes forced to act in concert when colonial questions became major international issues, but otherwise it was perfectly possible for them to work either in ignorance or in opposition. The ambitions and views of civilian bureaucrats and military officers did not always mesh. Even more frightening was that within certain branches of the armed forces there was no symmetry between general plans for mobilization and eventual war, and the actual policies pursued by the men of action in the field or at sea.

During the mid-1880s, when France was committing considerable numbers of her metropolitan armed forces to overseas campaigns, the plans of the general staff were switching from an essentially defensive posture *vis-à-vis* Germany to a more offensive strategy.[11] Certainly the difficulty successive governments had in restructuring the armed forces so that the military could undertake both continental and imperial missions raises questions about whether national ambitions and general defence plans were properly coordinated. While emphasis in both the general defence plans and various army infantry regulations was placed on the need to adopt offensive strategies against Germany, debates continued in parliament about whether mobilization in time of war would be possible given the extent of overseas commitments.

A more coherent link between actual external policy and projects for modernization and reform *appeared* to exist in respect of the navy but, here also, the plans to make the *marine de guerre* able to fulfil overseas missions were developed only some time after the renewed interest in colonial expansion. Many plans were developed to give the navy important power projection capacities, but these were not carried out at the time of expansion. In fact, while a number of naval officers persistently pointed out the relative decline of French naval power in the 1870s and 1880s, parliament was extremely reluctant to grant credits for the navy. The essential tasks of the navy in the event of a European war had long been established as threefold: the defence of the coasts, protection against possible blockades and the transport to the metropole of forces stationed in Algeria.[13] A number of French naval officers in the 1880s, later known as the *Jeune Ecole*, began to elaborate more adventurous doctrines relating to the use of naval power that in many senses anticipated the writings of the American naval propagandist and historian Alfred Mahan.[14] Members of the *Jeune Ecole* strongly believed that sea power was the source of all power and that to assure France's position in the struggle for power that was taking place, command of the seas and of sea lines of communication was vital. France therefore needed a naval procurement programme that would give the navy the means both to acquire and defend French interests abroad.

For many of these officers, the demands of commercial competition with England in the mid-1880s were deemed sufficiently important for France to adopt a more aggressive naval policy which would allow France to defend external positions, and assure the protection of vital commercial routes. Resentment of English naval supremacy was high, and numerous officers in the so-called *Jeune Ecole* argued in favour of establishing further naval bases overseas which would help to paralyse the movements of the English navy. Yet these enthusiasts had their critics. Ambitious plans to increase the size of the navy and create better installations abroad were regularly rejected by ministers and, within the navy, a number of admirals felt that the search for facilities overseas seriously impinged on French capacities to sustain a sound coastal defence. Especially after the passage of the Naval Defence Act of 1889 which called for increases in the size of the English navy, many in France took the view that competition with England would be fruitless and chose instead only to ensure superiority over the combined naval strength of Germany and Italy.

The difficulty in getting ministerial approval for appropriate procurement decisions that would give France a navy matched to French political ambitions would eventually pose serious problems. By the mid-1890s the disparity with England had widened, this despite the fact that many propagandists had argued for major increases in French naval strength. Yet at the same time that this relative decline of French naval power was taking place, France had posed serious challenges to the British Empire by the pursuit of expansionist policies in Africa and Asia.[15] While the *Jeune Ecole* had proposed procurement policies that matched France's declared and evolving overseas ambitions, conservatives in the navy had blocked plans which, in their view, would have badly compromised France's abilities to defend its coasts in Europe. This particular battle between continentalists and imperialists had its analogues throughout French political and bureaucratic society.

The move towards further imperial expansion which began in the 1880s affected bureaucratic politics quite profoundly, and in particular the relationship between those responsible for foreign policy as a whole and those responsible exclusively for colonial issues. It was only in 1894 that a Ministry for the Colonies was created. Before that the department for the colonies was attached to the Ministry for the Marine until 1889, when it became part of the Ministry of Commerce. The Quai d'Orsay always opposed the creation of an independent ministry for the colonies on the grounds that colonial policy had to be considered part and parcel of foreign policy. Once a Ministry for the Colonies was created, the rivalry between it and the Quai d'Orsay immediately became great. Little co-ordination of policy took place and in some instances, when decisions could not be taken jointly, one ministry would simply arrogate to itself the power to take the action it saw fit in respect of France's external commitments.[16]

The fact that the army, the navy and the central diplomatic machinery in the 1880s and the 1890s did not have either consistent or co-ordinated policies that might support a policy of expansion underscores the point that France's experience of expansion during that period was less a centrally directed policy than a series of events which Paris tried to influence only from time to time or in periods of crisis. The Colonial Department would be forced to work with the Ministry of Foreign Affairs when it was clear that there would be important international consequences for France. This was often the case on the West African coast, for example, where the presence of other European powers meant that the central bureaucracy needed to subordinate local questions to the larger issue of managing safely the competition with other actors.[17] But in remote areas, explorers could act freely not only in situations of Parisian indifference but also when the individuals concerned knew that there was no easy way for Paris to impose its will.

For the most part, events of discovery and pacification were a result of the enthusiasm of certain explorers and officers and were justified by ideologies developed by propagandists and certain political leaders in the absence of either popular or bureaucratic consensus. In a sense there was a strange alliance between the officers in the field who had an intense sense of their own potential contribution to the grandeur of France, and political leaders in France who supported the colonialist cause and therefore the often spontaneous actions of the colonial troops, but who also stood to lose office if overseas adventures failed.

The idea that men in the field had to lead the colonial enterprise had already been evident in the mid-nineteenth century when France was pursuing campaigns in Algeria. It is well illustrated by the answer of General Bugeaud to orders he received from Paris forbidding him to begin the conquest of Kabylia: 'I have received your message. It is too late. My troops have begun to march... If we are successful the government and France will have the honour. In the opposite case, the entire responsibility will fall on me. I accept this.'[18] Many years later Marshal Lyautey would say at a meeting of the *Société de l'Histoire des colonies* that the whole secret of efficient colonial expansion was to 'take the initiative, conceive and take action without waiting for orders from "up Above" which never arrive or are negative. For those "up Above" it was always necessary, in the construction of our magnificent colonial estate, to present them with a *fait accompli*.'[19] Certainly the *faits accomplis* in distant lands with which the French parliament was often seized did not please everybody. Many thought that French patriotism was best demonstrated in France rather than in Tonkin or Madagascar. Yet the examples of military officers using minor frontier disputes in distant outposts as pretexts for making further conquests in the name of France are legion, especially in West Africa in the 1880s and 1890s. Often local chiefs would side with ambitious French officers to help them defeat a local rival or traditional enemy. Taking advantage of such regional disputes French officers were often able to exceed their instructions without need for further reinforcements to expand French overseas territory. Thus annexations often took place because the opportunity for them arose, rather then because this corresponded to either a political or an economic grand strategy.

In many areas of the world, especially perhaps in Africa, expansion was at least partially driven by the aspirations of those who thought in terms of overseas Eldorados and who held strong assumptions about both the practical and abstract gains to be had overseas. Military officers who usually became the first administrators in African territories could claim that the external pacifier that France provided for bloody inter-ethnic disputes proved the worth of France's civilizing mission. Others might argue (again often only after the fact) that expansion would create new commercial opportunities for France. Even where military conquest did not hasten commercial development (in Central Africa the resultant political instability actually retarded commercial possibilities) it could always be presented as a victory for France's image in the world.[20] This argument, by far the most important and persistent, was only possible because of the existence in France of a political culture which gave support to the idea that without an empire of prestige France would be nothing in Europe.

The Ideology of Expansion in the 1880s

The French defeat at the hands of Germany in 1870 did not immediately produce the urge for imperial expansion which was to possess a number of European states during the 1880s and 1890s. After 1870, French politicians, whose concern with questions of empire like that of all French citizens (with the exception of soldiers and sailors directly involved) was minimal, worried themselves with the problem of how best to reassert French power on the European continent, and specifically with the issue of how the lost provinces of Alsace and Lorraine could be recovered. The nationalism which formerly had been virtually the exclusive preserve of the navy became widespread, and the whole of French public opinion, whose xenophobia had in other eras been directed mostly toward the British, now became Germanophobe.

It was generally thought, by the few who in the decade after the Franco–Prussian war directed their minds to the question, that no amount of successful adventurism in Africa or Asia could relieve the pain of a military disaster in Europe which was not accepted by anyone as final. Even later supporters of the policy of colonial conquest believed with the French minister of foreign affairs, Gambetta (who eventually in the late 1870s became one of the great promoters of colonialism) that Alsace-Lorraine should be thought of always and spoken of never.[21] The ability of those who defended the colonialist cause to win their case against those who thought that all French resources should be devoted to the German problem depended on the argument that colonies were a means to the same end: increased French power *vis-à-vis* the continental enemy. But this argument took some time to take hold and only really did so at the end of the imperialist era.

For many, the pursuit of Empire was something which cost money better spent on preparing the revenge against Germany, and would wrongfully take public attention away from fighting the principal enemy on the continent. For the anticolonialists, French power could only be judged by the capacity of France to influence political outcomes in Europe; for others, the expansion of France's domain in Africa and elsewhere would create new measures of international power and status favourable to France. Few easily accepted this latter argument. The idea that power outside Europe could both compensate for lack of power within Europe, and boost whatever power was in any case possessed there, the concept of the inter-relationship between European and Imperial power, never really took hold in the France of the 1870s. Cabinets persistently took the view that questions of Empire were of peripheral importance to the affairs of the metropole. No French foreign minister of the 1870s could say as did Lord Roseberry in 1892 that 'our foreign policy has become a colonial policy.'[22] As late as 1897 De Lanessan, the former governor of Indochina could claim: 'We have been pushed towards distant enterprises largely by a need to give an occupation to the army and to the marine.'[23]

Yet the intellectual foundation to justify a new surge of imperial expansion was beginning to be laid in the 1870s, by parliamentarians, economists, geographers and men of letters who themselves held a certain image of French power that needed an imperial dimension to be fulfilled. Some of this propaganda and ideology had its sources in established territories overseas, where colonists made appeals to those in the metropole to recall that their future could still have an African aspect. The archbishop of Algiers, Monsignor Lavigerie, even launched a direct appeal to refugees of Alsace-Lorraine to cross the Mediterranean and develop a new France, 'an African France', which was 'as French as the France you have lost and ready to welcome you'. Africa would be a refuge, a place to start again, for if 'In France everything seems finished, in the immensity of Africa, on the contrary, everything is beginning.'[24]

This appeal to a missionary zeal, from a missionary, was also the call of geographers who insisted that explorations might have a political utility that went beyond the obvious 'scientific value' of overseas exploration. The geographical societies became important places to discuss the colonial idea, and membership in them grew from 780 in 1873 to 2,000 in 1880 and 3,500 in 1881.[25] The various societies that grew up in the cities of the provinces concentrated as much on political issues as on the science of geography. Some of these groups, like the *Société de géographie commerciale* served to finance overseas expeditions, as well as convincing public opinion of the need for expansion, sometimes focusing on the commercial gains that would result.[26] These arguments themselves often led to discussions in parliament about the possible need to extend preferential trade agreements to acquired colonies or to develop clear protectionist policies. It was left to the free traders to point out the then still tiny fraction of foreign trade that the colonies represented. Yet the general contention that colonies would halt French decline in an economic as much as in the political sense was almost always part of any public apology for a policy of colonial acquisition.

Still, the theme that France must expand in order to avoid falling into political and social decadence was the central idea of those who began to write about colonies in the 1870s. Typical of the sort of writing that began to emerge was a book of 1874, entitled *De la colonisation chez les peuples modernes*, written by Paul Leroy-Beaulieu, an economist, whose arguments were quickly picked up by journalists and other publicists. In a celebrated passage of his work, Leroy-Beaulieu argued that colonization represented the 'expansive force of a people', and that those who colonized first would rank first: 'A people who colonize are a people who establish the basis of their grandeur and supremacy for the future.'[27] In the preface to the second edition of his work Leroy-Beaulieu went further: 'colonization is for France a question of life or death: either France will become a great African power or it will be, in one or two centuries, only a secondary European power.'[28] Leroy-Beaulieu's basic tenet was that France should pursue a defensive policy in the continent of Europe, but that abroad, only a policy of expansion could satisfy France's legitimate needs. These sorts of arguments quickly found their way into journals which were read by the intellectual elite and large sectors of the bourgeoisie. Publications such as the *Revue des Deux Mondes*, *L'Economiste Français* or *Le Temps* became filled with articles by colonial enthusiasts.[29]

While some works would focus on the need to strengthen French prestige and others on the economic utility of overseas possessions, there were numerous articles which caught the public eye and were intended to appeal to the French sense of adventure. These sometimes also may have tested the French sense of humour. In 1874, Captain Elie Roudaire developed a plan in the *Revue des Deux Mondes* to connect the salt lakes south of Tunisia and Algeria with the Mediterranean. By extending the lakes into a large inland sea, the climate would change and this would help to fertilize the adjacent desert.[30] Adolphe Duponchel, who was an engineer, published a pamphlet advocating the construction of a trans-Saharan railway. This idea was taken quite seriously in 1879 by Admiral Jean Jaureguiberry, then Minister of the Marine, who felt such a railway might help to consolidate French political influence in the Upper Senegal and Niger regions.[31]

He was aided in the advancement of this ambitious railway project by Louis Freycinet, the Minister for Public Works, who felt that such a railway would be an essential piece of infrastructure which would allow France to increase trade and commerce in Africa. Jaureguiberry and Freycinet worked together to convince parliament of both the economic and political merits of the railway project. In the debates in parliament dealing with the trans-Saharan project, speakers consistently referred to the need for France to take advantage of her geographical proximity to the African continent and to undertake projects which, no matter how ambitious, would help to secure France's place among the great powers seeking to establish positions there. Maurice Rouvier, rapporteur on one of the budget debates dealing with the Duponchel idea, gave fervent expression to the notion that France had to be in Africa or be nowhere:

France, which is closer to the African continent than the majority of other nations, more interested than them in the future of the continent because of her possessions in Algeria, Senegal, Gabon and other positions established on the West African Coast; France cannot allow herself not to take part in this movement which brings Europe to African regions whose riches we are only now understanding. Does not the concern for grandeur and the interests of our nation demand that we place ourselves at the head of this movement?[32]

While parliament did not want to approve such a risky grand design as a fully fledged trans-Saharan railway, it did give credits for an expedition to Upper Senegal, which helped to set off the new phase of French expansion in West Africa. An examination of the contemporary documents supports the view that this new expansion had very little central control and barely any regional supervision. After Jaureguiberry had sent instructions to Colonel Desbordes, in charge of the campaign to reach Kita in Niger as part of the mission that parliament had approved, the Governor of Senegal sent his own message which emphasized the difficulties of the mission but also contained phrases which delegated near total power to the colonel: 'You enjoy complete liberty of action in the Upper River from a military, political and economic point of view; the distance that separates us during the dry season prohibits me from interfering in the interests placed in your hands.'[33]

While the pursuit of French glory, when it again began to manifest itself nearly ten years after a humiliating defeat at the hands of Germany, was without much concern handed over to the military, quite stormy debates took place in Paris about the virtues of the imperialist cause. In the capital, nationalists confronted each other over continental and overseas priorities. Initially, few believed that an imperial role could be subordinated to the need for a strong role in Europe. Fewer still believed that it was possible to combine both continental and overseas missions. In 1891, a professor at the *Ecole Coloniale*, Louis Vignon, wrote a book on the expansion of France in which he argued that while Great Britain was a maritime power, and Germany a continental one, France needed to assume both missions:

how is it possible to ask that France renounces one of these two policies, that she choose one of these, which would be to abandon something of herself, part of her heritage that has been slowly acquired by preceding generations[34]

But such views, which became the language of colonial advocates in the 1890s, as a whole array of colonial organizations and pressure groups were being founded and were successful in making their voices heard, were not current in the 1880s. Then, the debates on the orientations and the sources of French power (often the same debate) were intense and acrimonious.

The ascendency of the colonialist cause and its success – even if temporary – in winning over those whose main concern was Germany was in large measure due to the fact that Léon Gambetta (President and Minister of Foreign Affairs 1881–2), long considered one of the political figures most closely associated with those calling for a *revanche* against Germany, eventually became himself a supporter of imperial designs. He had even given hints of this soon after the defeat of 1870, long before he was to encourage Jules Ferry to pursue an imperialist policy. In a speech he gave in Anger on 7 April 1872 Gambetta spoke of the dangers of the then accepted policy of *recueillement*:

To truly retake the position in the world that belongs to it, France cannot accept to lean back on itself: it is by expansion, by a *rayonnement* in the life outside, by the place we take in the general life of humanity that nations persist and last; if that life were to end, it would be the end of France.[35]

In the course of his 'imperial education' Gambetta was to elaborate three basic justifications for expansion.[36] One concentrated on the need to develop France's external commerce and essentially relied on old mercantilist arguments that did not suit the era of free trade. The law of July 1861 by which the regime of Napoleon III did away with the stringent protectionist measures of the *pacte coloniale* was regretted and the hope that new reserved markets could be found to increase French economic power animated a number of colonial enthusiasts who rallied round Gambetta.

A second basic argument proceeded from the assumption that colonial expansion would be useful to solve some of France's social ills. The *Gambettistes* in many instances supported those who argued that to preserve France's social institutions it was necessary to colonize. The pursuit of colonies was a way to calm domestic instability and reaffirm the validity of

French structures. For some *Gambettistes*, social peace in the industrial age was a question of finding outlets for otherwise divisive tendencies. One strong supporter of Gambetta, Joseph Reinach, wrote in a book published in 1882 that it was necessary to expatriate those who had no future in France but could make a new future for France overseas. From dangerous elements that created social disunity it was necessary to create a force for progress and grandeur for the mother country. For writers such as Reinach, colonial expansion was a way of solving some of France's social problems; an attitude which the political opponents to Gambetta probably found to be a poor substitute for a coherent domestic social policy. Naturally, the leading colonizers themselves sometimes argued that living away from France allowed them to make better use of their energies. Lyautey was to argue at Oran in 1907, for example, that he was a convinced colonialist precisely because it allowed him to escape from the horrid internecine disputes of the metropole. Many of those who stayed in their Paris armchairs advanced the idea that France would be saved by her colonies; Emile Zola wrote romantically 'of that other France, of the Sudan'.[37]

But the most important argument advanced by the most vocal of Gambetta's supporters was undoubtedly patriotic. It concentrated on the need to ensure that France would not be found lacking in a competition which was engaging the primary powers of Europe. Gambetta's support of the Tunisian expedition in 1881, defined by Gambetta as an operation of prestige that would mark the re-entry of France into international politics, sparked off four years of near-colonial fever in France, during which the arguments of patriotism and prestige dominated the debate on imperialism. Essential to this new and essentially fragile consensus on the need for imperial expansion, was the tacit admission that assymetries in the European balance of power mattered less when one put the European situation in the context of a global balance. Success overseas would provide a form of compensatory power for relative weaknesses in Europe. While the radicals and the monarchists were not easily drawn to this argument, the Opportunist wing of the Republican Party was perfectly able to support projects that would enhance France's prestige, though that support would be withdrawn once it was clear that external adventures were not properly controlled or proved dangerous. A colonial policy which won France position on the world stage would be the next best thing to the direct collection of reparations from Germany.

For some supporters of the colonial policy, expansion was the last chance for French power. It was argued, for example, that the abandonment of the expedition to Tunis would be noted by other European states. A diplomatic dispatch from the French Embassy in Berlin in 1881 argued that 'if we give a new sign of weakness we will be reduced to the rank of Spain.'[38] The eventual decision of the new President of the Council, Jules Ferry, to mount the Tunisian expedition, against the advice of the Ministry of War and a former president, Jules Grévy (who thought that Tunisia was not worth '*un cigare de deux sous*') naturally required Ferry to develop a coherent justification for new overseas activities.[39] In the event, Ferry became the most famous nineteenth-century exponent of French imperialism. Largely under his direction and with the support of Gambetta, France undertook expeditions to Tunis, and to Tonkin, to the Gulf of Guinea and to Upper Senegal, through the Sudan, Niger and the Congo. Later successes in Madagascar and Morocco owed their political justifications to the sorts of arguments which were honed in the 1880s during the height of republican influence on foreign affairs.

The vocabulary and the images used by Jules Ferry (President 1880–1, and 1883–5) to justify expansion were by the early 1880s part of the pool of ideas on which a whole army of colonial propagandists were constantly drawing. These were largely focused on the concepts of prestige and of mission with which French imperialism would be so closely associated. In one procolonialist journal, the *Journal des Débats*, Gabriel Charmes, who wrote often on the colonial question, gave a basic justification for expansion which combined the language of power politics and competition with the images of prestige and grandeur in a manner which would be henceforth the hallmark of the French imperialist instinct:

The time is past when it was enough to be a great nation in Europe to be assured a future and to hold a preponderant place in history. The struggle of races and of peoples has from now on the whole globe as its theatre: each advances towards the conquest of unoccupied territories. Soon all the places will be taken...in the middle of this general expansionist movement, of this universal push, it would be the case that a France which stubbornly chose to take abdication for *recueillement*, on the pretext of having lost provinces in Europe, would lose again her prestige and her possessions on the Mediterranean.[40]

For those who would always recall the embarrassing position in which France found herself in Europe, having ceded two provinces by treaty and reduced within frontiers that were unfair constraints on a great nation, there were also those who reinforced in the minds of doubters the importance for France of remaining active elsewhere, especially given that revisionist policies within Europe were for a time excluded by all as a realistic course of action. These propagandists did not, as they naturally hoped, capture the public imagination – the public, eventually would be more impressed by defeat abroad than by initial conquest – but they held positions of influence within government which influenced the structure and the style of parliamentary debate on these issues. A preface written to a book on English colonial policy by Alfred Rambaud, a *chef de cabinet* of Jules Ferry, gives an indication of a logic of imperial expansion conceived intentionally to defeat those who thought that French activity could only concentrate on the European continent:

If there is a people for whom it is a necessity in these times to make a great effort to reconstitute its colonial Empire, it is surely the French people. After having filled the world with its activity...it finds itself enclosed at home by frontiers of iron and moreover by the new situation of Europe...such a people...could not but be exasperated by its impotence, the warrior instincts would be transferred into internal quarrels, into bloody intrigues, class hatred, perhaps even civil war.[41]

These two quotations perhaps sum up best the full force of the republican argument: French prestige and the need for national unity required a policy of expansion. But the vision put before the French parliament was never so passionate as when the need for overseas Empire had to be defended at a time of apparent crisis or after an overseas failure. It is for this reason that the parliamentary debates of 1885, held when France's policy in Tonkin had resulted in more conflict with China than had been anticipated and quite serious diplomatic problems with England, are worth citing. Fanned by fears expressed in the press that a French defeat in China would be 'another Sedan', senior figures of Ferry's opposition, who had for some time considered his colonial policy dangerous, and who wished for a whole range of reasons of domestic policy to see the end of his rule, succeeded in bringing him down. In famous debates of July 1885, after Ferry's fall, the colonialist and anticolonialist arguments were put forward with a vigour that would permanently affect the way in which the value of overseas power would be debated.

Jules Ferry's sweeping defence of his policies took into account industrial, commercial, humanitarian, social and moral questions but the central and most remembered argument was driven by nationalist sentiments. His definition of a great nation needing to act abroad and to refuse any hint of abdication for fear of dropping to the third or fourth rank was a powerful image. He also sought to reconvert parliament by showing that no other image of France could be acceptable:

The republican party has shown that it has well understood that one could not propose to France a political ideal similar to those of Belgium or Switzerland something else is needed for France: it can not simply be a free country, it must also be a great country exercising over the destinies of Europe all the influence that belongs to it, that it should spread this influence over the world, and take wherever it can its language, its customs, its flag, its arms, its genius.[42]

This desire to achieve or maintain great-power status by overseas activity would be displayed many times by French leaders, even long after the period of decolonization, but the sense that French national power had to be measured by the range of overseas activity was not a given of the colonial age. A few days after Ferry's speech, Georges Clemenceau provided the essence of the opposition rebuttal:

you pretend to open up commercial routes yet at the same time there are other nations near us who having not made any expenditures on colonial acquisitions enter into battle with us on the ground that we have chosen. As they have budgets that have not been hurt by the costs of such expeditions they compete with us strongly and take away commerce from us even in our own markets.[43]

A number of opposition leaders and anticolonialists added to this basic economic protest other arguments that struck at the heart of popular French concerns. In the July 1885 debate it was an economist, Frédéric Passy, who made the most striking political point, one which probably most closely matched the views of the French public, still essentially pacifist and not easily swayed by the images of grandeur so eloquently conjured up by the procolonialists:

I believe that we, the opponents of these distant adventures, are better managers of the expansive force of the nation, better representatives of the national mentality, and of national patriotism, when we refuse to sacrifice for pure losses precious things – the gold and blood of France.[44]

Many of these anticolonialist arguments were presented by the radical left and the monarchist right for reasons of domestic politics. They succeeded in taking the wind out of the sails of the most ardent procolonialist politicians. At the same time they made the advocates of colonialism redouble their efforts to organize themselves and present a better case for expansion. The emergence of the *parti colonial*, a loose society of pressure groups, largely based in Paris and devoted to the colonialist cause, was a sign that the colonial cause was not dead. Throughout the late 1890s and the early part of the twentieth century it served to influence a number of politicians and was able to organize colonial expeditions and promulgate the need for an ever larger French Empire. Some of its members developed political doctrines to justify policies of foreign domination and eventually, though only some time after most French expansion was completed, it was able to instil in Frenchmen the idea that Empire was an important source of French power.

Colonial Propaganda, Doctrine and the Prewar Period

The members of the *parti colonial* worked within and outside parliament to promote the colonial idea. In the Chamber of Deputies, the *groupe colonial* (founded in the summer of 1892) was at times extremely powerful and could exert an important influence on foreign policy. It brought together deputies from all political parties united in their belief in the colonial cause. It played a leading role in developing the Fashoda strategy of the 1890s which sought to challenge British control of Egypt. The fact that the French cabinet did not know of initial expeditions to Fashoda in 1893 and despite approving an expedition in 1896 was surprised to find itself in 1898 seized with a crisis that almost led to war with England, was an indication of the lack of control the government had maintained on French foreign policy.[45] It also was some measure of the influence of colonial groups on some aspects of French foreign policy. As President Felix Faure remarked with some bitterness at the time of the Fashoda crisis: 'We have behaved crazily in Africa, dragged along by irresponsible people who call themselves colonialists.'[46]

Outside parliament, the *Union Coloniale Française* (founded in 1893) was able over a period to amass considerable riches and regularly published a journal called *Politique Coloniale*. It was mainly a society of businessmen who had important interests in the colonies and sometimes did not share the views of other colonial groups, such as the *Comité de l'Afrique Française* which, while having strong links with business circles, was motivated mainly by nationalistic sentiments. The *Comité* was formed in 1890 and was both the most serious and the most influential of the colonial groups. Its focus was less on spinning out propaganda or on organizing lavish dinners to discuss colonial issues, than on providing subsidies for treaty-making expeditions to Africa. The *Comité's* great ambition was to unite France's various African possessions in the Sudan, Congo, Algeria and Tunisia to create an African bloc. It worked discreetly and closely with government to make further expansion in Africa possible.[47] It had an especially close connection with the Ministry of the Colonies. Senior members of the *Comité*, notably Eugène Etienne and Théophile Delcasse, came to occupy leading positions in the Ministry. The *Comité* strongly supported the idea of challenging British power in the Upper Nile and was actually opposed on this issue by the *Union Coloniale* who did not feel that French business interests could be advanced in the Upper Nile, and could not approve of an expedition that engaged only questions of national prestige.[48]

In the latter part of the nineteenth century and as the twentieth century opened the highest priority of the *parti colonial*, and particularly of Eugène Etienne, was the addition of Morocco to the French Empire. The initially very cautious policy of the Quai d'Orsay towards Morocco was transformed by Etienne who believed that the future of France lay in establishing a protectorate over Morocco. Such a protectorate could not be 'shared' with anyone since the security of Algeria intimately depended on complete French control in the region. This was claimed as a matter of right, Etienne arguing in 1898 that it was necessary for France to assert influence over Morocco where France had 'incontestable rights'.[49] The eventual creation of a protectorate in 1911 owed much to pressure on the government by the *parti colonial*, which was nevertheless annoyed that it was established at a price. The Agadir crisis of November 1911 which ended when Germany chose to recognize the protectorate in return for a slice of the French Congo reconfirmed that colonial expansion would always have to take into account the interests of other European powers. For some, the bargain that was struck also served to establish in the minds of colonialists clear areas of priority for French power. The right wing parliamentarian Maurice Barres made a vital distinction when he remarked on the bargain: '*Le Maroc: question nationale. Le Congo: question coloniale.*'[50]

The idea that North Africa was of more direct importance to France than was Black Africa would endure for over fifty years, though later some would also see in control over Black Africa a means of ensuring the great-power status of a 'larger France'. French control over North Africa, assured with the acquisition of Morocco, gave France considerable power in the Mediterranean region. No area in Black Africa could offer the same geopolitical advantages to France. France's prestige in North Africa was directly related to military power, and French control in the area, in turn, was of great strategic value to France. Later in the twentieth century, the bloc of francophone Black Africa, protected by French control of North Africa, would begin to assume greater importance as statesmen would see in the vast holdings of French West and Equatorial Africa symbols of French prestige.

In any case, the various expansionist policies pursued by French governments from the 1880s to the early part of the twentieth century eventually required a broad guiding doctrine that went beyond simple assertions of the need to enhance French prestige or specific calculations about the regional balance of power. If overseas influence would help give France greater status in comparison to those other European powers who had been slow or ineffective in the race for colonies, it would nevertheless be important to develop a coherent ideology which properly incorporated colonies into a national design. The ideologies of overseas influence and the doctrines of colonial management developed by French publicists eventually became more than an explanation for French power; they became mechanisms for the perpetuation of French influence.

Much of the writing produced by members of the *parti colonial* as the struggle took place to acquire possessions and influence in Africa, the Middle East and Asia centred on developing such ideologies of control and domination. These would generally, at least in the first instance, not distinguish between types of overseas possessions, a tendency against which Joseph Chailley-Bert (a secretary general of the *Union Coloniale Française*) argued in a book he published in 1902. He was struck by the numerous vague phrases that were customarily bandied about whenever colonies were discussed: axioms and pronouncements on *les colonies, la politique coloniale, la mise en valeur des colonies*. He argued that it was fruitless to consider the colonies as a bloc to which a single set of images or policies could apply and that it was necessary to distinguish between various types of colonies according to age, population, resources and their utility to France. A failure properly to distinguish types of colonies had led to mistakes. No other imperial power had the same tendency to group all their possessions in the same way:

it is worth declaring that there is no bloc, that the theory of the bloc in colonial matters is false; and moreover it is a theory that exists only in France. Dutch and German authors are shocked at our linguistic confusions, source of our errors of conduct. The English do not permit themselves a theory of unity on their colonies; and neither their authors nor their legislators would dream to see in India, for example, anything else but a possession: the word colony here would appear to them a solecism.[51]

Even today, in their view of those countries, particularly in Africa, where they continue to have influence, the French persist in treating these states as part of a bloc, a unity with whom relations are assessed on the basis of general rather than individual attitudes. It is difficult now to speak of a French policy towards Senegal or Gabon, easier to understand however how specific decisions taken in respect of these countries are part of a general strategy for Black Africa. This certainly has its roots in some of the colonial theories of the nineteenth century which emphasized the inherent unity and symmetry of African possessions. These doctrines were elaborated in part to suggest ways in which administrators could view their colonial mission, in part to create in France a 'colonial opinion'; that *sentiment imperiale* which French colonialists believed was what made the British Empire great.

The first and most basic colonial doctrine to be implicitly accepted by most Frenchmen who had anything to do with colonies was 'assimilation'. It was certainly taken on by the republicans who guided French expansion in the 1880s. They accepted the idea of assimilation as part of official colonial practice. The policy of assimilation essentially was both a statement and an expectation: it stated that the colonies were a natural prolongation of the metropole, provinces *outre-mer* which should receive institutions and administration similar to that of France. The historian Charles-Robert Ageron has described those who believed in assimilation as:

dominated by the spirit of Roman law that impregnated all institutions and by the tradition of unity dear to the French spirit, republican statesmen had no greater concern than to transport to the colonies the whole administrative and judicial machinery ... of the metropole.[52]

This attitude of mind was often criticized. The bonapartiste deputy Jules Delafosse argued in 1891 that 'we colonize only in order to indulge in the export of our bureaucracy.'[53] But the expectation that the assimilationists nurtured to justify their export of bureaucracy was that in the process those who were colonized by France would in some senses become French; they would be assimilated into French ways of thinking. This would not only enhance French power, by creating abroad a community of like minded individuals who would naturally support France, it was also a means by which to consolidate power in the colonized areas. As Arthur Girault, one of the strongest advocates of assimilation, put it in his book *Principes de colonisation et de législation coloniale*, published in 1894:

The policy of assimilation is the ... security ... which prevents rupture. To the man whom we prevent from being the first in his country because his country is a colony, one must offer him in exchange the possibility of being the first *chez nous*. In the people whom we wish to prohibit the expression of local patriotism, we must inculcate the love of a common fatherland, the cult of the Empire.[54]

The concept of assimilation therefore had within it the idea of a *France d'outre-mer* which could be created by a successful *mission civilisatrice*. Assimilation meant that the colony could become an integral part of the mother country 'with its society and population made over to whatever extent possible in her image.'[55] The extreme version of assimilation which sometimes found its way into the speeches of certain parliamentarians or the writings of some publicists had it that assimilation could lead to the granting of French citizenship to colonial peoples. This complete view of assimilation was never really carried into practice. As Alistair Horne has pointed out, in Algeria, where the concept of assimilation was perhaps most strongly advocated, given that so many Frenchmen did come to see in Algeria an extension of France, 'by 1936, after seventy-five years of "assimilation", no more than 2,500 Muslims had actually crossed the bar to French citizenship.'[56]

While some colonialists took to the doctrine of 'assimilation' easily and supported it as a guiding principle of French colonial activity, others preferred what came to be known as 'association' as a more appropriate doctrine. Assimilation was the doctrine preferred by those who felt a public need to justify colonialism; association was adopted by those who had actually to administer colonies, for whom the high ideals of assimilation were both abstract and dangerous. One of the main advocates of association, Jules Harmand, argued in his *Domination et colonisation* published in 1910 that association was 'indirect administration, with the preservation but improved governance of the institutions of the conquered peoples, and with respect for the past'.[57] Also strongly supported by General Lyautey in Morocco, who prided himself on not interfering unnecessarily with local rulers, the idea of association became the staple description of French colonial practice especially in the interwar years. As early as 1905 the Ministry of Colonies actually decreed that it was necessary to substitute the policy of association for the policy of domination.

Central to the idea of association was the concept of co-operation. Assimilation was dangerous in the eyes of the 'association theorists' because forcing people to adopt French culture might inspire resentment and revolution. Association would create the possibilities for a more mutually beneficial exchange between the metropole and the colonies. The idea was that the management of colonial areas would be more effective if the native and Frenchmen worked together within the framework of native institutions. This relationship was to be founded on the basis of 'fraternity' not 'equality' but co-operation would help ensure that the native would not believe that his sense of self was lost within the French Empire. As it happened, neither of these doctrines was ever really practised as the theorists suggested: assimilation, because overseas colonies were never integrated into the French state; and association, because French colonial administration in most instances came to exercise direct rule.

Whatever the differences between the two doctrines, the words that described them, assimilation and association, did naturally imply an intimate link, in different forms, between the metropole and overseas possessions. That link was not profoundly understood by the French public before the

First World War, but the experience of the war brought home to many the elemental contribution that colonies could make to French power. During the war the Empire had provided over 500,000 soldiers to fight in Europe and about 200,000 workers for metropolitan industries.[58] The idea of the *force noire* had been launched in 1910 by a French officer, Colonel Mangin, who felt it was necessary for France to draw on the Empire for its fighting force. This was not new; the *tirailleurs sénégalais* had fought in the Franco–Prussian war, but the republican governments had not built on this experience. Mangin was a strong advocate of colonial conscription. In his book of 1910 he exalted the idea of '*la plus grande France*, which goes from the North Sea to the mouth of the Congo' and he argued that the peoples of all this area should be prepared to contribute directly to the defence of metropolitan France.[59] The estimates made of the possibilities of recruitment in Africa by the followers of Mangin – certain colonial administrators and some officers of the general staff – were hopelessly exaggerated. There was much less available manpower in Africa for the defence of France than many of the enthusiasts believed. The section of the French officer corps responsible for developing war plans never calculated, in any case, that Africans would be used in Europe. The French *état major* in the prewar period only envisaged that Black Africans might have to replace white soldiers in North Africa.

Nevertheless, slowly, in the immediate years leading to the war, there was some recruitment of soldiers in both North and West Africa. Despite the recognized overestimation of the manpower available for recruitment, and the acknowledged lack of planning, once the war began, efforts were increased to recruit Black African soldiers for the war in Europe, and as early as 1914 African soldiers were brought to France. The High Command, who viewed such use of African soldiers as experimental, and as a palliative to the then governor general of the *Afrique Occidentale Française* (William Ponty), who wanted French West Africa to play its role in the defence of the motherland, eventually came to view African participation in the war as a necessity.[60] This effort at recruitment was accelerated later in the war, though there were some colonial administrators who began to object to this practice. This was largely because African troops were sometimes brought into the front line with almost no training and the results in African death tolls often reflected this lack of preparation. By November 1917 the Empire had provided 330,000 wartime recruits, with the largest contingents – 90,000 and 85,000 men respectively – coming from West Africa and Algeria.[61] There were some officers who considered that further recruitment in the colonies would be fruitless since African troops were thought unsuitable for European fighting. Even though they may have had potential, there was little opportunity to train them adequately for warfare in the trenches. A mixed opinion on the value of African troops was provided by General Micheler: 'These troops are certainly very brave, but their value depends upon their leaders, and if the leaders disappear, all that remains is a flock ready to go astray.'[62] Despite these assessments, by late 1917 the manpower problem was becoming serious and, it fell to the former opponent of Empire, Georges Clemenceau, to renew efforts at recruitment. In a report he received on taking office he was told:

There are two Frances – metropolitan France and colonial France – who should properly form a single entity. The former represents forty million inhabitants, the latter fifty million. Logically, these ninety million human beings, representing a total population equal to that of the continental German Empire, should have been equally represented in the front line. We could have achieved this result if we had made preparations in peacetime – and unhappily we did not – for the systematic organization of our native military forces.[63]

Here was the most forthright argument for how Empire could help compensate for lack of power in Europe. It was able to convince someone for whom the abstractions of an empire of prestige had never had much attraction. It resulted in a new recruiting drive, which was organized by a black deputy from Senegal, Blaise Diagne (the first African to sit in the French parliament) who was specially appointed as *Commissaire de la République* for the purpose. By the end of 1918 France had 200,000 black troops in the army, 125,000 of whom were used in combat at the Dardanelles Straits, on the Bulgarian Front and on the Western Front.[64] The experience of the use of Africans in this way for the war in Europe was to have profound effects for the vision Frenchmen were to have of the place of colonies in national life.

War and the Enduring Images of French Power and Africa

In seeking the sources of the binding nature of the relationship between France and Africa, the images of Franco–African unity which were thrown up by the First World War hold more importance than some of the abstract doctrines developed in the previous years to explain the nature of France's links with the colonies. By the end of the war, some tangible evidence had been provided of the way in which Africa could serve as a source of power for the French state. The dispatch of men and materiel from Africa to Europe in the service of French national interests on the continent gave a practical display of the way in which Empire could strengthen France's continental position. The integration of African troops in the European battlefront, even if often ineffective and sometimes disastrous, would help to support the later arguments of propagandists who would speak of the essential unity of France and the Empire which the theories of assimilation and association were meant to advance.

If immediately after the war there was little discussion about the role of overseas possessions in national life – all political effort was concentrated on managing the consequences of the Versailles treaty – the effect of the war on the nature of colonial propaganda would nevertheless be very important. The official doctrines of assimilation or association did not capture the imagination of journalists, publicists or politicians who would address themselves to Empire. More often, geographical metaphors would dominate. Hence, the ideas of *France–Afrique* and *Eurafrique* which began to be used reflected a special interest in the African dimension of Empire and of French power.

As colonial interests in the Orient and Asia began to fade, a tendency which was incorporated in a pre-war phrase that gained some currency: '*Lâchons l'Asie, Prenons L'Afrique*', French territories in Africa became increasingly invested with properties which would contribute to the reinforcement of national grandeur. Propagandists and politicians alike alternatively referred to the importance of maintaining the unity of *France–Afrique* or of *Eurafrique* in order to sustain French influence on the world stage and French power in Europe. It was these visions of France's overseas power which subliminally affected the attitude of the French state to the retention of influence overseas. The ideas that flowed from the use of these terms – many of them quite outstandingly superficial – are important because they indicated an acceptance of the view that Africa was an integral part of France, an attitude which would naturally infect the process of decolonization. The use of these terms, which were developed in the interwar period, but which even now retain some limited currency, symbolized the importance of influence in Africa as an indicator of French strength. For the proponents of continued development of France's African possessions, the terms *France–Afrique* and *Eurafrique* helped to reinforce the notion that Africa was a special reserve of national energies and power. If there is one psychological legacy of the late nineteenth- and early twentieth-century French imperialist expansion in Africa it is the idea – incorporated in these two terms – that France and Africa could form a mutually beneficial bloc which would be able to defend French grandeur against a hostile world.

3

The *France–Afrique* and *Eurafrique* Ideas

It has been remarked that the French public was not interested in colonies except to the extent that they 'entered into national projects'.[1] For colonies to be of interest – for the strange and, in the popular mind, savage territories of Africa to hold the public imagination – they had to be of use, or enter into some grand scheme. Drafters of such grand schemes could only expect to interest public opinion when there had been a recent experience that would help to suggest that French national power or prestige could have overseas sources. The image, some would say myth, of the *force noire* battling in Europe for the mother country provided scope for post-First World War propagandists to reassert the importance of Africa for national security. But the projects and ideas they promoted had still to be defined in terms which had historical meaning, and could be placed within a geopolitical context.

By the end of the First World War, France had expanded her Empire in Africa. Most politicians turned their minds to continental questions, but colonial enthusiasts laboured to consider ways in which France's possessions and interests in North and tropical Africa could be merged. The aesthetic desire to create an indissoluble whole of imperial possessions lying south of the French hexagon led, as it did in the 1880s, to the development of often fanciful projects for the *mise en valeur* of the colonies. These are not worth examining, but the labels by which some of thse designs came to be known served a political and cultural purpose which colonialists would find important. These designs, which were by and large concentrated only on Africa, served to bind that continent into an imagery of national prestige which would solidify over time. France's Middle Eastern interests may have been thought of greater importance than possessions in tropical Africa which were poor and could offer little economic advantage. Yet the Middle East never became absorbed into an idea, an *image* of a geographical whole which linked it to France. Indochina, which before the war had been able to fire the colonial imagination, remained important economically, but the vision of a South East Asian Eldorado had long disappeared.[2] After the war, if people considered the need to develop overseas possessions, to incorporate them in a new national project, they thought largely of Africa, which could be absorbed into a geopolitical grand design.

Africa's place in a French geopolitical design had somehow to be described. The colonial doctrines of assimilation and association had their uses as guides to colonial administrators and offered vague descriptions of the aims of French colonial policy. But neither of these doctrines could be expected to serve as an inspiration for a determined overseas policy in Africa. These doctrines could explain the intended relationship between France and native populations, but they did not, in and of themselves, explain why France wanted such a relationship. For some, colonial policy was an aspect of power politics and of a general world policy, and those who felt the need to emphasize the link between France's role in Africa and France's greatness spoke of the large 'unity' that was formed by France and her possessions in Africa. When the concept of a 'larger France' was focused on Africa, when politicians or publicists wished to declare France great in part because France had been 'extended' into Africa, reliance was placed on images of a Franco–African entity which would symbolize the greatness of France. The mere idea of *France–Afrique* as a single geopolitical whole, was often implicitly or explicitly offered as the goal of continued French activity in Africa. Sometimes the image of *Eurafrique*, initially German in origin, was conjured up by Frenchmen who believed that France could lead the other Europeans in Africa. The *France-Afrique* and *Eurafrique* notions were important only insofar as they symbolized the intensity with which Frenchmen believed that links with Africa were indissoluble. These labels were often devoid of political content, and when they were descriptions of political programmes, these tended to be impractical.

The *Eurafrique* design posited a policy of European co-operation in Africa, and had both historical and intellectual roots in the nineteenth century. It was sometimes presented as an alternative, sometimes as a necessary complement to the idea of a greater France which was part of the *France–Afrique* notion. Both these myths became the subject of debate in the interwar years and were later taken up after the Second World War. While the concepts themselves seemed eccentric, both *Eurafrique* and *France–Afrique* could be made to have policy implications. People talked about political unification of France and Africa or of Europe and Africa, and even if this talk was abstract it reinforced the idea that France (or Europe) belonged in Africa. Both these notions were especially powerful because they were not only accepted, but sometimes even promoted by distinguished African leaders. The concepts of *France–Afrique* and *Eurafrique* were therefore not only politically useful at home, in attracting people to a grand design of overseas control, they were also helpful abroad in helping to secure, amongst elites, overseas support for a policy of control disguised by the language of common destiny. It must be underlined that the actual proponents of the myths of *France–Afrique* or *Eurafrique* were often marginal figures, both intellectually and politically, but the arguments they put forward nevertheless helped to evolve ideas about the French relationship with Africa which were of lasting significance.

This chapter will examine the interplay of these two notions, looking first at how the *Eurafrique* idea was developed in the prewar period, and then at ways it was later taken up as a slogan by both French propagandists and African leaders. It competed with, and was sometimes awkwardly used as a synonym for, the more nationalist notion of *France–Afrique* which implied an exclusive control by France of African interests. Some writers used the term *Eurafrique* to refer to ways in which Europe could co-operate in Africa, others used it to explain ways in which France could lead European activity in Africa, yet others would, even more ambitiously, argue that France, because of her unique interests in both Europe and Africa, was in a special position to lead both continents. *France–Afrique* was a term deployed by both propagandists and politicians to refer more specifically to the need to ensure that African material and human resources could be developed to service French needs. It later became used by those who wished to create practical agreements, as the prospect of decolonization approached, to link Africa more efficiently to France by economic, juridical and military means. Both concepts applied to all of Africa where France held influence, but both initially clearly focused on the need to link France and Europe to North Africa. The attraction of both concepts was that once, after the end of the Algerian war, French influence in North Africa was dissipated, they could be used to describe France's continuing relationship with Black Africa, and as we shall see, all leaders of the Fifth Republic, at one time or another, used these concepts in their speeches on Africa.

The Roots of *Eurafrique*

The political origins of the *Eurafrique* idea can be traced to the Berlin Conference of November 1884 on West Africa, at which the great powers of Europe managed some of the conflicts in which they were then involved on the African continent. The aims of the various participants were, in fact, quite distinct. Bismarck's aim at the conference was to gain freedom of commerce in the Congo, freedom of navigation on the Congo and Niger rivers, and some agreement about the formalities of valid annexaton of territory in the future. Many at the time thought that Bismarck simply hoped to keep the other powers occupied in Africa while he planned consolidation of German power in Europe. The British, especially H. Percy Anderson, head of the African department at the Foreign Office, hoped to ensure that any further French expansion in Africa would not cut off potential markets, or increase French political or military power. Ferry's concern, equally, was to a large extent economic, though it proceeded from strategic considerations: he refused to discuss the application of the Free Trade principle to the Gabon, Guinea or Senegal.[3] The conference is often wrongly perceived as being concerned with the partition of Africa, yet questions of sovereignty were never formally dealt with. Its interest here in relation to the future idea of *Eurafrique* is that the conference itself displayed the tensions between those in favour of detente in Africa, and those preferring competition, or, put another way, it served to distinguish the 'internationalists' from the 'scramblers'.

While in one sense the conference's principal act – the creation of the Congo Free State – can be seen as giving the 'scramble' international sanction, in that the belief emerged that Africa was to be partitioned peacefully in accordance with the principle of Free Trade,[4] viewed another way, the conference showed that a common European activity in Africa to the benefit of all Europeans was possible, and that such activity would ensure peace in Europe. In this sense, the Berlin Conference can be seen as the first true act of European co-operation in Africa. This was something of which many Europeans had dreamed for some time. Indeed the intellectual roots of the *Eurafrique* idea can even be traced to 1876 when Victor Hugo wrote in a manner which would give the modern reader cause for shock:

The time has come to note that Europe has Africa beside her. The time has come to tell this group of nations: 'unite yourself, go south.' In the 19thC. the white man made of the black a man, in the 20thC. Europe will make of Africa a world. Remake a new Africa, render the old Africa malleable for civilization. That is the problem, Europe will solve it.[5]

Very soon after the Berlin Conference, the co-operative spirit which seemed to animate European attitudes to Africa dissipated, and a number of the crises which occurred in the immediate prewar period were centred on Africa. Aside from pressing on politicians the need for effective use of the *force noire* there were few occasions during the war when the French *parti colonial* and its supporters could have an influence on policy. But whenever they could, the *parti colonial* tried to remind the politicians waging the war that questions of Empire were questions of national prestige, and that those aware of the colonial issue were in the best position to stand as interpreters of the national will.

They were naturally concerned about Germany's intentions in Africa as Chancellor Bethmann Hollwegg had expressed a desire for the 'creation of a continuous Central African colonial Empire' which would necessarily involve the annexation of much of French Equatorial Africa. The *Comité d'Afrique Française* hoped for territorial repartition in Africa during the war, and particularly looked foward to recovery of the Congo, lost to Germany in 1911. In 1914, some high officials even placed the colonial question as a high priority. The foreign minister, Gaston Doumergue, announced early on that 'it is on the African continent that our most considerable interests are engaged and that our action covers the most extended territory.'[6] Many colonialists argued the need during the war to enlarge the African Empire as much a possible. But others, in a reversal of the late nineteenth-century argument that French possessions in Africa helped to compensate for loss of territory in Europe, argued that Germany, if deprived of her African possessions, might turn against France after the war. The editor of *Le Temps* Philippe Millet argued: 'The most grave danger is that Germany, expelled from Africa, will return with all her wrath against her neighbours, and especially against France.'[7] By the end of the war France had recovered Congo and received mandates over Togo and Cameroon.

The various negotiations that had led to this last repartition of Africa also raised new questions about the future of French and European activity in Africa. For France, the consolidation of her sub-Saharan African Empire (which delighted the Ministry of Colonies, while others considered the receipt of mandates over Syria and Lebanon more important), turned the attention of many figures towards how France's African Empire (particularly on the shores of the Mediterranean) could be brought closer to France. Creating a strong Franco–African unity was of enormous importance for a large group of colonialists. There were also some who wished for greater collaboration with other European countries in the postwar era to ensure a growth in general European power. This posed two sorts of questions for Frenchmen: Should the European powers co-operate in Africa and create something approaching a Eurafrican entity; or should areas in Africa be cultivated for the boost they could give to national power? The answers given to these questions helped to define the policies later to be followed by the French government both within Europe and in Africa.

Eurafrique and *France-Afrique* in the Interwar Period

Among the first to address in writing the problem of European co-operation in Africa at the time of the war was the British pacifist E. D. Morel. Morel's work did not directly influence French thinkers but it is worth reviewing briefly because many of the ideas he presented would be marshalled by French colonialists in the 1930s and later. In a small book published even as the war was on, Morel argued that the only way in which Africa could be removed from the sphere of future European embroilments would be for a common African policy to be worked out by the interested powers. Asserting that the peoples of Africa had been made to suffer for Europe's sins, Morel insisted that it was a common European duty to ensure that history did not repeat itself. More importantly, perhaps, Morel added that '...the very fact of international action being designed to this end will...assist Europe in ridding herself of one of the most dangerous incentives to international tension.'[8]

The means to such an end was the neutralization of the greater part of Africa and an internationalization of commercial activities within the neutralized areas, in other words, a reworking of the positions taken at the Berlin Conference of 1884 but subsequently abandoned, by which an area was excluded from the effects of disputes between the signatories, and a Free Trade zone created. While not all of Africa could be part of such a scheme – South Africa as a Dominion was inextricably linked to Great Britain, as the Mediterranean possessions of France, if only for reasons of security, were tied to that country – much of the rest, what Morel termed 'non-colonizable Africa', would have to be opened up to all European powers if the peace of both continents was to be maintained. Since Morel's concern was that all countries be treated as equally as possible in any arrangement affecting relations between Europe and Africa, he made it clear that German fears and concerns should be taken into special account:

A stable future for Europe requires...that Germany should continue to enjoy rights in non-colonizable Africa on a scale at least comparable with that possessed by her before the war, and that no obstacle be placed in the way of an extension of her control in this area of which Germany could legitimately take advantage.[9]

In Morel's plan for an international arrangement by which the European and African continents would be assured, if not of perpetual peace, at least of relative tranquillity and prosperity, we have the origins both of the policies of colonial appeasement of Germany that would be debated in the interwar years, and of the Eurafrican idea which would not be known by that name until a decade and a half later. When, at the end of the war, Germany was stripped of those rights in Africa which she possessed, there were still many in Britain, and some in France, who felt that the diffusion of German power through Africa was fundamental to any European security arrangement. The mandates system of the League of Nations set up after the Versailles peace conference was for those who, like Morel, believed in the internationalization of rights (and duties) in Africa, the denial of the projects in Africa they thought essential. The French economist, Charles Cide, to take one example, argued in the *Revue d'Economie Politique* in 1919 that the peace treaty had wrongly deprived Germany of her sources of primary materials in Africa. He regretted that the peace treaties had not created a supranational colonial regime of which Germany could form a part.[10]

In France, where the fear of Germany and the perceptions of continental tension were naturally more acute than in Britain, the idea that international activity in Africa and European security were inextricably linked was not the majority view, and only interested some colonial propagandists. In Britain, only a handful of Foreign Office officials bothered to consider the issue of German colonial revisionism. When Franco–German co-operation was eventually revived by the 'Locarno Spirit' inspired by Aristide Briand in the mid-1920s, it was inevitable that some would see in this the basis of both European unification, and European co-operation in Africa. Still, it tended to be Central Europeans, rather than the British or the French, who advocated the Eurafrican idea in the 1920s. It was also inevitable that the idea of 'Africa for the Europeans' would have a warmer reception in Germany than in France.

Just as, before the war, many policies of conciliation with Germany had begun with agreements in Africa, the argument went, so would it have to be in the postwar era. Several publicists in the early and mid-1920s spoke of the need for European unification, which inevitably would require some policies of collaboration in Africa. Given the infrequency of French public interest in colonies it is not surprising that some of these ideas originated outside France. It was an Austrian writer, Richard de Coudenhove-Kalergi who spoke most enthusiastically of the possibilities of a *Pan Europa*, in which a European Federation would be extended to all African colonies of European nations (with the exception of those held by Great Britain). Such a federation would serve European interests both by ensuring a constant supply of raw materials, and by diverting the energies of nations without colonies to another field of action. This provided economic as well as political reasons for the foundation of a Eurafrican entity.[11] A geopolitical idea par excellence, the fortunes of the *Eurafrique* concept became dependent in the interwar years, on the extent of Franco-German desires for a European detente.

For most of the 1920s there was little or no public interest in colonies in France and the discussion about the value of colonies continued to take place only in specialized circles. But from time to time politicians would refer to colonial factors in speeches. Their consideration of the political purposes which colonies could serve naturally reflected the prime concerns of the day, especially the search for new conditions of European security. The French politician Joseph Caillaux, probably one of the most enthusiastic supporters of a Franco–German entente raised at various points in 1925 and 1927 the prospect of a Franco-German customs union and rarely was the colonial question far from his mind. He once suggested the establishment of 'Franco–German projects in a grand style with co-operation in the colonies'.[12] In the latter part of the 1920s some radical politicians and socialists proposed policies to return colonies to Germany or common projects for the exploitation of African resources. But it was not until 1930, when Briand's proposals for a United States of Europe became a subject for debate, that those in favour of the *mise en valeur des colonies*, to use the term of the one-time Minister for Colonies Albert Sarraut, would combine with the internationalists in support of the *Eurafrique* concept. Henry de Jouvenal, writing in the *Revue des Vivants*, struck a theme which would become even more familiar in the mid-1950s when he insisted that: 'in taking the initiative of a European Federation we have revived the perspective of a colonial federation. The European federation presupposes an African bloc; the *mise en valeur* of all Africa by the associated Europeans.'[13]

In 1930 and 1931, as considerations of a United States of Europe and the prospect of collaboration in Africa were beginning to be raised with some seriousness, Frenchmen were also celebrating the greatness of French *national* power in Africa. During this period there were celebrations of the centenary of the expedition to Algiers, the fiftieth anniversary of the protectorate over Tunisia and the fiftieth anniversary of the definitive establishment of French power in the Congo. The *parti colonial* spent many years preparing the largest of celebrations, the International Colonial Exhibition, held in 1931 in Vincennes. While most of the Exhibition dealt with French colonies, protectorates, or mandate territories, other countries also mounted certain displays at the Exhibition including Denmark, the United States, Italy, the Netherlands and Portugal. Though Palestine and Hindustan were represented, it is notable that Great Britain did not directly participate. Despite the international character of the Exhibition, its clear purpose in French official eyes was to celebrate, before Frenchmen, France's extra-metropolitan reach.

It was in fact the ultimate tribute to ideas of a greater France.[14] Organized with the assistance of Maréchal Lyautey, inaugurated by the French

President Gaston Doumergue and by the Minister of Colonies Paul Reynaud as well as his Senegalese undersecretary Blaise Diagne (one of the great early political symbols of assimilation), the Exhibition attracted over 34 million visitors in a little over six months. Paul Reynaud's opening speech clearly gave an indication of the patriotic purposes of the Exhibition:

The essential purpose of this Exhibition is to give to Frenchmen a consciousness of their Empire...It is important that each one of us considers himself a citizen of *la plus grande France* of five parts of the world. Metropolitan France is the largest territory of Europe after Russia. It is nevertheless only one twenty third the size of the French Empire.[15]

The Colonial Exhibition of 1931 brought to the majority of Frenchmen, who had never had it, the sense of Empire and of the glory of France that for members of the *parti colonial* was expressed most emphatically through the *possessions d'outre-mer*. The very fact that the phrase *France d'outre-mer* began to enter the language gave an indication that Frenchmen were perhaps beginning to think imperially. One highly placed French observer of the Exhibition argued that for years Europeans and particularly Frenchmen had regarded Empire with nonchalance. The virtue of the Exhibition was that it had wakened Europeans from this dangerous stupor:

Directly by the force of the actual displays or indirectly by the movement of ideas that it inspired, the Exhibition has rehabilitated the work of Europe as colonizer. As a result, it has placed the elites on notice against those who would advise them to abdicate on the pretext that this work was bad or finished.[16]

In this passage Governor-General Olivier revivified the idea that Europe had a mission to fulfil overseas which it could not abandon. More often, observers of the Exhibition referred openly to the boost it had given to France's sense of national power. This sense of national power could rarely be discussed, however, without broader geopolitical questions being raised. For as soon as the concept of French power overseas and especially in Africa was considered, it was necessary to think of ways in which the French Empire, and those of other powers, affected the stability of Europe. Some of the more committed supporters of the French Empire argued that overseas possessions contributed not only to national prestige but also to the general strength of Europe.

In his *Grandeurs et Servitudes Coloniales*, of 1931, Albert Sarraut argued that 'The European edifice rests on colonial pillars.'[17] If Europe was to live in the peaceful conditions envisaged by the League of Nations, if it was to resist the threats being made by the Russians to its colonial pillars, then European unification was necessary:

If the colonizing peoples are the first interested in the defence of the colonial *oeuvre*, all of Europe does not have a lesser interest, as its future depends on it. Side by side, with, the colonizing nations, the Federation of the states of Europe should unanimously devote its great force to the same cause, its attention to the same problem.[18]

While some of the early believers in a European federation thought that it was only through this sort of international co-operation that German ambitions could be curtailed, and her legitimate fears appeased, others added to this the concern for limiting the potential influence of the communist threat. This threat was frequently raised by such writers as Sarraut to justify the formation of the 'Holy Alliance of Imperial Powers', which it was becoming fashionable to propose.[19] Those who shared a fear of a communist threat to Europe would have to ensure that rivalries overseas did not divide forces needed to defend freedom in Europe. In this debate of the 1930s there was an unclear distinction between those who felt that other European powers had to be co-opted into a general defence of Empire against outside threats, and those who felt that France should protect her national interests overseas alone.

For some, to preserve 'la plus grande France', celebrated by Paul Reynaud's opening speech to the Colonial Exhibition, other European countries would have to be called in to save it. The memory of the role played by the colonies during the 1914–18 war may have made it easier, for those who might not otherwise have had the inclination, to support Euro–African federations, though there were others, for the same reason, who insisted that only France could be responsible for its Empire. Reynaud's speech at the opening of the Colonial Exhibition made little appeal to the 'European' element of Empire, and he sought, rather, to remind Frenchmen that they should all feel citizens of a larger France.[20] The vision of a France of one hundred million inhabitants spread over five continents of a *France-d'outre-mer* constituting an indissoluble whole, did much to allay fears that France was a great power on the wane.[21] The sense of national celebration that accompanied the 1931 Exhibition was but an extension of the feeling held by many Frenchmen since the end of the war, that the decline of French power on the continent could only be compensated for by a rejuvenation of the Empire. Sarraut's theme in his *La Mise en Valeur des Colonies Françaises*, published in 1923, was that only through the exploitation of raw materials in the colonies could France remain a major force in world affairs, and in 1927, still four years before the Colonial Exhibition, Octave Homberg paid homage to French colonialists, arguing that: 'It is thanks to her colonies that France, despite her badly closed wounds, is still a world nation, and not a small European nation, a sort of tourist reserve for all those who are able to benefit from her financial distress...'[22]

If writers such as Homberg ever thought of uniting the continents of Europe and Africa, or of the essential complementarity between Europe and its overseas territories, they did so only in the context of the particular relationship of France to her own colonies. These did not share with the Eurafricanists the desire for formalizing the common European links with the continent by making appeals to federationist ideals. Standing against those who might have favoured forms of colonial appeasement of Germany, coupled with European unification, the more traditional colonialists argued simply for a more powerful *plus grande France* to counter the various threats to which the metropole and its overseas territories might be subject. Equally, among those promulgating the unification of Europe, there was a division between those who saw the importance of colonies to a European movement, and those who thought the problem of overseas territories irrelevant. In a book written in 1931 called *L'Europe contre les patries*, Drieu de la Rochelle argued that Europe could only be strong if it formed a complete unit, and that this would have to come about by including Africa in a huge unity that would rival North America. On the other hand, Gaston Riou, a writer who was equally keen on European unification and wrote two books on the need for unification in 1928 and 1929, never mentioned the question of colonies.[23]

For at least four or five years after the Colonial Exhibition however, at which Paul Reynaud had even made a brief allusion to the possibility, which shocked some, of European collaboration in the solution of overseas problems, the idea of Eurafrica gained some ground. Its most famous proponent in France, and the inventor of the *Eurafrique* neologism, was Eugène Guenier who wrote *l'Afrique: Champ d'Expansion de l'Europe* in 1933. In this, as in some of his earlier writings of the late 1920s, Guenier argued that there was a need to unite Africa and Europe, to link the future of the two continents together so as to avoid the senseless breaking up of nations, and to ensure that the evident intercontinental complementarity could be preserved and managed. Africa, as the natural extension of Europe, as its provider of vital materials, was an indispensable partner of Europe, which in its turn was valuable to Africa as a supplier of finished goods. The 'solidarity' which therefore existed as a matter of course between the two great land masses, if cultivated, would ensure the economic prosperity of both continents. The notion of *Eurafrique* as an economic bloc, to be distinguished from Eurasia or the Americas, ran throughout Guenier's writings, and could be found not only in the work of other French eurafricanists of the mid-1930s, but also in the plans of colonial revisionists in Germany.

A leading official of the *Kolonialpolitisches Ampt*, H. W. Bauer, considered the development of African resources as a task to be carried out through the common effort of all European countries, and that co-operation between Europe and Africa would produce an economic bloc similar in potential to that of Greater East Asia and the Western Hemisphere. A Eurafrica thus formed, would be an ideally self-sufficient economic unit.[24] Like French thinkers on the subject, some Germans believed that expansion outside Europe and the management of economic relations between Africa and Europe were the key to recovery within Europe.

Guenier's argument for *Eurafrique* was certainly the archetypal one. Not confining himself to economic or strategic issues, Guenier appealed to the most general of considerations, and argued that because of the geographical proximity of Africa to Europe, the creation of a Eurafrican entity was inevitable, and further, that it was only through such a federation that both European civilization and African society could be made to prosper. But his vision of a single Eurafrican continent emerging after twenty million Europeans had crossed the Mediterranean, and which would be the guarantor of peace and security for the nations of Europe (whose division into states he deplored) proceeded from such ahistorical reasoning that it could not be taken seriously by politicians. Still, his thought had become sufficiently part of the pool of ideas on which colonialists drew that the Eurafrican myth could hold some sway for those seeking a *modus vivendi* for the beleaguered nations of Europe. The Congress of Africanists, held in Rome in the spring of 1938, addressed the question of how European civilization could be saved, and came to the conclusion that 'the operating principle must be Africa for the Africans and for the Europeans', an attitude which French politicians of the future would later adopt.[25]

Empire, National Security and the Second World War

In the period immediately preceding the Second World War, politicians and publicists alike began making increased reference to overseas territories. France began to think imperially. Even the Popular Front government of Léon Blum in 1936, which rejected the vocabulary of Empire, did intensify the propaganda of a *France outre-mer*, creating a *Comité de la France d'outre-mer*, and even encouraging school teaching which emphasized the French *mission civilisatrice*.[26] In 1936, also, military planners were beginning to take into account not only the question of the aid France might get from Empire in the event of war but also the risks to which overseas territories, especially North Africa, might be exposed in the case of war. An army memorandum by General George in 1936 put the dilemma clearly:

It must be considered that the integrity of North Africa presents the same interest as the integrity of the whole of the national territory and that the sacrifices that may be imposed by this cannot be avoided without creating a gap in our defensive armour... a direct threat to North Africa would mean that it would cease to be a reservoir of forces and instead become a vulnerable point in our Empire.[27]

In 1937 army plans included, for example, the possible dispatch of troops to the south of Tunisia and northern points in Morocco to guard against possible Italian attacks which might emanate from Libya. But many of the improvements in local infrastructure and communications which would be necessary to ensure that military plans such as the *plan Tunisie* could be carried out were never implemented. A plan launched in 1938 to accumulate stocks and improve communication networks had barely begun to take shape at the outbreak of hostilities in 1940.[28] Nevertheless, by 1938 the Empire did begin to figure prominently in speeches and some military staff work took place to assess how the Empire could help serve French needs in a crisis.

The previous lack of effort in this respect is illustrated by the discovery in 1938 by Georges Mandel, the Minister for the Colonies, that the Empire provided France with only 4 per cent of its raw materials, a fact that seemed to run counter to much of the economic propaganda about the Empire advanced by the more enthusiastic French imperialists. Mandel tried to develop projects for the development of mines in the Empire, and the *Conseil supérieur de la France d'outre-mer* engaged itself in encouraging such development, noting that choices in this area should 'be guided by the special needs of national defence'.[29] But nothing much came of this project, as French industrialists were concerned that the creation of advanced industries in the colonies would lead to dangerous competition with the metropole. Despite the lack of a practical policy towards the Empire which would serve the ends of national power, the French press in these years began to pick up the themes of Empire and played on images of French power *outre-mer* that recalled the experience of the First World War. The idea that the colonies could provide France with 500,000 workers and 2,000,000 soldiers again became part of the political currency.

No more than the vast claims sometimes made about the economic and material resources of the Empire, did these figures about potential military contribution seem to reflect accurately the level of preparation made. A Ministry of War publication in 1939 entitled *L'Empire Français* stated that the indigenous colonial force now in the armed forces amounted to 75,000 men, 45,000 of whom were stationed in the colonies. The proclamation of General Buhrer, Chief of the Colonial General Staff in January 1940 that 'the Empire could provide up to 6,000,000 men in the event of war', seemed clearly fantastic in the light of official figures that could have been, but were not, the object of public scrutiny and criticism.[30] The idea that the Empire was a huge reservoir of men and of minerals became, even against publicly available evidence, a fact accepted by an ever larger portion of public opinion. As Christopher Andrew and A. N. Kanya-Forstner have argued, as the Second World War drew near, 'Most Frenchmen rallied to the defence of the Empire because they expected the Empire to rally once more to the defence of France.'[31]

Because of the approach of war in the late 1930s, whatever the importance of the Eurafrican idea for some colonial specialists who hoped for a detente between France and Germany, the tensions of these years meant that the question of colonies was raised exclusively in the context of their strategic utility to the metropole. As Hitler's claims became better understood, the question of colonial appeasement which had had some support in the mid-1920s was expressly ruled out by a large body of opinion. On the right, especially, nobody thought it right to exchange colonies for peace. While in 1911 it had seemed reasonable to give up the Congo for a stake in Morocco, Black African compensations to Germany were no longer considered acceptable. One right wing publication argued: 'To give up the Cameroon is to precipitate war. This is not a colonial question, it is a question of life or death for France.'[32] Already, Black Africa was beginning to achieve a greater status in the panoply of France's overseas possessions. This was in part linked to a perception that the natives were unquestionably loyal to France. At a time when France seemed weak, the attachment of Black Africans to the mother country would be an important source of confidence and strength.

In the late 1930s more and more Frenchmen, particularly politicians in the Radical Party, saw in Empire the single guarantee that France was still a great power. Many also argued that to preserve this Empire it was necessary to ensure that there would be no rivalries in Europe which would put the Empire at risk. Speaking at the Radical Party Congress in Marseilles in 1938, one politician, Raymond Réthore, spoke for the party as a whole on this point:

We radicals dismiss the policy that France should fold itself back to its frontiers, and for the simple reason that there should be no such policy possible for a country which has a vast colonial empire ... the defence of our distant possessions can only be done in Europe by a policy of a coalition of alliances and collective security ... It is this policy and this policy only which is right for a great colonial power, because to be a colonial power it is important first to be a power.[33]

Yet in the face of clear external challenges to the French Empire (such as Mussolini's claims in 1938 to Tunisia and Djibouti), and growing evidence of France's economic and military inferiority on the European continent, the defence of Empire became strident. This defence was in the last analysis animated by a feeling that France's flagging continental power could be revived from overseas. By 1939, the idea that salvation could come from Empire was entrenched. In a radio broadcast of 29 March 1939, President Edouard Daladier spoke of how Empire meant power:

The French force? It is present in the whole world. It is the measure of this immense Empire which is the African bloc, intangible, yet a type of central armour, whose affectionate attachment to the mother country I myself was recently able to measure.[34]

The approach of war saw a weakening in those versions of the Eurafrican idea which stressed the need for European co-operation in Africa. The political priority at such a time was for national rallying cries. Notions of Eurafrica could not serve this purpose; but the careful cultivation of the *France–Afrique* notion could help nurture national confidence, badly bruised by the process of appeasement. The preservation of *France–Afrique* would be tantamount to the preservation of France.

The beginning of the war, while perhaps providing fodder for those marginal eurafricanists who had believed that an international federation could in some way have prevented conflict, tarnished the concept of *Eurafrique* which had been taken up by Hitler. While Nazi plans for expansion were focused on Europe, Hitler occasionally expressed the view that an organization might be created to preserve European interests in Africa. In speaking to Pierre Laval in June 1940, he argued in favour of the need for the creation of a Eurafrican community modelled on the sort of relationship existing between North and South America.[35] There is also evidence that Hitler raised the subject at the Montoire Conference of October 1940, at which the Vichy leadership officially proclaimed that their policy would be one of collaboration with Germany. Certainly the fear that any Eurafrican association created by the Germans, a *Eurafrique* with a 'K', so to speak, would be inimical to French interests, meant that during the war and for at least a short time afterwards little thought was given to realizing the grand design of such fanatics as Eugène Guenier.

The fear that the United States or the Soviet Union might make incursions into a continent which 'belonged' to Europeans animated some, like the French writer Gentizon to remark: 'Africa is us. Europe has known it, modelled it, and fashioned it in its image.'[36] But by and large the exigencies of the war meant that few in France thought that a Europe of the future should co-operate in Africa, if that meant losing title to something which contributed so fundamentally to both national prestige and power. The fact that for the Vichy government the possession of Empire constituted the last remaining sign that occupied France was still a sovereign nation, that the Empire constituted 'France's last card', and equally the view of de Gaulle's that the crime of the Armistice was that the government had capitulated 'as if it did not have an Empire', meant that most felt after the war that the possession of exclusive spheres of influence in Africa or Asia was to be treasured.[37] During the war, Vichy and Free France competed for favour in Africa, and the changing loyalties of North African and Black African territories immediately affected power struggles in and for France. De Gaulle's eventual success in winning over Black Africa to his cause served to reinforce the value of overseas power for the metropole's position in Europe. Peoples' attitudes in France were later shaped by the conventional wisdom contained in Gaston Monnerville's remark of 1945 (when he was President of the Commission of Overseas France) that 'Without Empire France would today only be a liberated country. Thanks to her Empire it is today a victorious country.'[38] In Africa, there was no doubt a nascent understanding that if Africans could affect the destiny of France in Europe, there might be a chance for Africans to affect, and prepare for, their own destiny in Africa. But this challenge to the authority of France would take some time to develop, and in the immediate aftermath of the war what was most clear for Frenchmen was the need to retain possessions in Africa.

In the last years of the war and for some time immediately after it, the idea of Empire as a continued source of French power and sovereignty was rarely questioned. Even the communists accepted this notion, one leader arguing in 1944 that France, which was 'in Algiers and in Tunis as much as in Marseilles is and must remain a great African power.'[39] In August 1945 the French minister of colonies gave the following summary assessment: 'During the war that has just ended it was in the Empire that French liberty survived, it is by the Empire that France constantly persevered in the struggle, it is from the Empire that the French forces of liberation were launched.'[40] These arguments supported the notion that for France to remain a European power it had also to remain an imperial and especially an

African power. It was this perception that largely contributed to an official French desire to hang on to imperial possessions even at considerable economic, political and in some instances, military cost.

Eurafrique and France–Afrique towards De-colonization

While during the war and for the first five years afterwards some practical steps were taken by civil servants in Britain and France to co-ordinate policies towards their African territories, this received no public attention. The attempt by such civil servants to rationalize economic policies and bring a European dimension to the management of colonial territories foundered because of the political impediments to the sharing of colonial responsibilities and influence.[41] Still there was a re-emergence of Eurafrican thinking in the 1950s. As could be expected, when the prospect of European unification was becoming real, and the evident antagonism between the United States and the Soviet Union was forcing people to revise their notions about the place of Europe in world affairs, the idea of Eurafrica was launched again.

The writings of an Austrian, Anton Zischka, whose major book was translated into French as *Afrique, Complément de l'Europe* (1950), did much to revive the Eurafrican ideal in some quarters. In France, Pierre Nord's *L'Eurafrique, Notre Dernière Chance* (1955) put the problem in more striking fashion than had Zischka, whose argument had been framed almost exclusively by economic considerations. Proceeding from the premise that the failure of the French to support the European Defence Community was inconsequential in comparison to the need to forge a Eurafrican community, Nord suggested that all of Europe's strategic, economic and political problems would be solved by a link with Africa. With Africa supplying the necessary raw materials, Europe had a chance of competing with the United States and the Soviet Union. The military possibilities offered by the huge expanse of Africa could not be ignored by a continent needing to develop and test atomic weaponry. The creation of a Eurafrican entity would make possible a reconciliation between France and Germany.[42]

None of these specific arguments was brought out by the unpredictable Raymond Cartier, who in 1953, had reached a much larger audience through the popular journal *Paris-Match*, and who put forward the now familiar and hackneyed theme that Europe needed the African continent ('as a prolongation, and as a complement') for its raw materials.[43] This theme was echoed throughout much of the popular and highbrow press in this period. Writing in the *Revue des Deux Mondes* in early 1954 one contributor put the argument plainly: 'We should understand our common interest. *Eurafrique* is a necessity. We, Frenchmen, need Africa almost as much as Africa needs us. We must not indulge those who for reasons of personal ambition or ignorance oppose this union.[44] By 1956 Cartier had changed his earlier position and considered that France should pull out of Africa as quickly as possible. In *Paris-Match* articles Cartier argued that overseas possessions had become too costly for France. This argument was later to bear his name and became known as *cartièrisme*. But *cartièrisme* did not win much favour with such staunch defenders of the French presence in Africa as Jacques Soustelle. In February 1955, Soustelle, who had been appointed Governor-General of Algeria argued in Algiers that:

France is at home here, or rather, Algeria and her inhabitants form an integral part of France, one and indivisible. All must know, here and elsewhere, that France will not leave Algeria any more than she will leave Provence and Brittany. Whatever happens, the destiny of Algeria is French.[45]

In late 1956 Soustelle argued in The French National Assembly that the loss of Algeria would be the loss of Africa, and that in losing Africa, France, which he considered a 'Eurafrican power', would lose her 'future' at the same time.[46] It was statements like these which were to create the atmosphere for the fatal crisis over Algeria suffered by the Fourth Republic. For the French eurafricanists, all of the North African territories of France, but particularly Algeria, were considered inseparable from France, a myth which would eventually be incarnated by the phrase of General Raoul Salan, Commander-in-Chief in Algeria, who liked to argue that 'The Mediterranean passes through France as the Seine runs through Paris.' Visionary ideas like this ensured that the struggle to keep Algeria French would be bloody.

Those eurafricanists who were not directly concerned with the specific problem of Algeria were concerned about East–West relations and the effect these would have on the European presence in Africa. Much of the writing on Eurafrica of the mid-1950s concentrated on the problem of Cold War rivalries, and the articles to be found in journals such as *Eurafrique-Alger*, which specialized in explanations of the Eurafrican thesis, played up the perceived threats of both the United States and the Soviet Union on Europe's *chasse gardée*. An article published in 1955 ominously entitled 'L'Eurafrique devant l'Armement Sovietique' sounded the urgent call for integration:

It is the fear of danger that hooks Europe to Africa while reason should have for some time pushed one continent to the other as they complement each other. But it is not too late. If the sense of common danger forces us to accept the European solution: a collective organization of Empire, then nothing would be lost... If Europe wishes to live and radiate again, if it does not want to abandon itself and perhaps never again cast a shadow, it will be necessary for it to accept the idea of an integrated Africa.[47]

The fear of American and Soviet pressure on Europe led some military men too, towards the Eurafrican solution which was now being steadily transformed from a means by which the European powers could live with each other, to a system of defence of European civilization. Since every European state had its own vision of the shape an intercontinental system would take, it was suggested that every state possessing colonies should first work independently on the problem of integration. Taking up where President Millerand and Maréchal Lyautey had left off in the 1920s, argued one writer, France should begin by reinforcing the links between France and the Maghreb territories and then join with the Belgians and Portuguese who would help by uniting their colonies, and finally integrate these areas with Great Britain and her South African territories.[48] Once such an association was created (and it was rarely explained what legal form *Eurafrique* would take), all sorts of economic possibilities were open. One writer, in Great Britain, displaying a mixture of political sensitivities, suggested that the Europeans could work to change the course of the Congo river, develop hydroelectric projects, exploit Moroccan minerals, all so that Europe would cease to be 'dependent on American capitalism, the victim of Asiatic Communism'.[49] For another, French, writer, the Sahara was the key to a Franco–Eurafrican Community. While the French government should retain its overwhelming interest in the area, argued J. M. Lattre, it should allow foreign capital (principally from other European countries) to enter so that the desert could be properly exploited. Eventually, just as a European Coal and Steel Community and a European Atomic Energy Community had been created, so, in the future, a Eurafrican Petrol Community or a Eurafrican Iron Ore Community could be established for the mutual benefit of both continents.[50]

What gave these characteristically superficial and rhetorical writings some degree of legitimacy was the implicit support they received from Black African writers who felt that after the abandonment of the more pernicious forms both of European colonial practices and African nationalist sentiments an effective partnership could, and should, be created between the two continents. Writing in 1953 on the need for European unification, Léopold Sedar Senghor claimed that:

The Europe which must be created does not stop in Marseilles or Sicily, it is in reality two continents which are complementary, that is Europe and Africa, in reality it is a political, economic and cultural eurafrican community which must be formed. That this word was used by the nazis is not a reason for our abandoning the enterprise.[51]

Senghor's vision was of a Eurafrican entity led by France. Because 'the vocation of France is an African one',[52] France could only realize her full potential by an association with the Africans which, by replacing the Colonial Pact, would make the creation of a European union easier, the improvement of living conditions in Africa more likely, and the position of France in the world more secure, since: 'a Eurafrican France of 88 million inhabitants would be in the first rank, as much by the number of its inhabitants as by the resources of all sorts it would control.'[53] In this bald appeal to well-established concepts of French power *outre-mer*, made by a Black African leader of the highest distinction, one sees the roots of the very special relationship with Black Africa which would permit French power to be wielded there with particular efficacy even after formal decolonization. This 'greater France' of the postwar order which Senghor advocated could only be built by Africans strengthening links with Europe and France. Senghor often argued in the early 1950s that many Africans did not as yet want separation from France and wanted to co-operate in the construction of a Eurafrican enterprise which would be to the mutual benefit not only of France and her colonies but, more broadly, of the two continents which were natural complements of each other.

While the construction of Eurafrica was an economic need, it was also a political one affecting the peace of the world as a whole. In later writings Senghor began to play up the 'Third Force' theme which would become central to the Eurafrican idea, and which held some appeal for those Europeans who thought in terms of distancing themselves from the two blocs. In 1955 Senghor made this element in his argument clear:

What is interesting about the Eurafrican problem is that the two continents, because they are opposed, like a man and a woman, are also complementary, while the two antagonistic blocs think only of victory and prepare themselves to achieve it... [Europe and Africa] can constitute a larger force of culture proceeding from peace.'[54]

The centrepiece of Senghor's argument was, therefore, that if the European states could abandon the economic and cultural imperialisms that had formerly governed their policies toward Africa, then the possibility of building on the evident 'symbiotic' relationship that existed would be greater, and a single Eurafrican continent might emerge distinct from the large blocs to the East and West which were threatening to push the world into new dangers. Proceeding from what he would often describe as humanistic considerations, Senghor's Eurafrican ideas nevertheless would have practical consequences, and though in essence a literary man, tending always toward the abstract, he did make recommendations for actual political action which would lead to proper links between Europe and Africa. As a member of the French National Assembly during the Fourth Republic, Senghor fought in the mid-1950s for a revision of the constitution he had originally helped to draft. He hoped that the French Union (established in 1946) would not be defined, as it originally was, in largely sentimental terms, as the group formed by the people of France and those of the colonies, but in stronger juridical terms, as a confederation of states who desired association with each other.[55] His concern was that the Union thus formed should be based not only on the terms of the constitution, but also, more generally, on a contractual agreement between different nations which would have meaning in international law. De Gaulle's French Community of 1958 (examined in the next chapter) did not entirely fulfil his hopes, but Senghor saw it as a step in the right direction toward the sort of federation he thought appropriate.[56]

How these types of arrangements could fit into the broader goal of a Eurafrica, and not just a Franco–African Community, was a question Senghor, like others, could only address with difficulty. Certainly, the provision for association agreements between the European Economic Community (EEC) and overseas territories contained in Part IV of the EEC Treaty, went some way towards the creation of an economic Eurafrican association. The tensions created by the question of which should be given pre-eminence, bilateral relations between France and her colonies, or multilateral relations between 'Europe' and Africa, would always remain, despite the hope of some that these could eventually be dissipated. In the latter part of the twentieth century, while France retains a special relationship with her ex-colonies, it is also true that Europe presents a coherent and largely favourable image of itself to the developing world largely through the aid policy of the European Community towards the African, Caribbean and Pacific (ACP) states.

In the early 1950s, whatever the practical problems associated with the creation of a Eurafrican entity – and they grew more complicated as various African territories pushed towards a severing of links with the former European overlords – great hopes for a Eurafrican federation continued to be held out by enthusiasts of the European Community. The culmination of this process was the Eurafrican Conference in Strasbourg of 1961, which brought together European and African parliamentarians to discuss political and institutional forms of co-operation and economic problems, as well as technical assistance and cultural exchange plans. All the delegates to the Conference paid tribute to the themes of complementarity and solidarity which had emerged over time as the *leitmotifs* of Eurafrican thinking. Some, like the Netherlands delegate M. van der Goes van Naters, thought grandly that the only mistake the Conference might make was to underestimate the possibilities of the Afro-European 'symbiosis'. Others, like René Pleven, were more modest, and insisted only that the Conference should aim at establishing general principles which would provide the foundation of a Eurafrican association. M. Pleven, whose enthusiasm for the European Community was very great indeed, offered one very significant warning to those African states who were unwilling to create new ties with the nations of Europe, when they had just broken the old ones:

If you hesitate to accept our offer of association what will be the alternative? It would be bilateral accords, alliances of which the most dangerous will not have a name; in brief the transfer to Africa of a competition which it is in the interest of no one to develop again on the African continent.[57]

Pleven then presented the proposed Eurafrican association as a solution both to the misfortunes of Africa created by imperialist activities, and to the problems of Europe which had sometimes been caused by rivalries in Africa. He gave notice that bilateral agreements between European states and African countries were inimical to the proper working of Eurafrica, and that tacit alliances, or spheres of influence, would put the African continent in the same position as it had been before decolonization. In so doing, Pleven revealed how difficult it was to realize the grand design of *Eurafrique*, about which so many had spoken for fifty years. In the case of France, while politicians would often refer to Eurafrican premises, the bilateral arrangements of which Pleven spoke, which would inevitably help to promote the idea of a powerful *France outre-mer*, would in the end be the preferred system of post-colonial management.

Fundamental to the growth of the Eurafrican idea over time had been its aesthetic appeal, which could not be so great when the African continent underwent the process of decolonization, just as the states of Europe were considering ways in which they could go beyond the nation state and form an integrated whole. For the government of the Fifth Republic, struggling with the Algerian problem, needing to establish a means for dealing with the demand for decolonization, attempting to give some meaning to the French Community, the question of creating Eurafrica was naturally affected by the sorts of tensions Pleven described at Strasbourg in 1961. Drafting a compromise between the maintenance of bilateral relations, and the creation of multilateral ones, was to prove difficult if not impossible.

The Eurafrican idea, then, had been an intrinsic part of the French, and general European, colonial myth. At the Congress of Berlin in 1884, concerned with laying down rules for common, as opposed to competing policies in Africa, the various proposals made were advanced with the suggestion that closer links between the two continents should be encouraged, and that the management of these links by the European powers would be to the mutual benefit of all. Similarly, the policies of colonial appeasement of Germany, and the proposals for European unification of the 1930s, were often accompanied by statements on the value of creating *Eurafrique*, a concept which was defined with greater precision and enthusiasm. After the Second World War, the Eurafrican myth became associated with solutions advanced particularly by French writers to help Europe escape from the evils of the Cold War. The formation of *Eurafrique* became a strategic and economic necessity for those trying to combat the influence of the superpowers. Written and spoken about by publicists and politicians in times when the perception of national power was on the decline, or when European power generally was thought to be on the wane, the Eurafrican myth was discarded by those in France who were confident that no European decline into decadence was to be feared.

For those who believed that French power could never decay, the Eurafrican myth was quite irrelevant. But other myths of various types were raised to give support to claims of great-power status. The idea of *France–Afrique* was often raised to counter assertions that French power was weakening. The image of *France–Afrique* easily entered into popular political vocabulary. There were, throughout North and Black Africa, specific problems with which France had to deal, specific challenges to French authority. These would require specially tailored responses. When French control in North Africa was challenged, in the 1950s, the imagery of *France–Afrique* was transposed to apply to the francophone Black African bloc. Again, as the struggle for decolonization became intense, French politicians had to manoeuvre carefully (and in Black Africa did so successfully) to preserve the image that the destinies of France and Africa were in some way united. French foreign policy in Africa would never escape from the sorts of fictions that had originally been invented to justify French influence there and were later put forward to maintain it.

The process of decolonization which was to be debated after the war was largely managed by one man, Charles de Gaulle, whose own vision of power in Africa was influenced by the role Africa had played in supporting the Free French. For him, the idea that Africa was a source of French power was a matter of fact not myth. The idea of sharing power in Africa with other powers would mean implicitly for him the sharing of part of French sovereignty. If Africa were to become independent then it would be important, where possible, for the link with France to be firmly created and the mechanisms for a post-decolonization Franco–African relationship to be put in place. The notion of *Eurafrique* would have some enduring relevance to this process, but in the initial stages, for decolonization to be the assertion of power which de Gaulle eventually meant it to be, the myth of *France–Afrique* was a more useful guiding force. In turning now to an analytical treatment of ideas of French power during the process of decolonization in Africa, it is important, still, to keep in mind the ideas of Franco–African and Eurafrican unities that in subtle ways guided the actions of those who had to deal with the evolving situation in Africa, conceding power or influence in small increments and only where absolutely necessary.

4

Decolonization and the Assertion of Power in Black Africa

The colonial consensus which existed in France at the close of the Second World War was such as to make decisions in favour of granting independence to overseas possessions extremely difficult. The important contribution that overseas possessions had made to France during the war years seemed to confirm not only the maxim that French continental power could achieve its salvation from Empire, but also, more importantly, the idea that France's activity overseas (including its 'civilizing mission') was appreciated and accepted as necessary by the indigenous peoples. More particularly, France's huge African Empire (see table 4.1) was seen as an important source of prestige and state power as well as an arena in which the *mission civilisatrice* could continue to be held up as a noble end of French policy. Detractors of Empire in the postwar years would in some way have to deal with these two common perceptions of Empire. Both of these perceptions were deployed in 1945 by the head of information in the French Ministry of Colonies who tried to explain why France could expect to receive support, in times of need, from its overseas possessions:

It is a great recompense, a stunning justification of the past, this loyalty shown in the most difficult of circumstances by all the people which France has brought together. Whatever may have been the errors, the negligence, the abuses, which may have characterized colonization (no less than any other great historical enterprise) it must have been the case that France accomplished its generous, emancipating vocation and conquered the affections of these peoples, for them to come to the defence of French liberty at a time when France trembled without force, and her prestige appeared defeated.[1]

In short, who could question the civilizing mission, who could doubt the importance of Empire to France, if France seemed to have been saved, at least in part, by the willingness of the colonized peoples to come to her aid? If the Second World War brought home to Frenchmen the value of Empire it also confirmed them in their confidence that close links not only should, but could be maintained. In 1954, François Mitterrand declared austerely that there was 'from Flanders to the Congo but one law, one Nation, one Parliament'.[2] This type of confidence was disturbed by rebellion in Algeria and Indochina. Decolonization became very quickly a question needing debate, but most Frenchmen discounted the idea of independence for colonies as unacceptable and even wrong. The fact that less than twenty years after the war, by 1960-2, a majority of Frenchmen had become anticolonialist was no minor development. When considered against the background of the colonialist mythology incorporated in the remarks quoted above this transformation in attitude, shared as it was by a large elite, was all the more impressive. As the historian Jean-Baptiste Duroselle once noted, it was curious that Frenchmen would come to accept 'as a historical necessity a phenomenon which contradicted all the education Frenchmen had received – by which France, better than any other country, was said to have accomplished a civilizing mission in exchange for which the colonies would increase French power,...and her wealth...'[3]

This development was possible precisely because decolonization itself was eventually presented as a great historical act and because that act would prepare France for a new period in her development during which French power overseas would be considerably reduced in some areas but sustained in others. In the end, French power was maintained most conspicuously in Black Africa. There, independence was intentionally granted as a 'gift' whose acceptance by the newly created states was implicitly meant to ensure a close relationship with France which would ultimately strengthen French prestige, even as this prestige was being whittled away in Algeria.

Certainly the specific forms of decolonization, especially in Africa, have affected the nature of post-colonial relationships. France suffered two wars, in Indochina and in Algeria, and numerous interventions in Madagascar, Cameroon, Tunisia, Morocco and various other places in the attempt to keep the French flag in distant outposts. From the beginning of the Second World War onwards, much of French overseas policy concentrated on holding territories and peoples within the French orbit Syria and Lebanon were effectively lost to France sometime after the British and Free French invasion of the mandate territories in 1941 when they were appearing to offer facilities to Germany. After the Free French reneged on a promise to grant independence to them, Syrian and Lebanese nationalists, benefiting also from divisions between Britain and France, were able to gain formal sovereignty at the end of 1941. Both achieved further freedoms from French control after general elections were allowed in 1943, and following clashes between demonstrators and French forces in 1945, all French forces were withdrawn from both countries in 1946 at which time each had gained full independence. In neither Syria nor Lebanon did France have an opportunity to re-establish the influence she had earlier acquired.[4] The struggle in Indochina was a battle against communism, and once that battle was lost, and then taken up again by the Americans, the strong links between France and the region were basically severed. In the protectorates of Tunisia and Morocco, France's struggle against reform might well have been very strong were it not for the fact that Algeria, as a department of France, demanded more attention. In 1956 independence was granted to the protectorates because opening two more fronts at a time of growing conflict in Algeria would have been impossible. Decolonization in Algeria was difficult and tragic because of the way the problem was internalized. The commonly accepted phrase *Algérie Française* did not have within it the sources of a liberating and enlightened policy. In contrast to all these other situations, the process of decolonization in Black Africa was relatively easy, and though there were many tensions and some armed conflict which helped to accelerate the process, it was one which allowed for a good deal of post-imperial influence to be maintained.

This chapter seeks to analyse how decolonization in Black Africa was managed to ensure that there would be a persistence of French influence there which would remain more special than French influence elsewhere. It will examine how France's general interests in maintaining power in Africa became necessarily focused on sub-Saharan Africa and how the language of Franco–African unity was adapted to apply essentially to the emerging states of francophone Black Africa. The very fact that the French-speaking peoples dispersed through West and Central Africa could be referred to, without opposition, in terms which evoked links of common language and destiny rather than in terms which described facts of geography or specific national history, should be seen as testimony to the enduring hold France would have on its ex-colonies in Africa. Because the 'area' of francophone Black Africa could still be subject to plans involving the creation of Franco–African structures, the leaders of francophone Black Africa would be seen as ones who could be co-opted to enhance France's reputation and carry forward the imagery of a continuing French role in Africa. With these leaders, French power could be maintained and a favourable post-imperial relationship based on sentimental as much as juridical ties, could be nurtured and developed. Much of this was possible because of the way the leadership of the Free French had been able to establish, even as the Second World War was being fought, some of the basic premises on which a new Franco–African relationship would be built.

The Brazzaville Conference: Reconfirming France's African Power

In the mythology of Gaullism, the Brazzaville Conference of 1944 attended by French colonial governors to discuss reform of colonial institutions was the first step towards eventual decolonization. It was certainly not seen that way by the key figures who helped to organize the conference, René Pleven, de Gaulle's Commissioner of Colonies or Henri Laurentie, the chief of political affairs for the commissioner. Nor did the French administrators who attended the conference consider that they were discussing ways of creating the conditions for self-government. For General de Gaulle, as leader of the Free French, the French Empire in Black Africa represented four things: a source of men; territory which gave substance to his idea of a still 'independent' France fighting for the freedom of the metropole; legitimacy for his personal position as the leader of this movement; and a

4.1 The French African Empire on the eve of the Second World War

Territory	Status	Capital	Size (sq.km)	Population
Tunisia	Protectorate	Tunis	156,000	2,600,000
Algeria	Department	Algiers	2,205,000	7,235,000
Morocco	Protectorate	Rabat	399,000	6,296,000
French West Africa (AOF)ᵃ	Colony	Dakar	4,702,000	14,703,000
French Equatorial Africa (AEF)ᵇ	Colony	Brazzaville	2,487,000	3,423,000
Cameroon	Mandate	Yaounde	422,000	2,389,000
Togo	Mandate	Lomé	57,000	736,000
Madagascar	Colony	Tananarive	592,000	3,798,000
Reunion	Colony	Saint Denis	2,500	209,000
Somalia Coast	Colony	Djibouti	21,700	46,000

ᵃAOF= Senegal, Mauritania, Guinea, Ivory Coast, Sudan, Niger, Dahomey, Upper Volta
ᵇAEF= Gabon, Congo, Oubangui-Chari, Chad.
Source: Adapted from Alain Ruscio, *La Décolonisation Tragique, 1945–1962*, Edition Sociales/Messidor, Paris, 1987, p. 16

place which could again be 'attached' to France after the war to help make France great again. Against the background of increasing American pressure during the war on the imperial powers to consider ways of retreating from Empire, the *Comité Français de Libération Nationale* (CFLN), de Gaulle's Free French organization established in Algiers in 1943, began organizing the Brazzaville Conference. But it did so to defend the idea of Empire and restructure its institutions to ensure its survival.

The attention devoted to Empire by de Gaulle during the war and the desire, where possible, to preserve both its unity and its attachment to France was inherent in the very history of the Free French movement and in the problems thrown up by a divided France. Speaking in London to the Royal Institute for International Affairs in 1947, Henri Laurentie, by then Political Director of the Ministry of Overseas France, made clear the mutually beneficial relationship that seemed to develop between the Free French and sections of francophone Africa:

The appeal which General de Gaulle launched in London against the capitulation and the Vichy regime had two results: firstly, it cut the French Empire temporarily in two; secondly it gave the French colonies a sense of their own importance and responsibility. This division of the Empire, far from promoting the dislocation of France's possessions, emphasized a pressing need for unity; never was the principle of unity more appreciated than during this period of separation. On the other hand, not only were the French colonies aware for the first time of the role they could play in wartime, but more important, they also served as an operational base for the Free French Government... Thus the French colonies enjoyed an audience and a prestige which had never before been theirs.[5]

In this relationship built up during the war some of the roots of post-imperial Franco–African co-operation can be seen. As in the First World War, a great many Black Africans, mainly from French West Africa were mobilized; about 130,000 in 1939–40 and a further 60,000 from 1943 to 1944. Despite the burden this imposed, especially great given that during the war West African exports fell dramatically since so little could be sent to occupied France, there was little resistance to French rule. Though economic conditions were bad, and the war effort substantial, francophone Black Africa still by and large felt that a connection with France was important. Most, in the end, felt that this France should be Free France.

In fact, loyalties first committed to the Pétain regime in Vichy were quickly switched in many parts of Black Africa to de Gaulle. Félix Eboué, the black Governor of Chad declared for de Gaulle on 26 June 1940 and Chad was soon followed by Cameroon, the Middle Congo and Oubangui-Chari. Governor Masson of Gabon chose to remain faithful to Pétain, but by November 1940 Free French troops arrived in Gabon and after Masson's suicide, Gabon could be claimed by de Gaulle. Senegal did not join the Free French cause until the allied landing in North Africa on 8 November 1942. But by the time German and Italian troops left Tunisia on 13 May 1943, all of French Africa was essentially committed to the Free French. In West Africa, pictures of Pétain disappeared from schoolrooms and offices. In many territories it became an offence to have a poster of the Vichy leader on the wall. Africans were effectively instructed to oppose the government in Vichy and support the 'rebellious' Free French. In 1943 de Gaulle was able to establish the CFLN in Algiers which would later become the *Gouvernement Provisoire de la République Française* (GPRF).[6]

Even though the headquarters of the Free French movement was established in North Africa, its sentimental home was probably further south. In 1940 de Gaulle had established the Council for the Defence of the Empire in Brazzaville. This small town was one of the sources of de Gaulle's personal independence and would later be seen as one of the places from which a new France was born. Thus it was right that Brazzaville be the place where a meeting take place to discuss the evolving relationship between France and colonial Africa. The idea of this conference was probably discussed between de Gaulle and René Pleven in 1943. Others, like Henri Laurentie, also played a role in conceiving the idea.[7] By 13 October 1943, plans were well enough advanced to announce the conference and issue invitations for the last week of January 1944. By this time, some small reforms had begun to take place in francophone Africa, prudently managed by Félix Eboué, nominated the Governor-General of French Equatorial Africa in November 1940 and enjoying de Gaulle's full confidence. These reforms were not major (a few local communes had been given increased budgetary powers) and Eboué himself believed that while local customs had to be respected, a policy of association between France and Africa based on the principles of indirect rule was still the best means of governing these colonial territories.[8]

It is in this context that the Brazzaville Conference must be analysed. Though imperial reform would have its place in de Gaulle's conception of a *rénovation nationale*, he would still wish to impose limits to it and he would not easily yield to pressures, which at the time had mainly American origins, for the unravelling of French control in Black Africa. Formally, the Brazzaville Conference brought together French colonial governors to 'assure the progress of the French populations on the African continent'. Virtually all the discussions centred on the nature of the relationship between France and her colonies in Black Africa, North Africa being intentionally excluded. De Gaulle came to the conference after having paused 'with deliberate solemnity' at the other African cities that had declared for him: Dakar,

Conakry, Abidjan, Lomé, Cotonou, Douala and Libreville, and in so doing he gave public notice of the need for France to keep its colonial links in Africa.[9] On arrival in Brazzaville, he was received by Félix Eboué, twenty other Governors-General and some assorted observers. With the exception of Reunion, Madagascar and Somaliland, official representation at the conference was restricted to those from continental Black Africa. The only black man present, however, was Eboué himself, who was there in his capacity as a Governor-General, not as an African. This fact, naturally, put limits *ab initio* on the radicalism of the ideas that would be proposed.

The conference itself, which lasted from 30 January to 8 February 1944 was presided over by René Pleven, and while de Gaulle put in an appearance at the beginning and near the end most of the discussions took place without him. The subjects covered included economic development, native policy, administrative reform in the colonies, and forms of colonial representation of the colonies in a postwar French constitution. Most of the work of the conference took place in commissions. Much of the debate referred to questions of colonial doctrine. Words like assimilation, association and federation were bandied about in debate by speakers in search of ways to define the evolving relationship between France and her Black African colonies. Much of this discussion was quite vague. Many years after the conference Henri Laurentie was to describe it as 'a tissue of contradictions. No real doctrine came out of it. Doctrine came afterwards.'[10] The opening addresses of de Gaulle and Pleven, which focused on the sentimental attachments between France and Black Africa and which implicitly re-affirmed the paternal role that France still had to play in Africa, effectively set limits both on the breadth of the doctrinal changes and on the legal and administrative reforms that might be mooted in more detailed discussions to follow. One passage from Pleven's opening remarks nicely illustrates the basic ideology that underlay the discussions:

In greater colonial France there are neither peoples to enfranchise nor racial discrimination to abolish... There are populations which we intend to conduct, stage by stage, to a political personality, and for the more developed to political rights, but this will still mean that the only independence they will want will be the independence of France.[11]

Certainly some of the documents presented to conference participants encouraged the delegates to think carefully about the conditions of the native. The general programme which stated the aims of the conference emphasized that 'the indigenous peoples are the base itself of our colonies ... nothing could be done against their wishes' and that sometimes in the past 'the true interests of the Africans had escaped colonial administrators.' Thus the conference was meeting 'to prepare a solid and happy future for francophone Black Africa'.[12] Statements like these, including criticisms of some aspects of past administrative practice, fostered the later myth that decolonization was begun in earnest at Brazzaville. In fact, the implicit aim of the conference was to discuss the African as an individual and as a member of a group, and his incorporation into a specifically French world. The Free French desire for independence would be one in which the Africans would share.[13] The question of whether the Africans themselves might wish independence from France was not seriously debated.

The document produced at the end of the conference summarizing the political recommendations of the delegates stated as a matter of *principle* that:

The purpose of the work of civilization accomplished in the colonies leaves out all idea of autonomy, any possibility of evolution outside of the French bloc, the eventual establishment, even in the distant future, of self government is to be excluded.[14]

The conference did produce some basic colonial reforms and a few shifts in policy were proposed which would be later adopted to different degrees by French administrators. There was a call for provision of better health facilities, the establishment of primary schools in each village and the improvement of communication networks as well as a general appeal for greater economic development and industrialization to raise the African standard of living. It was proposed that forced labour and certain legal codes specific to native populations be abolished (measures which were eventually adopted by the First French Constituent Assembly in April 1946). Some changes in social and economic policy were also proposed and it was recommended that where possible there should be greater decentralization of administrative arrangements.[15] Despite this, the overall political effect of the conference was to tie Black Africa's future closer to that of France. This was certainly the view of the Americans, who, given their interest in seeing the imperial powers make rapid progress in the granting of further freedoms in the colonies, followed the conference with interest. The assessment of Ralph Bunche, a State Department official who followed colonial and trusteeship questions, is worth noting:

Brazzaville clung tenaciously to conventional French policy of integration and assimilation of the colonial territories and their peoples ... there was no compromise with the basic principle that French Africa belongs solely to France and is an exclusively French affair. There was no recognition that France owed any account-ability to the international community in the conduct of her colonial affairs nor that the international community had any valid interest in such affairs... The French were clearly thinking in terms of strengthening the bonds of empire, of drawing the natives into closer communion with France and French institutions. It would seem that the French dream of a united France, with one hundred million Frenchmen, has not been dissipated.[16]

This dream of a larger France extending into Africa certainly continued to grip the leadership of the Free French who had every reason to believe that the essence of French influence in Black Africa would remain unopposed. The Brazzaville Conference served effectively to consolidate that influence and surround French power in Black Africa with an aura of progressive thinking and possible reform. If the language of the concluding document ruled out the possibility of drastic change, the nature of the conference itself, during which the form of France's political relations was discussed, made it possible for Gaullists later to build a myth of the 'spirit of Brazzaville'.

That myth, which would later earn de Gaulle the epithet of *'l'homme de Brazzaville'*, had as its main feature the idea that Brazzaville was where the notion of future decolonization was given birth. In fact, Brazzaville constituted a different sort of historical milestone. It was the place where the French leadership grasped that in Black Africa, adroit use of the language of unity ('federation', 'union', 'assimilation', 'association') could still be used to hide, or to camouflage, the bald facts of effective suzerainty and continued power. Brazzaville should be seen not as the place where decolonization began, but rather as the place at which a specific style of managing power was implicitly adopted which would serve France well at the true moment of decolonization in Black Africa. While in Algeria the problem of decolonization was aggravated by the images called up of an Algeria which was an integral part of France, in Black Africa, decolonization would be eased by the fact that there was time to adapt language to a changing situation. The path from essential 'unity' through to loose 'union', 'community' and finally to 'co-operation' could be followed with only a minimal loss of real power and influence. Since distinguished Black African leaders from Félix Eboué through to Houphouet-Boigny of the Ivory Coast agreed to take part in various stages of this gradual development, decolonization in Black Africa would take place in an atmosphere of reform rather than revolution.

French Union to the 'Loi-Cadre': Rearranging French Power

The ambiguous result of the Brazzaville Conference meant that it was still necessary after the war for French leaders to consider the possible options for the organization of the post-war Empire and to choose from these one which best suited the French desire to retain the greatest degree of control over colonial affairs at the most reasonable possible cost. In his speech to the Royal Institute for International Affairs in London in 1947, Henri Laurentie outlined the choices that were available after the Brazzaville Conference:

From then on the French had a choice of two solutions: the one being to apply to all their possessions the general principles of internal native policy which they had promulgated, waiting for progress sufficiently marked to admit of the creation of a federal system; the other to establish at the outset a kind of union elastic enough to permit each territory to develop without hindrance. Though it might have seemed more reasonable to favour the first solution, they did in fact choose the second.[17]

At this time, decolonization was a concept totally foreign to the French ideology. It represented, to the extent that it was given any consideration, a meaningless renunciation of responsibility for areas which were thought incapable of self-management. At least in the case of Black Africa, there was no pressure on metropolitan France to give decolonization much thought since the colonized peoples themselves were not making any organized demand for liberation from France. Members of francophone Black Africa's elite, the *évolués*, even often subscribed to the arguments of the *mission civilisatrice* with greater enthusiasm than did French colonial administrators themselves. The Congolese Jean-Rémy Ayoumé concluded an essay written in 1944 on 'Westernism and Africanism' with these remarks:

To sum up, we favour the extension into Africa of Western civilization in its entirety. One may, if need be, momentarily restrict this extension for practical, transitory reasons stemming, for example, from needs that must be satisfied immediately. But in our view the extension, without any discrimination, gives rise to no irrefutable or decisive objection.[18]

Given these sorts of attitudes in the colonies of Black Africa, the postwar impetus in the metropole was for the redrafting, not the rejection, of the imperial design. Though the views of Black African leaders about their own rights quickly evolved after the end of the war and in fact directly influenced the wording of the constitution of the new Fourth Republic, Black African leaders were more than willing to collaborate in the creation of a new French entity designed to bring together France and its colonial territories. The blueprint initially accepted was the French Union.

The French Union was established by Title Eight of the new French Constitution of 13 October 1946 which gave birth to the Fourth Republic. In the early stages of the constitution's preparation (January 1946), de Gaulle resigned as the President of the Council then in existence largely because he thought that the negotiations for a new constitution would give too much power to the parties and not enough to the chief executive. Once the final version of the constitution was adopted in October he would also complain (in line with Laurentie) that it had not established a federation with a strong centre, and that the pre-eminent position of France was not sufficiently guaranteed. He was obviously worried that the French Union did not sufficiently safeguard the metropole against nationalism in the colonies and that this would have a divisive effect. During his years in 'exile' de Gaulle would elaborate on his precise preferences as to the form of links that should have been created in 1946, and the French Community which he created in 1958 (analysed below) corresponded slightly better to the system he was advocating in 1946. Clearly, the 1946 French Union was more 'confederal' in nature (each of the component parts themselves theoretically retaining an individual identity) than federal (where the autonomy of the members would be clearly circumscribed) but these sorts of legal distinction were not perfectly reflected in the final form of the constitution.[19] Title Eight was full of ambiguities, something that Henri Laurentie, a clear proponent of federalism, was to highlight later in noting that it 'bears the mark of the hesitation between the trend towards a federal system and the classic leaning to unity and assimilation.'[20] As it happened, this ambiguity would allow French statesmen and propagandists concerned with the importance of France's overseas territories to argue that the constitution effectively tied these areas to France and therefore that the Union essentially confirmed France's overseas power.

The creation of the French Union in 1946 had, in fact, diverse and sometimes paradoxical implications. In eliminating from French constitutional vocabulary the idea of Empire, it also brought the overseas territories 'closer' to France. The preamble of the 1946 constitution stated that:

France, together with the overseas peoples shall form a union founded upon equality of rights and duties, without distinction of race or religion. The French Union shall consist of nations and peoples who combine or co-ordinate their resources and their efforts in order to develop their respective civilizations, increase their well-being, and ensure their security. Faithful to her traditional mission, France proposes to guide the peoples for whom she has assumed responsibility into the freedom to administer themselves and to manage their own affairs democratically; rejecting any system of colonial rule based on arbitrary power, she shall guarantee to all equal access to public service and the individual or collective exercise of the rights and liberties proclaimed or confirmed above.[21]

The articles of Title Eight expanded on these general principles but in ways which left considerable scope for scholars to find contradictions and inconsistencies in the texts. The French Union was declared one and indivisible, though it is clear that the status of the overseas territories and departments was lower than that of the metropole itself. Much of the apparently liberal language of the constitution was obscured by the more detailed articles which followed and which limited the independence of the Union's constituent elements and the exact rights of representation or citizenship that they might claim. If de Gaulle and members of his party were to criticize the terms of the Union's constitution and the types of links it established, for most of the French people the Union only confirmed the general permanence of France's colonial heritage. The themes of France's imperial past were easily identifiable in the language of the Union which, whether confederal or not, seemed basically to reaffirm the existence of a *France outre-mer*. De Gaulle, himself, who was unimpressed by the Fourth Republic's constitution, could still support the idea of the Union (if not its exact terms) and in Bordeaux on 15 May 1947 deployed familiar imagery in its defence:

For us in the world as it is and as it is going, to lose the French Union would be a blow which could cost us even our independence. To protect it and to nourish it, is to remain great and, as a result, free.[22]

The establishment of the French Union was therefore seen as a necessary step towards the unification of a larger France. The act of bringing diverse overseas territories close to France was a foreign policy equivalent of protectionism, insofar as it helped to insulate these territories from 'foreign' pressures. French writers could romanticize about the Union even as there were tensions within it which would lead to its fragmentation. In 1954, an article on the elements of an overseas policy appeared in the still imperially minded *Revue des Deux Mondes* in which the author reaffirmed principles of integration which were being severely tested in Algeria:

The whole future of the new construction of the French Union, created by the Constitution of 1946, depends on the success of this policy of humane integration. It is in the extent to which our populations *outre-mer* will accept to integrate themselves in French universalism that the ambitious project of the constitution's authors will be fulfilled: make them accede to a modern civilization through a peaceful evolution, without having them suffer the crises and disturbances of a nationalism generally inspired from the outside.[23]

If Frenchmen were to see in the French Union a modernization of the colonial myth, overseas native leaders would see in it the promise of more radical reforms whose pace they would wish to accelerate. The cultivation of a political consciousness in Black Africa by some of the senior members of the *évolués* class forced French leaders to revise the forms of overseas control. Yet because the pressure from Africa was managed by members of the elite who had an interest in maintaining a close connection with France, the degree of pressure brought to bear on the metropole remained a function of a basic need to maintain some ties with France. It was this that most clearly distinguished Black Africa from other territories of the French Union and that ensured that the force of the Black African pressure would still allow for gradualist responses from the metropole designed to maintain a special relationship. While the French Union was immediately put under pressure by nationalists in Indochina, and would later be the object of rebellion in Algeria, for a long time it served as an adequate answer for Black Africa whence the nationalist pressures were containable.

The focus of Black African nationalism after the Second World War was in the Ivory Coast, though developments in Senegal would also affect the nature and the coherence of West African resistance to colonial rule. The most important political group in the Ivory Coast was Houphouet-Boigny's *Parti Démocratique du Côte d'Ivoire* which had as its power base the large coffee and cocoa planters' voluntary association, the *Syndicat Agricole Africaine* (SAA). It was in his capacity as party president that Houphouet was elected to the first French Constituent Assembly which allowed him to take part in debates on the French constitution in 1946. When the second Constituent Assembly adopted in 1946 the new French constitution, which was less liberal than many Africans had hoped, Houphouet and others organized a large conference in Bamako in October 1946 to co-ordinate policy towards France among various Black African political groups. There was some pressure from the French to prevent this meeting from taking place and this was sufficiently great to result in a boycott by some important groupings, the most potentially influential of which was the contingent from Senegal. The most important outcome of the conference was the creation of a new inter-territorial party, with Houphouet at its head, called the *Rassemblement Démocratique Africain* (RDA) which soon affiliated itself with the Communist party in France. This link with the communists led to a Paris-based policy of repression managed by the Socialist deputy Paul Bechard who in 1948 was appointed Governor-General of the West African Federation, and by Laurent Pechoux the socialist governor of the Ivory Coast. Activists were persecuted and elections rigged. By mid-1950 the pressure had become considerable and Houphouet was convinced in July 1950 by the then Minister of Overseas France, François Mitterrand, to sever his ties with the communists in France.[24] This allowed French officials to claim to Americans concerned about the spread of communism in Africa that France knew best how to deal with the problem. The Political Director of the Quai d'Orsay argued to George McGhee in September 1950 that 'the most effective way to counter communist tactics in French Africa is to persuade the native groups (a) that their aspirations for self-government be realized within the framework of the French Union, and (b) that their best interests, materially and otherwise, lie in close co-operation with France.'[25]

Sometimes this required more than moral persuasion. But in Black Africa, the use of force by French officials was able to change policies and even help reshape loyalties towards France, in a manner which would become impossible in Algeria. This was possible in the Ivory Coast, and ultimately throughout much of francophone West and Central Africa, because African leaders perceived that their own positions were dependent on favourable links with France. The party Houphouet-Boigny led was not a unified one, but its weakness was not the reason it eventually succumbed to French pressure. As Tony Smith has shown, Houphouet-Boigny, as a Catholic and large landowner, was not the sort of person to mobilize the peasantry and conduct guerrilla warfare. In 1953 he would open a fair in the Ivory Coast by remarking to members of the African bourgeoisie: 'If you don't want to vegetate in bamboo huts, concentrate your efforts on growing good cocoa and coffee. They will fetch a good price and you will become rich.'[26] Houphouet recognized that economic success for his people required co-operation with France and this no doubt affected his decision in 1950 to move away from the communists.

The RDA would continue to have important followings with influential leaders throughout West Africa, but it never became the sort of mass movement which could move the people effectively against France. It was a symbol of political consciousness, but not a revolutionary front. The only other influential political group in West Africa at the time was Senghor's *Bloc Démocratique Sénégalais* (BDS) created in September 1948 and quite separate from the RDA. This was inevitable, given Senghor's effective break with the movement led by Houphouet at the Bamako conference which Senghor did not attend. The BDS was a large heterogeneous group including civil servants, intellectuals, peasants and members of the marabout brotherhoods.[27] It was a national party which Senghor tried to expand, creating links with groups in Dahomey, Togo and Upper Volta, but it never became a true inter-territorial rival to the RDA.

With different views of the future of Black Africa and working from different political bases, Senghor and Houphouet-Boigny campaigned (largely in Paris) to convince French officialdom of the need for more reforms in the colonies. It was this metropolitian intriguing which most affected the process of decolonization in Black Africa and the nature of post-colonial links. Houphouet and Senghor, the first a landowner, the second a 'French' intellectual, both of them deputies in the French parliament, shared a general strategy even if they were divided on the future shape independent Black Africa might take. They both felt that the best way to control and influence French interests in Africa was through their knowledge of the French parliamentary process and of the central administration as well as through their personal contacts with influential French politicians. Rather than force a mass rebellion, these leaders would work for decolonization from above. Moreover, while their pressure for reform would be constant, it was brought to bear with the full understanding that their own power in a liberated Africa would remain a function of their links with France.

These political developments in Black Africa of the late 1940s and early 1950s remained only of marginal concern to French leaders occupied with the war in Indochina and the need to 'maintain order' in Algeria. The reality of a larger France was under growing threat just as the imagery used to define it was becoming more dramatic. For Gaston Deferre in November 1953 it was a basic axiom of political life that 'France without the French Union will no longer be an important world power'.[28] But three years later in 1956 it was Gaston Deferre, as Overseas Minister, who pushed through the *Loi-Cadre* which established autonomy in the colonies. The nature of this reform which brought the day of decolonization closer, would also help to transform in the mind of French officialdom the relationship between the idea of French power in Africa and the structures that allowed its practice. The loss of formal control would not necessarily be accompanied by a loss of real power. In a book published in 1955 by two colonial civil servants, one of whom (Claude Cheysson) would become a minister of foreign affairs many years later, the idea that power could still be maintained in new forms was nicely spelled out:

The Frenchmen, who is a good colonial administrator... is sincerely convinced that the French presence is wrapped up with the exercise of authority, the maintenance of troops and the flag. The day when these trappings are taken away he believes the game will be finitely lost; and his compatriots in France share this view. It is therefore an urgent task to clarify through objective studies, in interested *milieux*, specialized organizations, large industrial enterprises, commercial and banking groups, the press, students, that the establishment of large technical and economic assistance programmes for the associated territories and states, the establishment of a long term policy, would be in vain if French public opinion were not first convinced of the possibility for France to be present in new forms, as fruitful as those of the past, but better adapted to current conditions, and as a consequence more durable.[29]

This passage perfectly illustrates the perception that reforms which might lead to a loss of authority could be transformed by an enlightened administration and political leadership into a positive policy intended to create more durable conditions for continued influence. It effectively set out the basic direction that French policy towards Black Africa would take: evolutionary reform intended to 'modernize' the forms and content of French influence and power in the weaker part of France's Empire. As the conflict in Algeria became more bloody and as the divisions between France and the Algerians became bitter, the unstated assumption of much of French policy was that French relations with Black Africa would have to be saved from a similar disaster.

The *Loi-Cadre* was the first serious step in this direction. In 1954 the Minister of Overseas France in the Mendes-France government, Robert Buron, had begun exploring the idea of self-government for the territories of Black Africa but his relatively ambitious ideas were discouraged. Buron's successor in the government of Edgar Faure, Pierre-Henri Teitgen, allowed the development of internal autonomy in Togo which was to lead to near total independence by 1958. It was on the basis of this successful experiment that Deferre in 1956 decided to accelerate the pace of reform.[30] Some of the thinking that went into the *Loi-Cadre* was no doubt influenced by the fact that Houphouet-Boigny (as Minister of Health in the cabinet of Guy Mollet) was able to impress officials in the French government with the need for change and suggest the form this change might take.

The *Loi-Cadre* was specially designed so as not to undermine the 1946 constitution establishing a one and indivisible Union but in practice it provided for a major administrative decentralization. The law granted universal suffrage in the territories and the establishment of governing councils empowered to administer local public services. Only questions affecting 'sovereignty' were still to be dealt with by the French. These would include a good number of issues: foreign policy, defence, currency and tariff matters as well as higher education and the control of radio stations. Yet the important point was that such transfer of power as did take place was to the benefit of the individual territories rather than of the large federations of French West and Equatorial Africa. Houphouet-Boigny was a forceful proponent of this solution which would eventually leave him at the head of the Ivory Coast, while Senghor opposed what he would later refer to as the 'balkanization' of Africa. This reform made it possible for local leaders of individual territories to see themselves as future leaders of independent states. It also ensured that these states would be weak.

For those in France who clung to traditional concepts of centralization these reforms had serious drawbacks. In words which perhaps revealed more about the politics of the Fourth Republic than about the changing nature of French overseas policy, George Bidault complained that 'Soon there will be governments everywhere except in Paris.'[31] The *Loi-Cadre* was seen by some as a challenge to the idea of an indivisible Republic, and the near dissolution of the African federations (which continued to exist in law but whose existence had minimal effect on local politics), was seen by a few as reducing Paris's control over the Africans. Yet, in the end, these reforms probably helped to maintain French power, since the small states which were to emerge a few years after the passage of the *Loi-Cadre* would in practice still be reliant on France.

The text of the *Loi-Cadre*, adopted by the National Assembly on 19 June 1956, contained important principles for electoral reform, the establishment of local government councils, and the enlargement of the powers of the territorial assemblies. It authorized the French government to put forward formal decrees related to these proposed changes. In January 1957 thirteen decrees were submitted to parliament for approval and the intensity of the debate on the decrees testified to the growing strength of African feeling on the need for autonomy. Senghor, who was to abstain on the vote, complained that the decrees did not go far enough: 'Instead of the true autonomy that we wish, the decrees only bring us a semi-autonomy, toys and lollipops which we do not want because we are not children.'[32] French newspaper reporting on the debate hinted at considerable bitterness. The left wing *La Dépêche de Midi* published in Toulouse argued that 'To find a compromise that preserves the French Union, it has proved necessary to prolong the difficult debate on the overseas territories. The liberalism of the government has been answered by the overbidding of some of the African deputies.'[33] The debates were certainly made difficult by the new status given Togo on 24 August 1956, a status which had just been offered to Cameroon, namely, near total independence outside the French Union. Yet, the National Assembly refused to go too far in granting important powers to the territorial assemblies on the grounds that it was wrong to give individual territories responsibility for services they could not afford to maintain. Thus, as Edward Mortimer has argued, 'whether or not it was so intended, the decision to create governments at the territorial and not at the federal level acted as a brake on the transfer of power from French to African hands.'[34]

While the *Loi-Cadre* pleased few people entirely (French or African) it did change the structure of the debate in Africa. If in 1956 and early 1957 discussions centred on territorial government and autonomy, by late 1957 the subjects became federation and independence. Independence began to be seen as an inevitability and the question African leaders posed themselves was whether in the future it would be right for the new individual states to join in an equal federation with France (Houphouet-Boigny's view) or whether (as Senghor wished) a responsible federation of the African states should join France in a loose confederation.[35] But if the debate had moved, thus creating further pressures on policy makers in Paris, it was still shaped by a desire for the establishment of a new relationship with France, and this reflected the peculiar character of francophone Black African nationalism. The leaders of Black Africa wanted independence, but as René Pleven had said in the 1940s, that independence, in the African view, would still require some connection with France and some share in the special 'independence' of France. It was still up to Charles de Gaulle, on his return to power in 1958, to restructure the Franco–African relationship while working carefully with the existing cast. There would be no need to surrender to 'enemies' in the colonies. Efforts instead could be concentrated on finding new rules for collaboration between a France weary of other colonial struggles and a leadership of Black Africa which saw itself as having a stake in the re-establishment of French prestige.

The French Community and the Establishment of *France–Afrique*

Following the passage of the *Loi-Cadre* decrees there was renewed political activity in Africa. None of the great African political parties was yet calling formally for independence, but a more thorough reform of the institutions governing Franco–African relations was universally deemed necessary. In September 1957 the RDA held a large conference at Bamako, birthplace of what was still the most important African political party. The conference brought out some sharp differences between the delegates on the form future relations with France should take.

Much of the discussion at the conference was centred on the type of federative institutions that should be created in Africa. Some, like Sékou Touré (future president of Guinea), who was clearly looking forward to the prospect of independence, called for the establishment of federal capitals at Dakar and Brazzaville. The creation of a federal executive was for Touré a step towards greater autonomy for the African territories since it would give Africans direct control over budgets still basically directed by a French High Commissioner. For Houphouet-Boigny, himself a member of the French government, if there was to be a federation it had to be a Franco–African one, based on full equality between Frenchmen and Africans, but centred in Paris. For Houphouet, reform of Title Eight of the French Constitution was the only way of satisfying African concerns, but he had no truck with arguments which suggested a total break with France. As leader of the Ivory Coast, (with Gabon one of the few potentially 'rich' territories within French Africa) Houphouet was also concerned that a federal government would too severely drain the Ivorian economy which in any federation would be a major contributor to a federal budget.[36] These financial questions did not seem to affect Touré's calculations in the least, despite the fact that Guinea too would probably be a net contributor to a federal budget. He was largely motivated by a conviction that African unity was a precondition for advancement. For Houphouet, movement towards a Franco–African Community was the best way forward, and in suggesting such a course he majestically thrust aside any arguments that might have been based on the spirit which had been evoked, far away in Asia, at the first non-aligned meeting at Bandung in 1955:

I think that we are made, Frenchmen and Africans, to succeed in this unique experiment, the only one of its kind in the world. The particular message which Africa brings is one of fraternity in this world, it is the opposite of the hatred, of that spirit of vengeance which was expressed in Bandung against the former colonizing peoples.[37]

It was therefore in a spirit of collaboration with the former colonizer that the next steps towards decolonization would be taken. The authority of Houphouet-Boigny was not sufficiently shaken by the different views expressed during the Bamako conference for him to lose his ability to influence the process of reform in Paris. This process was in part accelerated by the crisis in Algeria, which in and of itself would affect perceptions about how to deal with the territories in Black Africa, but also by the fact that in May 1958, following serious riots in Algiers, Charles de Gaulle (*l'homme de Brazzaville*) was called to Paris to try to solve the Algerian problem, a task which would lead him to create a new government and a new constitution. The need to create a new French Republic coincided with a long felt need to reform offending parts of the 1946 Constitution and to establish a proper structure for the management of relations between France and Black Africa. For members of the Black African elite like Houphouet-Boigny, the atmosphere of reform mixed with crisis which prevailed in France in 1958 strengthened their position for it encouraged them to press for the changes they wished while allowing them to claim to their opponents that only their voices of reason could command attention in Paris. A special relationship could therefore be nurtured between de Gaulle, who was trying to preserve French greatness, and African leaders who knew that if they could share in the creation of a new France they would also have a part in its success. The bonds first created by the period of the Free French movement and strengthened by the passage of time which helped to mystify their value, made it possible for de Gaulle to control the initial stages of constitutional reform as it affected Black Africa.

After 1 June 1958, when de Gaulle was formally voted into power by the National Assembly, following President René Coty's invitation to him to form a government, movement on constitutional reform was rapid. On 3 June a law was passed stating the five main principles on which a new French Republic would be based, the fifth of which stated that 'the Constitution should allow for the organization of relations between the French Republic and the peoples associated to it.'[38] In July 1958 an interministerial committee which included Houphouet-Boigny established that there should be a federal system to bring together France and the overseas territories.

These ideas were further discussed at the end of July within the Consultative Constitutional Committee, whose African members included Senghor, now leader of the newly formed *Parti de Regroupement Africain* (PRA), Lamine-Gueye also from Senegal and the PRA, Gabriel Lisette of the RDA who would represent Houphouet's point of view, and Philibert Tsiranana, the future president of Madagascar. Before this committee, de Gaulle defended his particular idea of a new federal state. Senghor defended his own concept of a confederation and bitterly argued against de Gaulle's suggestion that any African proposal which differed from his constituted a proposal for secession. But this dispute was solved by a suggestion of Tsiranana that the new constitution should put forward a French Community (rather than federation) bringing together a free association of states (rather than a 'community of free peoples'). The final document adopted in August 1958 therefore set aside federal language, yet the proposed Community (in which France was to be one state among many) would still be basically directed by France. The Community would not provide for independence in Black Africa, but it would allow, in de Gaulle's words, for 'evolution' within the member states.[39] The draft constitution establishing the French Community was to be presented to the French and African peoples in a referendum on 28 September, and to promote its terms (some of which remained ambiguous) de Gaulle undertook an African tour in late August which allowed him, at a time when tensions between France and Algeria were becoming more severe, to promote his ideology of Franco–African solidarity.

This trip to Africa was intended to rally support for the new constitution and de Gaulle did not mince words in his effort to ensure that his vision be accepted. Between 21 and 28 August he visited Fort Lamy, Tananarive,

Brazzaville, Abidjan, Conakry and Dakar. Following a brief stop in the birthplace of the Free French movement in Fort Lamy, it was in Tananarive that he first hinted of the consequences of a state choosing to become independent once it had entered the 'Community on a federal model' that he offered. Once such a choice were made then the newly independent territory would have to follow 'by itself, its own destiny', and the clear implication of this was that it might lose the support of France in so doing.[40] Tsiranana is said to have told a journalist after hearing de Gaulle speak that 'When I let my heart talk I am a partisan of total and immediate independence, when I let my reason speak, I realize that it is impossible.' [41] In Brazzaville, later to be dubbed by historians as the 'sanctuary of colonial Gaullism', de Gaulle expanded on this idea that independence would mean separation from the Community, but here he did so to show the audience that independence was not ruled out and that a 'yes' vote would not forever close the door to further freedoms. In explaining the proposed Constitution he remarked that:

If within this Community a given territory, in the course of time, after a period which I do not specify, feels itself able to undertake all the burdens and duties of independence, that is its affair, for it to decide through its elected Assembly, and by a referendum of its people. After this, the Community will act to prepare the transfer of powers to the territory becoming independent, and it would follow one route and the Community would then follow its own.[42]

After a carefully organized and warm reception in Abidjan, de Gaulle arrived in Conakry to meet the resistance of Sékou Touré, who announced that the people of Guinea would never renounce their right to independence and that they preferred 'poverty in liberty to wealth in slavery'.[43] To this challenge de Gaulle responded simply that France would draw her own conclusions from a negative vote in the referendum. His 'Adieu Guinea' on leaving Conakry was to prove a final farewell. In Dakar, where de Gaulle was greeted with numerous banners demanding independence and asserting the need for African unity, he made a firm statement very much intended as a threat to deter others from destroying his conception of mutually reinforcing Franco–African unity. Speaking to the crowd and referring directly to the demonstrators he remarked:

If they want independence, they can take it on 28 September... We are not in the era of the demagogues... We put no obstacles before anyone... If we are told 'no' we will draw the conclusions. If we are told 'yes' we will be brothers to take the road side by side, the road of great destinies.[44]

Throughout French West and Equatorial Africa the results of the 28 September referendum were overwhelmingly in favour of the French Community. Only Sékou Touré led his people away from de Gaulle's concept. Two weeks before the referendum took place he signalled this 'intention' clearly by remarking that Guinea would vote 'no' 'to a Community which is nothing but a rebaptized French Union, old merchandise with only a changed label. We will vote no to inequality. We will vote no to irresponsibility. As from 29 September, we will be an independent state. We will take total responsibility for our affairs.'[45] This statement was radically different from the signal Houphouet-Boigny had given his voters earlier in August when he said, referring to de Gaulle's trip to Abidjan: 'Tomorrow will be a great day for all of us, Metropolitans and Africans, when we will make a choice which will be, I hope, the one which has always been the purpose of my struggle, that choice that I have on my lips and in my heart: a Franco–African Community equal and fraternal.'[46] The difference between these two views was that between the leader of a colonial people who fell into the tradition of revolutionary leaders who wished for a clear break with former colonial masters, and a leader of a territory who, despite his use of the language of struggle considered that close co-operation with the former colonizer was important for his own nation's development. This latter view of Houphouet was the one followed by nearly all of francophone Black Africa and was the basic choice which allowed for the perpetuation of French influence in Africa. In this sense, it is true to say that francophone Black African leaders controlled the process of decolonization and moulded it to their own needs.

Following the September referendum de Gaulle was able to put the French Community in place. Guinea was left alone to pursue its own independent course. The French withdrew their administrative and other aid almost immediately, stating that since Guinea had said no to the constitution it could no longer expect French assistance of any kind. For the next quarter of a century, Guinea would be left to decline into near total poverty under the authoritarian rule of Sékou Touré. One of the potentially richest states of francophone Africa became a model of mismanagement. Its relative misery would serve as constant reminder to other African states, who would receive French aid, of the advantages of staying within the French orbit.

The terms of the French Constitution of 4 October 1958 established the rights of the states which had become members of the Community, and specified the limits on sovereignty imposed on each state. Article 78 of the Constitution declared that matters of foreign policy, money, communal political economy and finance, strategic raw materials policy, justice, higher education, external and common transport, and telecommunications, would be ones for decision by the Community as a whole. While this may have implied on paper that all members of the Community would have equal powers, in practice it meant that the French Republic, as the only independent state in the Community, would control all these questions. The Community was governed by a number of institutions which in theory disposed of communal powers: a presidency, an executive council, a senate and a court. However these organs could not be separated either juridically or in practice from those of the French Republic at large, and it was in part against this sort of control that Sékou Touré had rebelled.[47] De Gaulle's idea of a Community founded on 'legality and the equality of the people it comprises', while appearing to lead to a federal organization, in fact resulted in little more than an extension of the French Republic. For this reason, even representatives of territories which had voted in favour of the Constitution, like Senghor, felt that the Community had to be considered as only a step towards true independence.

The creation of the Community was, in the words of one French journalist, 'the last gasp of the policy of assimilation'.[48] It may well have been that de Gaulle had hoped, also, that the Community could serve as a model for future relations with Algeria. But almost as soon as it was established the all too obvious irrationality and inherent contradictions of the Community and its various institutions served to increase pressures within the Black African states for true and complete independence. By late 1958 leaders in Mali began to speak of plans to establish a Mali Federation, which would include Upper Volta, Senegal and Dahomey. Though this plan failed, by the summer of 1959 Mali announced that it would seek independence in confederation with France. In December 1959 de Gaulle accepted this request and began negotiations with Mali to 'transfer the necessary competences' to the new republic, which became fully independent on 24 June 1960. This followed passage of a law on 4 June 1960 which permitted all member states of the Community to become fully sovereign. The acceptance of the principle that Mali could become independent while staying within the Community set off a chain reaction as much in French Equatorial as in French West Africa. Shortly after Mali, Madagascar became independent, and the rest of francophone Africa soon followed. In September 1960, France sponsored twelve Black African states to UN membership, and the French Community, as originally constituted, became moribund.

What did not die, in this final rush to independence, was the juridical link with France. The states which had become independent still wanted to collaborate with France. In a debate in the National Assembly on 9 June 1960, as the Black African states were achieving independence, Mamadou Dia of Senegal, called for a close Franco–African relationship on new terms:

This is the occasion to render solemn homage to France which has known how to keep all the promises it made including the absolute duty to decolonize and the imperative of co-operation. France is in the process of succeeding in the best possible way in her mission as tutor.[49]

All the states that became independent during this period (fourteen African states plus Madagascar) signed new 'co-operation' agreements with France. Some like the Ivory Coast, Dahomey, Niger, and Upper Volta (who had formed a regional organization as the Conseil d'Entente), Mauritania and Cameroon, signed co-operation agreements only after independence and formal recognition at the UN. The others signed agreements at the same time as they claimed independence. Michel Debré, de Gaulle's prime minister, had sent a letter on 15 June 1960 to Leon M'ba of Gabon which typified the spirit which still reigned in the French government about the need to hold on to a special relationship with the new African states. It was not so much that France wished such a relationship, but that it was expected:

We give independence on the condition that the state once independent engages itself to respect the co-operation agreements it first signs. There are two systems that come into play at the same time: Independence and the co-operation agreements. One does not go without the other ... I will be obliged if you would please, in acknowledging receipt of this communication confirm to me that on the proclamation of independence by the Republic of Gabon, the government of the Gabonese Republic will proceed to the signature of co-operation agreements... [50]

While, as noted above, some states chose to defy this simultaneity – independence, but only with co-operation – the fact remained that all of the former Community states accepted that even as sovereign states there had to be a basic juridical link to France. That link, through co-operation agreements, continues to this day. De Gaulle's policy of co-operation with Black Africa became, thus, one of the basic aspects of his overseas policy but also, more generally, one of the ordering principles of his foreign policy. One French jurist has described this policy in relatively cold, almost legal terms:

as a mode of international relations which implies the establishment of a policy (hence a strategy and a tactic) followed over a certain period of time in order to render more intimate, thanks to permanent mechanisms, international relations, in one or more determined areas, without challenging the independence of the units in question.[51]

The policy of co-operation in fact was a means of holding on to influence in

Black Africa even if it was often presented as a general leitmotif of French foreign policy. The agreements codified the still sentimental attachment between France and Black Africa. They put on a legal footing the continued role that France would play in the protection and internal development of these states. And since these new 'contracts' were freely entered into, even if there was some pressure to do so at the time of independence, they allowed France to claim to the outside world that French policy in Black Africa was in virtually every detail not merely accepted by the states in question but also requested by them. The very word co-operation disguised the practical effect of the agreements: continued development and other aid on the part of the former colonial power in return for continued loyalty and special favours on the part of the newly independent states of Black Africa. The effect of undertaking in 1960 a coherent policy of co-operation has been well summarized by Albert Bourgi, one of the foremost authorities on Franco–Senegalese relations:

In a country where the mere idea of confederation had two years before been considered subversive, the new type of relations installed by France, under the name co-operation was aimed to temper the consequences of a process of independence that had become irreversible and to prolong, if not to consolidate beyond the indispensable political and juridical changes, the multifarious presence of the former colonizer: presence of a great number of technicians for some time, of its army in key strategic locations, control of economic and financial life, guaranteed outlets and sources for certain articles, a huge monetary zone based on the Franc and finally a cultural and linguistic hegemony.[52]

The establishment of a policy of co-operation with independent Black Africa can therefore only be seen, both in its detail and in its general effect, as a successful assertion of power by France over the former colonial Empire. Not only was influence preserved, but also France was praised by the Africans for the liberalizing spirit which it seemed to display in the process. In contrast to the tragedy of Algeria, French leaders were able to deal with change, and had time to shape it to their advantage.

The co-operation agreements, which were concluded mainly in 1960 but also in 1961, 1962 and 1963, guaranteed most of the important rights that France had formerly held because of conquest and the nature of imperial power. Some of the agreements were on political issues which the French Community had formerly tried to address: foreign policy, defence, strategic materials; others included technical assistance provisions in terms of either personnel or equipment. In some instances economic and financial agreements, and in others juridical problems such as the organization of local justice, were dealt with. Some agreements could be described more as contracts, others as international treaties. Nearly all of the new states signed agreements that covered economic, financial, political, military and technical assistance questions. The agreements were either strictly bilateral as in the case of Senegal, Mauritania, the Malagasy Republic and several others; or multilateral and organized on a regional basis as was the case with the Ivory Coast, Dahomey and Niger in one group and Chad, the Central African Republic and Congo Brazzaville in another (which Gabon later joined). The exact terms of these agreements will be discussed where relevant in subsequent chapters, but here it is important to explain generally how they affected the new-found sovereignty of the francophone African states.

Though the first generation of co-operation agreements were subsequently revised in the mid-1970s on African demand, and while there would be later rejections of the more stringent terms, in their initial form, the agreements gave overwhelming privileges to France. The political aspects of the co-operation agreements provided not only for considerable exchange of information between France and the signatory state but also for consultation in matters of foreign policy. This clause and the policy which flowed naturally from it would allow France to organize, for example, bloc votes in the fora of the UN in support of French positions. The military accords provided in various cases for fully fledged defence agreements, technical military assistance accords, and base rights in francophone Africa. In some instances they also covered the transfer of primary resources and strategic minerals, obliging the signatory state not only to give France priority in the purchase of such resources, but also, where relevant, to buy certain products from France rather than turn to other trade partners. In the economic domain, France promised to aid the economies of the signatory states and to provide such financial support as was necessary to cover certain parts of local administrative expenses. The agreements also gave the signatories mutually preferential treatment in trade matters. Since virtually all the states signing co-operation agreements also became members of the Franc Zone, their currencies were tied to the French Franc, and therefore to the Bank of France.

The effect of these various agreements was to link, in large measure, the political, military, economic and financial policies of the new states to the decision-making process in Paris. There was little coercion in this process, for most of the leaders of the new states who had pressed for decolonization by skilful manipulation of the French political system which they well understood, knew that their own status within their countries depended on the quality of aid and assistance they could get from France. In the same way that senior African leaders had struck deals with politicians in France during the process of decolonization, so they made special arrangements for themselves as independence became a fact. The form of French influence in post-colonial Black Africa is rooted in the nature of the special decolonization process that took place there.

For the most part, the leaders of francophone Black Africa shaped their own decolonization and the method chosen was gradualism in preference to rebellion. This was because the Black African leaders had a stake in their connection with France and in metropolitan prestige. They perceived no interest in destroying France's image of herself as a great power while they achieved juridical independence. In cleverly managing their own process of decolonization, these leaders allowed France certain residual economic, military, and cultural influence, but they also claimed for themselves a particular status in French foreign policy to which they cling and which French leaders ignore at their peril. Black African leaders were able to secure for themselves arrangements through the co-operation agreements that helped sustain their own power base and gave them a degree of influence over the French political agenda. At the same time they gave official sanction to a post-imperial role for France that would enhance France's status in the international system. De Gaulle was able to assert French power in Black Africa because he had the good fortune to work with African leaders who wished to collaborate with him in return for a special place for their countries in French external policy.

Decolonization, French Power and International Relations

As it was defined at the time, the general process of decolonization ended only in 1962 with the signature of the Evian agreements with Algeria. The Algerian problem was great because it was an internal one both in the juridical and political sense. Algeria was controlled by the Ministry of the Interior and was also substantially populated by Frenchmen. Despite his cry in May 1958 – 'Vive l'Algérie Française' – de Gaulle became convinced of the need for decolonization in Algeria more quickly than some of his supporters, (who later turned on him), either expected or desired. What was special about the process of decolonization in Black Africa was that the language of unity that had formerly been used primarily to refer to North Africa became transferred *mutatis mutandis* to the territories of Black Africa. The images of *Eurafrique* and *France–Afrique*, or similar terms which called up the same sense of unique destiny, became applicable to the French Community, and later to Franco–African relations in the age of 'co-operation' between France and Black Africa.

As retreat from North Africa and especially Algeria became inevitable,

Black Africa was increasingly invested with the important political 'properties' formerly held only by Algeria. So much so that when, in the closing years of the twentieth century, French politicians refer to Africa, they almost always mean the francophone states of Black Africa. It is perhaps unsurprising that de Gaulle should have tacitly engineered this process. When France was losing her foothold in the Levant in 1943-4 de Gaulle's appearance in Brazzaville helped to consolidate Free French influence in Black Africa. In 1958, when Algeria was cracking, much of de Gaulle's overseas efforts were directed towards the creation of the French Community to strengthen ever more essential links with Black Africa. As this was accomplished, appeal was often made for Franco–African solidarity because of the need jointly to defend against external pressures. Similarly, France's commitments in Africa were often presented to allies as just cause for public stances which emphasized the politics of independence more strongly than those of alliance. The public positions taken by de Gaulle and his ministers with respect to Black Africa between 1958 and 1962 reflected general foreign policy concerns and forcefully shaped the future course of France's global policy. Indeed the management of decolonization itself considerably affected the way in which France's influence would later be proclaimed.

The French Community was immediately presented by de Gaulle as an instrument of mutual security and in his appeal to African states he incessantly pointed to the need for collaborative action against external threats. In Tananarive on 8 July 1959 he remarked:

We are united because we are free men and because we wish to remain so. Freedom is won... but it also must be defended. How can we do this if we are isolated, forced to stand alone, while the threats weigh on the whole world and to repulse them... strong means are required. Our Community is the condition of our security.[53]

If the French Community was the condition of both French and African security it was also the case that France's need to defend all of Africa pushed her toward a policy of independence. To explain why France had chosen in early 1959 to withdraw the French Mediterranean squadron from NATO jurisdiction, the Foreign Minister Maurice Couve de Murville remarked in the National Assembly in December 1959 that:

One fact is ... for the Free World and especially for France, the growing importance from the point of view of defence, of African problems. North Africa and the Community impose on us duties and responsibilities which are heavy. However, Africa is not covered by NATO. Our forces in Algeria, our forces in Black Africa and Madagascar have never been and could never be part of the Atlantic organization. Our naval units in the Mediterranean will be in time of war, the only link between those forces and the metropole.[54]

At least while the Algerian war was on and before full decolonization in Black Africa, France's African vocation played a determining role in France's wider foreign policy. Once this process was over, it was inevitable that French global policy would centre on European affairs. A successful overseas policy had always been a means to greater status in Europe and it was natural for long-established priorities to reassert themselves. Once the defeat in Algeria had been absorbed and the new system of *France–Afrique* negotiated with the leaders of Black Africa was in place, France's African vocation, which was concentrated in Black Africa, became integrated into France's broader designs. Speaking at the end of 1963 de Gaulle defined the general orientations of French external policy:

France, because it can, because all invite her to, because she is France, must follow in the middle of the world a policy that is global. During the course of the year that is about to begin, France will work on the great tasks that occupy us. The Union of Europe... the progress of the developing countries and above all those which, in Africa, are already linked to us through special agreements and those that will do so on that continent or on others. Finally, a contribution to the maintenance of peace.[55]

France's African vocation therefore became 'officially' part of France's general global mission. Almost no French official of the Fifth Republic has been able to make a foreign policy speech without remarking on how the strength of French relations with Black Africa in the post-colonial era shows French commitment to the practical aspects of the North–South dialogue and reflects France's enduring prestige as a world power. Sometimes the 'privileged relations' between France and North Africa are referred to as important, but by and large it is 'Black Africa' which has become the repository of France's post-colonial effort and also the source of the prestige which French leaders still perceive derives from an active overseas policy. French international relations may become increasingly centred on ensuring that France remains a leading power in a united Europe. But as a symbol of power, an effective and persistent influence in Black Africa is almost as important as possession of nuclear weapons and the status France enjoys as a permanent member of the UN Security Council. The nature of French military, economic and diplomatic policy towards Black Africa is carefully gauged to ensure the perpetuation both of French influence in Africa and of France's position as an important power which such influence helps to bolster. It is to each of these three practical aspects of French power in Africa that we now turn.

5
French Military Power and Black Africa since 1960

From the end of the Second World War, France's commitments in the African continent have had a major impact on the formulation of French declaratory policies as well as on the substance of defence plans. Immediately after the war, the defence of North Africa and of the French Union virtually received a higher priority than the defence of Europe, where a fresh outbreak of hostilities seemed unlikely.[1] Once negotiations on the Atlantic Treaty began, France made substantial efforts to use the Atlantic framework to retain her colonial possessions, by insisting that the United States consider giving greater commitments to Allied interests outside the treaty area. The reluctance of the United States to do so, (despite the initial inclusion of Algeria within the treaty area), must be seen as one of the root causes of France's later desire for independence within the Atlantic Alliance. Since many of France's major military responsibilities remained in areas not covered by the Alliance, it would eventually appear proper and logical that France take a more aloof stand in respect of direct collaboration for European defence. France would 'independently' prepare for her defence within Europe, just as she was forced to stand 'alone' in defence of her outside obligations in Africa.

Immediately after the war, events in Algeria and emerging nationalist problems in Morocco and Tunisia dominated French military thinking. North Africa was seen as a vital strategic area, closely linked to France's principal interests in Europe. Defence of the countries along the North African littoral was considered vital for the preservation of NATO interests in the Mediterranean. Aside from their own installations and garrisons in these territories, the French allowed the Americans to have five air bases in Morocco and military thinkers repeatedly emphasized – as did political apologists for the concept of *Algérie Française* – the essential indivisibility of the Mediterranean area whose stability was a key to Western security. A classic statement which reflected French geostrategic thinking in this respect was provided by General de Monsabert in a *Foreign Affairs* article of 1953, in which he argued that North Africa's importance lay in:

its central position at the point where the Mediterranean and African facades of the African and European continent meet. Without North Africa Europe cannot breathe and cannot act unless it be to retreat ... the real frontier of Europe, then, is the ancient Roman limes bordering the Sahara. From Casablanca to Berlin, from Kiel to Gabes everything interlocks and because it does the whole area constitutes a single and indivisible theatre of war.[2]

Once the protectorates of Tunisia and Morocco were granted independence all energy was focused on Algeria, and once Algeria became independent, it was acknowledged that the defence of Western interests in the Mediterranean would have to rely, at least in part, on a carefully managed diplomatic and economic policy towards the new North African states. While the Soviet Union must have hoped that it could arrange facilities for its Mediterranean squadron in these countries, it did not succeed in gaining the sort of port access it wished and the West feared.[3] While the French evacuated their large port at Mers-el-Kebir in 1968 they did so having signed a military assistance agreement with Algeria, which was followed, in 1973, by agreements with Morocco and Tunisia. After the Maghreb countries became independent, French military assistance and arms transfers still followed, but this has not been the subject of the sort of grand strategy that politicians and generals felt necessary in the 1950s. While most Western strategists would view with considerable alarm the establishment of Soviet bases in these countries, the clear desire of the Maghreb states to retain their independence, and the close links many Western countries maintain with North African leaders has made it possible for the West to secure its basic interests in the Mediterranean without an overly ostentatious military policy.

As France's individual position and strength in North Africa began to fade, French leaders, and particularly de Gaulle, saw in Black Africa the one area where France's military power could still be relevant, and where its acceptance would symbolize the retention of unique national influence. French military assistance towards Black Africa has been relatively inexpensive and insofar as it has been exclusive has helped to maintain French influence. With France's economic and other aid, military assistance has helped to keep alive the notion of France as a benevolent great power. France's military power in Black Africa has only occasionally been related to general military strategic aims though it has certainly made it very difficult for the Soviet Union to establish herself in West and Central Africa. The significance of French military power is largely political, in that it reflects the fact that other states still 'need' French assistance, and that, generally, these states accept, and in some instances even enjoy, being within a French sphere of influence. French military policy in Black Africa has been at least in part directed to keeping alive the historical idea of *France–Afrique* so badly damaged after the loss of *Algérie Française*.

The French Community had codified the idea of a unitary global defence of France and the African states close to her. Even in the post-colonial world, the defence of francophone Africa and the defence of France herself have often been presented as co-extensive aims. Certainly the military expression of French power in Black Africa has been the most important in sustaining France's post-colonial influence in the region. The need to keep a military presence in Africa has been considered a central geopolitical aim. In the view of one analyst writing in the 1960s, the strong links between the metropole and the new African states overseas were justified not only by the various political, cultural and economic interests which France had there, but also because if France did not act to preserve these interests others would take her place. He added that: 'The building of African states must proceed with us, otherwise it shall proceed against us.'[4] Because the cost of military aid to these small, weak countries in Black Africa has remained quite low, while the political benefits have been perceived as substantial, all governments of the Fifth Republic have seen military aid to Black Africa as an important constant of French external policy.

This chapter analyses the post-colonial military agreements between France and Black Africa, the general lines of French military policy since decolonization, the structure of present French–African security relations, the objectives of French military intervention, and the constraints, both political and military that operate on France when she chooses to intervene with military force in Africa. What emerges from these considerations is that the Franco–African security relationship is a principal determinant of French power in Africa, and that despite specific defeats on the African continent, French military policy has shown itself to be adaptable to changing conditions. This has ensured that to the degree that French military power continues to be accepted by the African states themselves as an essential part of their own security, France's African 'vocation' can still be held up by French leaders as an essential aspect of French state power.

Military Agreements

The military agreements concluded with Black African states in the first year after decolonization were of two kinds: defence agreements which gave African states the opportunity to call on France for direct security assistance; and military co-operation agreements (not necessarily linked with the defence accords) by which France promised to provide African states with technical advisers, place students in French military schools and transfer (at no cost) military material and equipment to help form national African armies.

In the military domain, the principal aim of the French government in concluding the agreements was to maintain its influence in Africa while preserving its ultimate freedom of action. The French government wanted the right to keep bases and facilities in francophone Black Africa and Madagascar, the ability to ensure its supply of raw materials from these countries, as well as the right to abstain from sending forces to the continent if it chose.[5] Twelve African states signed defence agreements between 1960 and 1961: Central African Republic (CAR), Chad, Congo, Gabon, Senegal, Madagascar, the Ivory Coast, Dahomey (now Benin), Niger, Mauritania, Togo and Cameroon. Some of these agreements were bilateral, others were multilateral. Mali refused to sign any military agreement and, while it retained some agreements with France, it generally had a more aloof attitude towards the connection which perhaps reflected some of the tensions created by the break-up of the Mali Federation in 1960. Mali did, eventually, sign a military co-operation agreement in 1977. Upper Volta (now Burkina Faso) demanded the dismantling of French bases and refused to sign a defence agreement, but did grant France overflight, staging and transit rights. The analysis offered by *Le Monde* on 9 March 1961 is instructive on the reasons for this:

The fraternity of arms between Africans and Europeans in the course of the two global conflicts has created common links. However, some French soldiers have intervened in local problems, particularly those who in October 1959 wished to aid the Moro-Naba, Emperor of the Mossis, to overthrow the government. The memory of that influence remains, and however meagre French forces may be - they are limited to two garrisons at Bobo-Dioulasso and Ouagadougou - the co-existence of the two armies is no longer accepted by the Upper Voltan capital.[6]

These fears of the domestic role that France might play in the African countries with whom she had defence or military co-operation agreements were not shared by many other states. A number of African leaders wished the French military to provide for their own personal security. In the event, all the countries which originally signed defence agreements, with the exception of Togo and Dahomey, also sought protection from France against internal as well as external threats. The decision to intervene to solve disputes was reserved to the French President, and French response to appeals to help was not considered as being automatic (table 5.1).

Table 5.1 Military agreements between France and African countries

Defence Agreements	*Year of Signature*
Cameroon	1974
CAR	1960
Comores	1973
Djibouti	1977
Gabon	1960
Ivory Coast	1961
Senegal	1974
Togo	1963
Military Assistance Agreements	*Year of Signature*
Algeria	1967
Benin	1975
Burkina Faso	1961
Burundi	1969
Cameroon	1974
Central African Republic	1960
Chad	1976
Comores	1978
Congo	1974
Djibouti	1977
Gabon	1960
Libya	1978
Madagascar	1973
Mauritania	1976
Mauritius	1979
Niger	1977
Rwanda	1975
Senegal	1974
Seychelles	1979
Togo	1976
Tunisia	1973
Zaire	1974

Defence agreements provide for signatories to call on France for direct military assistance, but Paris is not obliged to respond positively.

Military assistance agreements are not necessarily linked to defence agreements. They provide for training, technical assistance and transfer of military equipment.

Annexes to the defence agreements sought to give more tangible meaning to the claim that the defence of France and that of Africa were linked. This was clear in raw materials policy. Most states signing defence agreements with France also undertook to keep the French government informed on the general measures taken to ensure the continuance of research, exploitation and trading of such materials as liquid and gaseous hydrocarbons, uranium, thorium, lithium, beryllium, helium and various other minerals and compounds. The French government was given priority in any sales made of these materials, and the African states undertook both to facilitate the provision of these materials to France and to refrain from trading them to other states when required to do so by defence considerations.[7]

The military arrangements established between France and her ex-colonies assured France exclusive action in francophone Africa. Article 2 of the second annex of the defence agreement between France and Gabon, for example, stipulated that the 'Gabonese Republic, in consideration of the help granted it by the French Republic, and in order to assure the standardization of armaments, engages itself to call exclusively on the French Republic for the maintenance and renewal of its materials...'[8] This article recurred in numerous agreeements with other francophone African states. While this provision came to be ignored from time to time (in the case of Gabon, for example, by the purchase of *Cascavel* light tanks from Brazil), a habit of turning to France for military assistance was established early on, from which escape was difficult even to consider, let alone justify. Most of the agreements also allowed African soldiers to serve in the French army or French soldiers to serve with the armies of particular African states. The fact that Frenchmen could wear the uniform of an independent African state and that Africans could serve in the French army to defend French interests, perpetuated the sense of a Franco–African solidarity which went beyond mere protestations of complementary interests.

But while the defence agreements provided for regular consultation between France and her African partners on defence questions, French planners never lost sight of the primacy of the French position in any of these arrangements. The principal reason that the French government had demanded that African states sign agreements was to ensure that French bases on that continent remained secure. In a document written for the *Centre Militaire d'Informations et Documentations Outre-Mer* in 1961, General Revol wrote that 'it is evident that bases are necessary to us - first to go to the aid of those of our African partners who might be in difficulties, but equally to hold on to our place in the world.'[9] In the event, the need to develop an African military infrastructure with communication links and bases determined the policies of both the French and the Africans.

Throughout the 1960s French strategic planners saw their principal overseas commitments as being divided among three large zones: the Indian Ocean (which included Madagascar and Djibouti); Central Africa (comprising the ex-West and Central African French colonies); and the Pacific area. Military commands were organized to take the strategic unity of each of these areas into account.[10] The Central African Zone was itself divided into three - Zones d'Outre-Mer (ZOM) - with headquarters at Dakar, Abidjan and Brazzaville. The Indian Ocean ZOM had its headquarters in Tananarive. Throughout Black Africa and in Madagascar the French maintained five categories of military facilities at the time of decolonization: principal bases at which elements of all three branches of the armed forces were stationed; intermediate bases which allowed the French to move comfortably around the continent; replacement bases which could be built up if a principal base were lost; security garrisons which were established on an *ad hoc* basis; and places where staging rights were automatically granted. The most important principal bases were at Djibouti, Dakar, Diego-Suarez and Fort Lamy (now Ndjamena) but those at Port Bouet (Ivory Coast), Libreville (Gabon) and Bangui (CAR) were also significant. In 1960 there were over one hundred French garrisons in Black Africa and Madagascar. In this sense, perhaps not very much had changed from the height of French colonial power in francophone Africa, when the extent of French military activity was often commented upon by bemused travellers. One, in 1935, had remarked that:

Perhaps the thing which surprised me most in French West Africa was the excessive militarization of the country. In any conglomeration of any size was a barracks; and it was comparatively seldom that an hour passed without hearing a military bugle. Indeed the bugle has completely ousted the tomtom as a background to local color.[11]

After 1960 the French had reason - indeed in some respects were forced - to withdraw this heavy garrisoning of Black Africa, and indeed now, despite a still important French presence, there are only six French bases in Black Africa. [12]

This physical retreat from Africa, which began soon after decolonization, was made possible because of changes which were taking place in the African military structures themselves as a result of French technical assistance, and because of improvements made in the French ability to act overseas. All French colonies except Guinea signed military assistance agreements which were aimed at building national armies and providing logistic support. Instruction to local armies was openly declared to be in the French interest since it was 'one of the most efficient ways of guaranteeing the maintenance of (French) influence in the new armies'.[13] Training of the developing African armies was done by technical advisers and armaments were provided by the French government which, in order to organize military co-operation properly, established a *Bureau d'Aide Militaire* or a *Mission d'Aide Militaire* in each country having co-operation agreements with France. The French initially preserved the right to enlist new African volunteers directly and retain those not called on by their national armies, thus giving further substance to the sometimes vague political claim that African defence considerations were indistinguishable from French ones.

All these activities were run by the French Ministry of Co-operation (the defence agreements are run directly by the Ministry of Defence) established in 1961, whose sole reponsibility was the management of relations with the African states and Madagascar as provided by the co-operation agreements. By a decree of 18 May 1961, a Council of African and Malagasy Affairs – consisting of the President, the Prime Minister, the Foreign Minister and the Minister of Co-operation – was created to ensure that the regional policy undertaken by France in Africa was managed with the direct participation of the highest government officials. This Council no longer operates, but the retention of an adviser at the Elysée Palace with sole responsibility for African affairs has ensured that African policy is determined at the top level of government and informal meetings do take place weekly at the Elysée between representatives of those parts of the administration having an interest in African affairs. By the end of 1961, then, the elements of a long-term policy were in place, and thought was given to making the deployment of French power in Africa more subtle. The cost of maintaining and supplying bases in Africa was high and, after all, francophone Black African armies were being created which could do much of the work previously done by France. So, French troop levels in Africa were progressively reduced from 58,000 to 21,300 in the two years following 1962, and again from 21,300 to about 6,400 from 1965 to 1970.[14]

This troop withdrawal was compensated for by the creation in 1962 of the *Force Interarmées d'Intervention*, about which de Gaulle spoke in 1961 to a group of Army representatives in Strasbourg:

As the relative distance between the continents seems to become smaller, there is no conflict or danger anywhere which can fail to affect a world power, and therefore France. Furthermore, in new forms, adapted to our century, France is, as always, present and active overseas. As it happens, her security, the aid that she owes to her allies, the support that she has decided to give her associates, can all be challenged in any region of the globe. A ground, naval and aerial intervention force created to act at any moment, no matter where, is therefore altogether necessary.[15]

The creation of the *Force d'Intervention* grew from a belief that it would be both politically more acceptable and more effective from a military point of view than French troops on the ground in Africa. While important strongholds in Africa would be retained, the French military presence would be gradually reduced and in this way become more acceptable to public opinion both at home and abroad. Yet the new system did not mean that there was a significant decline in the French ability to guard Africa. From 1962 onwards, French military policy in Africa was based on power wielded on three levels. First, the immediate defence of African territory rested on the *Armées Nationales* which were being developed in African states with French help. Second, the African-based French *Forces d'Outre-Mer*, stationed at various points in francophone Africa which had been singled out by the defence and co-operation agreements as French military posts, would provide further cover if required. These local French forces depended quite heavily on the system of bases established in 1960 and 1961. Third, the *Force d'Intervention Interarmées*, stationed in the south of France, would provide fast and powerful land, sea and air reinforcement to the *Forces d'Outre-Mer* in the event of a crisis. The link between the *Forces d'Outre-Mer* and the *Force d'Intervention* was considered from the beginning as necessarily close, with the former securing the bases which would serve the *Force d'Intervention* on its arrival from France. As one military authority explained, this two-tier French system of forces would serve as a deterrent to any aggression in Africa inimical to French interests. Writing (anonymously) in *Frères d'Armes*, an official periodical devoted to Franco-African military matters, he asserted that: ' "deterrence" has found in contemporary military vocabulary a new life: the possibility of rapid and massive intervention in distant places has meant we can reduce our external forces.'[16] This conventional deterrent force, while owing its evolution to political considerations, was to become part of a graduated system of defence which could be put into effect by an African country having links with France.

Military Intervention and Policy

Before 1962, and while the Gaullist system was being put into place with the decolonization of francophone Black Africa, there had been a number of interventions in the ex-colonies, and it was to these that the defenders of the *Force d'Intervention* would point in justifying its creation, both because the proven instability of the area required such a force, and because, being an evident improvement on the previous military arrangement, its value as a deterrent would be high. The strategic importance of some francophone countries, often exaggerated by those who were most enthusiastic about suppressing local revolts, meant that French forces were quite active during the early 1960s in attempts to stamp out internal rebellions which might lead to the disintegration of French influence (table 5.2). In Cameroon, the French gave considerable support to government forces fighting the *Union des Populations du Cameroon* (UPC) which was itself receiving help from the Soviet Union. At some points during the early years of the UPC insurrection, 300 officers and NCOs were operating as military assistants to the Cameroon government and managing the Zone de Pacification du Cameroon (ZOPAC) which the French government had set up to control the rebellion.[17]

Similar operations took place from 1956-1963 in Mauritania. In 1958 French troops had entered the Western Sahara to restore order and, after *Opération Ecouvillon* had proved successful, French troops stayed in the newly-independent Mauritania to keep the peace until co-operation agreements had been signed to keep the peace. Smaller-scale interventions also took place in 1960 in Gabon and the Congo to end conflicts between the nationals of the two countries, and later also in Chad and Niger to quell internal disturbances. Throughout this period there was also activity by some French soldiers in Africa, often independent of direct government instructions (as in the case of Burkina Faso cited above), to control or influence, in favour of perceived French interests, local unrest. Even in the early 1960s, French soldiers garrisoned in Black Africa sometimes acted without specific instructions from Paris. However, none of these interventions or security operations associated with the process of decolonization received as much publicity as did the French intervention in Gabon in February 1964 to support President M'ba.

In accordance with the defence agreement with Gabon (which implicitly provided for the personal protection of the Gabonese president) French forces intervened to put down an uprising led by the leader of the opposition party. As France had not intervened in Togo during the disturbances which followed the assassination of President Olympio in 1963 (ostensibly because there was no defence agreement yet concluded) and having not sent troops to Congo-Brazzaville during the troubles in the same year (supposedly because the President preferred to resign rather than call in the French), the intervention in Gabon came as somewhat of a surprise. It indicated, however, that when a francophone African leader close to France needed help, France would be willing to use military force to sustain him in power.

Table 5.2 French military interventions in Black Africa since decolonization

Country	Date	Type
Cameroon	1959–64	Action against UPC insurgents
Mauritania	1961	Suppression of revolts
Senegal	1959–60	Local suppport to President Senghor during the breakdown of the Mali Federation
Congo	1960–2	Suppression of riots
Gabon	1960, 1962 1964	Suppression of riots Prevention of military coup against President M'ba
Chad	1960–3 1969–1975	Suppression of minor uprisings War against FROLINAT
Djibouti	1976–7	Operations *Louada* and *Saphir* against Somalian irredentism
Mauritania	1977	Intervention against *Polisario*
Zaire	1977–8	Supppression of Shaba rebellion
Chad	1978–80	War against FROLINAT
Central Africa	1979	Operation *Barracuda* in suppport of David Dacko against Bokassa
Chad	1983–8	Various operations in suppport of President Hissein Habré
Togo	1986	Operation in suppport of President Eyadema

This list includes only the most obvious interventions and does not refer to discreet military actions like reinforcement of garrisons, rapid increases of military aid etc., which have occurred from time to time during all this period and have often been as effective as direct military intervention with externally based forces.

The excitement surrounding the Gabon affair led to a review of France's military policy in Africa, and a decision was made to accelerate the withdrawal of troops from African soil, and more obviously to rely on the deterrent value of the *Force d'Intervention* to preserve French interests. These slight changes were explained to the National Assembly's Commission on Foreign Affairs by the Secretary of State M. Habib-Deloncle, without reference to Gabon and entirely in terms of the economic advantages of maintaining fewer troops in Africa. The French ability to ensure regional security, he went on to imply, would be more effective if it were based on a healthy policy of economic co-operation with France.[18] The French policy of economic aid to Africa flowed from suggestions made in a major foreign aid report of 1963 as well as from de Gaulle's own inclination continually to prove France's sympathy for contemporary movements favouring third-world independence and development. As he put it in a press conference in 1964:

Naturally France, despite the ordeals that have sometimes deadened or weakened her, plays a considerable role in this vast evolution. That is a result, no doubt, of the positions which her policy, her economy, her culture, her force have allowed her to gain in all parts of the world.[19]

After 1964, French military policy in Africa concentrated on local training of armed forces and on a policy of deterrence led from the metropole. After the several upheavals in Africa that had taken place between 1958 and 1964, de Gaulle's priority was to reduce Franco–African relations to a problem of management: an instance of North–South relations which was efficient and productive of goodwill.

More or less satisfied that relations between France and Africa were secure, de Gaulle spent less time in the middle years of his Presidency making pronouncements in favour of Franco–African solidarity. Concerned with giving substance to the policy of detente and co-operation with other powers which became central to France's general foreign policy after 1964, de Gaulle's hope, largely fulfilled, was that France's African policy could be marked by the quiet nurturing of a privileged relationship.

Unfortunately France's African partners were not always as obliging as French leaders might have liked. Even though there were no French military interventions in Africa from 1964-1968, a return to a 'business as usual' policy with the ex-colonies was sometimes upset by internal disturbances and external pressures. In 1965 and 1966 alone, there were *coups d'états* in Dahomey, the Central African Republic, and Upper Volta, as well as in other African countries of interest to France, such as Algeria, Burundi and Congo-Léopoldville. Showing particular concern about events in the CAR and Upper Volta, M. Peyrefitte, the Information Minister, declared to the Council of Ministers on 5 January 1966 that: 'the events which have taken place in Bangui and Ouagadougou are of a kind which can affect the French policy of aid and co-operation which can only function in a context of order and legitimacy.'[20]

Followed the next day by a public statement from the President in the same terms, this was both a general warning to other African states that the continuance of French aid would be dependent on their being able to keep their houses in order, and a specific threat to Colonel (later Emperor) Bokassa, and Lieutenant-Colonel Lamizana that, unless they proved themselves to be fair and legitimate rulers, French aid to them might well be interrupted. At least for a short time after the late 1965 coups the *Fonds d'Aide et de Coopération* (FAC) of the French Treasury did not consider any new dossiers from either the CAR or Upper Volta.[21] A form of economic deterrence was therefore implicitly coupled with the *Force d'Intervention's* military deterrence of upheaval in an attempt to ensure that France's *chasse gardée* would stay loyal.

By 1968 and 1969 French policy in Africa returned to centre stage. The threat made to the territorial integrity of Chad by the revolt in the northern provinces of Boukou, Ennedi and Tibesti (BET) in 1968 became the first major test of the credibility of France's guarantee to African states close to her. A decision not to intervene would gravely affect her reputation on the continent. The protection of French interests in such neighbouring countries as Niger and the CAR (both of which contained potentially important uranium deposits), was also seen as requiring French action in Chad. Finally, the belief was strongly held that if Chad were to break up, violence would inevitably spread to other states of West and Central Africa, thus threatening a number of France's vital interests. French military involvement in Chad, which has since followed its own irreducible logic, was seen early on as being inescapable and symbolic of France's general commitment to the security of francophone Africa.

The principle of territorial integrity defended in Chad with a major military intervention in 1968 seemed, at least formally, to stand in direct opposition to de Gaulle's policy in supporting the Biafran secessionist movement in Nigeria in the same year. In this case, geopolitical requirements overrode consistency. Though the French government never officially recognized the Biafran government of General Ojukwu, French support for it, which extended to disguised arms transfers made through Gabon and the Ivory Coast, was evident and extensive. President de Gaulle's private view (not necessarily shared by the Ministry of Foreign Affairs), was that the break-up of Nigeria, a potential African great power, was in the French interest. As a potential African regional power, a strong Nigeria could make France's policy in West Africa more difficult to implement. As Edward Kolodziej has pointed out, France was prepared to defend this geopolitical interest even when its defence might put French economic investments at risk. Most French investments in Nigeria and the oil drilling concessions extended to SAFRAP, France's government-controlled oil company, were in areas controlled by the federal Nigerian government. These concessions were eventually suspended, and diplomatic relations briefly severed, when the central government won the war.[22] While support for Biafra's claims of self-determination was designed to be geopolitically useful, it did serve to damage France's Africa policy. Division among francophone states on French policy towards Nigeria and within the French government, eventually persuaded de Gaulle to allow the Nigerian civil war to take its own course. But France's interference in the civil war tarnished French–Nigerian relations for some time and served to create in the minds of Nigerians a permanent suspicion of French policy towards West Africa. For many years following the Biafran fiasco, French–Nigerian relations were strained even if economic exchanges were relatively healthy. Only the sale of considerable amounts of military equipment in the 1980s put these relations on a completely sure footing.

The Pompidou Variation on Policy

By the time de Gaulle surrendered power in 1969, a tradition of post-colonial French–African relations had been established. While French influence on African affairs was strong under de Gaulle, Gaullist policy was not nearly as directly interventionist as later myth has asserted. The slow disengagement from Africa that de Gaulle had begun in 1962 and then continued after 1964 had been interrupted only by the rather spectacular events in Chad and Nigeria. When Georges Pompidou came to power, having announced that his foreign policy would be marked by 'continuity and opening', his intention was to make even less obvious the French military presence in francophone Black Africa (though maintaining its effectiveness) while establishing French influence in areas where in earlier years it had been dormant. Aid reports written during the Pompidou presidency stressed the need for France to extend her economic activity beyond the francophone African states. Within France's traditional sphere, Pompidou adopted a relatively more mercantilist policy than had his predecessor, choosing to send aid primarily to countries who could later help France rather than sink money into countries whose ability to absorb finance was not matched by the strength necessary to make significant purchases from France.

Generally, the policy which Pompidou launched in Africa served more to remind people of the link between French action in the region and France's broader policy on the world stage than to further precise French aims on the continent. That is, use made in foreign policy speeches of the existence of healthy Franco–African relations by government officials often appeared more important than their management. Pompidou's aim (evident also in the 'Mediterranean policy' he directed) was to separate the superpowers in their activities outside Europe. African states in particular were to be assured of independence from outside influence. For this, the *Force d'Intervention* was a perfect instrument, all the more so because it was part of an integrated system of defence whose main purpose was deterrence of the Soviet threat. The value of the *Force d'Intervention* was, in Michel Debré's formulation, that it served the more general aims of French defence policy. As he put it: 'We cannot consider that our deterrence policy against attack on our territory is credible if we stay passive in the face of threats which, though they weigh on lands and peoples outside our frontiers, still touch us directly.'[23]

The implication was that, if France was seen to be indifferent about threats to her African partners, her policy of nuclear deterrence would be less convincing. In any case, France's determination to uphold the interests of francophone African states, which often prevented subversive movements from taking hold, was openly presented as a valuable contribution to Western unity. Though Pompidou's sentimental attachment to Africa was less than de Gaulle's, his hold over the continent was similar, even if the juridical basis of it was slightly altered at African insistence.

Revision of the Co-operation Agreements

Over a decade after independence some African states made plain their desire to revise the co-operation agreements they had signed in the first years after decolonization. In July 1972 Niger announced that it wanted to withdraw from its defence agreement with France and soon afterwards Togo, Congo, Mauritania, Madagascar, Cameroon and Dahomey all requested changes in or cancellations of their agreements, arguing that it was time for the normalization of relations between France and her ex-colonies.[24] For the third time since 1958, the French government was forced to restructure its relations with francophone Black Africa and the collective revolt on the part of these states against the arrangements of 1960 showed signs of a new African consciousness to which the French government had to respond. Rather than belonging simply to a Franco–African or Eurafrican entity, African states were beginning to see themselves as members of an emerging 'Third World'.[25] Accordingly, in requesting changes in the political, economic and military co-operation agreements which had been signed with France, the African states sought to have removed those clauses which most restricted their freedom of manoeuvre.

In the case of military agreements, the most significant result of the reforms which took place in the mid-1970s was that few states maintained fully-fledged defence agreements with France. Of the twelve states which originally signed such accords only Senegal, Ivory Coast, the CAR, Gabon, Togo, and (more secretively) Cameroon, remained loyal to the old agreements even if cosmetic changes were made in some cases. The new agreement signed with Senegal on 29 March 1974, for example, essentially reproduced the arrangements of 1960 with the exception that no reference was made to France ensuring Senegal's internal security. Also, the French military base at Dakar was to be formally handed over to the Senegalese authorities although France would continue to have rights at the base. The substance of Franco–Senegalese relations remained unchanged. France would still provide substantial military assistance to Senegal and French officers would still serve in the Senegalese armed forces. Equally, if Cameroon did not sign a new defence agreement, neither did it formally renounce the old defence pact. From the mid-1970s on, French forces on the African continent were maintained only in Senegal, Ivory Coast, Gabon, the CAR and Djibouti. Other states which formerly had accepted French troops on their soil as part of their defence agreements (such as Chad) asked for them to be removed, even if they wished to continue to receive military aid from France.

The most radical change which took place in Franco–African military arrangements at this time was in Madagascar, where the new regime demanded the withdrawal of all French forces from the base of Tananarive, and was prepared to provide extended rights only on a renewable basis to the naval base at Diégo-Suarez which came under Malagasy control. The risk evident in this arrangement forced the French to withdraw completely from Madagascar by 1975. Interests in the region were only assured some time later when Djibouti in 1977 (after independence) signed a defence agreement with France, thus enabling her to keep a naval presence near the Indian Ocean. In 1978 the Comores Islands also signed a defence agreement with France which allowed the French to maintain control of movements in the Mozambique Channel. Also, the French Indian Ocean Force was transferred to the French Department of Réunion which has since been the object of some complaint by Malagasy authorities.

In general, the renegotiation of the co-operation agreements in 1973 took place in a cordial atmosphere. France's military and political strategy in the region was not seen to be adversely affected by the African call for revisions. While reference was still made to communal defence in the agreements which were renegotiated, it was clear that the maintenance of certain facilities in Africa was related as much to France's geopolitical demand for an 'African presence' as to the particular need to defend certain territories. As it happened, the Pompidou government could make changes in the military co-operation agreements confident that the solidarity of the Franco–African 'bloc' would still be essentially unchanged, especially since the most important states made only minimal demands for reform. The closeness of Franco–African relations, even during this period when their structure was being altered, was demonstrated by the request made in 1973 by President Diori of Niger for a Franco–African summit conference bringing together the French President and Heads of State of francophone African countries. The first of what was to become a series of annual meetings, the 1973 summit, which was attended by a number of more important African leaders, showed that the aura around Franco–African affairs had in fact changed little. It was clear that both France and the francophone states continued to recognize that a special relationship existed between them. Enough states recognized that this special relationship required a military aspect for the broad lines of French military policy in Africa to remain intact.

Giscardian Military Policy towards Africa

In fact, the arrival of Giscard d'Estaing to power brought an end to the policy of military disengagement from Africa which had lasted for nearly a decade. The language used during the Pompidou presidency by Prime Minister Debré had indicated that France had a role to play in defence of Western interests in Africa. For Giscard, the display of French military power in Africa was an even more important indicator than it had been for his predecessors of France's position in the international system. Giscard did much, especially from the middle of his term onwards, to strengthen France's military power in Africa. From 1960 to 1978 yearly military aid to Africa remained essentially static, but between 1977 and 1978 French military assistance jumped from 414 million francs to 644 million and has climbed steadily since then.[26] These amounts are still only a tiny fraction of the total amount spent by France on defence, but Giscard's decision to increase military aid to Africa was a symbol of his commitment to the notions of Franco–African unity. This came to be reflected both in the increased number of Africans receiving training in French military academies and in the growth in various other forms of military assistance. (tables 5.3 and 5.4) His early decision to increase the effectiveness of the *Force d'Intervention* was made in the almost certain knowledge that French military power in Africa would be increasingly needed. Giscard, in proposing that France's special mobile force be expanded, argued that France should have an intervention capability which 'corresponded to her stature as a modern state'.[27] Several changes therefore had to be made in French military arrangements.

After 1975 French power in Africa was divided between bases in Senegal, Gabon, CAR, Ivory Coast, Djibouti and Réunion. The *Force d'Intervention* which had drawn simply from the 11th Parachute Division in the South-west of France and the 9th Marine Infantry Division in Brittany was thought to be in need of restructuring and soon after Giscard came to power it was decided to develop the 31 *Demi Brigade* in Provence with lighter and more mobile weapons as an adjunct to other forces. An attempt was made to increase the firepower of the *Force d'Intervention* while retaining its mobility.[28] But despite the improvements made in France's intervention capacity it became increasingly clear that French military solutions could not hope to bring any sort of permanent political settlements in areas where conflict was endemic. Moreover, the scope of French military power was such that, even for quite limited operations, outside help was often required even if it was rarely sought by French leaders concerned about maintaining French independence.

The various French military interventions in Africa in the late 1970s were made for humanitarian, political, economic or strategic reasons, some of them motivated by a combination of these. The continuing dispute over the Western Sahara drew in the French forces twice. In December 1977 the French intervened against *Polisario* in Mauritania to secure the release of French prisoners, though the action taken seemed far in excess of what was necessary for this limited purpose. A further intervention in May 1979 helped to create a temporary pause in the conflict, though the sporadic negotiations which followed did not produce a lasting solution. France provided logistic support to the Chadian Air Force in June 1977 after a new offensive by rebel forces, and sent troops to Chad in April 1978 to give further support to the government. These were only withdrawn in May 1980 after the establishment in 1979 of a new transitional government. Soon after French troops left, Libyan troops entered Chad, briefly occupying, much to the embarrassment of the Giscard government, the capital city of Ndjamena. Libyan troops left in late 1981 but would later return. Again, while French intervention had initially helped to stabilize the conflict, the complexity of the Chadian problem and the number of African and other

Table 5.3 Numbers of African officers training in France

	1982	1983	1984	1985	1986	1987	1988
Benin	123	156	126	106	103	170	123
Burkina Faso	100	126	116	92	51	48	37
Burundi	39	43	44	35	21	23	27
Cameroon	142	156	153	113	184	130	169
CAR	34	44	62	30	36	54	46
Chad	88	23	32	52	51	81	101
Comores	–	17	21	29	21	39	42
Congo	154	274	136	181	87	113	158
Djibouti	80	120	121	101	87	84	71
Gabon	152	223	240	230	226	219	197
Guinea	–	2	1	–	150	72	68
Ivory Coast	220	320	272	286	285	326	269
Madagascar	104	94	156	117	79	140	93
Mali	26	36	38	38	36	49	62
Mauritania	94	163	128	151	131	135	129
Mauritius	–	6	4	6	7	5	9
Niger	63	62	80	55	60	40	41
Rwanda	23	47	15	34	33	30	33
Senegal	151	174	152	92	144	123	109
Seychelles	–	–	1	1	–	1	–
Togo	73	93	83	98	99	157	144
Zaire	106	47	15	20	30	35	40
Total	1,772	2,226	1,995	1,909	1,921	2,077	1,968

Source: Ministry of Co-operation

Table 5.4 Military co-operation budgets (millions of francs)

	1982	1983	1984	1985	1986	1987	1988
Military assistance (personnel)	316	331.8	400	412.8	531.3	533.8	554.3
Direct aid	248.8	236.7	256	247.8	299.5	232.4	213.3
Training	95.3	108.6	145.3	145.3	123.5	116.3	112.8
Total	660.1	677.1	801.3	805.9	954.3	882.5	880.4

Source: Ministry of Co-operation

states who could claim that their interests were at play, meant that solution of the problem was impossible.

Perhaps more surprising than the repeated interventions in Chad, however, were the two expeditions to Zaire in 1977 and 1978 in support of President Mobutu and against the forces of the *Front de Libération Nationale Congolaise* (FLNC) who twice invaded Shaba province. French relations with Zaire had improved after Giscard's visit in 1975 when he announced his pleasure in being in the biggest francophone country after France. A country producing 6 per cent of the world's copper, 30 per cent of all industrial diamonds and far more cobalt than any other country was one which France could not ignore. Having entered into the Franco–African family by virtue of her participation in the annual Franco–African summit meetings, Zaire was more or less assured of French support.

The first FLNC invasion in March 1977 brought a measured French response: advisers were sent to organize the defence of the mining town of Kolwezi, arms were sent to Zaire's army and transport aircraft were provided to fly in Moroccan forces, who did all the fighting. In May 1978, after a second FLNC infiltration, the French sent 600 Foreign Legionnaires and 100 parachutists, who were followed by three more companies in the ensuing weeks. The French and 1,750 Belgian troops were flown in by aircraft from the US Military Airlift Command, using the French bases at Dakar and Libreville to refuel.[29] While the immediate task of the troops was to save European lives, the humanitarian justification for the intervention was not the one first stressed by France. Rather, support for the government of Zaire, with whom France had secretly signed a military aid agreement, was the main reason advanced for French action. Yet Giscard's claim that he was keeping the continent free from great-power rivalry did not hold water with the Gaullists, who observed with dismay that without American support French action would have been impossible.

While most Frenchmen agreed that action in Zaire seemed appropriate to defend French interests in Africa, other instances of France's militarism in Africa came in for harsh and widespread criticism. French military support for David Dacko, who deposed the self-styled Emperor Bokassa of the CAR in September 1979, met with some approval, but the fact that French troops stayed in the CAR afterwards was a cause of concern. In a major debate on African questions in December 1979, M. Pierre Messmer put forward the most cogent explanation of why so many thought Giscard's policy misguided:

To be tolerable, any use of force in Africa must have an indispensable motive and be strictly limited in time and space, that is, brief and punctual. That was the case in

Zaire; it was not in any of the other three interventions in Chad, Mauritania, and Central Africa. The fact that their prolongation is demanded by the interested governments is an explanation that cannot satisfy us.[30]

France's military activism in Africa during the Giscard presidency was matched by active political involvement. More and more African states attended the annual Franco–African summit meetings during the late 1970s, and Giscard often claimed that France stood at the head of a 'Eurafrican' entity whose economic, political and military borders would exclude the superpowers. Giscard's strong personal links with several African leaders helped to rekindle the ideas of an 'imperial presidency' that had been so evident in the early part of the Gaullist years. The African dimension of Giscard's foreign policy became an important domestic issue in France following revelations that the President had been given diamonds by Bokassa. Yet the active military policy that the Giscard government pursued, which earned for France the perhaps unfortunate epithet of 'gendarme of Africa', served to reconfirm that France had a post-imperial mission overseas which few other ex-imperial powers could match. The extension, even in the military domain, of France's influence beyond its former Empire (into Zaire for example) was proof of France's enduring ambitions in Africa. In 1979, Giscard's foreign minister, Louis de Guirangaud, affirmed that 'Africa is the only continent that is still to the measure of France, within its reach. It is the only one where it can still, with 300 men, change the course of history.'[31] It was this spirit which the socialist administration of François Mitterrand inherited, and wished to transfigure in its own image.

The Legacy Left to Mitterrand

The Mitterrand government came to power in 1981 wanting to change France's African policy much as it wanted to affect other aspects of France's foreign and domestic policy.[32] The pre-election document, which defined what form socialist policy in Africa would take, outlined several changes which needed to be made in the political, economic and cultural fields.[33] In the military sphere the document stated that the whole question of the French military presence on the continent would have to be reviewed. The socialists argued that France's African policy had too often ignored the domestic policies of many African regimes:

The historical links which unite us with Africa make of the peoples of that continent privileged partners in a co-operation which should cease to be adapted to the exigencies of local oligarchies, themselves in the service of private interests in the metropole. With the African governments, all the military co-operation agreements should be renegotiated.[34]

Military co-operation agreements would be renegotiated on a case-by-case basis and attempts would be made to reinforce regional inter-African defence agreements which in turn might bolster the capacity of the Organization of African Unity (OAU) to solve Africa's problems without having recourse to outside help. Having accused the Giscard administration of behaving like a 'pyromaniac fireman' in Africa, the Mitterrand government, when it took office, implicitly seemed to renounce the possibility of further direct military intervention on the African continent. In the event, it became difficult for the Mitterrand government to make radical changes in policy. Soon after taking office President Mitterrand had quickly to arrange for discreet military aid to be given to Cameroon which was then being threatened from within. Of the states retaining defence or technical assistance agreements with France, none took up earlier implied offers of the socialist party to have them further revised.

In the early years of the Mitterrand administration, French military policy came to follow certain principles which were developed over time as much by accident as by design. Any military involvement in Africa would take place only at the express request of an African leader and preferably only in conjunction with African forces. France would honour her defence agreements but never use force to solve internal disputes. In conformity with these imperatives, the first Mitterrand government supported the Senegalese intervention in The Gambia in July 1982, but instructed French forces to stay in their barracks when, in September 1981, David Dacko of the CAR was overthrown by General Kolingba. The hesitation evident in the French decision to intervene in Chad in the summer of 1983 (when Zaire also established a presence) grew out of these self-imposed constraints. French policy at the time was to bring armed conflict to an end without using direct military force.

But from the time of the decision to intervene in 1983 onwards, the French government was forced to keep an important military detachment in Chad. The military presence which was created to deter further Libyan action in the south of Chad (analysed later in this chapter), put French armed strength at the service of the government of Chad to preserve territorial integrity. But over time it also made French foreign policy in the region hostage to the decisions taken in Ndjamena. The semi-permanence of the French presence in Chad contrasted sharply with the only other direct military intervention by France during the first Mitterrand administration.

In September 1986, France sent 200 French parachutists to Togo (from Gabon and the CAR), shortly before a Franco–African summit meeting was to take place, in order to put down an internal uprising that the government of Lomé claimed was inspired by opponents of the regime in Ghana. This use of French force showed that France was still very concerned to help African leaders close to her, and proved the political utility of a willingness to demonstrate French power in Africa. The extended French intervention in Chad, whose form was initially the subject of considerable bureaucratic debate, demonstrated the continued need France had for effective intervention forces. Indeed, despite early socialist rhetoric, the government did much both to sustain and then to improve France's capacity to bring military power to bear on the African continent, and the level of security assistance to Africa offered by François Mitterrand was effectively even higher than that provided by France in the Giscard years.

The Present Structure of French-African Security Relations

While no substantive changes in the juridical structure of Franco–African relations have taken place since the reforms of the Pompidou years arising out of the need to renegotiate the co-operation agreements, the Mitterrand government put its own stamp on French security policy in the 1984–8 Military Programme Law, and the bulk of these changes were built upon in the ensuing four-year plan of 1988–92. [34] Its principal innovation lay in the reorganization of the armed forces and in particular, the creation of a new intervention force, the *Force d'Action Rapide* (FAR). The establishment of this new intervention structure was an attempt to reconcile France's African (and Middle East) military vocation with the need to be able to come to the aid of France's allies in Europe. A rapid action force which could contribute both to the maintenance of peace in the Third World and to the conventional defence of Western Europe would reflect France's position as a 'Eurafrican power'. As the FAR has developed, analysts and policy-makers have asked whether it primarily serves France's European needs (and therefore brings France closer to her NATO allies), or whether the new force, in strengthening France's intervention capability, merely emphasizes France's existing guarantee of support to her African allies. In principle, French leaders have insisted that the FAR can do both at the same time. Its establishment gave meaning to France's defence policy which in the words of Mitterrand's first

Defence Minister, Charles Hernu, was contained in the phrase 'independence and solidarity'. French military power would allow France to act (on her own volition) in defence of countries politically close to her. Like other elements of the French armed forces, the FAR also would serve a symbolic purpose. At the end of 1983 a group of civil servants in the Ministry of Defence noted that the existence of the FAR and the doctrines governing its use would allow France to keep her place in the world:

The FAR is an expression of our will, of our capacity to be a nation with worldwide interests and a universal vocation; neither hegemonic superpower nor mediocre province, France and her civilization must continue to bring to the world her message of liberty and independence in the service of peace.[36]

In practice, given the relative unlikelihood of an outbreak of hostilities in Europe, the restructuring of France's intervention forces was of greater immediate relevance to overseas commitments, even if some of the units assigned to the FAR were more appropriate for action in Europe than in the African bush or in desert wars. The anti-tank division (with its *Force d'Hélicoptères Anti-Char* or FHAC) is specially designed to fight alongside NATO forces attempting to contain Soviet Operational Manoeuvre Groups (OMG). Action by the FAR in Central Europe, beyond the reach of French supply lines, would depend on substantial NATO logistical and air support.[37] The implication of the FAR's creation is that the Mitterrand government, more than any of its predecessors, chose to give substance to the axiom that the conventional defence of France was inseparable from that of its West European neighbours. This was given further support when in 1987 the government announced the creation of a Franco–German brigade which could be used alongside the FAR.

Still, while the FAR has a politico-military significance for the European theatre, the continued instability of third-world states who desire outside support means that the FAR is likely to be used most often for overseas tasks. The modernization of France's intervention capability will allow France to conduct more effectively the type of operations overseas that she has traditionally seen as necessary. The creation of the FAR has not, however, changed the dimension of France's extra-European power, or the substance of her regular military relations with African states. There are still potential challenges for which the FAR by itself would be an inadequate instrument, while the nature of Franco–African military co-operation has been untouched by the recent structural reforms.

Table 5.5 France's Rapid Deployment Force

4th Aeromobile Division	Three combat helicopter regiments (*Gazelle*, with HOT, *Puma*, support helicopters) One infantry regiment with *Milan* anti-tank One command and support regiment One support regiment (Super Pumas)
6th Light Armoured Division	Two light-armed regiments (with AMX-10 RC) Two infantry regiments on armoured personnel carriers One artillery regiment One engineer regiment One command and support regiment
11th Parachute Division	Six infantry regiments One light-armed regiment One artillery regiment One engineer regiment One command and support regiment One support battalion
9th Marine Infantry Division	Two motorized infantry regiments Two light-armed regiments with anti-tank squadron One artillery regiment One engineer regiment One command and support regiment
27th Alpine Division	Six mountain infantry regiments with *Milan* anti-tank One light-armed regiment with anti-tank squadron One artillery regiment One engineer battalion One command and support regiment

Source: Service d'information et de relations publiques des Armées, France, and Military Balance, 1988-1989, International Institute for Strategic Studies, London, 1987

The FAR and Africa

The FAR comprises five divisions and a logistic formation totalling approximately 47,000 men: the 9th Marine Infantry, the 11th Parachute, the 6th Light Armoured, the 27th Alpine, and the 4th Aeromobile Divisions. The 9th and the 11th are untouched Divisions of the former *Force d'Intervention* (mostly *Troupes de Marine*); the 6th Light Armoured Division is an outgrowth of the 31st Brigade (some of the Foreign Legion is linked to this Division); the 27th Alpine Division is assigned to the FAR more or less intact; and the 4th Aeromobile Division is a totally new formation (see table 5.5).

The reorganization therefore does not materially affect the *Troupes de Marine* who have traditionally acted overseas.[38] Nor has it affected the special structure of the Foreign Legion, which numbers 8,500 men, and often operates alongside the FAR particularly in African contingencies. Though the FAR has been joined under a single commander it is not intended to fight as a unit and the separate divisions do not often exercise together. A large manoeuvre took place in June 1985, code-named *Farfadet*, including 12,000 men from all three services, and as the FAR was improved over the next few years bigger joint exercises took place. The FAR is conceived as an army corps divided into a general staff with its command and support elements and the five separate combat divisions. Its principal communications are provided through a RITA system and *Syracuse* stations. In wartime it would have a special logistics brigade attached to it with 6,500 men and 2,000 vehicles. Yet it is not truly an independent army corps able in the European theatre to take on an enemy for long without other logistic or communication support. Rather, the FAR provides a command structure and a reservoir of forces from which a commander may draw for deployment in areas of crisis.

The only thing all five divisions have in common is their relatively high mobility. Of these five divisions, the 4th Aeromobile was isolated as the most important for combat in Europe. Composed in part of three regiments of combat helicopters (*Gazelles* and *Super Pumas*), the 4th Division has been presented as a valuable potential complement to NATO forces trying to contain Soviet attacks into Western Europe. The 27th Alpine Division also has a more obvious mission in Europe than in Africa, though because of its light armour it would be expected to see combat only in mountainous, wooded or urban areas. In the event of war in Europe, however, the other three divisions, although more accustomed to overseas action, could be deployed in the European theatre. Recent changes in the structure of the 9th Marine Infantry Division (providing it with lighter equipment and better organization) would make it easier to operate alongside some of the other divisions of the FAR, notably the 6th Light Armoured Division.

While the precise conditions under which the FAR would act in Europe remain necessarily somewhat ambiguous, given France's general attitude to NATO, the FAR's overseas missions have been given clear definition. Its first is to guarantee the security of French citizens abroad. Its second is to protect the territorial integrity of the *Départements Outres-Mer* (DOM) and the *Territoires Outre-Mer* (TOM). Third, it should be able to defend energy and raw material supplies as well as France's commercial routes. Fourth, it must fulfil the defence and co-operation agreements which France has signed with other states. And, fifth, it must be able to participate in international peacekeeping missions.[39] The president's capacity to act quickly in the event of some overseas crises has been increased by the fact that nearly all members of the FAR are professional servicemen. Under French law, short-term conscripts may not be sent overseas without parliamentary approval. The professionalization of France's intervention capability means that a large force may now be sent overseas without parliamentary debate.

This has not gone uncriticized. In February 1984 the *Mouvement Information pour les Droits du Soldat* (IDS) issued a communiqué stating that 'with the professionalization of a quarter of our armed forces...the government has given itself an intervention capability of a colonial type – without the parliamentary debate considered a democratic minimum.'[40] The professionalization of France's intervention capability has nevertheless been seen by the government as an essential reform and, on the basis of recent experience, has been extended to include certain types of technicians. In the summer of 1983, when the Mitterrand government was mounting *Opération Manta* for its intervention in Chad, it was unable in the first instance to send a refuelling detachment as the technicians were all conscripts. It has since ensured that essential logistic units of this kind are made up entirely of professionals.[41]

While the size of the FAR (47,000 men) is double that of the old *Force d'Intervention* (by the end of Giscard's term of office this included the 11th Parachute Division at 15,000 men, the 9th Marine Infantry Division at 7,600 and the 31 (full) Brigade at 3,500) there are still considerable limits to its ability to act overseas. The 1984–8 Military Programme Law guaranteed the Air Force 450 combat aircraft, but its transport capacity remains low. Any rapid overseas action obviously requires a large transport capacity and the French have been forced to rely almost exclusively on their *Transall* aircraft for this purpose. At the end of 1984, all the planned twenty-five of the second generation *Transall* (C–160S) (which can be refuelled in the air) were in service to complement the forty-eight first generation aircraft (in service since 1967 and due to be phased out between 1995 and 1998). Neither the first nor the second generation *Transall* is truly adequate for France's overseas needs. Aircraft of the second generation can deliver a payload of only eight metric tons over 5,000 kilometres; the maximum payload of sixteen tons is deliverable over a distance of only 1,800 kilometres.[42] Even with its refuelling capability, the *Transall* would require the use of staging bases for a distant overseas intervention. In 1987 the French government received two of the six C-130 Hercules cargo planes it had succeeded in buying from the US and this with a payload of fifteen tons over a 4,500 kilometre distance will be of some help. The French government has long dismissed the idea of trying to buy American C-141 *Starlifter* aircraft on the grounds that some basic problems would not be solved by its acquisition. In any case the US Air Force felt that it needed all its C-141s (now out of production) for use by the Military Aircraft Command. The French government has chosen instead to augment its military transport capabilities by relying on national civil air lines to provide aircraft at short notice for specific missions. An agreement concluded on 22 February 1984 with Air France and UTA obliges them to provide aircraft to the French armed forces with twelve hours notice. Further light transport aircraft (ATM 42L or CN 235) may be procured in the early 1990s to ease France's transport burden.[43]

In the light of these deficiencies, the *Commandement du Transport Aérien Militaire* (COTAM), which is in charge of all logistic and tactical missions associated with military transport, clearly needs to improve its carrying capacity and certain criteria for a new transport have been established.[44] A transport aircraft for the year 2000 would have to be capable of certain tactical manoeuvres and support of ground troops, and suitable for the carriage of troops, freight, medical supplies or casualties. Yet the procurement of major new transport, either through French development, or a joint European project is still only a very long-term possibility.

While airlift is therefore likely to be a problem affecting France's intervention capability until well into the next century, sea transport presents fewer problems. Any intervention action by sea will, of course, be considerably slower than transport by air but the sea does offer some advantages: transport can usually be effected without violating areas of national sovereignty; the cost is lower; and the range of material which can be transported is more varied. Distance is less critical and the establishment of a sea presence can often help to complement the deployment of ground forces.[45] The 1984–8 Military Programme Law made provisions for the improvement of France's sea transport capabilities. Three new *Foudre*-class landing ships were ordered, to be delivered in the early 1990s. These ships, of about 10,000 tons displacement, are intended to maintain the Navy's capacity to transport tanks overseas and any other material not easily transported by air.[46] Plans to develop a nuclear-powered aircraft carrier to replace *Clémenceau* have also been put into effect since the 1984–8 Programme Law was presented. On 6 February 1986 the French Defence Minister signed the first authorizations for the building of the *Richelieu*, and when this is deployed it will give France a greater capacity to establish an overseas presence.

Nevertheless, given that France's links are often to landlocked African states, it is difficult for the French to exploit the advantages of sea transport. For the intervention in Chad in 1983, some equipment was transported by sea to Cameroon and then taken overland to Chad, a process which took some time to organize and put into effect. Without relying on US transport aircraft, or on the goodwill of a number of African states, it will be difficult for France in the forseeable future to deploy an interventionary force much larger than that sent to Chad in 1983 – which was the largest overseas expedition launched by France since the Algerian War. At the height of the peacekeeping mission about 3,475 troops from all three branches of the armed services were present in Chad and over the first thirteen months that French troops were there (before being withdrawn and deployed again) almost 10,000 men completed a period of service.[47]

Even if certain types of African contingencies could be dealt with by sea, the French will still have to rely extensively on air transport for the initial stages of any intervention in Africa. They must also rely on the co-operation of African states politically close to France for the prolongation of any intervention. The present capacities of the French interventionary forces are such that though they can be very effective for long-term peacekeeping operations (as in Chad or the Lebanon), their capacity to fight long and intense wars on the African continent is very limited. The FAR is primarily a 'first aid' instrument, able to put down uprisings or invasions not involving sophisticated opposing forces.

The FAR and Parachute Assault Capability

French military action in Africa may be of two types: long-term peacekeeping activity; and short-term firefighting action. The rapid mounting of a major expedition is subject primarily to the capacity of the target states to receive French forces at the same rate as they can be dispatched. If there are airstrips large enough to accommodate civil aircraft, then troop deployment can be expected to take place rapidly and efficiently. One of the advantages of

French action in Chad in 1983–4 was that French engineers were able to rebuild the Ndjamena airstrip so that large civil airliners could land there. While such work has civil implications, it naturally increases France's capacity to bring in an intervention force rapidly when required. In 1988 the French reworked the airstrip at Abeché near the Sudanese border and also committed themselves at a cost of about $17,000,000 to totally modernize the airstrip at Faya Largeau so that it could receive both large military aircraft and civilian airliners. In late 1988 it was decided to use some of this money for non-military reconstruction in Chad.[48]

Though it would be wrong to suppose that the French have an interventionist *idée fixe*, action is taken where possible to improve the quality of African military infrastructures (for a variety of motives). Over the course of France's period in Chad, for example, increasingly sophisticated equipment has been put at the disposal of French soldiers to combat the rising Libyan challenge. To take but one instance, the installation of a *Centaure* radar in Ndjamena and the deployment of *Hawk* missiles in the capital made it possible for France in September 1987 to intercept and destroy a *Tupolev 22 Blinder* that Libya had dispatched to bomb the Chadian capital, when only a few months before France had been demonstrably incapable of such air defence of Ndjamena. Throughout Chadian territory French troops have deployed military materiel of a quality that formerly was never needed for African conflicts. France is also willing to supply the Chadian army with the most recent French equipment (like *Milan* anti-tank missiles) when necessary to meet the rising capabilities of enemy armed forces. This special long-term experience in Chad means that it can now be expected that any French military intervention could be quickly mounted, effectively deployed within twenty-four hours, and could rely on close interoperability with local armed forces.

In general, France is continuing to upgrade her intervention capacity and is making efforts to improve her capacity to land troops in all conditions. In principle, all troops of the 11th Division are parachute trained. Having seized and cleared an airfield, these assault troops could then be followed by air-landed elements of the FAR. Moreover, in each regiment of the 11th Division there are units who have been trained to conduct intelligence-gathering or minor combat roles deep behind enemy lines. These 'pathfinder' troops might well be sent into a crisis area before other troops of the 11th Division are deployed. These units, which are known as *Commandos de Renseignement et Action dans la Profondeur*, are specially trained to drop onto hostile territory in order to secure military installations (including airstrips) which could then be made available for French reinforcements. In peacetime there are only some 200-400 such specialist troops operational at any time, far too few to engage in a long-drawn-out war without immediate support. Troops forming the *Détachements d'Assistance Opérationelle* (DAO) are specially trained to conduct intelligence missions within enemy territory. There are DAO units in three regiments (the 1st RPIMa, 2nd RIMa and 3rd RIMa).

The most specialized of these French units to have operated in Africa is the 1st RPIMa (*Régiment Parachutistes d'Infanterie de Marine*). This unit (not belonging to the FAR) is at the direct disposal of the French President. It can be used for rescue missions or sensitive intelligence operations. In practice, however, for a mission such as the Shaba rescue, these commandos are likely to lead, possibly with *Jaguar* aircraft support, to be reinforced as soon as possible by additional troops from the 11th or 9th Divisions. So long as African armies or insurgent bands remain small and dispersed, the French can remain reasonably confident of their 'firefighting' capacity even though, in the first instance, it may rely on the unique abilities of only a few hundred troops.

The creation of the FAR has in no essential way changed the means by which France deploys force in Africa, even if recent reforms have improved France's ability to manage its overseas power. New communications systems now allow French commanders to work more effectively with marine or air forces supporting African land operations. In late 1984 a new satellite was launched by the Ariane rocket with two military communication channels. The *Syracuse* network, operational from the beginning of 1985, allows for secure, jam-free communication between fixed and mobile stations.[49] As a result, the French President can (in principle, though there have been failures), communicate directly with French forces deployed in Africa, something which is often essential, given the political sensitivity of much of French military policy. There remain, however, certain natural restrictions to the deployment of French power in Africa.

Logistics and Prepositioning

The logistical problems associated with any substantial military action overseas are immense: the organization of the initial intervention must be such that in the first instance units are able to act autonomously; and, once forces are deployed, they must be able to take advantage of stocks which have been prepositioned overseas. The maintenance of prepositioned stocks in key areas of interest to France naturally saves a considerable amount in initial transport costs, but all French action in Africa since decolonization has been *sui generis*, and it is impossible to calculate the amount or type of equipment which in the future the FAR would have to take with it in order to ensure success.[50] French forces intervening in countries having defence agreements with France (and, in certain cases, having signed military assistance agreements) will be able to make use either of local stocks or (in countries where French forces are stationed) equipment in the inventory of the French *Force de Présence* (see below). In other cases all supplies would have to come directly from France and this might require the case-by-case negotiation of appropriate overflight or transit rights with the countries involved.[51] The transport of heavy equipment (such as tanks) can perhaps be effected by air but this will always be extremely expensive. In the past, the cost of such transport has sometimes exceeded the book value of the cargo. The type of intervention naturally affects the organization of its support. For a rapid intervention as in Shaba, everything is sacrificed to speed and the stocks taken in with the troops are minimal. For more deliberate peace-keeping missions, such as the 1983 Chad operation, after the first stage of rapid troop deployments has passed, most of the resupply is done by sea and a substantial infrastructure has to be set up in the host country to deal with supplies.

Forces Stationed Overseas

The French forces stationed in certain African countries (and not part of the FAR) include the 23rd BIMa (*Battalion d'Infanterie de Marine*) in Senegal, 43rd BIMa in the Ivory Coast and the 6th BIMa in Gabon, as well as the various marine infantry troops in Djibouti. Some of the troops stationed in Djibouti are from the 13th Division Blindée de la Légion Etrangère (Tank Division). In addition, some FAR troops are semi-permanently deployed (on a rotational basis) to the CAR. All are in a position to co-operate with troops coming from the metropole. The defence agreements signed with each of these countries explicitly prohibit France from using the territories of the signatory states for interventions elsewhere but, by special agreement, France may use her facilities in these countries as staging posts. During the 1983 intervention in Chad, for example, the garrisons in Gabon (near Libreville) and in the CAR (in Bangui and Bouar) effectively served as rear bases for French action. The French forces permanently prepositioned in Senegal, the Ivory Coast or Gabon may be redeployed elsewhere for a French intervention though local leaders do not like this.

In extreme circumstances, therefore, the French would ask the host government if the forces stationed there could temporarily be moved to another theatre. The political importance of these forces, however, which serve as a deterrent to internal unrest, is such that leaders prefer that any forces used be replaced by units coming from France unless, as has happened from time to time, their absence from their home bases would be very brief (as for the Togo intervention in 1986). The French government will ask for 'permission' to redeploy these troops only in circumstances where there is an immediate need. Even the transfer to other parts of Africa of certain pieces of equipment at the disposal of prepositioned troops would cause some concern locally and this, again, would normally be done only on the understanding that replacements would be sent as soon as possible. The *Jaguar* fighter aircraft based in Gabon, for example, would (in principle) only be transferred to another field of action with the approval of the Gabonese President, who would have to balance the relevance to Gabonese interests of a specific French action against the problems associated with the temporary absence of French aircraft from the country. If the mobility of the FAR is restricted by transport problems, that of the prepositioned forces is partly, if not unduly, constrained by the juridical terms which govern their actions in the host countries. Nevertheless, the existence of permanent French garrisons increases the reach of the FAR and allows it to have at least some capacity to intervene in almost any African area of direct interest to France.

Elements of the FAR arriving in Africa are able to act effectively with other French units stationed there and with African armies because of the manner in which training and exercising of these forces is organized. Elements of the FAR are often sent abroad as rotating units (*unités tournantes*) to complement other French forces permanently stationed there. This rotation of personnel gives the FAR direct experience of African conditions and makes large exercises of metropole-based forces (in collaboration with local armies) much simpler. As the training of African troops is, in the case of those countries having defence agreements with France, coupled with participation in Franco–African joint exercises, interoperability problems are reduced, though not entirely eliminated.

National Armies, Joint Manoeuvres and the FAR

The creation of African national armies grew out of objectives set down by the French government at the time of independence in the so-called *Plan Raisonnable*.[52] Its aim was to create small national armies to replace French forces and to contribute in some degree to the maintenance of internal and external security. French policy was, and remains, to train national armies so that they can work closely with French units and effectively serve as branches of the French Army overseas. The *Plan Raisonnable* made clear that the establishment of African national armies and the reorganization of France's overseas defence were inseparable. In fact, the *Plan* was drawn up without any consultation with the emerging states of Africa. This emphasizes that the French originally saw the role of national armies and French security interests as co-extensive.[53] But when the French made their major withdrawal from Africa in the mid-1960s, the national armies they left in place were weak, disorganized and inexperienced, hence the continued need for substantial French technical support. Certainly the maintenance of French officers and NCOs as technical advisers to various African armed forces guarantees a degree of complementarity between the French and African armies which is indispensable to France's influence in these countries (table 5.6). So, too, does the training of large numbers of African

Table 5.6 French military assistants in Africa

	1986	*1987*	*1988*
Benin	11	9	9
Burkina Faso	11	8	8
Burundi	28	28	28
Cameroon	71	70	69
CAR	80	77	76
Chad	38	41	41
Comores	26	28	28
Congo	14	14	13
Djibouti	108	102	97
Equatorial Guinea	2	4	4
Gabon	117	114	111
Guinea	14	30	25
Guinea Bissau	2	2	2
Ivory Coast	73	73	74
Madagascar	7	7	7
Mali	8	8	8
Mauritania	61	62	62
Mauritius	2	2	2
Niger	55	57	55
Rwanda	20	19	20
Senegal	32	33	32
Togo	76	76	78
Zaire	108	105	105
Total	964	972	958

Source: Ministry of Co-operation

officers in France. Furthermore, the general policy of military co-operation pursued by France ensures that African armies remain dependent on France for the replacement of equipment. While the second generation of co-operation agreements allows African states to turn to other suppliers if they wish, it continues to make economic and general political sense for most African states to keep the French military connection.

By her policy of co-operation, then, France is able to control the size and capabilities of most francophone African armies. Arms transfers remain at a modest level and the general policy is to supply only those types of equipment which the Africans are able to maintain themselves. An attempt is made to transfer equipment which has civilian as well as purely military uses and only very rarely does the French Ministry of Co-operation give the Africans equipment which has been recently developed. The preference is to transfer armaments which are appropriate for African conditions and which are not expensive to maintain. France often refuses African requests for equipment either because the equipment demanded is too expensive to be transferred through the medium of co-operation arrangements, or because it does not correspond to the perceived needs of the state concerned, or because the French have other priorities on the continent. Each African state connected to France by a co-operation agreement makes its annual requests through the local French Head of Military Co-operation who passes the requests on to Paris. The Ministry of Co-operation then distributes aid as it sees fit to all the countries under its jurisdiction, thus subordinating particular African demands to France's general strategy for Africa. It is worth recalling that most French sales of arms are to the Maghreb countries and to the Middle East, areas where France's diplomatic power is important but not nearly as absolute as it is in sub-Saharan Africa. Francophone Africa is therefore not a market for France's arms industry, though certain more advanced pieces of equipment, such as *Mirage* and *Alpha-Jet* fighters are occasionally sold to the richer states. The others have largely to satisfy themselves with what the French decide to give them, a fact which allows the French to ensure that appropriate military balances are kept in the region.

There is, therefore, a conscious attempt by the French in their dealings with African countries to develop a common military policy. Careful not to overendow African armies, the French are able to ensure that it is difficult for one country to launch an attack on another. The fact that France maintains agreements with so many countries also serves as a stabilizing factor in that leaders would be uncertain whom the French might support in any interstate conflict which might occur and consequently they are likely to be deterred from letting any dispute lead to war. The likelihood that African states may diversify their arms suppliers in the coming years will no doubt weaken French ability to temper bellicose tendencies in Africa. Moreover, France's reluctance to be involved in minor African conflicts might mean that states could reasonably count on French neutrality. The outbreak of the short war between Mali and Burkina Faso in December 1985 is a case in point.

Still, where France has troops prepositioned, there is a more immediate capacity to deter conflict. The closeness of French–African relations in these cases also means that French officers can stay well abreast of developments which may lead to conflict. The main effect of the French presence in these countries is, nevertheless, to further the co-operation between the French and the local armed forces. The military relations with states in which France has prepositioned troops are intended to ensure that France is able to act alongside local forces with ease. Interoperability is obviously generally high because the troops have been trained and equipped by France but compatibility of forces still varies from country to country. French local forces are best integrated in Senegal where French action has been most intense. Contingency plans for operations within Senegalese territory have been developed to a reasonably sophisticated if not elaborate degree and joint manoeuvres have taken place consistently. In the realm of communications technology, however, the Senegalese are significantly behind the French in their ability to use the more important systems and this is recognized as a problem which could affect joint operations. The same is broadly true of the Ivory Coast, with whom the French have the next best military relations, and with Gabon, where the integration of forces is good, but not as complete as in the case of the other two countries.

The discovery and solution of the types of problems and inefficiencies which might affect joint operations take place through the system of joint manoeuvres which are essentially of two types. First, there are the national manoeuvres, in which the armed forces of the African country exercise with the French *Forces de Présence*. The armies of Senegal, Gabon and the Ivory Coast almost never go on a major exercise without including French troops. These exercises have been increasingly linked to specific local security needs. The *Moanda 1987* exercise held in February 1987 in Gabon, for example, brought together the French 6th BIMa with elements of the Gabonese security forces to develop techniques to defend the uranium and manganese mines near Franceville.[54] Second, there are bilateral manoeuvres, which the French organize on average once a year. These include elements from the local African army, French forces stationed in Africa and units of the FAR which come from the metropole. These are costly and complex but deemed to be worthwhile because they are demonstrations of political solidarity as much as tests of military effectiveness. Again the most important take place in Senegal, Ivory Coast and Gabon. In the CAR, where the French forces are labelled *Eléments Français d'Assistance Opérationnelle* (EFAO), and are rotated once every four months from the FAR, the French units hold small exercises almost on a weekly basis, and undertake major exercises around the country once in their tour. Full bilateral exercises sometimes take place in countries with which France has defence agreements but in which there are no prepositioned forces. This, for example, was the case for *Katcha 83*, a bilateral manoeuvre held in the north of Togo in June 1983 which involved metropole-based troops of the FAR and also elements of the EFAO coming from the CAR.[55]

The first large Franco–African exercise took place in 1965 (*Gaur VI*) in south-east Senegal, and emphasized techniques of counter-guerrilla warfare in the bush.[56] This exercise brought out the importance of proper acclimatization of French forces coming from the metropole. The institutionalization, after 1974, of a system of rotating units in Africa was designed to give elements of the intervention force direct experience of African conditions for periods usually of four months.[57] In this way, prepositioned troops are able to work with those coming from France and, over time, units normally stationed in France will benefit from the experience of their colleagues based overseas. However, as only a relatively small percentage of the metropole-based force is involved in this process at any given time, and as such units are usually sent regularly only to Gabon and (more recently) the CAR, there are limits to the benefits which can be gained from this experience. Any substantial military intervention by France in Africa may still suffer in its initial stages because of acclimatization problems. In reality, the only troops who may be able to operate effectively in an African conflict are those which are stationed in Africa, those which have been in Africa for six to eight weeks, and those just returned to France after an African tour - no more than a few thousand men.

The first major exercise (*Alligator III*), to demonstrate France's transport difficulties, took place in the Ivory Coast in 1967.[58] Most French troops were transported by sea and disembarked on the Ivory Coast. Commentators afterwards pointed out that France was in need of more transport aircraft to fly in troops quickly. The exercise was watched by observers from Niger, Dahomey, Togo, Mauritania and Upper Volta. It was therefore also a form of training for professionals from these countries. It is now less usual for countries not participating in a bilateral exercise to show such interest, a fact which points to the distance that many of France's ex-colonies now wish to keep from the more obvious manifestations of French power in Africa.

In the many exercises that have taken place since the 1970s, a tradition of collaboration with African armies has been established. These exercises have also allowed the French to test new weapons on African soil. They have proved as challenging for French as for African troops, primarily because troops coming from the metropole are forced to adapt themselves to several different generations of equipment. During the *N'Diambour III* manoeuvres in Senegal in November 1982, for example, French soldiers used AMX 30 tanks (introduced to African soil for the first time) and AMX 10 RC infantry vehicles together with older vehicles, such as the AML, now used only by French-supplied armies overseas.[59] Though the different generations of combat equipment in the FAR and African armies do not pose serious problems, they do require a certain versatility on the part of soldiers involved in any joint action. Of more concern, as was demonstrated in the bilateral manoeuvres which took place in the Ivory Coast during 1984, is the question of communication.[60] Radio equipment in African armies is often incompatible with more modern French systems, so that liaison between elements of French and African armies is often awkward.

Over time, the bilateral exercises have helped the French and the Africans to develop complementary forces which would be useful in meeting certain African contingencies, but these exercises have not necessarily improved the capacity of African armies to fight well independently. It is doubtful whether any francophone African army could, even today, successfully mount a major expedition outside its own territory although the Senegalese, for example, have tried to gain international recognition for their armed forces and have participated in peacekeeping operations far from national territory (in Chad and the Lebanon) and an intervention (Gambia) much closer to home. Troops from Zaire have twice been sent to Chad and were also sent to Togo in 1986. Zaire's rapid action force (the 31st Parachutist Brigade) was created with French assistance but it is not yet an expeditionary force of the first order. For the most part, the capacities of francophone African armies are modest and uninspiring. While their ability to put down internal disputes is adequate defence against an external aggressor would in most instances require outside help, and francophone African leaders of countries closely affiliated to France openly declare that defence in such contingencies depends on French support.

Political Implications of French Training and Co-operation

French military co-operation with francophone African countries has created a dependency which is in the service of French political interests but not always to the long-term benefit of African countries. There is no question that, but for the French policy of co-operation, the countries of francophone Africa would have derisory armed forces and would have greater problems maintaining internal order. An additional benefit of French forces stationed in African countries is that they regularly perform important civilian tasks – such as the building of bridges and the repairing of roads – which has an important impact on the economic welfare of the states concerned. French policy has thus served development and security needs but it has also made it difficult for the Africans to rid themselves of the French connection, especially at some of the higher levels within national armed forces. The institutionalization of military aid by France to francophone African countries, the regularity of free arms transfers and the system of military training both on the ground and in French military schools have made it unusual for most francophone states to look elsewhere for military assistance. Many would argue that the type of collaboration which has taken place between France and some of her ex-colonies has made these African countries overly reliant on French technical advice. Rather than train their own people, particularly for specialized posts, the Africans have often allowed Frenchmen to hold positions which, in a more developed society, would normally go to a national. Instead of formation of national cadres at the highest levels, a policy of French substitution has been followed, a policy which was unavoidable in the early years, but less evidently so now. The task of reducing direct French military assistance while retaining the general French security guarantee is now seen as an important challenge facing many francophone African armies.

The penetration of French officers and other specialized personnel into francophone African armies and governments clearly provides France with certain strategic advantages including general intelligence gathering and knowledge of local conditions but it also brings with it the danger that the French personnel can be implicated, even if only indirectly or circumstantially, in the internal feuds and struggles for power of the African states to which they are posted.

In April 1984, for example, when the Presidential Guard rose against the government in Cameroon (where no French forces are stationed) some French officers who had contacts both within the Guard and the army were expelled from the country after the Cameroonian army put down the revolt. In this specific case the expulsion apparently took place for reasons that were unconnected with the uprising. But it remains the case that French military advisers could find themselves involved in the disputes within the African armies whose uniform they may wear and perhaps particularly between elite presidential guards and the regular army. If the presence of French armed forces in certain African countries can, in certain circumstances, serve as a deterrent to major internal unrest, the position of technical advisers within most francophone African governments is a form of permanent intervention (even if entirely benign) whose political effects are unpredictable.

The activities and positions of French technical advisers abroad can be the cause of strained relations between France and the African state concerned. They may also suffer as a consequence of strained relations. The role of French advisers or permanently stationed troops may be questioned by African governments in times of tension. Yet as a rule it is the Africans who insist that French military technical assistants wear the uniform of the host country and this seems to reinforce the mutual sense of trust which normally obtains. Despite the fact that French officers wearing an African uniform effectively report both to their African commanding officer and to the local head of the military co-operation office, this does not cause many problems as African leaders still tend to consider that French interests and their own are generally co-extensive. How long this generally happy relationship can continue is a matter for conjecture.

The younger francophone African leaders now in (or soon to come into) power in many states are bound to take stock of the fact that their countries are linked to one military supplier and that the French presence on their soil has become a fact of internal political life which cannot be ignored. The overt desire of these younger leaders (to some degree held, though more discreetly, by their senior colleagues in more conservative states) is for the progressive 'africanization' of their own armed forces and society. Such an 'africanization' is likely to take place first with respect to civil rather than military advisers as the cost of the former is borne largely by the host state.[61]

The fact that French military advice and aid is given free to those states which have signed military assistance agreements is a powerful argument against change, but leaders in those states which have traditionally been less close to France will attempt to find ways to make more subtle (less obvious) their reliance on French aid, even if a complete rejection of French military assistance is unlikely for most. Though in some of the states that host

French bases there are occasional denunciations of this presence from journalists or opposition groups, no major hostile acts have ever taken place, a fact which reflects the deeply held conviction among many in Black Africa that a French presence is still necessary.

For France, the main challenge of the next few years will be to maintain her ability to project power into the African continent to the degree required by her obligations towards her African partners and in a manner consistent with French priorities and interests. French military aid to Africa must be seen as one element of France's overall strategic policy rather than simply as a contribution to the elaboration of particular policies and capabilities within the states to which such aid is directed.[62] French presidents have been fortunate in that their decisions to deploy force in francophone Africa have traditionally not encountered strong opposition from African leaders. Many of the latter support French military action because they see French force as the ultimate guarantee of their own positions. These leaders are therefore happy to cultivate the sense of mutual solidarity which makes the use of force on the continent, for a variety of purposes, still widely acceptable. Even the official entourage of the OAU President Moussa Traoré let it be known to French journalists after a visit to Ndjamena in 1988 that they believed it right that the new French government of Michel Rocard continue the policies of the preceding government in Chad, and argued that failure to do so would obviously injure the credibility of French diplomacy in Africa [63]. But French presidents may well become reluctant to order African political change if there is a perception that they have become prisoners of their close relations with African leaders.

It may become more rare that French national interests coincide with the specific security needs of African leaders. So long as French force can be shown to serve a broad, rather than merely a sectarian purpose, French presidents will not hesitate to use force in Africa to defend the basic interests France has in supporting regimes close to her. But these interests are changeable, as is France's ability to defend them. If certain areas in Africa have become important in the past, others may become more important in the future. The purpose of France's interventionary capability is bound to be affected by both domestic and external factors, and these will also affect France's ability to deploy her power. France's incentives to act and her capacity to do so will not always be in balance. For this reason, in the years approaching the twenty-first century it is likely that France's incentives to deploy force in Africa will be shaped as much by the constraints that may emerge on the effective use of force, as by the political interests the use of force is meant to serve.

French Military Intervention: Incentives and Constraints

French policy towards Africa, more than any other aspect of France's external policy, remains the *domaine réservée* of the President. While many government institutions in France have reason to deal directly in African affairs (the Ministry of Foreign Affairs and the Ministry of Co-operation attached to it, the Ministry of Defence and the Treasury), the President's own advisers at the Elysée Palace play the most important role in maintaining personal contacts with African leaders and in discreetly paving the way for public negotiations on African political and strategic problems. All of the leading figures in the French government have access to the basic intelligence provided by the armed forces on external crises in the form of the *Bulletin Hebdomadaire de Situation* (BHS), and consultation throughout the government organs on African policy is considerable.

But, traditionally, it is in the office of the President that the most important decisions on African policy are made, and this is a reflection of the fact that African affairs are still considered to affect the heart of French state power. In fact, the constitutional powers of the President in matters relating to foreign policy have helped the French government to escape censorious domestic debate on military policy in Africa. While the structure of French–African relations puts certain pressures and responsibilities on the French government, the decision to deploy force in Africa rests largely on the President's personal commitment to Africa. The experience of *cohabitation* between March 1986 and May 1988 when Mitterrand was President and Jacques Chirac, Prime Minister, meant that, briefly, the Elysée and Matignon shared responsibility for African affairs. Both Mitterrand and Chirac (who re-employed de Gaulle's old adviser Jacques Foccart), retained personal advisers on Africa. No major disputes on Africa took place between the two leaders, though in September 1987 when Jacques Chirac (without consulting the President) decided to send transport aircraft to the Congo to help Denis Sassou N'Guesso quell internal unrest, Mitterrand is said to have reminded him that such a decision could only properly be taken by the President.[64] When Michel Rocard became Prime Minister in 1988, it was again the case that (despite the presence in Matignon of some advisors on Africa) the President held all the cards relevant to African affairs. The role of the President in African affairs is likely to remain paramount, and the choice to use military power in Africa will rest with the head of state so long as the constitution of the Fifth Republic remains unchanged.

Each president, certainly, has put his own stamp on France's African policy. After the struggles arising from decolonization and with the exception of the conflict in Chad, President de Gaulle preferred to use diplomatic and economic rather than direct military pressure to maintain French interests in Africa. While President Pompidou visited Africa more frequently than did his predecessor, his fascination with it was less and French militarism was notably absent during the Pompidou years. The habit of inaction continued during the interim period following Pompidou's death. When Niger's President Hamani Diori was replaced in a *coup d'état* in 1974, French forces, which might have been expected to support Diori, stayed at home. During the Giscard presidency, active intervention in Africa became an integral part of France's security policy and during his tenure he opened up relations with African leaders who had previously been less close to France. As a consequence, France assumed further responsibilities in Africa. The personal relationship between Mobutu and Giscard, which confirmed France's ability totally to replace Belgian influence in her ex-colonies, was a principal cause of France's two Shaba adventures in Zaire. When Mitterrand came to power, some African states, worried by the rhetoric of the socialists, thought that the French security guarantee might be over, and some of the leading conservative African leaders lobbied Paris to make certain that this would not be the case.

The fact that France chose to send a force to Chad in August 1983 satisfied right-wing francophone African leaders who desired a continued role for France in Africa. Some fears re-emerged in late 1984 when it was clear that the Libyan presence in Chad, after the French withdrawal, remained substantial. On the other hand, the style of the intervention and the manner in which the French attempted to bring the warring factions together mollified most, if not all, of the left-wing francophone leaders who still have their suspicions about France's 'imperial' design in Africa.

As the French seek to present their military policy in Africa solely as a stabilizing force, they are conscious of the criticisms that their actions might attract from the left in Africa, as much as they are concerned that the right would criticize a policy of renunciation. The principal political challenge facing France's military policy and the president who formulates it, is to seek as wide an acceptance of it by African leaders as possible, in a way which does not constrain France's ability to determine her own foreign policy for the region. French political/military strategy, artificial as it may sometimes seem, is to maintain simultaneously a policy of independence and a reputation for solidarity. These are the *leitmotifs* of France's European policy, and they are no less important for her African one.

Incentives

Direct French military intervention in Africa is likely to take place only in very well-defined circumstances. The protection of French civilians embroiled in an internal conflict or directly attacked by forces of the state in which they live is the only situation in which a French military response can be considered almost automatic. In virtually all states of francophone Africa there are thousands of Frenchmen working in both official and unofficial capacities and their protection is something to which all French governments have naturally been firmly committed. However, the threat to expatriates must still be real before troops are likely to be deployed. During the *coup de force* in Cameroon in April 1984, Frenchmen were certainly put in danger, but French forces were put on the alert in neighbouring states as much because there was a possibility that the Cameroonian president might invoke the defence accords for his own reasons, as because French citizens might be in trouble. In all cases where the protection of French citizens has been cited as a reason for military intervention (e.g. Mauritania and Zaire, both in 1978) there have in fact existed broader (if undeclared) political or economic motivations for French action.

The principal political justification for intervention has always been based on geopolitical criteria which have in turn sometimes been affected by broad symbolic considerations. Military interventions which take place exclusively on French initiative and without outside help allow France to 'exercise her full sovereignty on the international stage'[65] and hence France's ability to answer African demands for assistance supports this political need. While the military agreements with African states do not formally guarantee that direct military aid will be given when asked, the network of treaties itself raises the presumption of a French 'guarantee', at least to those states having signed defence agreements, as opposed to merely military technical assistance agreements. While reference is rarely made to these states as 'allies' (more usually the term is 'partners'), there is a deeply-ingrained feeling that a legitimate request for aid, especially where it is supported by other African governments close to France, must be answered positively. A refusal to act in a clear case of aggression could well result in a political defeat for France in Africa, but then so also could a hastily-organized intervention in support of an unpopular leader.

This is why the letter of the actual agreements between France and her African partners must not be taken too literally. Freedom of action is one of the vital principles of France's Africa policy. For French military intervention to take place it is not necessary that there exist a formal defence agreement between France and the African country concerned. Some analysts have argued that, because there has been a general shift from fully-fledged defence agreements to 'mere' military assistance pacts since 1974, the scope of French action on the continent has been reduced commensurately. In fact, France has intervened as often in countries not having defence agreements with France (Mauritania, Chad and Zaire), than in those with whom she has been, from a juridical point of view, more closely allied (Gabon, CAR and Togo). The 1983 intervention in Chad actually went beyond the terms of the miliary co-operation agreement, as Article 4 of the agreement expressly prohibits French military personnel in Chad from participating directly in operations of war or 'in the maintenance or re-establishment of order or legality'. In the event, President Mitterrand admitted that the French peacekeeping force in Chad had a mandate which went beyond the terms of the co-operation agreement. He declared publicly at the time that the primary justification for the French intervention lay in the fact that the legitimate government in Chad had requested it. Later, at the Franco–African summit meeting in Burundi in December 1984, Mitterrand added that France had met Habré's request for help because France believed it necessary to maintain a 'balance of power' in the Central African region. The French commitment to the territorial integrity of Chad has taken on a special symbolic importance and the fact that a previous Chadian government had decided for political reasons to scrap the defence pact has in no sense undermined French resolve to show that it can on request defend the country from outside attack.

The existence of a broad network of military agreements with African states has therefore created an implied commitment to African security which is often unaffected by the precise terms of these agreements. The defence accords remain useful, in so far as they allow for staging posts in Africa which make the use of the FAR in other areas possible, but it is not to these accords that one should look in order to determine the extent of France's military commitments. As noted above, the creation and the constant further training and equipping of African armies has meant that African states see it as natural and normal that they should turn first to France for outside security assistance. While there is no juridical obligation to respond to calls for help (none of the defence agreements obliges France automatically to act) a French government would normally agree to send military aid of some kind if an external power were involved in the conflict. This was the case when France sent troops to Zaire in 1978 and to Chad in 1983. It was not so obvious in Togo in 1986 but a case of external involvement (Ghana) could at least be made credible.

Some French leaders, however, have become increasingly concerned about France's reputation for being the *gendarme* of the African continent.

When he was President of the Foreign Affairs Committee of the National Assembly in 1983, Maurice Faure publicly complained that African states were relying too much on France and called for a revision of France's attitude to African security. No such revision has taken place, despite the view of many in the French Socialist Party that France should abandon her military policy on the continent. Jacques Chirac as prime minister of a newly elected right-wing government in 1986 several times made clear that France's military commitment to Africa would not waver. Recent experience, however, has revealed an increasing French desire to involve other African states in any French military intervention. In general, the French have adopted (in respect of their Western allies) an emphatically bilateral approach towards Africa. While the French have often relied on American help in providing logistic support for their African operations, they are unlikely to wish to collaborate more directly with the US or with other Western countries in an African policy which, in principle, is meant to promote the idea of French independence. On the other hand, the legitimacy of France's own action is bolstered by the participation, even if only at a symbolic level, of African troops alongside French soldiers in a conflict overseas. The fact that Zaire sent troops to Chad in 1983 strengthened France's argument that she was not violating principles dear to the OAU. Had it not been for the accord arrived at between Colonel Gadaffi and King Hassan II in the early summer of 1983, the French might well have hoped for Morocco also to provide substantial military (and therefore political) support for French action.[66]

In the future, it is increasingly likely that national and international support for French actions overseas will only be secured if a number of African states call for French military intervention. It would be better still if at least one African state not a party to a given conflict sees its own interests as sufficiently affected to warrant its direct involvement, and if action taken by France can be limited both in terms of space and time. Traditionally, the domestic political costs of French action overseas have not been unacceptable. In fact, President Mitterrand's popularity was at its highest in October 1983, when *Opération Manta* in Chad had succeeded in creating a military stalemate. When some French troops were accidentally killed by Libyan-placed mines in mid-1984 there was considerable public questioning of the reasons for and purpose of the French intervention, but this was not enough to create pressure on the government to force a change of policy. Nor was the cost of the operation (about $400,000 a day) an issue of great public concern.

Yet the fact that France's commitments in Chad could be determined by the strength of Colonel Gadaffi's will to remain there did meet with some public disapproval. Having chosen a policy of deterrence in Chad, Mitterrand could not withdraw his own forces until the Libyan threat was gone. Colonel Gadaffi was permitted to become master of France's fate in the country. Ironically, however, Mitterrand's policy came in for the harshest criticism when the government pulled back French troops after the Franco–Libyan withdrawal agreement of 17 September 1984 was signed, without properly monitoring the Libyan withdrawal, which in November 1984 was revealed to be incomplete. The withdrawal pact caused a serious rift in French–Chadian relations as Habré's government was informed of it only after the fact. When US satellites picked up the continued presence of almost 3,000 Libyan troops and about fifty tanks in northern Chad, French policy came under harsh criticism from a number of African states. It was only with great difficulty that Mitterrand avoided an overly damaging discussion of the Chad issue at the December 1984 Franco–African summit meeting in Burundi. Almost all African states felt it necessary to ask whether France's 'guarantee' had been devalued by her mishandling of the withdrawal.

The desire to show strength clearly drove French policy later, in February 1986, when Gadaffi again chose to test French resolve. In the period since 1984, Tripoli had worked to improve the military infrastructure of the territories it occupied in the north of Chad with the rebel forces. The airstrip at Ouadi Doum (between Faya Largeau and Fada) was reinforced to receive major military transports. In mid-February 1986, new confrontations took place at Ziguey and Oum Chalouba between Chadian and rebel forces. French aid to Habré in the form of artillery pieces, light arms and AML 90 *Panhard* vehicles followed. On 16 February a Libyan *Tupolev* 22 attacked Ndjamena, calling into question the efficacy of local air defence. In France some military experts regretted in public that France did not possess Boeing AWACS systems which could have given advance warning of the attack. Eventually (as noted earlier) radar installations were deployed to the capital.

Soon after these attacks, France mounted *Opération Epervier* to reinforce Ndjamena and sent six *Mirages F-Is* and four *Jaguars* to help establish air superiority around the Chadian capital. Habré began receiving more aid from the US, while France stepped up her efforts to reinforce various Chadian strategic points in the south of Chad. In 1987 this effort was vindicated as Habré's forces, with discreet aid from France, were able to conquer Ouadi Doum. Later in the year they managed to gain control of Faya Largeau, and implanted themselves temporarily in the Aouzou strip on the Chad/Libya border, capturing on the way numerous Libyan tanks and other Soviet-supplied heavy equipment which had proved useless in desert conditions. Throughout this period Habré had been able to rely on France for support, and the French government, reluctant to risk a direct confrontation with Libya, nevertheless had little choice, given the logic of Franco–Chadian relations, but to carry on helping Habré in the hope that he might finally bring peace to Chad. The eventual re-establishment of diplomatic relations between Chad and Libya in 1988 seemed then to vindicate government policy in Chad and silence some critics of French policy.

Still, the experience of French policy in Chad also underscores the fact that unquestioning domestic support for France's African policy can no longer be assured. If the series of French interventions in Africa since 1975 have conditioned international public opinion to accept France's 'Africa mission' as one of the facts of contemporary international politics the French public is more likely now to challenge the continued value of the government's obligations when these seem open-ended and uncontrollable by politicians. Such opposition is unlikely to be crippling, but French governments have to be wary about extensive military commitments in a country like Chad. Any serious loss of French lives in the Chadian desert might cause the public to question whether French grandeur would be immediately damaged if France did not choose to guarantee the territorial and political integrity of a country whose boundaries and leadership are likely to remain under constant challenges.

There seems, at least, to be 'only one Chad' in Africa. In no other country could one have expected French troops to be deployed so often, in such numbers, on behalf of so many different leaders, for so long, and with so little ultimate effect on regional stability. The political commitment to Chad should be thought of as being separate and distinct from the commitment to other francophone African countries. Chad has a special claim on France and her own internal logic. After Chad, the governments of Senegal, Ivory Coast, Gabon, Cameroon, Togo and the CAR can be relatively certain of French support in the event of an external attack on their countries. On the other hand, support by the French public in cases of internal upheaval is by no means certain.

The latter is very dependent on the precise circumstances as well as on the state of relations that may exist between France and the country concerned at the time. If France's commitment to Chad is justified partly on geostrategic grounds – her collapse would endanger the security of neighbouring countries politically close to France – support is given to the other states listed above primarily because these countries themselves symbolize the success of France's distinctive policy of decolonization and because, in the main, the leaders of these countries are close allies of the French government.

The core states have been politically close to France since decolonization. Even if their direct economic importance to France is not great, their importance to France's reputation in Africa is undeniable. It is these states which push the Chadian 'domino theory' at France with most insistence. Though Senegal is thousands of miles away from Libya, her leaders feared the destabilizing influence of Gadaffi's revolution and argued throughout the 1980s that West African states could become subject to Libyan influence even if Libya's military power was not such as to allow it to control directly the leadership and populations of distant states. Traditionally, the core states of francophone Africa have seen French intervention in Chad as proof of a continued willingness by France to protect them. Although French intervention in Chad stems from a specific commitment, it also serves to underwrite a more general policy for all of francophone Africa. So long as the leaders of the core states desire French support and so long as they see the defence agreements as essential elements of their security policy, then France is bound to treat her implied commitments seriously. But the strength of these implied commitments can vary.

The presence of French troops in some of these countries serves to deter internal upheaval or *coups d'états* only to the extent that subversive elements believe that the French will protect the leader in place. For example, so long as Houphouet-Boigny remains in power in the Ivory Coast, he can be sure of protection afforded by French troops. But the mere presence of French soldiers in a francophone African country does not necessarily shield a leader from internal revolt, as David Dacko, himself put in power with the help of France, discovered when French troops did not move to support him when General Kolingba mounted a *coup d'état* in 1981. In the future, French leaders are likely to become increasingly concerned about being accused of ordering Africa's internal affairs. The commitments that France now has, either to individual leaders or to certain states, are unlikely to be expanded in any formal sense. Some analysts have argued that the system of defence co-operation agreements with francophone Africa should be extended to other states of Africa as well as to some in the Middle East if France is to protect her political and economic interests in these regions.[67] But the cost of such an expansion of influence (even if it were possible) and the political burdens this would imply strongly militate against France launching a programme of political adventurism in Africa or elsewhere. There have been times when states outside the francophone African family, such as Guinea Bissau in 1988, have sought a defence agreement with France, but the government has always shown itself wary of signing new defence agreements in Africa. History has determined certain allegiances. While France may be in a position to do something to protect her interests elsewhere, such a commitment would not receive the same approbation in other countries as it has in the core states of francophone Africa or in France itself. Securing rights outside France's present sphere of influence would also mean assuming new duties and if France is to maintain her general policy of independence it is necessary for her to ensure that she does not become too susceptible to African pressures for purely African interests.[68] While some French defence experts would like France to have a wider interventionary capability, few French government officials would like to see an expansion of French security commitments.

While French military intervention in Black Africa has taken place primarily to ensure the safety of French nationals (some 300,000 live and work there), to keep in power certain friendly political leaders, or to maintain a general balance of power in West and Central Africa, it is often suggested that the preservation of economic interests might be the true cause of French military action. Yet the countries of francophone Africa are generally poor and even if many of these countries do place most of their export orders with France, much of this trade is paid for with aid originally given by France. France's most important client in Black Africa by the 1980s was, and is still, Nigeria. If most francophone African countries are economically dependent on France, France's own trade efforts are beginning to concentrate more on larger markets elsewhere. In recent years trade with francophone Africa has declined sharply as a proportion of total French trade, even if it remains an important market.[69] This is not to say that France would be indifferent to problems which affected the economic interest of the government or of private companies, but only that such a threat would not be the sole or the primary cause of French military action.

This is equally true in the case of strategic minerals, many of which France receives in substantial quantities from Africa. The most important of these is uranium which France imports primarily from Africa. Two semi-public organizations, the *Bureau de Recherches Géologiques et Minières* (BRGM) and the *Compagnie Générale de Matières Nucléaires* (COGEMA) help to organize the discovery and development of uranium deposits in Niger, Gabon and the CAR and French companies have worked alongside other Western enterprises in Senegal, Mali, Guinea, Mauritania and South Africa.[70] The activities of BRGM and COGEMA are aided by the fact, noted earlier, that many of the co-operation agreements signed with strategic mineral suppliers ensure that France remains a 'privileged partner' of these states.[71] It is true to say that political relations with countries such as Niger and Gabon are maintained in part to ensure the continued supply of uranium to France but it would be wrong to presume from this that France would inevitably intervene militarily in Niger or Gabon merely to assure uranium supply, especially as the present glut in the world uranium market means that France could readily turn elsewhere.

In any case, it is unlikely that a decision, for instance, by the existing Gabonese government to restrict uranium exports to France severely could take effect without seriously damaging Franco–Gabonese relations and the Gabonese economy. Though the present regime in Gabon has not hesitated to criticize French policy, it has little incentive to damage relations beyond repair. Equally, if there were serious internal unrest in Gabon, an attempted *coup d'état* or an external attack which, if successful, could affect economic relations with France, the Gabonese President would almost certainly invoke the defence accord, an act which would allow France to claim that she was protecting her own interests in the name of a wider cause: namely the security of Gabon. France certainly has economic interests in a variety of francophone African states but in none of these countries is the interest so great, or so exclusive, that France would use military force solely to protect it. France's economic policy (see chapter 7) itself is directed with a view to ensuring the internal stability of her close African partners. Furthermore, the diplomatic and political tools which France has at her disposal make it easier for her not to rely immediately on a military instrument to safeguard special economic interests.

Constraints: the Limits of French Power

The decision to use military power on the African continent has therefore traditionally been seen as a last resort. With the reduction of French forces based on the continent and the consequential need to rely more on forces based in France, whose use could less easily escape public notice and possible criticism, the French have been particularly concerned to ensure that any military intervention in Africa had a motive which was easily explained to the domestic public. During the Giscard years this concern did not always seem evident, but it certainly existed. It became more important when Mitterrand came to power as was shown by the hesitation of the government before it intervened in Chad in 1983, and also the moderation shown by the government in February 1986 when Gadaffi ostentatiously tried to provoke France in Chad. The direct involvement of Libya in the conflict after 1983, however, virtually ensured that other Western states would support France's intervention. As against its own announced policy of non-interference in the internal affairs of African states, the French government had to balance the possibility of an American response which would call into question France's special and exclusive role in francophone Africa.

American pressure to intervene, which was itself encouraged by African demands, gave France less choice than the government would have liked, but international opinion in favour of intervention, thus accumulated, implicitly helped to justify French action. For most of the ensuing period there was close consultation between France and the US in Chad, though sudden increases in US military aid sometimes put pressure on France to increase her own activity. Because 'independence' is such a crucial aim of French policy, however, tensions have been known to arise in US–French relations when both have sought to aid the same Black African state. French leaders have somtimes shown a distaste for overly collaborative military action with other Western powers in Africa if only because the whole purpose of France's Africa policy is to preserve an exclusive 'field of action'. Despite this, when the military requirement for co-operative action has existed, particularly in Chad in the late 1980s, the French and the Americans have been able to collaborate effectively.

Earlier French decisions to intervene in Africa hardly required the government to take seriously into account its own capacities in comparison with those of France's likely adversaries. For the most part, this continues to be the case for the countries of West and Central Africa. The armed forces of many of these states tend to reproduce the ethnic and religious divisions of the societies they are meant to defend. Often the army may distrust members of the gendarmerie or other paramilitary forces who were created to help the central government establish an internal balance of power. These divisions and tensions reduce the ability of many African states to fight effectively against an external force.[72] While the richer states of Africa have been able to buy some sophisticated equipment, their capacity to use – and, more importantly, to maintain – such equipment is often questionable. Use of mercenaries or technical advisers from states outside the continent may increase the effectiveness of African armies for a time, but their actual combat capability remains, for the most part, inconsistent and unpredictable.

This said, France can no longer assume that her military power allows her free rein. Her virtual monopoly of the air, previously assured by *Jaguar* and combat helicopters such as the *Alouette* or *Gazelle*, is now restricted by the fact that African states are gaining access to modern anti-aircraft weapons. In Chad, France has been forced to deploy very sophisticated military equipment to be sure of the upper hand. Furthermore, the speed with which France is able to intervene in Africa is affected not only by the availability of suitable transport aircraft (a problem already referred to) but also by her capacity, at short notice, to negotiate overflying rights with states whose support for French intervention cannot always be assured.

Constraints of these kinds make it necessary for France to equip her African forces with the most sophisticated armaments in order to ensure supremacy over local forces, even though the most advanced European equipment is not always suitable for use in all African environments. Of course, in the particular case of the francophone African countries with which France has special links, France's arms-transfer policy ensures that francophone states cannot present a challenge to French forces and this is one reason why French military capacity and influence is highest in countries to which she has transferred the fewest arms.

Even if some of France's actual or potential military actions in Africa may require her to confront forces of a well-equipped African state (Libya in the case of Chad, Nigeria in the event of a possible conflict with Cameroon), it is still a fact that the military power of the USSR is in no direct way brought to bear on francophone Africa. Though the USSR has diplomatic, political and economic links with a number of these states (including some nominally Marxist–Leninist regimes like Benin and the Congo), such links are in no sense incompatible with the connection that most of these countries retain with France. Though the USSR also has military contacts with a handful of francophone states, she has not transferred to them a substantial amount of military equipment. Her activity in West and Central Africa, primarily because of the extent of French influence, has been only sporadic and symbolic. In fact, the USSR seems tacitly to have accepted the *de facto* spheres of influence that exist in Africa. While the USSR was able to exploit the vacuum created by Portugal's withdrawal from southern Africa in 1975, she has not sought directly to oppose Western influence when it was well-established. During the Zaire crisis in 1978, for example, the USSR appears to have stopped military support to the FLNC as soon as French and Belgian troops were deployed to Shaba province.[73] In the one case where Soviet military aid has been substantial (Libya) the experience of 1987 showed that the heavy equipment she had transferred to that country was totally ill-suited to the environment.

For the most part, the French are still able militarily to deal with the forces they are likely to confront in Africa, even if this ability is likely to decline slowly over time. As the major external power operating in francophone West and Central Africa, France is in a strong position to influence the management of regional security problems. Yet the French neither desire nor are likely to receive a great deal of allied assistance in large-scale problems. Discreet co-operation with the Americans has often taken place there, but it is doubtful whether either party, for differing reasons, would like to translate this into outright collaboration. The Americans would be reluctant (despite French fears) entirely to 'replace' France in Africa, or to send troops to an area previously the preserve of France, while the French, who like to de-emphasize the East–West dimension of African conflicts, would not want to be responsible for introducing the Western superpower into the African theatre.

At present it is questionable whether the French would be able to sustain a long-drawn-out war on the continent, except at a totally unacceptable cost. Furthermore, if an African conflict were to break out at a time when French forces were needed in a combat or deterrent role on the European continent, France's European commitments would naturally outweigh any possible African ones. The whole point of the FAR is that all of its elements, including those which have had only an African role hitherto, could be used anywhere outside French borders to defend French interests and these will always be greater in Europe than in Africa. In any case French leaders are now sensitive to the fact that a policy of intervention in Africa is not often a useful solution to the problems which affect the continent. Aid is therefore given – in a manner which is admittedly not disinterested – to those states which are seen as stabilizing forces. Hence the support given to the 'core' states and to those which, like post-Sékou-Touré's Guinea, might be wooed back into the French camp. At the same time, African states who know they have been 'useful' to France in this respect hope for an economic *quid pro quo* for the positions they have taken. Thus, Finance Ministers of the CAR forcefully argued in 1984 that as the CAR was allowing millions of francs worth of military equipment to pass through its country in order to supply French forces in Chad, the French should not 'hide behind IMF structures' when considering their economic support of the CAR. In this sense, and in others, one notes that 'carrot-and-stick' policies can be used by both sides of the Franco–African partnership.

The range of factors which determine French policy in Africa and the volatile nature of the continent's politics has made it difficult for France to be as much in control of her destiny there as many observers have presumed. Though France has a policy of economic co-operation, she has no strategy for development and equally, though she has a tradition of military assistance, France can provide no answer to the continent's security problems. Many years after decolonization the French have wisely chosen to renounce their previous 'right' to impose political solutions in areas in which France is still directly involved. But the increasing complexity of certain African security problems, their almost definitional intractability, has even made it difficult for French leaders to suggest effective compromises and possible changes. Though French military aid, in all its forms, is still needed, it is recognized as being an inadequate tool for the solution of many security problems which confront African states, which increasingly wish not only to take stock of the particular types of problems which beset them, but also to take steps to manage them on their own.

6
France and Regional Stability in Africa

Francophone African States suffer from a variety of internal and external disturbances which directly affect their stability and security; a great many of these cannot be adequately addressed by the use or threat of force. All these states struggle even to maintain a capacity to manage their own internal affairs: bureaucracies, even if large, tend to be disorganized. The strength of a regime is often linked merely to the efficiency and personality of its leader, a fact which facilitates contacts with other countries and organizations, both on the continent and beyond, insofar as the distinction between president and state is often merely juridical. Yet it remains an important priority of all francophone African leaders to render less fictitious the concept of independent statehood in Africa: to create enduring legally based links with others in order to further development of both a political and an economic kind. Even if the connection with France provides an important cement to fragile state structures, francophone African states rightly place increasing emphasis on more sophisticated forms of inter-African co-operation. The sense that African stability must be built regionally as much as on a national or individual basis, and that such co-operation need not detract from the intensity of relations with extra-continental powers or organizations is an increasingly important element in francophone African calculations. Before going on in later chapters to analyse French economic and diplomatic activity on the continent, and how this sometimes affects existing regional structures, it is worthwhile to pause and show how even in the military domain, francophone Africa is beginning to establish important international structures. Their agendas and their purposes offer useful guidance to how francophone states perceive their own security. This chapter will therefore briefly examine some of these regional arrangements, which may in the long term have important salutory effects on international relations in West and Central Africa.

One must begin, inevitably, with the proposition that the various African states with which France has military agreements have complex security concerns. While the fear of external attack is in some cases the driving force of defence policy and of military dispositions, the leaders of most francophone African states perceive threats which are intimately bound up with domestic political problems. These can naturally be aggravated by ethnic and other links which cross national frontiers, and this serves to complicate the formation of appropriate national security policies. The astute deployment of military force is therefore rarely a sufficient condition of stability. Despite the apparent strength of the French military 'guarantee' to many of these states, it cannot help to deter all forms of local or regional threat. Local leaders have an obligation to themselves to seek internal or regional solutions to problems which the link with France does not help to manage. France has an interest in seeing progress towards further regional co-operation since she has no incentive to become embroiled in local power struggles or to be caught having to decide between two states when she may wish to maintain close relations with both.

In the late 1980s, it is evident that the fragility of most francophone African states (economically, politically, militarily) is nearly as great as at the time of decolonization. Not since the period 1963–6, when there were thirteen *coups d'état* in francophone Africa, have these states seemed so unstable.[1] To the extent that there has been a greater diffusion of power in African states this has often merely created new poles of opposition. While there has been an increase in regional organization, interstate tensions still can arise, and can be all the more acute given that they occur between ostensible allies. The essential paradox of regional stability in West and Central Africa is that leaders are forced to build their nations in a way to solve domestic disputes and ensure internal unity, yet the nationalism that this can sometimes inspire is antithetical to the creation of better regional links which would dampen interstate suspicions and rivalries.

Types of Security Concerns

The security problems that leaders must confront can be roughly divided as follows: ethnic disputes and separatist problems; border conflict; insurgency caused by immigration or foreign propaganda (often referred to in francophone Africa as 'intoxication'); and disaffection caused by overly austere economic policies or natural catastrophes. There are few states of francophone Africa who fear a direct military attack from another state; of greater concern are the activities of agents of a foreign power, or of domestic forces which have fallen under the influence of a hostile foreign state.

The external threat posed by Colonel Gadaffi's Libya was the principal cause of concern in the early and mid-1980s. Gadaffi's action in Chad in 1983–4 (as well as the French response) were watched carefully by the leaders of all francophone states who often raised the spectre of Gadaffi with the same vigour as did President Reagan. Though few states, with the exception of those bordering Libya, need fear a direct attack, the falling of certain African states such as Chad or Niger under Libyan influence would pose a threat to other francophone states, particularly those having a large Muslim population. While some francophone states, such as Zaire, have taken a direct military interest in the Chad conflict, other states have perforce had to limit themselves to encouraging the French to defend their interests against the designs of an aggressor they widely accept to be as ambitious as his declaratory policy suggests.

The specific fear of Gadaffi has often been linked to a general uneasiness about the political power of Islam. Even in francophone African states where there is a strong Muslim presence, this Islamic heritage has never been used to help forge a national consciousness. Yet it is becoming increasingly difficult for secular leaders to ignore the Muslim communities in their countries. Still, popular Islam (with which the colonizing force of the Third Republic was sometimes confronted) is taken by most francophone leaders as a challenge to state authority. The creation of Islamic organizations has sometimes therefore been encouraged by state leaders who hope in this way to sanction activity that takes place within identifiable associations while combatting any activity that takes place outside recognized structures. This tactic has proved particularly successful in Niger and Togo where Islamic organizations have supported the government.[2] Yet it is still the case that Islamic groups in these countries, as well as in Burkina Faso, Senegal, the Ivory Coast, Guinea, or Mauritania, in times of economic or political instability can oppose the secular power, and pursue activities which are both generally xenophobic and particularly 'anti-Western' in nature. Since Muslim forces are perceived to be easily manipulated by external powers, state leaders feel they must be extraordinarily vigilant of any overt religious behaviour by foreigners and often take firm action, as in Senegal in February 1984 when the Iranian Embassy was closed on suspicion of fomenting Muslim dissent. It is probable that in the last years of the twentieth century, as in the last years of the nineteenth, accommodating traditional Islam with animist or Christian beliefs will be an important priority. The skill demonstrated by President Ben Ali of Tunisia in the first year of his mandate (1987–8) in dealing with the Islamic factor was watched with interest by others in sub-Saharan Africa.

There are, naturally, many other semi-permanent sources of dispute. Despite the strictures of the Organization of African Unity (OAU) against challenging colonial frontiers, many states have serious border disputes which resurface from time to time. Border differences exist *inter alia* between Mali and Burkina Faso; Togo and Ghana; Senegal and Guinea Bissau; Nigeria and Cameroon; Nigeria and Chad; Niger and Libya; and many of these have resulted in armed conflict. The general permeability of borders offers, however, greater risks to stability than do the juridical disputes as to where these borders lie. The more stable a state, the more it is prone to potential unrest of this sort. The Ivory Coast, for example, serves as a magnet to migrant workers from neighbouring states who seek to earn money for their families at home. The presence of roughly 1.2 million citizens of Burkina Faso in the Ivory Coast was perceived as a security risk by Ivorian leaders in 1984–7 who feared the revolutionary policies of the then Burkinabé leader, Captain Thomas Sankara. The management of immigrant populations, as much as the control of *agents provocateurs*, has often been a high priority for francophone African leaders.

Though the 'masses' in the poor states of West and Central Africa are not likely to be moved to collective action against government elites, it would be wrong to ignore the potentially destabilizing effects of economic hardship. Continued drought in the states of the Sahel, for example, is accepted as a security risk, particularly in such badly affected states as Mali. Equally, the stability of commodity prices is essential for economies which have only one major export. Dramatic price fluctuations in cocoa or in oil deeply affect not only the national economies of the Ivory Coast and Gabon or Cameroon, but also the essential stability of the whole of both West and Central Africa. The events in Tunisia and Morocco of January 1984 when there were extraordinary riots following an increase in the price of bread and in Algeria in October 1988 when the cry for 'democracy' was joined to the cry of hunger, also indicate that burdensome pricing policies can have a catalytic (though perhaps useful) effect on internal order. The practical effects of certain forms of economic management are therefore a security consideration of the first order. While local populations might be willing to undergo certain economic sacrifices imposed from outside on the understanding that their lot will generally improve, a national consensus of this sort is likely to be delicate, and sporadic challenges to authority can easily take place if government promises do not hold good.

Economic reform successfully imposed on African states by outside powers or intergovernmental organizations sometimes carries the price of decreasing the ability of governments to satisfy their populations. African leaders are well aware of this danger and are often forced to argue that, since a deficit is 'cheaper' than destabilization, economic changes must proceed more slowly than sound financial management might suggest. The internal security of francophone African states, therefore, like that of many other third-world states, is to be seen as a consequence of a wide variety of policies both locally directed and externally shaped and not merely as a goal which can be reached simply by the shrewd management of military power. How capable outside organizations will be in balancing their fears of potential economic mismanagement of carefully allocated funds with their perhaps greater fear of anarchy resulting from overly restrictive financial and general economic aid will be a key factor determining the stability of francophone Africa. As France has sought to manage its own influence in francophone Africa, her leaders have generally been sensitive to the different factors that affect local stability and France's own regional power. To the extent that this power continues to rely on the fact that post-colonial leaders have chosen to invite French influence, it is vulnerable to the evolving priorities of old leaders and the emerging concerns of the new. But so long as regional security structures remain inadequate for the management of the totality of francophone African security concerns, French power is unlikely to be dismissed easily from either West or Central Africa. But these, sometimes very new structures, are worth looking at, because over time they will shape and affect France's role.

Regional Security Structures

As the security problems of most francophone African states are both varied and highly specific, it is difficult to imagine a grand strategy or a blueprint for peace which could assure the stability of the states of West and Central Africa as a whole. Unrest can result as much from the vagaries of internal policy as from personal distrust between leaders of neighbouring states having different political affiliations. Problems of this kind are not easily susceptible to pre-emptive solutions. Since the foundation of the OAU, African leaders have understood that a system of regional crisis management is critical but, alone of the five specialized commissions established to promote functional co-operation on the continent, the Defence Commission has achieved no success. In Africa, as elsewhere, only 'sub-regional' organizations have shown any promise for crisis management, and even at these levels, progress has only been modest.

The OAU

At the founding conference of the OAU in Addis Ababa in 1963, the various heads of state and government who had assembled drafted resolutions which recognized a role for the organization they were creating in the management of regional conflict. African states could be destabilized or threatened by border or territorial disputes, refugee problems, subversion, *coups d'états* as well as extra-regional aggression. While the instruments of the OAU provide no collective measures against any member or outside aggressor, the Charter does call on member states to co-ordinate and harmonize their general policies of defence and security. Though the OAU attempted in its early years to set up an African defence organization, no collective security measures have been taken and the OAU simply pretends to a role in conflict management through the Mediation, Conciliation and Arbitration Commission. This body has almost never been used by the member states.[3] Every attempt to create some sort of Pan-African defence system or armed force has failed. This has been because the OAU has not been able to deal with the different viewpoints of English-and French-speaking ex-colonies, conservative and radical states, or Islamic and secular Black African states.[4] Twenty-five years after the formation of the OAU, the disputes between these groupings in some respects have even increased. Referring to Libyan involvement in the Chad dispute and to the continuing Moroccan activity against *Polisario*, President Mobutu of Zaire frequently pointed out in 1984 that these were the two great problems that had affected the OAU. From this he drew the somewhat cynical conclusion that the OAU's problems were 'Arab' ones and proposed the formation of a separate Black African regional security organization.[5] Such remarks have done little to strengthen the standing of the OAU which has traditionally been more preoccupied with the solution of its own institutional problems, rather than those of the member states. The Organization did have some success in arranging a cease-fire between Algeria and Morocco when the two had a border dispute in 1963 and it was also able successfully to replace British with African troops after the UK intervention in Tanzania in 1964. But since its failure to play a role in the 1964 Congo crisis the Organization has been quite ineffective in mediating between African combatants or in helping to solve civil wars.[6]

At present the member states are united only on the issue of apartheid in South Africa, a policy which they are in any case in no position directly to change for the better. The various attempts to establish an OAU Defence Force have failed because of the lack of consensus amongst African countries as to the use to which such a force could be put. At the eighth session of the OAU Defence Commission, held in Accra between 26 and 30 January 1984, for example, members of the Commission realized that they could only discuss distinctly modest projects, such as the harmonization of military training programmes among African states, and the possible creation of a bureau of military experts to advise the Secretary-General on security problems.[7] Nothing of significance has evolved since then.

The diplomatic efforts of the OAU Secretary-General in recent years to solve the Chad or the Western Sahara disputes have come to nothing mainly because the parties concerned have distrusted the OAU mechanism or because regional African powers and states external to the continent have complicated the process by offering their own solutions which, while not necessarily incompatible with OAU approaches, have not been sufficiently well co-ordinated with them. Advances towards solving these problems have been made, of course, but not because of anything the OAU has done. In the case of the Western Sahara conflict, the UN has emerged as by far the most important external factor. Furthermore, the recent OAU experience has shown that the personality of the OAU Chairman is crucial to the Organization's ability to bring warring factions nearer a negotiating table: if his own neutrality is to any degree suspect, then belligerents prefer to ignore diplomacy altogether or use other fora. Since the OAU, unlike the UN, does not have regular or continuous sessions and since much of the consideration of individual political problems is taken on by special committees, all negotiation tends to be *ad hoc*, informal and subject very much to the availability of senior diplomats from the countries most closely affected by a particular crisis.[8] Many of the principles of the OAU Charter, such as non-interference in internal affairs and the acceptance of the territorial legacy of imperialism, are ignored by member states when these impinge on the pursuit of fundamental national objectives.[9]

Regional Alternatives to the OAU

In general, the adoption of regional security structures may offer more hope for the management of African crises than would reliance on an OAU which is often insufficiently committed. The OAU was not established primarily as a security instrument and lacks the institutions to take on this role. Its meetings can still be useful demonstrations of African solidarity in respect of particular international questions and its summits (when they take place) serve as important testimonies to the desire of African states to preserve certain basic principles of the Charter. It will, however, be some time before the OAU will be able to recover from such failures to keep the peace as were experienced by the 1981 OAU multinational force in Chad, which was badly equipped, under-financed and lacked a clearly-defined mission. Until the OAU is able to establish more durable institutions which might replace the present system of 'musical chairs diplomacy', the solution of security questions, particularly for francophone African states, is best left to regional leaders and regional organizations. The OAU Charter itself, in Article 2, stipulates that member states are to co-ordinate and harmonize their policies with special reference to co-operation in defence and security, and implicit in the whole of the OAU Charter is the idea that regional integration is a first step towards the realization of any pan-African ideal. In any case, the geography of Africa and the pattern of its communications make evident the need to consider continental security in regional terms.[10]

Both regional and sub-regional defence structures have been established in West Africa, though in Central Africa no such organizations exist. Francophone states in both of these regions have relied primarily on the French guarantee for their security needs, but for three reasons African leaders are becoming aware that it is important for them to take steps to assure their own security. First, while the French have generally been loyal to the defence and co-operation agreements they have signed with African states, the recent experience in Chad has reinforced the extent to which France remains a prisoner of her African partners. It is difficult for France to remain aloof from her African commitments and occasionally she is drawn into conflict at the behest of African leaders whose demands French leaders cannot refuse if links with other countries are not to be brought into question. While it is unlikely that France will unilaterally withdraw her support for the legitimate leaders of African states, they must be aware that it is becoming increasingly awkward for France to act as *gendarme* for the continent. Second, since the bilateral defence relations that francophone African states enjoy with France in no sense prevent them from establishing stronger security contacts between themselves, there is now an understanding that regional organizations must be strengthened if only to boost the general African sense of independence from external influence. Lastly, while the French military connection may be useful in the event of a major military crisis, such as an interstate conflict or violent civil war, French support may not be needed for more modest purposes – such as civil defence and protection of a country's resources. The improvements in regional capacities for these needs in West and Central Africa have been modest, but some lessons may be drawn from recent experience on which leaders at least in West Africa seem intent to build.

West Africa

The principal regional organization of West Africa is the Economic Community of West African States (ECOWAS). On 28 May 1981, at

Freetown, thirteen of the sixteen member states signed a Defence Protocol.[11] While the remaining three ECOWAS states did not sign the Protocol for ideological reasons, there was also some hesitation by such francophone states as the Ivory Coast and Niger who feared that the influence of Nigeria in the Community would be overwhelming. The view of others, such as Senegal and Togo, was that Nigeria's participation would allow her to play an important stabilizing.role, her power being such that it could serve as a deterrent of sorts against the aggression of external powers.[12] Nevertheless, the vast majority of francophone states persist in viewing Nigeria with suspicion, and doubt whether she is ever likely to be motivated by concerns shared by themselves. For their part, the Nigerians believe that the presence of French bases in parts of francophone Africa impedes their own progress towards regional great-power status, and argue that member states should work more quickly towards eliminating their contacts with states external to the continent. In fact, the ECOWAS Defence Protocol calls for all foreign troops to be withdrawn once ECOWAS can guarantee mutual defence, but this is a very long way away and none of the francophone states which accept a French presence on their territory is likely to allow the ECOWAS charter to interfere with the sovereign right of all states to chose their allies freely. Certainly the defence links these countries have with France could not be broken until regional defence is satisfactorily assured by other means.

As it happens, the latent distrust of Nigeria by francophone states, and Nigeria's own doubts and difficulties, have made it difficult for the ECOWAS Defence Protocol to become anything more than an instrument of declaratory policy. The essential surety provided by France simply has no realistic equivalent in either the language of the Protocol, or the deployable military power of the member states. In principle the Protocol envisages action, co-ordinated by the Defence Council created by the member states in three circumstances: defence of an ECOWAS member against aggression by a non-member state; mediation of conflicts between member states; and action of either a political or military kind in the event of internal conflict in a member state – though community forces would not intervene if the conflict remained internal. The present instruments of the Protocol are, however, insufficient for any action to be taken in time to manage a crisis successfully. It makes no provision for a standing army. While in theory units of the member states are earmarked to participate in an Allied force, these would still have to be organized and co-ordinated at the moment of the crisis, a procedure which would take some time.[13] The fact that the force would come from countries with diverse colonial backgrounds and different military traditions (and speak different languages) means that problems of the co-ordination of units and unified command are likely to remain. One has only to look at the Confederation of Senegambia to see how, even in the easiest of conditions, co-ordination between armies of different types is difficult. The Gambian Army, such as it is, exercises with the Senegalese Army, but many of its officers have been and still are trained in British military academies. Gambian soldiers, on the other hand, are tending now to be trained by the French. This in itself might not always directly affect combat capabilities – although there is a reasonable presumption that it would – but differences in outlook certainly slow the process of integration.

At a symbolic level, the ECOWAS Defence Protocol is an important step forward but few practical results are likely to emerge for some time. It is not easy to imagine anglophone and francophone states acting together to defend a member state from external aggression, and it is equally unlikely that the Defence Protocol itself would be invoked to allow for diplomatic action of a kind which would ease tensions among member states. All the ideological and political divisions which plague the OAU affect also the states of West Africa. While the prospects for establishing a solid regional security network through ECOWAS are higher than for the establishment of a continental system, it is probably only at the sub-regional level that the security threats to the francophone African states can be addressed.

The existence of the *Communauté Économique de l'Afrique de l'Ouest* (CEAO) [14] is in itself testimony to the fact that the French states are suspicious of Nigerian power and are more comfortable dealing with each other than with non-francophone states of the region. The adoption by ECOWAS of the Defence Protocol in 1981 spurred the francophone states to accelerate their own negotiations for the adoption of a CEAO Defence Protocol. As early as 1977, the CEAO states plus Togo signed the *Accord de Non-agression et d'Assistance en Matière de Défense* (ANAD). The negotiations during the following years to adopt a protocol of application went slowly. At the second meeting of experts at Nouakchott in April 1979, Mali and Mauritania, in a move directed against France, insisted that no progress would be made until foreign bases were dismantled and defence agreements with third states denounced. Countries closer to the French argued successfully that, as independent states, members of the ANAD should be free to conclude agreements with whomsoever they chose. It was only in 1981, shortly after the ECOWAS Protocol was signed, that the ANAD states were able to come to an agreement which made no reference to outside powers.

The ANAD Protocol[15] states as its objective the reinforcement of defence measures of the member states so as to increase stability in the geographic zone. Member states also agree not to use force to resolve their disputes.

Most of the principles of the UN charter and the OAU are reaffirmed in the Protocol but certain articles address questions of particular interest to the ANAD member states. Article 6 reaffirms the need to adhere to CEAO principles relating to the free circulation of persons between member states. However, Article 7 moderates this by stipulating that member states 'undertake not to shelter or tolerate on their territories active opponents involved in subversive actions of any nature whatsoever against another member nation.' States undertake to provide mutual aid and assistance for the defence of one another against any form of aggression. Though a standing army has not yet been created, some work is being done to establish an inter-allied command and member states have agreed to create an intervention force by assigning units of their own armies to the ANAD organization. The 1977 Accord set up a Conference of Heads of State and Government, a Council of Ministers and a Secretariat all of which play different roles in managing the organization.

By far the most innovative aspect of the ANAD is the attempt to set up a system to ensure that states are informed as to potential threats to their security. Even if there are no direct military threats, misunderstandings between states can still occur which may lead to destabilizing political disputes. To deal with these, confidence-building measures (CBM) – though they have not been called by this name – have been established. They are modest in scope, infrequently applied, and not always effective. But the fact that member states have seen the need to address mutual fears in an ordered way is promising and shows that the states of the ANAD have recognized that a broad range of concerns must be addressed if the signatory states are to be sure of the essential good faith of other states in their region. The aim of the types of CBM proposed is to reduce all threats of intervention with a view to turning the military power which exists in the member states into a collective defence potential. Unless such CBM are successful, there can naturally be no hope of developing any sort of allied defence capability which would cope with direct threats to the member states.

To address some of these primary concerns, certain preliminary actions were quickly taken after the signature of the ANAD. An additional Protocol dealing with non-aggression was adopted by the ANAD member states in December 1982. This stipulated that states should ensure that meetings between border authorities should take place regularly to discuss immigration problems. It also suggested that states should arrange for both information exchange and mutual assistance between police and security forces. It also envisaged the creation of a regulatory commission which would seek to find solutions to differences between member states. These CBM, internal to the ANAD, would help to ensure that states did not suspect each other of harbouring individuals who might be intending to act against them. As the security concerns of francophone states relate more to the fear of covert forms of aggression rather than direct attacks, these measures, if they could be enforced, would help to control subversion before it spread to the point where military force might be required to suppress it.[16]

At the eighth session of the Council of Ministers, held in Niamey in October 1983, the ANAD adopted two protocols which broadened to some degree, the scope of the Treaty. Set up to defend the economic interests of the CEAO by ensuring the essential stability of the member states, ANAD has attempted to make arrangements which would help to protect the natural resources of member states.[17] One of these protocols envisaged co-operation in matters relating to the protection of the CEAO economies; the other considered co-operation in civil defence. Economic protection covered poaching, the devastation of flora and the systematic plundering of territorial waters. Member states have, for example, discussed ways in which they could provide security for ship movements in zones under jurisdiction of ANAD states. The Civil Defence Protocol, on the other hand, seeks to establish structures to deal with such problems as drought, forest fires, floods and the threat of marine pollution. While these protocols did not address specifically military questions, they did help to give substance to the often declared need to link questions of security with those of economic development. [18]

Building on these initial developments the ANAD states agreed in October 1984 to establish a commission for the peaceful regulation of disputes between the member states. Each state is represented on the commission by two individuals, and the commission is charged with solving disputes by one of three methods: mediation, conciliation, or arbitration. Provision was also made for the establishment of a *Force de Paix* to which the signatory states would contribute at a time of crisis. At the April 1987 meeting in Nouakchott, the signatories formally established the *Comité Régionale d'Assistance en matière de protection civile* originally proposed at the October 1983 meeting in Niamey. Also in Nouakchott in 1987, the ANAD states agreed to set up a common fund to support any action taken by an inter-allied force in the military defence of the ANAD states or for their civil and economic protection.[19]

Still in its early stages, ANAD is thus both a military umbrella and a form of insurance against unforseeable risks.[20] Unlike NATO, it is not an alliance with a predefined military strategy. Nor is it set up against any particular threat. Rather, it is an organization which, by attempting to improve interstate co-operation on a number of diverse problems, is intended to reduce tensions between them and helps also to ensure internal stability.

Until 1985 ANAD was still very much an idea in search of sufficient finance and political will. It is still very badly financed, but the success it had in the establishment of a cease-fire in the first days of 1986, after the 'Christmas war' between Mali and Burkina Faso, demonstrated its potential utility in helping to solve regional conflicts. The way in which this conflict was begun, and the manner in which it ended, is indicative of the types of disputes which can lead to war in West Africa as well as the types of conflict which can be settled by mediation.

The two countries had come to blows as early as 1974 and 1975 over their frontier, whose final delineation was still before the International Court of Justice at the Hague in December 1985 when conflict broke out again. Military operations began in Agacher, 300 kilometres north of Ouaga-dougou, when Burkinabé officials tried in the beginning of December to conduct a census among the largely nomadic population. Malian officials opposed this act which they viewed as affecting the still undecided delineation of the frontier. Frontier skirmishes were followed by air bombardments deeper into the territories of both belligerents. The initial analysis of the conflict stressed its territorial aspects: the Agacher region is thought rich in manganese, natural gas and uranium, but Burkina Faso justified the conflict on the grounds that it was needed to combat Malian counter-revolutionaries who were trying to destabilize the regime of Captain Thomas Sankara. Houphouet-Boigny of the Ivory Coast offered his good offices and with the discreet help of France succeeded in convincing both belligerents that they should cease their armed conflict. Simultaneously, Nigeria and Libya sought together to organize a cease-fire, which they announced as having succeeded in an agreement on 29 December 1985. This agreement envisioned the end of hostilities, the withdrawal of all armed forces and the deployment of Libyan, Nigerian, Malian and Burkinabé observers alongside those of the OAU to monitor the cease-fire. The ANAD as a consequence accelerated its own attempts to arrive at an agreement between two of its member states. The idea that non-francophone troops and particularly Libyan ones could form part of an observer force within 'ANAD territory' was seen as a direct challenge to the ANAD as a sub-regional organization. On 30 December the ANAD itself was able to announce a cease-fire of its own making which the belligerents accepted. Only observers from the ANAD member states as well as from the OAU would be allowed to supervise the peace.

While France did play an important role behind the scenes, the ANAD's ability to organize itself to conclude an agreement in the face of competitive attempts to do the same by two important outside powers at least gave an indication that it was committed to the basic aims of its charter, namely, to regulate conflict among the member states. There remain many unanswered questions relating to the breadth and purpose of the organization. The treaty states are pledged to come to the defence of every member state. Since Mauritania is a member and could perhaps become embroiled in a North African dispute, would this sub-regional military alliance become involved in a conflict in another region? It is doubtful whether ANAD forces could ever be a match for the armies of the Maghreb states. Given the occasional conflicts between Togo and Ghana, for example, would Togo involve ANAD against an ECOWAS state with which all the other ANAD states were also allied? The organization played no role in 1986 when Ghana was said to have encouraged domestic unrest in Togo. Only French troops stifled conflict in that instance. It will take some time before the ANAD itself becomes a diplomatic and military force of real substance, able to deal effectively with all possible disputes in the region. It is true that the ideological differences between some of the ANAD states have not yet created severe problems or threatened the alliance as a whole although this must remain a matter of concern. Far more of a restriction is the economic weakness of the member states, which makes rapid movement towards a sound regional security system unlikely. Yet the ANAD states have shown some persistence in developing useful instruments for improved regional co-operation and francophone states in Central Africa have sought to emulate what they perceive as West African successes.

Central Africa

In general, the states of Central Africa are far less advanced in their attempt to co-ordinate activities so as to control security threats than are the West Africans. The first effort at Central African integration came with the attempt by the founder of the CAR, Barthelemy Boganda, to establish a Central African entity, which would include Chad, Congo, Gabon and Cameroon and which could resist the encroachments of both communism and pan-Arabism.[21] This grand design died with its creator in 1959, but since then some success has been achieved in establishing organizations with specific missions of a more pragmatic kind. While both regional and sub-regional economic and political organizations are in existence, they have not yet attempted to take on a security dimension. The existing institutions are either newer than those of West Africa, or, if long-standing, less capable of making serious attempts at military integration owing to the weaknesses of some of the local forces. Yet, if the more powerful Central African countries were to take the lead (as did Senegal and the Ivory Coast in West Africa), there is no reason why the Central African states, perhaps with some outside help, could not at least come to some agreements over CBM similar to those which are now being developed elsewhere, which would help moderate mutual fears and suspicions.

In the autumn of 1983, President Bongo of Gabon launched a new regional organization uniting francophone, lusophone and anglophone countries called the *Communauté Économique des États de l'Afrique Centrale* (CEEAC), its members being Burundi, Cameroon, the CAR, Congo, Equatorial Guinea, Gabon, Rwanda, Sao Tomé, Chad and Zaire. Angola was invited as an observer state. The organization is unlikely to be properly operative for many years and the striking imbalance of economic and military power between the member states will make progress slow. A non-aggression pact on the ECOWAS model might have a similar symbolic significance, but it would not go far to solve internal security problems. Since these states have quite different security concerns (the CAR and other neighbouring states might have some worries about Libyan intentions, while Angola has a large and powerful neighbour to the south which poses problems), any kind of military integration would be hampered by the variety of possible threats which the organization might have to address. Equally, the wide political differences of member states would make collective action of a military kind difficult. Still, the CEEAC states have sought to put improved military co-operation on their agenda. At a meeting which took place in Lomé in February 1988 (Togo which hosted the conference had observer status), delegates argued that there was a need in Central Africa to develop the types of instruments for settling border disputes and dealing with national catastrophes that West African states had already put into force.[22] The fact that Brazzaville served as a centre for negotiations on the Angolan/Namibian problem throughout 1988 indicated that regional actors were beginning to take a more direct role in the management of regional affairs. President Denis Sassou Nguesso of the Congo has certainly harboured major ambitions for his country as a diplomatic force in Central Africa.

Nevertheless, as with West Africa, the prospects appear better at the sub-regional level. The *Union Douanière et Économique de l'Afrique Centrale* (UDEAC), comprising Cameroon, the CAR, Congo, Gabon, Equatorial Guinea and Chad (as from December 1984) has many of the same purposes as the CEAO. Although it has made only limited advances towards economic integration of the sub-region, owing in part to the nationalistic aims of the stronger member states, the UDEAC could adopt some measures having a security dimension. While the Central African states fear less the imposing presence of Nigeria, which helped the francophone West African states to forget some of their differences and establish their own security system, there is no reason why, if Gabon, Cameroon and the Congo were to take the lead, a francophone system, with a clear geographic unity, could not evolve in Central Africa. However, such an organization would probably have little meaning unless Chad were to be affiliated with it.

Outside the UDEAC from 1968, Chad's reintegration at the end of 1984 was a sign that she sees her own problems as having a better chance of solution if they are considered with those of neighbouring states. Chad would certainly have to take part in any agreement similar to ANAD for Central Africa, given the important strategic role played by that country in the region. The various attempts in the mid-1980s by Denis Sassou Nguesso, to establish a round table of neighbouring states for the settlement of the Chad dispute could have been more easily realized if a diplomatic structure already existed amongst the Central African states whose defined purpose was the resolution of conflict. Of course, no regional security system in Africa in the forseeable future is likely to be able to prevent external aggression from taking place, but without formal structures for the discussion of security problems, even terminating a conflict by peaceful means at the regional level will be difficult. A permanent round table of UDEAC would have a far better chance of succeeding in the resolution of conflict than any *ad hoc* OAU committee, many of whose member states have little direct interest in the problems of the region.

Regional Security Structures and the Role of France

The network of defence and co-operation agreements maintained between France and the francophone African states is itself an important factor contributing to security within the states and in the region as a whole. The presence of French troops in Senegal, Ivory Coast, Gabon and the CAR helps to ensure that the governments of these countries are able to govern free from the risk of external attack. The French presence must also help to prevent internal upheavals in these countries. The French make a large and still irreplaceable contribution to regional security. At the request of the Africans, who may want to reduce certain types of bilateral links, the French have shown themselves prepared to give some aid directly to regional and sub-regional organizations. While institutions such as the ANAD were set up precisely in order to reduce dependence on external powers, some redirection of French aid to the secretariat may help speed the process. Since most of the countries concerned receive military and economic aid from France, aid given to multilateral security structures would not constitute a significant change in practice but it could foster a sense of regional responsibilities while helping to contain certain types of nationalist ambition. Beginning in 1985, some officials of the French Ministry of Co-operation started to have conversations with ANAD officials who wanted to strengthen the ANAD command structures, and French officials have showed themselves to be interested in giving material aid to integrated regional military units, but an organized programme of aid is distant.

The existence of the ANAD in no sense challenges French power on the continent. Its limited ability to serve as regional peace-maker even while France maintains close links with the member states is likely to assist France in management of its own obligations in West Africa. The institutionalization of a round table in Central Africa or of a fully-fledged defence organization would, equally, make it easier for France to handle its involvement in Chad and might even offer advantages to its own diplomacy in Southern Africa. France's diplomatic efforts to solve regional disputes throughout francophone Africa can only be facilitated by the existence of friendly organizations composed of states who, individually, still desire a bilateral relationship with France. Since that relationship will persist so long as the francophone states perceive a potential extra-regional threat to their security, and so long as the military agreements these states have with France are considered as part of a general policy of 'co-operation', nascent francophone security structures will help to diversify French influence more than dispel it.

Certainly this has been the case in the economic domain, where the development of regional economic organizations has been co-extensive with a continuing French policy of bilateral economic aid. Those regional economic organizations which exist have been developed in the context of an important French economic presence, and in the absence of French aid these structures would have to make important adjustments or even cease to exist. The pervasiveness of French technical and economic assistance in Black Africa guarantees a degree of continuing influence which France's military policy protects and embellishes. That military policy also has important civilian aspects: the training that France provides to African armies, the infrastructure work carried out in building roads and bridges, the medical units which are sometimes initially established by the armed forces, all serve to broaden the definition of military assistance. The security and territorial guarantee which French forces provide the states of Black Africa would, however, not carry much weight, and in certain cases might even be rejected, were it not for the economic aid France gives both to individual countries, and generally to that bloc of states which fall within the Franc Zone.

There is no public link between these two forms of aid, but for French state power to be maintained in francophone Africa, it has been thought necessary both to establish a practice of economic assistance, and to develop a broad concept, 'co-operation', to help sustain the idea that France belongs in Africa, and that it is natural for African states to acquiesce in that presence. These economic relations thus have their own logic, their own ideology and their own special history. This is also true of France's diplomatic practice in Africa. As in the military domain there is an important 'specificity' to French diplomatic activity in Africa. France's important influence on francophone Africa regional economic structures (through the mechanism of the Franc Zone) and her near replacement of certain African diplomatic forces (because of the enormous success of the Franco–African summit meetings), mean that France continues to have influence on both the bilateral and regional levels. France's economic and diplomatic weight on the continent will be an important determinant of francophone African stability and the cultivation of these roles, as well as of the justified impression of the relevance of French economic and diplomatic power to Africa since decolonization, will remain a constant of French external policy. This will be so even as pressures rise which make it more difficult for France to simply underwrite in economic and diplomatic (no less than in military) terms, the stability of African states.

7

French Economic Power and Black Africa

Since French overseas power was acquired in the service of French prestige and status – to satisfy a general will to grandeur rather than a specific need for riches – it was perhaps inevitable that the act of decolonization itself would not harm French economic interests. French imperial power rested on an ability to manage local structures and on the acceptance by native populations of French overseas rule. That power was not a function of the economic gain that France made from Empire, which as a rule cost, rather than earned, money. Throughout the French Empire France did have important economic interests, but Empire itself was not a means by which the French economy was strengthened. Even if the trade balance between France and her overseas territories would often appear strong, this was frequently compensated for by the transfer of public capital necessary to maintain even indirect rule.[1]

There were some periods of France's colonial history during which colonies were not a serious burden on the public purse. Trade, however, was not a vital pillar of French relations with her Empire, though trading activity and the efforts made to improve it were not entirely negligible. In the great period of colonial expansion between 1880 and 1913, French imports from the colonies (as a percentage of total imports) rose from 4.8 in 1880 to 9.4 in 1913, while exports to these areas as a percentage of total exports rose from 6.3 to 13 during the same period (see table 7.1).

Most of this activity centred on the main areas of France's 'first Empire': Algeria, the Antilles, Indochina and Senegal. In proportional terms, this corresponded to important increases, which were all the more valuable given that these markets (unlike those in continental Europe) were not subject to the potentially adverse affects of changing political circumstances. In Africa, most public expenditure in the latter part of this period was made to support the colonials in North Africa. Once these investments were made, imports

Table 7.1 Place of the empire in total French trade (millions of francs)

	Total imports	Imports from Empire	%	Total exports	Exports to Empire	%
1880	5033.2	244.6	4.8	3467.9	219.5	6.3
1890	4436.9	362.9	8.1	3753.5	296.1	7.8
1900	4697.8	363.6	7.7	4108.7	477.7	11.6
1913	8421.3	797.2	9.4	6880.2	894.8	13.0

Source: Jacques Marseilles, 'Les Relations Commerciales entre la France et Son Empire Colonial de 1880–1913', *Revue d'Histoire Moderne et Contemporaine*, April–June 1984, p. 288

Table 7.2 French exports of cottons and textile articles to the colonies (tons)

	1913	1937
Algeria	12,542	14,886
Tunisia	1,304	4,703
Morocco	462	376
AOF	876	8,707
Madagascar	3,378	5,368
Indochina	8,041	7,825

It is noteworthy that the Ministry of Foreign Affairs, in the case of Morocco, was unwilling to help the industry by forcing Morocco to give special treatment to French exports, a reluctance which inspired the anger of the Lille Chamber of Commerce.

Source: Jacques Marseille, *Empire Colonial et Capitalisme Français: Histoire d'un divorce*, Albin Michel, Paris, 1984, p. 195

of raw materials from this area became an increasingly important part of overall trade with Empire. In the period before the First World War, Empire held an interest both for the French state and some sectors of French industry. After the war, this began to decline and particularly after 1937–8, even if the state's political interest in colonies was high and would grow, the economic relevance of Empire to industrialists and financiers became less and eventually almost insignificant.[2]

In the mid- and the late 1930s some industrialists sought to take advantage of the economic bloc that the colonies offered them, and the French cotton industry was particularly successful in gaining access to markets, especially in Africa, at a time when those in Europe were beginning to close (table 7.2). But this case was special, and in the period immediately after the Second World War it was clear that because of the low degree of industrialization of the colonies, they could not buy what many industrialists needed to sell.

In 1948, the 'Plan for the modernization of overseas territories' declared that the 'Metropole should supply equipment and consumer goods while the territories should export to France primary materials: these are the respective missions of developed and young countries.'[3] But the fact of the matter was that this intended division of labour operated at a humble level of exchange. Furthermore, from the French perspective, it was not economically beneficial, both because the protected markets that did exist meant that certain sectors of French industry (like textiles) did not modernize as quickly as the world market situation required, and because often quite high prices were paid for imports from the colonies.

In the years leading to decolonization there was a growing realization that the withdrawal from overseas outposts would not seriously damage the French economy. In fact, many economic and financial administrators argued that the colonial market had not only become useless but was actually contributing to slowing the modernization of France's productive capacity. By and large, the struggle to hang on to overseas territories had little to do with economic considerations. For French relations with Africa, the political concepts of overseas power always overrode theories of economic necessity, just as the range and use of military power, which reflected political interests, was far out of proportion to the degree and importance of French economic interests in Africa. In those areas where France did have the most important investments at the time of decolonization there were naturally enormous efforts made to ensure that these would not be damaged by the sometimes vengeful politics of independence. Thus the 1962 Evian Agreements which brought an end to the Franco–Algerian war stipulated that French companies operating on Algerian territory 'would be guaranteed the normal exercise of their activities in conditions which would exclude any discrimination against them' and also that Algeria would 'provide for unhindered repatriation of earnings to France.'[4] Since 1962, French economic relations with North Africa, and Algeria in particular, have been substantial, and have often been held up – especially when France has paid above the market prices for raw materials such as Algerian gas – as an important example of successful pursuit of the North–South dialogue. Still, it could not be said that French economic relations with North Africa have become an integral part of French economic success. Nor have French leaders insisted that the 'privileged relations' that they feel exist between France and North Africa form part of an overall development strategy for the area.

In an examination of French power in Africa, the current nature of French economic policy towards Black Africa does, however, have some importance. This is not because of any special economic advantage that these countries bring to France. On the contrary, they are so poor as to offer no real direct economic benefit to France. Yet the economic relations that France has maintained with these countries since decolonization have not only been part of a general political strategy, they have been an element of continuing French state power in Black Africa. France's aid policy towards Black Africa has been presented to the (sometimes sceptical) public as a fundamental contribution to African stability. State structures have been developed (like the Ministry of Co-operation) whose principal responsibilities are to manage affairs with the ex-colonies of Black Africa. French economic aid to the countries of francophone Black Africa serves to balance the perhaps otherwise adverse local political effects of the deployment of French military power and helps to strengthen the hands of those members of the local political elite whose close connections with France are thought useful to the preservation of French influence.

It is important again in this context to underscore the fact that the francophone African states which are the objects of French economic assistance and development aid are generally weak. The political structures of these states, with some exceptions, are not strong enough to sustain long and well paced development policies, with specific projects carefully integrated into an ordered macro-economic design. There is equally an inherent sociological problem of inculcating new entrepreneurial attitudes both in the urban population and, further afield, in those working in the traditional agricultural sector. Generally, the gross domestic product of these countries is low and declining. Few Black African countries have developed an industrial capacity able to produce goods suitable for export. Many countries which were food exporters in the 1970s were by the early 1980s having to import food to meet basic needs. In 1980 the cereal production of sub-Saharan African states was 20 per cent lower than it was at the beginning of the 1970s.[5] African states continue to import (as a percentage of total imports), a tremendous volume of manufactured goods, while exporting (almost exclusively), primary products which are susceptible to major price variations. The dramatic fall in the price of cotton, for example, in 1985–6 and again in 1986–7, seriously affected the economies of Mali, Chad, Senegal, and Burkina Faso, just as the fall in oil prices in roughly the same period badly hurt Congo, Gabon and Cameroon.[6]

The major international aid agencies (World Bank, United Nations Development Programme) have sought, with difficulty, to facilitate a major transfer of resources to African countries and put in place increasingly precise sectoral development policies. France, who immediately after the independence of African countries gave bilateral support to francophone Africa, has more recently tried to co-ordinate her aid with that of the large agencies. In 1985, a Special Fund for Africa was created at the World Bank following a proposal made by France at a Franco–African summit meeting. French national lending bodies, such as the *Caisse Centrale de Coopération Économique* have made some efforts to ensure that aid goes for projects of which the international bodies would approve. Most of the francophone Black African states share economic problems with their anglophone and lusophone neighbours. It would be a mistake to suggest that the francophone countries have particular difficulties which are exclusive to them. However, the existence of the Franc Zone, which means that these countries have a common convertible currency (which *inter alia* ensures that they do not suffer the sort of hyperinflation so common among developing countries), and the tradition of bilateral aid provided by France, have created some order where otherwise there would be near total unpredictability. This has also created some dependence on France. Some forms of French aid, such as direct financial assistance for civil servants' salaries, involves France directly in the political economy of the African states to which she is closest. Despite the progressive multilateralization of aid to African countries, and the more frequent assertions (not always realistic) of political-economic independence by African states, France retains considerable control and influence on francophone Black African economies. Such influence is exercised through the numerous structures the French state has established to regulate France's aid and economic activity on the continent.

This chapter will therefore examine the state management of economic policy towards Black Africa since decolonization. In the future, it may well be that French regional power in the Mediterranean, and even more directly French security, will increasingly require France to ensure that her economic policy towards North Africa has a stabilizing influence. French security needs may push France towards again emphasizing relations with North Africa, developing policies to help insulate North Africa from external pressures which could bring governments hostile to France to power. There is a sense in which French policy towards the Maghreb since decolonization has been fashioned to preserve a continuing French interest in a peaceful Northern Africa. France's economic and diplomatic policy has been balanced, and every attempt has been made, against all odds, to remain on good terms, simultaneously, with Algeria, Tunisia and Morocco. But in the first three decades since decolonization, the idea of French power in Africa has been less related to a capacity to ensure that French metropolitan interests were not in danger in North Africa, than to a desire to foster development in the weakest area of the poorest continent where French power to control local events directly was still high. Thus, when French leaders speak of French development policy they invariably have in mind the specific aid packages negotiated with the Black African states who retain co-operation agreements with France.

France's economic policy towards francophone Black Africa has, in fact, formed part of an attempt to develop new measures of state power in the international system. The institutionalization of French aid to Black Africa has created a rhythm of French economic assistance, which in turn has reinforced loyalties between Black African leaders and France. The closeness of Franco–African relations thus nurtured has meant that francophone Black African leaders have been reluctant to turn to others for assistance. This basically bilateral relationship, despite its occasional burdens on France has generally helped French leaders to retain influence and, perhaps more important, a sense of enduring relevance and power. This chapter focuses, therefore, on the structures which make the management of French state economic power possible. The Ministry of Co-operation and the institutions related to the Franc Zone are the principal mechanisms for the exertion of French economic influence in Black Africa. Their management and the arguments deployed in favour of their continued existence have become a basic element of French power in Africa. Equally, while the francophone African states have begun to erect increasingly sophisticated stuctures for the management of regional economic relations, these can still be directly affected by French economic policy.

All would accept that France's economic and narrow strategic interests are probably more directly engaged in North Africa than they are in Black Africa. But since notions of French African power now only carry weight south of the Sahara, it is only in that area that France has developed anything approaching an economic strategy. Just as at the time of Empire, France has in the post-colonial world engaged her economy in Black Africa only minimally, but the economic factor in explaining French power has not been ignored. In the nineteenth century French imperialists argued that Africa was an important outlet for French commerce; in the late twentieth century, and mainly in respect of Black Africa, statesmen have insisted that development policy towards Africa helps to maintain French influence and status. Arguments based on economic questions have been affected by the appreciations and the sensitivities of the times, but they have been marshalled always to support a rationale for further state involvement. What is remarkable about French economic policy towards Black Africa since decolonization is less the volume of the transfers that take place, than the sophistication of the bureaucracy developed to bolster a policy which, while of clear help to the Africans, has also been substantially in the service of modernized concepts of French overseas prestige.

The Ministry of Co-operation and the Ideology of French Aid

President de Gaulle raised the idea of 'co-operation' to a principle of French foreign policy. It was a word and a programme with special relevance to the independent states of francophone Black Africa which had signed agreee-ments with France. The system of 'co-operation' (which others would less warmly but more accurately call 'aid') was intended to regulate the post-colonial system of *France-Afrique*. Since relations with Black Africa were run according to a particular juridical regime, and since Black Africa was to have a specific place in French foreign policy – because the French and Black African leadership both wished this to be the case – it was inevitable that an institution be created to supervise and manage the Franco–African relationship.

The Ministry of Co-operation was established with this in mind, though while it has prime responsibility for managing the co-operation agreements between France and Black African states, several other ministries, organiza-tions and personalities, not least the specialist African advisers at the Elysée, have an important say in policy for Africa. Still, the Ministry of Co-operation, which was created by government decree in 1961, with the dissolution of the structures of the French Community, was intentionally kept separate from the Ministry of Foreign Affairs, partly because it was thought wise to underscore the special relationship between France and Black Africa in this way. Certainly the leaders of francophone Black Africa wanted 'their' Ministry in Paris, to which direct appeal could be made in the event of some bilateral problem. Affectionately known to Black Africans by its address on 'Rue Monsieur', the Ministry of Co-operation has had a shifting, and not always easy relationship with the Quai d'Orsay (and in the early years with the secretariat responsible for African and Malagasy affairs attached to the Elysée), but remains one of the more important focal points of policy development for Black Africa.

Initially, the Ministry was created with special responsibilities for all the ex-colonies of the AOF and the AEF (with the exception of Guinea which had signed no co-operation agreement with France), but it has expanded its field of action over the years as co-operation agreements have been signed with other states in Africa. The history of the Ministry is at least a partial reflection of the general history of Franco–African relations since decolonization for, as we have seen, changes in the scope and substance of the co-operation agreements have followed new directions in policy initiated either by the French president or by Black African states. While the whole of France's policy of co-operation with Black Africa (military, economic, financial and cultural) has followed a centrally directed grand strategy, the economic aspect of this co-operation has been affected by a specific ideology. This is in part because various governments have commissioned development aid reports which have set out the broad goals of economic policy towards the countries falling under the responsibility of the Ministry of Co-operation, and in part because most governments have seen in development aid policy the linchpin of Franco-African relations, even though military policy often, necessarily, attracted more attention.

The Jeanneney Report

In 1963, the first of these reports was commissioned by the French state minister in charge of administrative reform (Louis Joxe) with a view to determining what changes might be needed in the structure and goals of a French policy of co-operation. Edited on the basis of a number of individual studies, the report was published in 1964 under the name of Jean-Marcel Jeanneney, president of the commission charged with drafting the report. Entitled *La Politique de Coopération avec les pays en voie de développement*, the report appeared the same year that *cartierisme* (the view that all development aid was wasted) was beginning to gather some support in Parisian intellectual circles. The report's conclusion, that the Ministry of Co-operation should be abolished and replaced by a whole series of other administrative structures with broadly the same purpose, was thought so curious that it was not published. The report suggested the establishment of a High Commission, an interministerial committee, a special treasury and a council for co-operation as well as a personnel agency to manage the work of technical advisers overseas. This would only have complicated a bureaucracy which many already thought overly cumbersome.[7] Despite the commission's view, which was not acted upon, that there should be some changes in the structures of co-operation, the report as a whole was largely in favour of the policy of co-operation which had only recently been instituted. Its importance lies in the fact that, as an explanation and justification of the Gaullist policy of co-operation, it effectively summarized both the ideology and purposes of aid policy. It did so drawing on well-worn notions of the purposes of French external policy. After arguing that 'human solidarity'

Table 7.3 Net public aid to development as a percentage of GNP

	1960	1961	1962	1963	1964	1965	1966	1967	1968	1969	1970
Australia	0.38	0.44	0.43	0.51	0.48	0.53	0.53	0.60	0.57	0.56	0.59
Austria	0.04	0.03	0.05	0.08	0.11	0.12	0.14	0.14	0.11	0.07	
Belgium	0.88	0.76	0.54	0.57	0.46	0.60	0.42	0.45	0.42	0.50	0.46
Canada	0.19	0.16	0.09	0.15	0.17	0.19	0.33	0.32	0.26	0.33	0.42
Denmark	0.09	0.12	0.10	0.11	0.11	0.13	0.19	0.21	0.23	0.38	0.38
France	1.38	1.35	1.27	0.98	0.90	0.76	0.69	0.71	0.67	0.67	0.66
Germany	0.31	0.44	0.45	0.41	0.44	0.40	0.34	0.41	0.41	0.38	0.32
Italy	0.22	0.15	0.18	0.14	0.09	0.10	0.12	0.22	0.19	0.16	0.16
Japan	0.24	0.21	0.14	0.20	0.14	0.27	0.28	0.31	0.25	0.26	0.23
Neth'lands	0.31	0.45	0.49	0.26	0.29	0.36	0.45	0.49	0.49	0.50	0.61
Norway	0.11	0.14	0.14	0.17	0.15	0.16	0.18	0.17	0.29	0.30	0.32
Portugal	1.45	1.73	1.26	1.46	1.48	0.59	0.54	0.54	0.54	1.29	0.67
Sweden	0.05	0.06	0.12	0.14	0.18	0.19	0.25	0.25	0.28	0.43	0.38
Swit'land	0.06	0.08	0.05	0.05	0.07	0.09	0.09	0.08	0.14	0.16	0.15
UK	056	0.59	0.52	0.48	0.53	0.47	0.45	0.44	0.40	0.39	0.37
USA	0.53	0.56	0.56	0.59	0.56	0.49	0.44	0.43	0.37	0.33	0.31
Total of CAD Countries	0.52	0.53	0.52	0.51	0.48	0.44	0.41	0.42	0.37	0.36	0.34

Source: French memorandum to the Committee for Aid and Development of the OECD, reproduced in Brigitte Nouaille-Degorce, 'Les Structures et les Moyens de la Politique de Coopération avec les Etats Africains et Malgache au sud du Sahara de 1958 a 1969', in Institut Charles de Gaulle and Centre d'Etude d'Afrique Noire, *La Politique Africaine du Général de Gaulle 1958–1969*, Editions A. Pédone, Paris, 1980, p. 89

required any French government to come to the aid of economically weak countries it emphasized that such aid was also necessary for the *rayonnement* of France:

Never in the course of her history has France resigned herself within her own borders; she has always shown the need to act well outside the hexagon. If she does not satisfy this inclination, she risks diminishing herself and suffering boredom. A *rayonnement* is necessary, which should be the work of men ready to expatriate themselves, and of a universalist culture.[8]

These basic sentiments were coupled with the assertion that aid policy would be useful to France in order to gain the diplomatic support of the developing countries:

France's potential for diplomatic action, whether in regional arrangements or in the debates within global conferences, will depend in part on the relations that she will have been able to sustain with developing countries.[9]

The report underscored that French public aid to the developing countries as a proportion of GNP was very high in comparison to that of other developed countries who were members of the Committee of Aid and Development (CAD) of the OECD but it emphasized the need to increase this aid. While French aid remained high in comparative terms it continued the decline begun in 1960. During the Gaullist period it nevertheless declined at a slower pace than was the case for the other major economic powers. Some of the smaller European powers during this period actually increased aid, but still not to the level of France. The only other member of the CAD that gave a higher proportion of its GNP to countries in the developing world was Portugal, which still had important colonial commitments in Africa (table 7.3).

Neither the administrative reforms nor the large increase in public aid called for by the report were taken up by the relevant authorities. Yet the direction and form of French development aid during this period did follow the implicit recommendations of the Jeanneney Report. First, that aid was concentrated on francophone Black Africa and was largely dispensed by the Ministry of Co-operation (between 1966 and 1974 and 1981 and 1986 this Ministry was not entirely independent of the Quai d'Orsay) having primary responsibility for the countries which had signed co-operation agreements with France. Most funds were disbursed through the *Fonds d'Aide et de Coopération* (FAC), created in 1959 and linked to Co-operation rather than to the Treasury. Loans and credit advances were organized by the *Caisse*

Centrale de Coopération Économique (CCCE) whose responsibilities only extended to those countries having signed co-operation agreements. The instruments for aid to Africa thus remained specific and essentially separate from those for all other developing countries.

The Jeanneney Report had argued that francophone Black Africa should receive priority though it should not have exclusive status. While there were always those who recommended that France should disperse her aid more widely, there evolved a broad consensus that while ideally French aid policy should be far-reaching, in practice it was only possible to have an effect in francophone Black Africa. Even de Gaulle, following a trip to Latin America in 1964, began to suggest that French aid policy should be extended to that continent, but his mind was changed by Jacques Foccart, the Secretary-General for African and Malagasy Affairs at the Elysée, who successfully argued that resources had to be centred on francophone Africa, where the political benefits of co-operation were most clearly evident.

Strong emphasis was maintained on bilateral rather than multilateral forms of aid. The Jeanneney Report had argued that in areas where France was not concentrating much aid, that aid should be co-ordinated with other actors, but implicitly accepted the inevitability of a bilateral approach for the African states closest to France. The fact that many of these countries became associated to the European Community did mean that for a time other European states were contributing to the development in Africa of francophone states. Initially no anglophone state was part of the arrangements arrived at after the 1963 Yaoundé Convention which established the conditions for EEC aid to Africa, a fact which contributed somewhat to the regional divisions between anglophone and francophone states. France clearly benefited from this insofar as some of the francophone states used EEC aid to buy products from France. The French policy of co-operation, which had clear political ends, operated in any case to perpetuate the African attachment to France. Certainly the preference for placing French state advisers in the administrations of developing countries reinforced pre-existing Black African tendencies to look towards the ex-metropolitan power for assistance.

The French doctrine of co-operation, as first practised, had several distinct characteristics.[10] Technical assistance was initially interpreted to mean direct administrative or highly skilled work by French professionals. Only very slowly was a policy of administrative substitution replaced by a training policy of African cadres and youth. For some years, French advisers effectively maintained the state apparatus of several African states. Even in the late 1980s, there are a few states, notably the Central African Republic, whose civil service is still run to a considerable degree by seconded French administrators responsible to the Ministry of Co-operation. Progressively, ministers in charge of co-operation policy (often at the demand of African states), have withdrawn technical advisers in favour of teachers and trainers who concentrated on strengthening the local system of education. From 1960 to 1969 there was a dramatic change in the numbers of those technical assistants who were teachers, and those who worked in all other sectors.

Table 7.4 Responsibilities of technical assistants of Ministry of Co-operation 1960–1969

	Teaching	Other Sectors	Total
1960	2,416	7,666	10,082
1961	2,794	5,890	8,684
1962	3,233	5,320	8,553
1963	4,040	4,709	8,749
1964	4,675	4,508	9,183
1965	5,182	4,268	9,450
1966	5,517	4,372	9,889
1967	6,121	4,248	10,369
1968	6,502	4,167	10,669
1969	6,274	3,880	10,154

Source: Ministry of Co-operation, Paris, France, cited in Brigitte Nouaille-Degorce, 'Les Structures et Les Moyens', p. 97

In 1960, slightly over 20 per cent of technical assistants were teachers, while by 1969 almost 60 per cent of the 'cooperants' were involved in teaching (table 6.4). Nevertheless, French 'cooperants' continue to play an important internal role in the administrations and bureaucracies of many African states. Just as French military technical assistants responsible to the Ministry of Co-operation play a direct role in some of the armed forces (wearing the uniform of the African country to which they are attached) so do civilian 'cooperants' occupy important administrative positions.

Great efforts have always been made by those directly concerned to emphasize the disinterested and apolitical nature of this type of aid. There are naturally occasions when French interests are inevitably strengthened simply by the presence of French nationals in the bureaucracies of these countries. But there are many in France who have wished to stress the technical aspect of French assistance and have therefore regretted attempts to make co-operation policy a part of foreign policy. In 1966 a French administrative reform did just that, by subordinating the Ministry of Co-operation to the Ministry of Foreign Affairs. A new *Secrétariat d'Etat aux affaires étrangères chargé de coopération* was created which exercised the same powers as did the former Ministry but these were delegated from the Ministry of Foreign Affairs. Among other things, this had the effect of forcing debates on the budget for co-operation in parliament at the same time as debates on the budget for foreign affairs. Africans were displeased with a corresponding loss of special status. As reviewed below, the status of 'co-operation' within the French government has since gone back and forth. Sometimes its activities have been subordinated to those of the Quai, sometimes it has had a completely independent position.

By the end of the Gaullist period after nearly ten years of co-operation and changes in the structures which managed French aid to Africa, the outlines of a continuing debate on co-operation had been drawn. Should that aid be aimed more to improve local structures? What should be the proportion of gifts to loans? What political aims were acceptable as part of a general co-operation policy? Should that aid become more multilateral? Should francophone Africa have a special status or should a development policy be created with relevance for numerous areas in the Third World? Subsequent presidents and ministers developed their own answers to these questions, and the aid reports produced under different administrations as well as the political debates which centred on Franco–African relations helped to shape the current structure of co-operation policy, which is still, nevertheless, affected by many of the old questions.

Gorse and Abelin Reports

In 1971 a French overseas administrator, Georges Gorse, tried to address some of these issues in a report which assessed the first decade of co-operation. It has remained unpublished though many of its conclusions have been widely and openly discussed. This new government report played down the role of co-operation in the perpetuation of French *rayonnement* and argued for some rethinking of French foreign aid to anglophone Africa. While the states of francophone Africa would have to remain the major recipients of aid and public aid to them should increase, the report also insisted that it was wrong to perpetuate the colonial divisions and act as if the anglophone states of Africa did not exist.[11] A lower proportion of aid should go to the departments and territories overseas to provide more funds for Black Africa. But the nature of this aid had to improve. The report was relatively harsh on some of the previous practices of co-operation, stating that in the past much aid had been badly applied and that there was a special need to assist rural development, industrialization, education and improved understanding of evolving demographic conditions. Also France had to internationalize her policy of co-operation. The Gorse report recommended increases of French contributions to the United Nations Development Programme, the International Association for Development, the Asian Development Bank as well as the Interamerican Bank, but still argued in favour of a bilateral aid policy for Africa.[12]

It is perhaps not surprising that these sometimes contradictory policy suggestions were not formally taken up by the Pompidou government. The Gorse Report's arguments reflected the complexity of the French debate on co-operation which has traditionally mixed political with technical considerations, images of grandeur with descriptions of the mechanisms for development policy. While the Pompidou government did try to make some shifts in a co-operation programme which still sought to remain faithful to basic Gaullist principles, both the form and substance of co-operation policy were eventually shaped more by external events than by positive decisions taken either at the Quai d'Orsay or Rue Monsieur. Pompidou leaned towards a more open policy for the anglophone states if only because he saw economic advantages in improving relations with countries like Nigeria and Kenya which potentially had more to offer France. At least in his declaratory policy he showed no political anxiety about other states beginning to help francophone Africa. In a speech he made in Cameroon on his first official trip to Africa in 1971 he said that 'to be the first among others is in any case more efficient and more durable than to be alone.'[13]

The creation of a distinct policy towards francophone Africa in the Pompidou period was affected on the one hand by the entry of the United Kingdom into the European Common Market and on the other by the general revision made in the co-operation agreements with Black Africa on African request. First, UK entry into the EEC meant that some of the anglophone African countries would begin to benefit from the aid disbursed by the Community. This would inevitably affect the nascent French aim to begin to penetrate these new areas. It also meant that some francophone African countries began to reduce their exports to France as they began to discover other European markets. A February 1974 report to the *Conseil Economique et Social* of the French parliament underscored the consequent need to maintain an important level of bilateral aid to the francophone countries even though it was inevitable that French participation in the multilateral structures of the Community would also rise.[14] Second, the need to renegotiate the co-operation agreements made French policy somewhat reactive at the end of the Pompidou period. In 1972 and 1973, the

French press was full of descriptions of the consequent 'crisis' in which French co-operation policy found itself. In fact, as we have seen in the military domain, changes were made in the agreements with considerable ease. None of these changes had a very substantial effect on the nature of aid given by France to those who still remained within the system.

However, in March 1974, the Minister for Foreign Affairs, Michel Jobert announced that there would be no separate structure for co-operation and that the work previously done by the secretariat would now be done by the Quai. He explained that 'this suppression was made in response to certain governmental requirements and to take account of the evolution of the modern world. It is necessary that France's foreign policy has the same face for all, even if that face is particularly friendly for some countries.'[15] This reform, which led to considerable disquiet among Black African states and caused President Senghor of Senegal to lament a possible disengagement of France from Africa and the beginning of the dismantling of French co-operation policy, was of little practical effect, since when Valery Giscard d'Estaing came to power in May 1974 he immediately reinstated a full Ministry of Cooperation. His parallel decision to eliminate the *Secrétariat général aux affaires africaines et malgaches* at the Elysée Palace (formerly run by Jacques Foccart), also strengthened the relative position of the Minister of Co-operation even though Giscard retained a personal adviser on Africa at the Palace.

The new Minister for Co-operation, Pierre Abelin, also authored the principal aid report of the Giscard administration which was published in 1975 and was intended to map out a modernized and more active co-operation policy. The report opened by defining three broad principles:

Principle of the universality of the French policy of aid to development; principle of the geographical limits of a privileged zone of co-operation; principle of the respect for sovereign choices made by the countries who are our partners: these are the three principles on which we should rest to enquire about the present and prepare the future of our policy of co-operation.[16]

The Abelin Report was published in the same year that the European Community signed the first Lomé accord with the African, Caribbean and Pacific (ACP) states which brought fifty-three states together and marked an important advance in European development policy. French editorialists, in the year before this major agreement was signed, speculated on the role for France in the middle of this new 'Eurafrican' enterprise. In September 1974 *Le Monde* had declared:

A policy of co-operation with Africa is in the interest of France, in particular for the extension of our language and of our influence. It is also in the interest of Europe which has in Africa at once a territory for common action and a geographic complement ... French–African co-operation placed in this broader context of solidarity between peoples on a regional level, as on the global level, can and should remain an essential element of French policy and of the dreams of young French-men.[17]

The broad recommendations of the Abelin Report were made in this spirit. It made clear that francophone states of Africa (whether former French or Belgian colonies) would be the preferred targets of aid. Any 'opening' to anglophone states of Africa, or to other continents would be a consequence of a new French willingness to participate in economic arrangements and projects formulated by the EEC, or by agencies of the United Nations, rather than of a very great expansion of bilateral aid programmes. The report brushed aside the evils both of neocolonialism and *cartierisme* and argued that Africa had to become a principal partner of Europe. Ideally, European involvement in Africa would become: 'a fundamental element of stability of a new *ensemble* linked by trade relations and reciprocity which would include, according to the vision of President L.S. Senghor, Western Europe, the Mediterranean and the African continent in its entirety.'[18] The report therefore emphasized that France's co-operation policy had to make some contribution to the evolving new international economic order. It was important to keep up the still high level of teaching aid, but also to make more advances in promoting industrial development in Africa. The report made few precise suggestions as to how this would be done, though it did make a recommendation for the establishment of a centre of research and innovation to help Africans industrialize. Like most of the other French official statements on aid, the Abelin Report was more important for the context in which it placed co-operation policy rather than for the proposals it made to improve its practice. In the event, the Giscard administration was marked by a considerable opening to the ex-Belgian colonies, and by efforts to improve the nature of project-related aid. It was also characterized, as will be seen in the next chapter, by large visions for new forms of co-operation between the African and European continents. The arrival of the socialists to power in 1981 resulted in an intensification of the debate on the purposes and form of aid policy, which eventually, particularly in the brief period of *cohabitation* between March 1986 and May 1988, brought French aid policy back to some basic Gaullist principles.

The Debates of the Mitterrand Presidency

The pre-election document of the Socialist Party criticized the Giscardian policy of co-operation on the grounds that it had become excessively mercantile. The relative weight of the credits given out by the *Fonds d'Aide et de Coopération* had declined in favour of the loans granted by the *Caisse centrale de coopération economique* to strengthen private firms. The poorer countries in Africa, the socialists argued, had been relatively ignored by French leaders more interested in a return on their investment than on a true policy of development.[19] The report argued that it was vital for France to broaden her aid policy considerably not only within the African continent but also beyond to other regions of the Third World. Aid should be directed towards the relief of misery, and should be indifferent to the political orientations of the donor state: only racist regimes (South Africa) could be excluded from a socialist co-operation policy. While the right-wing governments of the Fifth Republic had also centralized aid policy, putting it in the hands of two or three important state organizations and a few influential individuals, a socialist government would open up co-operation policy to Frenchmen as a whole, first by involving other government departments, second by encouraging action by trade unions and professional associations and finally by involving non-governmental associations. Increasingly, French aid would have to take on a multilateral aspect, through the European Community as well as the various UN agencies.[20]

Once in power the socialist administration sought to emphasize the globalization of French co-operation policy and the preference for a multilateral approach. Aid also was to be granted in order to encourage self-sufficiency in agriculture and the growth of small enterprises. Very quickly, and much to the annoyance of the francophone African leaders closest to France, the new leadership opened up contacts with progressive African states and to those outside the francophone *pré carré*. Symbolizing its new approach to co-operation the new government renamed the Quai d'Orsay the Ministry for External Relations and made the head of co-operation policy a *ministre délégué pour la coopération et du développement auprès du ministre des relations extérieures* thus eliminating the Ministry of Co-operation and placing its work under the authority of the Quai as had been the case from 1966 to 1974.

The architect of the new policy of co-operation (now officially incorporating for the first time the concept of 'development'), Jean Pierre Cot, had eighteen months in power as the new minister in charge of co-operation policy, and during that period inspired an important public debate on the form and purposes of French co-operation. His forced resignation in

December 1983 ('demanded' by a number of conservative African leaders), showed the influence that African states could still have on the formation of France's African policy, but more importantly, proved that the rhythm of Franco–African relations could not be easily changed. The declaratory and practical policies of Cot's new *tiers mondisme* ultimately had to be brought into line with long-standing political interests in francophone Africa.

While recognizing the importance of the historical links between France and francophone Africa as well as the inevitable need for bilateral assistance Cot unsuccessfully stressed the need to move away from these traditions. In the book he published on his experiences some time after his resignation he argued that one had to be worried about the fact that:

The accusation of neocolonialism [sticks] and threatens eventually to compromise a policy of solidarity towards the Third World. By maintaining an imperialist vision of our relationship with Africa, we may be reassuring some of today's friends, but we compromise our possibilities of action tomorrow ... Finally we must not forget Europe in our African enterprises. Europe's ambition is defined by the Lomé space, that is all of Africa... To take full advantage of this we must identify ourselves with the Lomé space and not let it be believed that we are using the construction of Europe as a useful way to complement the financing of our former Empire.[21]

Cot was not in power long enough to put his ideas into practice. During his tenure, credits for rural development went up slightly just as those for infrastructure declined, and some French non-governmental organizations did have increased opportunities to play a larger role in Africa. The enduring effect of Cot's brief tenure of office was the widening of the boundaries of the old debates on co-operation policy to include such issues as human rights and the moral aspects of development policy. On his departure, French co-operation policy began to centre a little more on the old francophone African *chasse gardée*. The new minister, Christian Nucci, developed no new lines of policy, though he was accused, after leaving office, of having been involved in the misappropriation of development funds. Generally, the thrust of France's Africa policy, including aspects of co-operation policy, was led from the Elysée and managed by Mitterrand's principal African adviser, Guy Penne.

When the March 1986 legislative elections brought in a right-wing government under Jacques Chirac, a different ideological approach was taken in France's co-operation policy. Again, a full Ministry of Co-operation was restored, and the new arrival to Rue Monsieur, Michel Aurillac, began to put in place a much more liberal policy drawing on a pre-election document that he had helped to draft for the Gaullist party of Jacques Chirac, the RPR. Its language brought back the confident imagery of the Gaullist years and re-established the primacy of Africa in the French scheme of Third World development:

Cooperation is for France a vocation. It is a natural dimension of her foreign policy. Having conducted to independence or to autonomy the states and territories which we opened up to Western civilization, France engaged herself, when they wished it, to help them to develop and to avoid disorder or totalitarian illusions. This philosophy of General de Gaulle is still relevant. It continues to inspire our policy and situates it at the other end of socialist conceptions viscerally motivated by an outdated ideology.[22]

The report argued for the importance of bilateral aid, the need to reduce the role of the state, the consequent value in encouraging private initiatives, and the importance of encouraging better conditions for trade. A new co-operation policy would emphasize aid to agriculture without ignoring the need for improved industrialization. The report called for the reinforcement of the main institutions of co-operation policy linked in different ways to the Ministry of Co-operation: the *Fonds d'Aide et de Coopération* (FAC), the *Caisse Centrale de Coopération Économique* (CCCE), and the Franc Zone. Once in power, the new government sought to make immediate increases in the amount of aid given, promising to reach a figure of 0.54 per cent of GNP in public aid (up from 0.52 per cent in 1986) and to make more money available to the FAC (whose budget of 1.5 billion (10^9) francs in 1988 was up 30 per cent from the previous year and 48 per cent from 1986) thus raising the percentage of gifts as compared to loans in French public aid. Lamenting the fact that less than 1 per cent of French foreign investment found its way to Africa, the Ministry sought to encourage French and African companies to co-operate more. To this end, a large conference of more than 700 people was held in January 1987 in Libreville bringing together French and African industrialists in the presence of ministers from twenty-six African countries. This meeting was widely criticized as an unrealistic attempt to convince French business of the value of investing in Africa at a time when the more experienced among them had come to a different conclusion. It was also derided by those who felt that there just were not enough African enterprises with whom French business could develop serious joint ventures.

In the slightly over two years that the Aurillac Ministry ran French co-operation it nevertheless succeeded in reasserting the special importance of francophone Africa in French aid policy, even as it built on certain links established by previous governments in lusophone and even anglophone Africa. The very different declaratory policies engaged in by Cot and

Aurillac, which represent the outer boundaries within which future governments will manoeuvre in developing a French co-operation policy, pointed
to the sometimes highly politicized nature of the French debate on co-
operation. Despite this tendency towards polemic, which did not result in
truly dramatic changes in policy, it remains the case that the many institutions
that effectively manage French–African economic relations, notably the
Franc Zone monetary system, assure a basic continuity of French–African
economic exchanges.

Not all the instruments of French economic relations with Africa, as we
have seen, are naturally resilient to the changing priorities of politicians, but
the system is so elaborate that deep and drastic changes in policy would be
required before the basic economic relationship between France and Africa
was changed. When the government of Michel Rocard assumed power in
mid-1988, the new Minister for Co-operation M. Jacques Pelletier argued
that it was impossible for France to abandon the 'mission' in Africa which it
had pursued for thirty-nine years. He underlined, however, that a good deal
of French aid would have to go to help the process of structural adjustment
in these countries, and that this aid would, *inter alia*, assure that the World
Bank and the IMF were not the sole 'masters of the game' in Africa.[23]
Maintaining a special economic relationship therefore remained an important political priority. That relationship depends on the various institutions
that disburse aid, but is primarily conditioned by the existence and management of the Franc Zone itself which assures a basic continuity in the nature
of economic co-operation between the member states.

The Institutions of French Aid and the Franc Zone

The existence of an independent organization for co-operation with the
states that have signed agreements with France creates an extra tool for the
promotion of a specific external policy towards these states, primarily still
the states of francophone Black Africa.

States falling under the jurisdiction of the Ministry of Co-operation
Angola, Benin, Burkina Faso, Burundi, Cameroon, Cap Vert, Central
African Republic, Chad, Comores, Congo, Djibouti, Equatorial
Guinea, Gabon, Gambia, Guinea, Guinea Bissau, Haiti, Iles au Vent
(Sainte-Lucie, Dominique, Grenade, Saint Vincent), Ivory Coast, Mada-
gascar, Mali, Mauritania, Mauritius, Mozambique, Niger, Rwanda, Sao
Tomé, Senegal, Seychelles, Togo, Zaire.

States which are members of the Franc Zone
Benin, Burkina Faso, Cameroon, Central African Republic, Chad,
Congo, Comoro Islands (Comoro Franc), Equatorial Guinea, Gabon,
Ivory Coast, Mali, Niger, Senegal, Togo.

The over 7,500 French 'coopérants' who work in these countries as teachers
or technical advisers linked to the Ministry of Co-operation implicitly
reinforce the utility of a close link to France. Black African leaders, many of
whom may choose to deal directly with the Elysée Palace, are in any case
aware that in the Ministry of Co-operation they have another *interlocuteur
valable* who is able to take their case to the president or prime minister. In
several senses, an independent Ministry of Co-operation is able to reinforce
the political interdependence between France and Africa.[24] The various
organizations that disburse financial aid, in different forms, to the states of
Black Africa, each of which has a slightly different relationship to the
Ministry of Co-operation, effectively direct a discrete aspect of Franco–
African economic relations which makes these relations less amenable to
dramatic change. They also, however, make these relations more difficult to
manage. Each has their own perspective, and each their own priorities. The
complaint by French leaders in colonial times that there was no one
organization responsible for overseas policy has its modern equivalent in the
sometimes exasperating complexity of relationships between the Paris-based
bureaucracies which have some role in France's economic relationship with
Africa.

While the primacy of the Ministry of Co-operation is beginning to
decline given the increasingly important role played by the Treasury, it is
evident that as the main deployer of personnel to Africa it has a relatively
privileged position. The technical assistance provided by the Ministry of
Co-operation guarantees a continuity of French presence in Africa. Also
important is the direct financial assistance (in 1988, 875 million francs) it
offers to support state structures in Africa and the payment of civil service
salaries. This gives it some direct influence in African affairs. Much of
France's development assistance to Africa is managed through the FAC, and
for the African states, the FAC is clearly the most important instrument of
financial aid, though the funds it disburses only amount to about 4–5 per
cent of all public aid given by France. Its budget has been in relative decline
since the early 1970s, though it was give a major boost in 1987–8. The FAC
disburses only loans, and falls under the responsibility of the Minister of
Co-operation even though it has a reporting obligation to the Ministry of
Finance. Its assistance has been traditionally concentrated on rural development and infrastructure projects with the rest of its funds going to support
teaching and training, health, cultural activities and information, and

industrial development. It has been criticized for not following through project aid sufficiently and for not having an overall development design for the African states to which it has given funds.

Of the structures managing French assistance to Africa the *Caisse Centrale de Coopération Économique* (CCCE) has remained most independent. It was founded in London in December 1941 as the *Caisse centrale de la France libre*. It was the treasury and the central bank for what became de Gaulle's *Comité Française de Libération Nationale* (CFLN). After 1944, and until 1958 when it took on its present name, it was the *Caisse centrale de la France d'outre-mer*.[25] The CCCE participated in the creation of a number of central banks and development banks in francophone Africa. It is responsible both to the Ministry of Co-operation and to the Ministry of Finance, but has a supervisory committee that is composed of individuals from the public and private sectors. It covers all the countries dealt with by the Ministry of Co-operation and a handful of others which the Ministry of Foreign Affairs has asked it to deal with, notably, but not only, the states of North Africa and Egypt.

The CCCE gives out loans and makes investments. To encourage the creation of medium-sized enterprises in developing countries it created a subsidiary in 1977, the *Société de Promotion et de Participation Pour La Coopération Économique* (PROPARCO), which provides technical assistance to companies. The agencies of the CCCE in the various countries in which it operates advise on the projects that might be financed and these are examined by a central projects committee in Paris. In 1986 the CCCE gave out about 2.5 billion francs in loans at extremely low rates of interest varying from 1.5 to 4.5 per cent. for a wide range of projects. Often, French companies will be involved in some of the work related to these projects, though local companies are supported where possible. The CCCE funds are provided largely by the Treasury, but it also borrows from the international market to finance its operations. While the Elysée, Matignon, Quai'd'Orsay or Coopération might seek gently to encourage it to begin working more, or less, in a given country, it has succeeded generally in insulating itself from pressures of this kind.

The CCCE was originally conceived to support the financing of large projects intended to turn a profit, providing investment financing for equipment and infrastructure. It has also supported various types of agricultural programmes. Typical projects which have attracted *Caisse* monies include, for example, the development of a palm-oil complex in the Congo, rubber plantations in Gabon, improvements in Chad's cotton industry and the development of a village water supply system in the countries of the *Conseil de l'Entente*. It continues to see these sorts of development projects as its primary aim, but by the mid-1980s it began to provide more structural adjustment aid. The *Caisse* has shown itself willing to give out non-project-related loans to countries suffering particular cash problems, but tends to do this in close consultation with the World Bank as well as the IMF, and seeks to ensure that such aid is given to countries engaged in economic reform or financial rehabilitation programmes approved by international lending institutions.

The work of all these institutions would be very different in character were it not for the existence of the Franc Zone. The Franc Zone links France to the African countries that are members of it in a way which ensures a basic monetary stability, and enables more effective use of the aid provided by France and also creates a solid base for regional trade between Franc Zone members. The creation of the Franc Zone has its origins in the protectionist policies introduced by France in her colonial Empire in the 1930s as a result of the economic recession. During this period only one currency was used in the African Empire and the Antilles which was directly linked to the franc. The structure was strengthened during the Second World War when the *Caisse centrale de la France libre* controlled the distribution of currency to the AEF. After the war, various 'colonial francs' were created, and by 1955 the main features of the system were in place.[26] The establishment of the French Community structure in 1958 saw the enactment of the main pieces of legislation governing the Franc Zone. A number of countries chose to leave the monetary zone immediately or soon after independence, such as Indochina, the states of the Maghreb and Guinea.[27] Mauritania and Madagascar pulled out in 1973, though Mali which had left in 1962, and demanded re-entry in 1967, was finally totally reintegrated in 1984.[28] The changing history of the Franc Zone membership, and most particularly the fact that states have re-entered and others, foreign to the system, have asked to be admitted, is itself testimony to the fact that despite the evident limits that membership places on the freedom to develop individual monetary policies, the system's stabilizing function is appreciated.

The Franc Zone and Regional Co-operation in Francophone Africa

There are fourteen members of the Franc Zone in Africa and the Indian Ocean. In West Africa, Benin, Burkina Faso, Ivory Coast, Mali, Senegal and Togo are members and form part of the *Union monétaire ouest africaine* (UMOA) created on 12 March 1962. They have given over to the *Banque centrale des états de l'Afrique de l'Ouest* (BCEAO) the power to manage their common currency. Five central African states, Cameroon, Central African Republic, Chad, Congo and Gabon, were in 1985 joined by Equatorial Guinea, now also member of the *Union monétaire d'Afrique centrale*, whose monetary affairs are managed through the *Banque des états d'Afrique centrale* (BEAC). The UMOA treaty as well as the monetary co-operation convention between France and the Central African countries both recognize the CFA franc (in West Africa this stands for the *Communauté financière africaine* and in Central Africa for *Coopération financière en Afrique centrale*) as a single monetary unit issued by a common financial institution. The fourteenth independent member of the Franc Zone is the Republic of the Comores which became a member of the Zone through a special monetary agreement signed in 1979.[29]

The most important feature of the Franc Zone is that the currency issued by these two regional African banks is guaranteed by the French franc, and this allows for holders of these currencies to exchange them freely, and without limit, for the French franc. The exchange rate between the French franc and the CFA franc is fixed at 0.02 French francs. This basic feature means that while there is a so-called vertical osmosis between the French franc and the CFA franc there is also a horizontal osmosis between the currencies of the CFA franc countries. This means that on a regional basis, there is freedom of unlimited transfer between each individual currency within the Zone and every other currency of the zone. Members of the zone agree to harmonize the regulations governing their national currency markets. The fixed exchange rate between the member states is a further major stabilizing factor which facilitates the activities of those having commercial relations with any of these states. All members of the zone have free access to the Paris currency markets.

These principal features of the Franc Zone are strongly affected by the residual control which France maintains over the activities of the regional African banks as well as by the economic conditions prevailing in France and the specific monetary policy pursued by the French government. No single organization regulates the monetary policy pursued by all members of the Franc Zone though there are biannual meetings of the finance ministers of all Franc Zone countries.[30] However, French government representatives participate directly in the various African organizations that manage the CFA franc, most importantly the mixed monetary committee, and the boards of the regional African banks. French officials help to determine the regulations at these banks. The level of French participation in these bodies varies since different agreements govern the French presence in West Africa, Central Africa and the Comores. Yet in all cases France retains an effective veto power over the modification of the monetary statutes in these organizations. Any suspension of the restrictive measures governing the release of credit by these banks, for example, could not take place without the approval of the French representatives at the relevant bank.

Since the late 1960s and early 1970s there has been an intense debate about the relative advantages and disadvantages of the Franc Zone for the member states. The terms of this debate have changed, however, and before examining in greater depth the more recent disputes it is worth pointing to this evolution. In the early 1970s the main argument deployed in support of the Franc Zone was the importance of the financing offered by France and the relatively guaranteed outlets which African states had for their exports at stable prices. At that time, detractors of the Franc Zone were concerned about the lack of autonomy possessed by the regional central banks in Africa symbolized by the widespread presence of French administrators in these structures. Also, constraints placed on the development of individualized monetary policies within the Franc Zone were criticized as a major block to economic development. While these arguments, which centred on long-term prospects for the Franc Zone states did not disappear from the debate, they were partly overshadowed in the mid- and late 1980s by arguments which focused on financial adjustment problems that needed to be addressed in the short or medium term. Supporters of the Franc Zone began to emphasize the value of the monetary rigour imposed by the internal regulations of the Zone. The stability and the automatic convertability of the CFA franc were also stressed. Detractors began to criticize the fixed rate of the CFA as effectively assuring an overvaluation of African currencies which was detrimental to the kind of financial adjustment process normally encouraged by such international institutions as the World Bank and the International Monetary Fund.[31]

According to the co-operation agreements which continue to govern the monetary relations between France and the member states of the Franc Zone, France undertakes to consult, to the degree possible, other members before changing the value of the franc. Franc Zone member states were surprised in 1969 when a devaluation took place without any consultation. After 1981, during the first Mitterrand administration, there were four devaluations of the French franc, yet in no instance were the Franc Zone consultative procedures put into effect. France has insisted that the inevitable need to prevent international speculation on the franc (potentially more destabilizing than any planned devaluation) would make consultation impossible in almost every instance. While there is almost no likelihood that this part of the co-operation agreements will ever be implemented in the way desired by African states, they are less concerned by the form, than by the fact that devaluations of the French franc have 'automatically' resulted in a devaluation of their own CFA franc in a way which appears indifferent to the specific monetary situation in Franc Zone member states and which can cause grave problems for those states needing to make external purchases in currencies other than the French franc.[32] However, none of the African countries has decided to negotiate a change in the fixed rate of exchange following a devaluation in order to preserve the relative value of the CFA. Another important immediate effect of any devaluation of the French franc relates to foreign exchange holdings and can be quite severe for Franc Zone members, since the African central banks will see their reserves, a large percentage of which are held in French francs at the French Treasury, decline with the devaluation of the franc.[33] While there are some compensatory measures which exist to dampen this effect, and while the Franc Zone countries have usually earned a fair rate of interest from their holdings at the French Treasury, it remains the case that some states, especially the oil exporters, have sought after such devaluations to keep their dollar earnings in American banks. While such monies are out of the Franc Zone channel, it equally makes them susceptible to falls in the value of the US dollar. Finally, French franc devaluations also have an effect on the level of the foreign debt carried by Franc Zone countries which is denominated in currencies (primarily the US dollar) other than the French franc.

The fact remains that despite the devaluations that took place between 1981 and 1986, most international financial experts still felt that the CFA franc was overvalued. International organizations such as the World Bank and the International Monetary Fund have argued that a more realistic exchange rate would help accelerate financial adjustment policies in these countries that are thought necessary. While it is a fair presumption that since the CFA exchange rate depends on the strength of the French economy, rather than on any of the African economies, the existing fixed exchange rate does not reflect prevailing economic conditions in the African member states, it does not necessarily follow that the rate is wrong. Certainly the complex relationship that exists between France and the member states of the Franc Zone makes it difficult to assess a 'true' exchange rate for the currencies of these countries.[34]

It is equally difficult to assess with certainty whether the inability of Franc Zone member states to use exchange rate manipulation as a tool of economic management is a clear weakness. Voluntary devaluations could theoretically be aimed at reducing domestic demand as a result of the increased cost of imports; improving the competitiveness of national industries in the international environment by effectively lowering the price to outsiders; or increasing the relative value of producing a certain good by guaranteeing to producers higher revenues in local currency thus encouraging them to produce more. The first of these aims has high costs in terms of economic growth, while the second and third are not so relevant to Franc Zone states, who have few small and medium size enterprises and whose foreign exchange tends, in any case, to be earned by the sale of primary products whose prices are fixed by world market conditions. The second and third aims can often be at least partly achieved by instituting national subsidies. It is unlikely therefore that Franc Zone states are deprived of an important control mechanism by the fact that their exchange rates are controlled by France.[35]

In the end, many of the arguments about the Franc Zone advanced from the perspective of the African states revolve around one broad political-economic question. Is the stability of the CFA franc, its easy convertibility, the horizontal osmosis it offers between African member states and the strict monetary regime the Franc Zone imposes, worth the relative loss of monetary sovereignty both nationally and at the central bank level, the vulnerability to French franc depreciations, and the inconvenience some-times attached to a fixed exchange rate? Most African leaders seemed to have decided that on balance the Franc Zone is worth the various restric-tions it imposes on the member states. Abou Diouf, President of Senegal, firmly stated in 1983 that: 'The advantages we derive from our membership of the Franc Zone are more important than the inconveniences. This is why there is no question, and this is true of other members of the *Union monétaire ouest africaine* ... of leaving the Franc Zone.'[36] The economic decline of Guinea after that country's withdrawal from the Franc Zone is widely cited as an example not to be followed. Mali withdrew in 1962, asked for re-entry in 1968 and only in 1984 was it possible for reintegration into the UMOA to take place. A non-francophone state, Equatorial Guinea has since joined, and it is known that anglophone states have made enquiries. Clearly, there is a perception that in monetary affairs there is strength in numbers, and the states which form the Franc Zone group continue to believe that their own individual position is bolstered by being part of the group. Increasingly, arguments about the value of the Franc Zone from the African perspective have thus focused on the fact that the economies of Franc Zone member states are opening up, and that they are able more easily to attract external finance.[37]

Throughout the 1960s, 1970s, and early 1980s, Franc Zone states exhibited certain marked advantages over other states in the developing world and particularly in Africa. While generalizations on certain indices can be made, it has to be recalled that there is an important difference in the size of their economies, that some have natural resources in the form of oil or minerals while others are entirely dependent on agriculture for their earnings. Still, membership in the Franc Zone affects them all in certain precise ways, and the development strategies of each of these countries have been quite spectacularly influenced by the fact of Franc Zone membership. The progressive growth of these economies from 1962 to 1981, accompanied by a comparatively low rate of inflation, is commonly explained by two important factors related to Franc Zone membership. First, the relative stability of exchange rates and the ready supply of currency whatever the individual balance of payments situation might be meant that Franc Zone states were protected from general shocks (e.g. 1971–3) to the international monetary system. Second, Franc Zone membership has helped these states to make relatively high domestic investments owing to the fact that high public savings were encouraged by limitations on financial advances by the central banks to member states, and by the fact that external capital could be attracted to these countries because of the convertability of the local currency. Indeed, most Franc Zone states have had economies more open to the outside then has been the case in non-Franc Zone African states.[38]

That said, most Franc Zone states, like most other African states, have reached the limit of their capacity to absorb capital. Subsidized public enterprises have funded unprofitable import substitution activities. The increase of activity by foreign enterprises has simultaneously led to unco-ordinated industrial development. Franc Zone states are thus now beginning to suffer many of the same problems as other states in the developing world, and while this has not led to an abandonment of the Franc Zone it has shown that it cannot insulate member states from problems typical of the developing world, particularly when, as began to be the case in the 1980s, the financial facilities offered by the Franc Zone began to be abused, resulting in larger state debts.[39]

From the French perspective, the advantages of leading the Franc Zone have become more political than economic. Clearly the Franc Zone is of benefit to French commercial firms (as it is to other foreign companies) and France's comparative advantage in trading with the francophone African countries is reinforced by the existence of the Zone, though the level of France's trade with francophone Africa has declined. The total value of the African currencies managed through the French Treasury is not very high: for West Africa 1.3 per cent and for Central Africa about 1 per cent of the total French money supply.[40] However, the economic crisis in Africa, from which the francophone states were in no way protected, especially given their more open economies, meant that by the mid-1980s the operating accounts of both the BEAC and the BCEAO were substantially overdrawn. Franc Zone states began demanding a moratorium or an annulment of debts, increased direct budgetary aid, greater support of African primary product exports and numerous specific monetary adjustments. Few of these demands were granted, and in particular, France was at first unwilling to set any precedent by writing off debts, raising the possibility of doing so for the first time in June 1988. By late 1988, France formally decided that it could cancel some of the debt of the poorer countries. The debate about the future of the Franc Zone, begun seriously in the mid-1980s, grew more intense. Financial experts became concerned over the cost of the Franc Zone, many considering that the Treasury could not, over the long term, provide the financial support needed. Beyond enforcing more strictly the monetary regulations of the Franc Zone, there are those who argue that the only future for the Franc Zone will lie in an internationalization of responsibilities for its management. However, most officials in government are highly sceptical about this sort of solution and believe that, as before, necessary adjustments can be made in the Franc Zone which can continue to satisfy African needs and at the same time protect France from those who might abuse the system. Indeed, for many, applying the rules more strictly is the simple, and only answer.

In the 1970s, when the various co-operation agreements were being revised, African states also called for reforms in the management of the Franc Zone. After 1972 there were thus fewer French administrators at the two central banks (whose headquarters were transferred from Paris to Dakar and Yaoundé), African states were given a greater freedom to take out loans, French credits were restructured to allow longer-term development, and African states were allowed to keep up to 35 per cent of their reserves in currencies other than the French franc.[41] This answered many concerns of the Africans. For the French, the thrust of the policy adjustments undertaken in the mid-1980s was a return to a slightly stricter system of management than took place in the 1970s. While neither the French nor the Africans felt, as a result of the economic crisis of the 1980s, that there was a need to again drastically reform the actual regulations of the Franc Zone, and while neither African nor French leaders question its essential value, there is more concern about its long-term viability. Those who wonder (mainly outside government) how the Franc Zone can survive into the twenty-first century have tended to propose two different forms of expansion, both of them relatively idealistic, but both also increasingly part of the continuing debate on the management of francophone African monetary affairs.[42]

The first suggestion is that the Franc Zone be eventually transformed into a larger system of African monetary integration. The Franc Zone is the only system in Africa which helps to co-ordinate African monetary policies. A pan-African system would still be linked to the French franc, but the particular exchange rates would be individually fixed. Fluctuations would be managed through a Central African monetary fund to which states would contribute from their reserve holdings. Each country would have its own currency but the CFA franc would serve as a unit of account as does the European Currency Unit (ECU) for European Community states. The African Monetary Fund created to manage this system would issue CFA francs and would deal directly with the French Treasury. The operations account mechanism managed by this fund would guarantee the convertabilty of the CFA franc, but each country would hold individual accounts and in the case of a long-term deficit this would result in alteration of the exchange rate for the country showing a deficit. Such a system, it is argued, would take better account of the heterogeneity of African economies and allow greater integration of them.

Others have argued that since two-thirds of the external commercial relations of the African states which are members of the Franc Zone are with the European Community, while three-quarters of French trade with Africa is now made outside the Franc Zone, it makes sense to further integrate the countries of the Franc Zone into a European monetary system by extending to Africa the ECU system. The attachment of the CFA franc to the ECU would theoretically allow for a greater stability in export receipts and a greater diversification of African commercial transactions. Whatever system of integration might reasonably be adopted to accommodate the CFA in the European monetary system would also no doubt partly relieve France of some of the current burdens of managing the Franc Zone. Whether such a Eurafrican monetary system could be attractive to France's European partners is doubtful, but in the late 1980s more and more French analysts began to argue that the future of the CFA franc might well lie with better links to the ECU. This, indeed, would also be logical given the existing links that bind Europe and Africa through the various Lomé accords.[43]

Even as French governments, in their general co-operation policy, have returned to Gaullist images of a privileged relationship with francophone Africa and a strong bilateral aid policy, analysts have argued for a greater internationalization of the Franc Zone structures which give general support to the whole French presence in Africa. In official circles, the proposal that the Franc Zone might be attached to the ECU, or that there could evolve a true African currency, tends nevertheless only to inspire ribald comment. The idea that France's European partners, who have difficulty agreeing on monetary questions amongst themselves, might accept to link the ECU to the CFA franc, is thought highly unrealistic. For most French officials, and especially those in the Treasury, which in the late 1980s became the most important French actor on the African economic scene, there is a need to supervise more directly the monetary policies of Franc Zone states, and make sure that countries stick to agreed practices. In addition, there is a need to review the nature of some bilateral structural adjustment loans and co-operate more closely with some of the international financial institutions. As long as these principles are followed, and the Franc Zone does not appear to lose France too much money, it is thought likely to be sustainable.

Whatever the outcome of the necessarily long-term re-evaluation of the Franc Zone that will occupy civil servants and outside analysts in the 1990s, it is evident that a strong political urge to maintain special links with francophone Africa of various kinds will persist. That urge will not necessarily be related to perceived imperatives of economic policy. As has been noted, French imports from francophone Africa have gone down just as has the overall value of French exports. While certain important primary materials, notably manganese, uranium, phosphates and natural gas, are still largely imported from various parts of Africa (see tables 7.5–7.11), and French firms continue to benefit from the various historical and linguistic ties between France and Africa, the economic advantages of the link with Africa are minimal.

Most French banks in the 1980s began to pull out of Africa. A number of companies who had made great fortunes in Africa, have begun to withdraw, keeping some offices open only for sentimental reasons. For the French state, the main interest in participating in francophone African affairs relates not so much to the protection of certain economic advantages, but more broadly to the desire to retain a basic structural influence in Africa. It is useful to recall that French aid is not provided mainly to improve France's commercial prospects. The African countries who are members of the Franc Zone who receive 50 per cent of all French bilateral aid (not including the DOM and the TOM) only represent 2 per cent of French commerce. Technical assistance in Africa financed by public aid does create a good deal of employment in France and Treasury loans do help to finance French exports, but it would be fanciful to suppose that France has major economic incentives to aid francophone Africa.[44] Yet this aid does produce political influence, and it has done so despite the fact that francophone African states have developed their own regional economic organizations. These organizations are therefore worth surveying, precisely to show that despite great attempts at inter-African economic co-operation, the role of France is paramount.

Table 7.5 France's imports of key African metal products (1,000s of tons)

	Aluminium			Copper			Uranium		
	1984	1985	1986	1984	1985	1986	1984	1985	1986
Cameroon	46.9	53.8	43.3	–	–	–	–	–	–
Egypt	4.0	7.8	2.9	–	–	–	–	–	–
Gabon	–	–	–	–	–	–	1.3	1.0	1.0
Ghana	0.2	–	0.2	–	–	–	–	–	–
Ivory Coast	–	–	0.2	–	–	–	–	–	–
Niger	–	–	–	–	–	–	4.3	3.9	3.7
South Africa	0.5	0.5	1.8	0.2	2.4	0.4	1.9	1.9	1.3
Zaire	–	–	–	13.3	14.6	12.7	–	–	–
Zimbabwe	–	–	0.1	–	–	–	–	–	–
Total	52.5	62.2	48.7	60.8	60.6	72.7	7.6	6.8	6.0

Source: *Marchés Tropicaux et Méditerranéens, La France et l'Afrique*, 5th edn, 25 December 1987, p. 3507

Table 7.6 French imports of key African mineral products (million tons)

	Crude Oil			Phosphates			Iron Ore		
	1984	1985	1986	1984	1985	1986	1984	1985	1986
Algeria	5.2	3.4	2.7	0.1	0.1	0.1	–	–	–
Angola	–	0.4	0.6	–	–	–	–	–	–
Benin	–	–	0.1	–	–	–	–	–	–
Cameroon	1.0	3.0	1.3	–	–	–	–	–	–
Congo	0.5	0.5	1.0	–	–	–	–	–	–
Egypt	2.5	1.6	1.7	–	–	–	–	–	–
Gabon	1.1	2.2	3.3	–	–	–	–	–	–
Liberia	–	–	–	–	–	–	1.3	1.1	0.6
Libya	3.5	3.0	2.1	–	–	–	–	–	–
Morocco	–	–	–	1.9	1.5	0.9	–	–	–
Mauritania	–	–	–	–	–	–	2.0	2.3	2.3
Niger	–	–	0.1	–	–	–	–	–	–
Nigeria	10.4	8.0	6.2	–	–	–	–	–	–
Senegal	–	–	–	0.3	0.2	0.3	–	–	–
Sierra Leone	–	–	–	–	–	–	0.1	–	–
Togo	–	–	–	0.6	0.5	0.4	–	–	–
Tunisia	0.7	0.4	0.4	0.3	0.3	0.2	–	–	–
South Africa	–	–	–	–	–	–	0.4	0.2	–
Total	24.9	22.5	19.4	3.2	2.6	1.8	3.0	3.6	2.9

Source: *Marchés Tropicaux et Méditerranéens*, p. 3507

Table 7.7 French imports of key African agricultural products

	Cocoa			Coffee			Cotton		
	1984	*1985*	*1986*	*1984*	*1985*	*1986*	*1984*	*1985*	*1986*
Angola	0.1	–	–	0.2	0.1	0.3	–	–	–
Benin	0.9	2.0	0.9	1.7	2.7	0.8	3.0	3.8	1.6
Burkina	–	–	–	–	–	–	4.5	3.6	6.4
Cameroon	5.3	3.2	4.4	23.3	15.8	20.1	1.0	3.0	1.3
CAR	–	–	–	7.3	5.9	5.6	5.1	2.7	5.2
Chad	–	–	–	–	–	–	6.6	1.6	2.8
Congo	–	–	–	2.0	0.7	1.3	–	–	–
Egypt	–	–	–	–	–	–	3.4	3.3	1.41
Ethiopia		–	–	9.1	5.6	7.4	–	–	–
Equato. Guinea	–	–	–	0.3	–	–	–	–	–
Gabon	–	–	–	0.8	1.2	1.0	–	–	–
Ghana	5.3	2.7	2.0	–	–	–	–	–	–
Guinea	–	–	–	0.3	–	0.8	0.1	–	0.1
Guinea-Bissau	–	–	–	–	–	–	0.3	0.3	0.5
Ivory Coast	32.0	28.8	24.3	58.1	72.8	60.3	11.7	11.2	8.7
Kenya	–	–	–	1.8	1.2	2.1	–	–	–
Liberia	–	–	–	0.4	0.8	1.1	–	–	–
Madagascar	1.7	1.6	1.8	23.9	16.9	22.0	–	–	–
Mali	–	–	–	–	–	–	10.9	8.4	9.4
Mozambique	–	–	–	–	–	–	0.1	–	–
Nigeria	0.5	0.7	1.0	0.9	1.6	–	–	–	–
Rwanda	–	–	–	2.4	2.2	2.0	–	–	–
Sao Tome	0.4	0.1	0.3	–	–	–	–	–	–
Senegal	–	–	–	–	–	–	0.1	0.1	0.2
Sudan	–	–	–	–	–	–	1.6	1.5	2.0
Tanzania	–	–	–	0.7	1.4	1.7	–	–	–
Togo	0.8	0.2	0.3	0.4	0.9	4.8	3.1	4.5	3.31
Uganda	0.1	–	–	14.1	11.1	13.1	–	–	–
Zaire	0.5	0.5	0.2	24.3	19.6	30.5	–	–	–
Zimbabwe	–	–	–	0.1	–	0.1	–	–	–
Total	47.6	40.1	43.7	173.2	161.3	177.6	57.6	47.0	48.6

Source: Marchés Tropicaux et Méditerranéens, p. 3506

Table 7.8 Destinations of French exports to Africa: Trend 1984–1986
(percentages)

	1984	*1985*	*1986*
Algeria	24.7	23.7	20.1
Egypt	8.7	9.7	8.2
Nigeria	8.3	5.4	3.4
Morocco	7.3	10.0	9.2
Tunisia	6.9	7.0	7.0
Cameroon	5.5	5.9	6.3
Ivory Coast	4.7	4.5	5.3
South Africa	4.6	3.8	3.5
Reunion	4.1	4.5	5.7
Gabon	3.5	3.9	.9
Senegal	2.5	2.5	.9
Congo	2.2	2.6	2.3
Libya	1.9	2.4	2.0
Madagascar	1.1	1.1	1.1
Mali	0.9	1.1	1.0
Sudan	0.9	0.8	0.3
Niger	0.8	0.9	0.9
Liberia	0.7	0.4	0.9
Benin	0.7	0.8	1.0
Mauritania	0.7	1.0	1.0
Other countries	9.3	8.0	14.1
Total	100.0	100.0	100.0

Source: Marchés Tropicaux et Méditerranéens, p.3504

France and Regional African Economic Arrangements

In the first years after decolonization, following the dissolution of the large federal structures of the French Empire (the AOF and AEF), smaller francophone African structures created just before independence helped to strengthen the local diplomatic powers of the larger states. In West Africa, the *Conseil de l'Entente* (Niger, Dahomey, Upper Volta and the Ivory Coast, founded in 1959), confirmed an important regional role for the Ivory Coast which wished to have access to the workforce of Upper Volta and

Table 7.9 Principal African suppliers to France

	Percentage			Rank		
	1984	*1985*	*1986*	*1984*	*1985*	*1986*
Algeria	25.5	22.3	28.1	1	1	1
Nigeria	20.3	16.4	9.2	2	2	3
Libya	7.3	7.4	4.2	3	4	9
South Africa	6.1	6.2	5.9	4	6	6
Egypt	5.5	4.1	3.0	5	9	10
Morocco	5.3	6.5	10.0	6	5	2
Ivory Coast	5.0	5.6	7.2	7	8	4
Cameroon	4.3	7.8	5.5	8	3	8
Gabon	3.8	6.0	6.7	9	7	5
Tunisia	3.8	6.0	5.6	10	10	7
Senegal	1.8	1.5	2.3	11	12	12
Niger	1.7	1.8	2.7	12	11	11
Congo	1.1	1.1	1.6	13	13	14
Madagascar	1.1	0.8	1.4	14	16	16
Zaire	1.0	0.9	1.6	15	15	15
Zambia	0.6	0.7	1.1	16	17	18
Reunion	0.6	0.4	1.2	17	20	17
Mauritius	0.6	1.0	1.9	18	14	13
Liberia	0.4	0.5	0.7	19	18	19
Mauritania	0.4	0.4	0.6	20	19	20
Togo	0.3	0.4	0.6	21	22	21
Guinea	0.3	0.4	0.4	22	21	22
Others	3.2	3.8	6.5	–	–	–
Total	100	100	100	–	–	–

Source: Marchés Tropicaux et Méditerranéens, p. 3502.

wanted to isolate Senegal. The *Conseil* in the early years served as a motor for the improvement of Franco–African relations (as indicatd by the signature of group co-operation agreements with France) and played an important role in the creation of other, larger, pan-African structures, such as the *Union africaine malgache* (1961), which in 1965 became the *Organisation africaine et malgache* comprising all the ex-AEF and AOF states minus Guinea and Mali, plus Cameroon, Togo, Madagascar and Zaire.[45] In Central Africa, the *Union Douanière Équatoriale* (UDE) (Chad, Central African Republic, Congo, Gabon, created in 1959), gave a similarly important role to Gabon, which under its structures was relieved of some of the economic burdens it shouldered under the AEF. Gabon also played the lead role in

Table 7.10 Evolution of the part of Africa in French imports
(percentages)

	1984	1985	1986
Cacao (beans)	90.8	86.2	82.4
Manganese ore	89.2	90.5	91.6
Uranium	69.9	48.2	40.7
Unground phosphates	68.6	67.7	54.5
Bauxite	55.5	45.7	52.4
Coffee (raw)	61.6	58.5	63.1
Aluminium	45.5	85.6	61.5
Sugar	38.3	42.9	44.4
Iron ore	18.3	24.5	19.5
Natural gas	31.8	27.2	30.7
Raw cotton	35.1	29.5	30.2
Unrefined oil	34.1	32.8	29.2
Timber and works	21.6	21.9	20.1
Fruits	18.2	14.4	20.1
Coal	27.1	32.9	12.3
All products	10.8	9.7	6.5

Source: *Marchés Tropicaux et Méditerranéens*, p. 3500

maintaining vertical ties with France, confirmed by all the co-operation agreements but also underlined, for example, by the acceptance by UDE states (plus Cameroon) of an investment code under which foreign private investment was guaranteed against the risks of nationalization and non-transferability of profits or capital.[46]

In the 1960s various regional and sub-regional agreements were signed and numerous bodies created both in West and Central Africa, of variable membership, ostensibly to manage international economic relations. These played insignificant roles during the Gaullist period, when the foreign economic policies of most francophone African states were defined to a considerable degree by their special relationship with France. The larger states, also, remained sceptical about the value of these organizations. Both the Ivory Coast and Gabon had actively participated in the dissolution of the AEF and the AOF at the time of decolonization. While they played important political roles in regional organizations (largely in the service of

Table 7.11 Evolution of the part of Africa in French exports
(percentages)

	1984	1985	1986
Flour	43.1	53.3	44.1
Pharmaceuticals	39.6	38.8	37.6
Railway material	23.1	34.8	28.0
Sugar and sugar products	21.7	17.2	21.8
Book-trade articles	19.7	16.6	16.4
Aerial navigation equipment	16.9	0.7	7.0
Automobiles and cycles	16.2	14.5	11.0
Machines, mechanical articles	15.9	14.5	12.5
Electrical materials	15.7	15.1	12.8
Chemical products	15.0	14.7	13.3
Milk products	12.5	11.1	11.8
Metallurgical products	11.6	13.8	8.8
Maritime navigation equipment	10.1	14.7	26.0
Paper and cartons	9.0	9.3	8.5
Plastic materials	8.1	7.9	6.6
Cereals	7.7	13.6	9.9
Petroleum products	6.1	6.1	5.2
All Products	11.8	10.6	9.6

Source: *Marchés Tropicaux et Méditerranéens, La France et l'Afrique*, p. 3504

their own national interests) they remained hostile to any re-establishment of mechanisms of financial redistribution or compensation which would work against their own pre-eminence.[47]

With the revision in the co-operation agreements in the early 1970s, 'africanization' of the regional central banks and the progressive decline of the place of France in the foreign trade of the francophone states of West and Central Africa, some new bodies were established and older ones were revivified. There was some expectation that many years after decolonization, regional economic affairs could be put on a sounder footing. But largely because of basic economic incompatibilities and the high priority many of the francophone states still place on their bilateral relationship with France, these bodies have not made major advances in regional co-operation.

The *Communauté Économique de l'Afrique de l'Ouest* (CEAO), founded in 1973 in West Africa, while having spawned a promising military co-operation structure (the ANAD, discussed in the previous chapter), has not been able to make more than modest advances towards regional integration. Some financial compensation measures were introduced (facilitated by the fact that all CEAO members use the CFA franc) which addressed some of the inequalities between the member states. Still, the Ivory Coast and Senegal remained the only significant intra-regional traders and this fact by the early 1980s began to affect the smooth working of the compensation measures. While there has been some advance in co-ordinating (limited) pre-existing trade, establishing new trade has been difficult. The heavily staffed secretariat has not yet been able to work efficiently to identify regional projects in the fields of infrastructure development, communications or agriculture, which could be the subject of common funding.[48] Because of its small size, however, it has advanced towards the development of a customs union more rapidly than the larger Economic Community of West African States (ECOWAS). Many of the anglophone members of ECOWAS, particularly Nigeria, persist in considering that the development of ECOWAS is slowed by the existence of what they perceive as the French-dominated CEAO. While a close analysis suggests that the difficulties of ECOWAS cannot be ascribed to the divisions between anglophone and francophone states (the former are sometimes quicker to ratify ECOWAS protocols), the Franc Zone system clearly facilitates co-operation amongst the member states. But it does so without preventing (it even may help) the establishment of trade links with those countries in Africa possessing unconvertable currencies.[49]

In Central Africa the *Union Douanière des États de l'Afrique Centrale* founded in 1964 and including all the former UDE states plus Cameroon, (Equatorial Guinea later joined) has been troubled by the nationalistic policies pursued by the member states. Relaunched in 1974 after several years of stagnation, during which there had been almost no rise in trade among the member states and little co-ordination in the important fields of agriculture and fisheries, the UDEAC nevertheless has made slow progress. Though a single tax system was put in place to govern intra-regional trade in manufactures, trade is conditioned by the highly uneven pattern of industrialization among the member states. In 1975 a development bank was created by the UDEAC states, the *Banque de développement des États de l'Afrique Centrale* with the express purpose of funding regional projects, yet the early recipients of funding were the richer and more industrialized states (Gabon and Cameroon) for projects which were not regional in nature.[50] By the late 1980s, when these two countries began to have economic problems (unemployment, decline of oil exports), they also called for the curtailment of the free movement of persons within the region theoretically guaranteed by the treaty.[51] The larger *Communauté Économique des États de l'Afrique*

Centrale (CEEAC) established in 1983 by President Bongo, which brings together ten lusophone, anglophone and francophone states (including UDEAC states) has tried to encourage the member states to buy from each other rather than from those outside the region. While the UDEAC sees itself primarily as a customs union, the CEEAC considers its goals to be centred on the development of broad economic policy. However, most of the CEEAC states do not pay their dues. Changing trade patterns in the region will take some time. In 1988 President Mobuto presented Zaire's decision to buy oil from Congo, rather than from other suppliers as a significant advance. The CEEAC states have recognized that more far-reaching improvements in regional trade can only be encouraged by the creation of an effective financial clearing house to manage the five currencies (Burundi franc, Rwandan franc, Sao Tomé dobra, Zaire franc and the CFA franc) which are used in the region.[52]

The principal economic organizations that exist in West and Central Africa have numerous obstacles to overcome before creating better regional trade and customs links. The francophone states within these organizations, linked to France through the Franc Zone, and the public economic aid as well as the technical assistance provided by the various French structures having special responsibility for Africa, will continue to look to France in times of crisis. Since they rely heavily on French professional advice - the regional organizations such as UDEAC and CEAO were strongly influenced by technical assistance offered by the French – francophone African states will still feel that they must deal with France, and sometimes through France, in managing their economic affairs.

These economic affairs will become harder to deal with, however, and France's capacity to sustain these states will be severely tested. Maintenance of a resolutely bilateral approach to francophone Africa will be difficult given the diversity and depth of the economic problems now faced by francophone states in Africa. More and more, French aid experts see that France should lead multilateral efforts and shape them to the particular interests that France wishes to defend rather than insist on a purely national approach as the only way of preserving influence. The tendency is to search for ways of alleviating a burden perceived to fall heavily on France while maintaining the political advantages of a highly visible national role. The need of African states to turn more and more towards IMF assistance in any case engages France in macro-economic policy. At the end of 1985, for example, France was forced to respond quickly, and positively, to a request from Senegal for 100 million francs of financial aid to permit it to conform to some of the economic management criteria called for by the IMF.[53] Since African states will continue to appeal to France in this way, it stands to reason that she will wish to co-ordinate her aid much more closely with international agencies. The requirement to evaluate more accurately the nature of project and financial assistance given to African states will effectively mean that a more comprehensive development strategy will have to be put in place by France if she is to remain relevant to emerging African needs. The offer of mere technical assistance will not be enough. Increasingly, France will have to orient her aid to ensure that these countries have a greater capacity to provide for their own economic growth. To do this, collaboration with other actors will be essential. Still, because of the complexity of the economic links between France and Africa, and the political difficulty of reneging on an implied commitment to support these states, the trend to multilateralization will still not sap the specificity of the French presence in Africa.

The many French organizations which dispense aid, manage technical and economic assistance, and administer financial and monetary structures of direct relevance to the various francophone African states linked to France strengthen the ties which exist through the co-operation agreements that are protected by French military guarantees. Many of these French organizations, as has been shown, have their origins in colonial structures. They have been modernized, and the reforms that have been made to their procedures have reflected French responsiveness to African demands for change. Yet their elimination, and the consequent termination of the 'privileged relations' which exist between France and Black Africa, would be a revolutionary act. This all the more so because the reach of these organizations and of French co-operation in general has been extended beyond the old French colonies to include the ex-Belgian colonies. Even lusophone and anglophone states have become the objects of French policy in Africa. Turning her back on francophone Africa is made more difficult precisely by the fact that leaders of these states are more alert to the possibility that France will engage herself from time to time outside the traditional *chasse gardée*.

This is why the nature and style of French economic support of francophone Africa cannot be appreciated without an understanding of the diplomatic context in which it takes place. African states are able to solicit support because they are aware of the value France attaches to being seen as central to African needs. It is to protect the French image in Africa and to deepen its impression that French leaders spend time speaking about Africa, travelling to it, and arranging for Africans to meet under French auspices. French diplomacy in Africa, built around the rhetorical flourishes inspired by the Franco–African and Eurafrican imagery which still have their place in French thinking about Africa, helps to nurture the ideology of unity which makes French power acceptable to so many African states. That diplomacy too, has had to adapt itself to a more interdependent and complex system of African international relations which is beginning to make French power on the continent more difficult to manage.

8
The Diplomacy of French
Power in Black Africa

French diplomacy in Black Africa since decolonization has traditionally operated on two quite distinct levels. On the one hand, there have been the personal links established between the French president and individual leaders of Black African states. In many cases, this has allowed bilateral inter-state questions to be addressed through conversations and personal undertakings rather than by diplomatic cables and bureaucratic assurances. President de Gaulle's special relationship with a number of African leaders (the strongest and most important of which was with Houphouet-Boigny), assured that special problems would be treated individually. Numerous were the African leaders who referred, without embarrassment, to the French president as *Père de Gaulle*. Even President Massemba-Debat of Congo-Brazzaville, who between 1963 and 1968 ran a socialist government (though in the latter years of his reign he strongly opposed the more radical measures proposed by his deputies), is said to have depicted the French and Congolese peoples as 'Siamese twins whom only surgical intervention could separate'.[1] All of de Gaulle's successors, and numerous politicians who have not reached the highest office, have cultivated their particular contacts in Black Africa and have invariably sought to present themselves as 'friends of Africa'. This fact alone speaks volumes for the perceived political importance in France of the African connection and for the boost to domestic political standing that politicians assume is there if they can present themselves, as did de Gaulle, as 'l'homme d'Afrique'.

On the other hand, against these carefully nurtured personal relationships which have stressed individual sentimental attachments, has been a rigorously institutionalized approach to Franco–African relations which in its early days emphasized foreign policy consultation and the homogeneity of bloc politics. The co-operation agreements initially signed by independent Black African states immediately on independence were criticized by some French parliamentarians when they were debated in the Senate and the National Assembly because their 'bilateral nature' sapped the sense of common purpose inherent in the structures of the French Community. But in fact, the accords were sufficiently similar (and some were multilaterally negotiated) to ensure that political co-operation among the signatories was, at least theoretically, possible. With six states, (CAR, Congo, Gabon, Madagascar, Senegal and Chad) the agreements stipulated that the signatories would 'compare points of view and endeavour to align positions and activities before taking any major decision', and the agreements with Ivory Coast, Dahomey, Upper Volta and Niger produced language which was almost as binding.[2] When the co-operation agreements were revised in the early 1970s, most of these political obligations of consultation fell into abeyance, but in 1973 the Franco–African summit meeting provided a new forum to discuss France's relations with the ex-colonies in Black Africa.

At the end of the 1975 meeting in Bangui the conference participants issued a communiqué which stated that 'the heads of state and delegation leaders have decided to give the Franco–African conference the status of a permanent institution. The principle of an annual conference meeting has been adopted.'[3] While many of the 'francophone family' metaphors used to describe France's relations with Africa have been used more sparingly, the political solidarity sought by both French and African leaders has been regularized by the institution of the Franco–African summit. This summit symbolizes an enduring relationship whose specific features are still a subject of sometimes fierce negotiation but whose broad lines have remained remarkably resilient to the passage of time.

From the French point of view, both the highly personal and carefully institutionalized forms of diplomacy with Black Africa are meant to serve the same end, and that end is almost indistinguishable from the means by which it is sought. The end is to perpetuate the image of a French role in Africa. This requires a policy of political seduction and is driven by the centralist notions of the French state and those who manage it. Stripped of the special diplomacy that accompanies French military and economic policy towards Black Africa, French relations with these countries would lose a great deal of their 'specificity' and hence their value.

From the African perspective, cultivation of a close relationship with France has provided some material rewards, in the form of an assured rhythm of both military and economic assistance, and also, though this French role has receded in recent years, an advocate for them in international fora. The most fundamental tension that exists between these basic aims of the French and the Africans (which are generally complementary, hence the durability of the relationship), is that while French statesmen invariably like to emphasize their policy towards francophone Africa as a bloc, individual African states still seek specially tailored attention. The close links these states have maintained with France have not deprived them of negotiating power. Rarely have francophone Black African states played East against West, more often they have set West against West, effectively threatening France with disloyalty by turning to others for aid if France did not respond as they wished.

In this sense, numerous Black African leaders have been able to play France's image of herself as benefactor and mentor against France. As a consequence, French leaders have sometimes been compelled to stoop to satisfy frivolous requirements in order to ensure continuity of the special relationship. This is not to deny the essential asymmetry, not only in power and resources, but also in interests, which conditions Franco–African relations. France's African policy is an important aspect of external policy and feeds an enduring sense of extra-continental purpose, but it is not the only outlet or source of national prestige. For the Africans, relations with France are central both to domestic life and to international (not least regional) relations. But this does not deprive the African leaders of tools to shape the policy that France takes towards them.

This chapter seeks to isolate the specific nature of French diplomacy towards Black Africa. It does not attempt to examine particular policies which France has pursued towards individual states, which in any case have almost always been fashioned as a function of a general strategy for francophone Africa. That said, it would be wrong to see in *every* French diplomatic act on the continent a carefully calculated move in a larger and perfectly conceived grand strategy. The general disorder of African politics as often as not makes this impossible. However it is the case that, since decolonization, individual links with particular African heads of state have been sustained with a larger purpose in mind. As in colonial times, General de Gaulle's approach to Black Africa reflected both a sense that personal relations with individual leaders was the best way to ensure broad support in Africa for France's policies and that for these connections to be of global use France had to be able to rely on Africa as a bloc. In this sense it is true that France's post-colonial diplomacy in Africa, like her initial imperial adventure there, has attempted to amalgamate special relationships in the service of a broader 'alliance'.

It is necessary to appreciate that this basic strategy has been facilitated by the extraordinary network of cultural and business links inherited from colonial times. Particularly when de Gaulle was in office, the French secret service relied on these links in its support of official government policy. More recently, France's ambitious policy in Africa has been driven by the increasing institutionalization of the personal relations between elites that characterized French power in Africa in pre-independence days. This has made the French position in Africa more invulnerable to changes in Africa's leadership and has given sustenance to a rhetorical policy which is sweeping and self-flattering. But it has also made the French position in Africa rigid and less adaptable to changing international circumstances. International relations in Africa may create linkages between the politics of North and of Black Africa where the history of French colonial activity and post-colonial strategy has erected dividing structures. Following the analysis of the nature of French diplomacy in Africa here, then, it will be necessary to ask in the conclusion to this book, whether the post-colonial development of France's general strategy in Africa will permit the perpetuation of French power, given changes in African international relations.

Since decolonization, there have been pressures on the Franco–African relationship that have thus far been resisted, but it is doubtful whether in the approach to the twenty-first century, France will be able to preserve in francophone Africa an exclusive field of action. The interests of other extra-continental powers and the degree to which they will choose to invest in francophone Black Africa will not be overwhelming, though they are bound to become a more important factor in French calculations. The ability of francophone African states to diversify and multilateralize their external contacts will not develop rapidly, but the threat to turn to countries other than France is now more persistently made. Nigeria's local capacity to establish a regional presence which, like a magnet, would draw francophone states closely to her is still only latent, and not yet a direct challenge to France, yet the basic power of Nigeria cannot be ignored. Domestic doubts in France about the *rentabilité* of France's African connection have emerged in the past and have not yet been distilled into forceful opposition, but it is reasonable to suppose that as the time of formal juridical independence of Black Africa becomes more easily counted in decades, Frenchmen will wonder whether they have the means to support an ambitious diplomacy in Black Africa. Certainly the combination of all these potential pressures, external, regional, and domestic, is likely to force France to work harder to maintain an environment in Africa conducive to the exertion of French influence without further conquest.

The threat from the Soviet Union is probably the least significant to France. If certain governments have adopted marxist-leninist ideologies in the late 1960s or 1970s (Congo, Benin, Madagascar), they have done so as much because of an appreciation of a French intellectual tradition of the left bank in Paris as because of the skilful work of Soviet operatives. Where the Soviet Union has penetrated more completely in francophone Africa – notably in Guinea – the example offered to other states has not been encouraging. Soviet technical and economic assistance is widely perceived as inferior to French, and if some of the Soviet Union's anti-imperialist rhetoric may have appeared more congenial to some left-leaning Africans, the consistency and quality of aid has rarely satisfied them. At a time when the Soviet Union is retreating from engagements in more obviously strategic areas, her diplomacy in Black Africa is unlikely severely to challenge French positions. The progressive return of Benin in the mid-1980s to France (just as the more dramatic return of Guinea), offers evidence of a certain durability of French influence. These countries 'return', however, with another experience, one which is not French, and they do not seek to be simply reintegrated into a French scheme of things.

The multilateralization of Black African links has not been very thorough. The need to deal with international aid agencies and the arrival of new national donors (the US, Canada) has, however, widened the ambitions of francophone African leaders. Gabon's President, Omar Bongo, spoke often in the mid-1980s, when French–Gabonese relations were unsteady, about the need to build a house with many doors, so that if ever there was a fire, other exits, besides the principal one, could be used. By this typically African metaphor, he meant to convey a willingness to search out other Western partners, if ever France became unwilling to provide Gabon with its perceived needs. In the late 1980s Chad, because of its battle with Libya, was uniquely placed to engage American interest, and often invited American military aid as a spur to France. Once the American card was played by Chad, France almost always responded positively to Chadian requests. This sort of brinkmanship has its limits – and France is not so hypersensitive to the activities of other powers as to jump at any request for assistance just because others might provide it instead. Also few Black African states are in a position to engage the interests of others. But insofar as Black African states will begin seeking other sources of aid, this can only, over time, dilute French power. Eventually, Black African states will develop habits of looking for as many sources of aid as possible. France will not, in any case, be able to fulfil all requests. A 'normalization' of the Franco–African relationship, which would mean that France would play a less overt role in the political economy of francophone Black African relations, and the African states would cease to see in France their only *interlocuteur valable*, is on the horizon.

As they negotiate more with outside powers, and as they begin to frame more carefully the conditions of French assistance, francophone Black African states will also have to ask themselves whether they can play an unhindered role within their own region. For most of the period since 1960, an intense fear of the power of Nigeria has helped francophone African states deal with each other, and has provided a special reason for their acceptance of a French residual role in West Africa. The need to counterbalance Nigeria has never been a declared policy of francophone

African states, but it is clearly implied by their willingness to reintroduce French political, economic and military power into the region. What is more important, the Nigerians have always perceived France as intent on acting as a countervailing force in West Africa. They have put pressure on the francophone African states to behave more independently of France. This, itself, may have helped to strengthen the links between weak francophone African states and their strong, extra-continental, protector. But if the perceived threat of Nigeria begins to wane, it will be another reason for francophone states to see that their future lies more in regional collaboration, than in a special relationship with France.

French diplomacy in francophone Africa since 1960 has been fashioned to reinforce the belief among Black Africans that a partnership with France offered the only hope for their own national development. Acceptance of this by the Africans has allowed France to pretend to a world role. The process of co-option has been facilitated by personal links between leaderships, and by the existence of the complex bureaucracy and state machinery, both overt and subtle, that operate in Africa. This 'abnormal' relationship between an ex-imperial power and her ex-colonies has been 'regularized' by the development of institutions which exist only to manage the Franco–African relationship. This has meant that even when particular relations with one or another African country seemed to be poor, the essentially good relations with the bloc of African states, which continued to rely on these institutions, could be held up as proof of the survivability of French influence.

The Gaullist Style of Diplomacy in Africa

After the end of the Algerian problem in 1962, de Gaulle's foreign policy concentrated on enlarging the scope of French foreign policy to give it a global dimension. Africa was not marginalized in this process, but rather began to occupy a more realistic proportion of the President's time. A system had been put in place, and it was up to diplomats and advisers to manage it, drawing where necessary on the atmosphere of warmth made possible by the enormous respect in which de Gaulle was held in most parts of francophone Africa.

The key vehicle for this relationship was the general secretariat for African and Malagasy Affairs run from the Elysée Palace and headed throughout the Gaullist period by Jacques Foccart. In constant competition with the Ministry of Co-operation and the Quai d'Orsay, Foccart's secretariat arranged the visits of leading African figures to Paris which were so important in the development of the special relationship with Black Africa. Foccart's personal influence was immense: he constantly received African heads of state and was able to develop a personal set of connections throughout francophone Africa (the *réseaux Foccart* as it came to be known) which allowed him to build up an independent basis of information on the political situation in francophone Africa. Foccart's network was intimately bound up with the activities of the official intelligence service, the *Service de Documentation Extérieure et de Contre Espionnage* (SDECE), which in the early years after decolonization played an important role in setting up intelligence services within a number of African states. Foccart ensured that principal agents in African capitals reported directly to him. Foccart also intervened in the choice of ambassadors, heads of the *Missions d'aide et de coopération* and directors of companies who had important activities in francophone Africa. Effectively, in each African country of importance to France, Foccart had a group of people who could provide him with his own reports to complement those received from other channels.[4] France's relations with African states were thus maintained on a number of different levels, most of these out of the public eye and beyond parliamentary scrutiny. African presidents felt able to call on Foccart and his network to help them to assess threats to internal security, and though his response would depend very much on the circumstances, this form of assistance inevitably involved the Elysée secretariat in judgements about the internal politics of francophone Africa and in assessments about how these might affect French interests.

As part of the defence agreements with these states, France promised to provide African leaders with the means to plan and prepare an appropriate national defence. This included the creation of security services in some states which put French intelligence in a strong position to assess both internal and external threats to these countries. From time to time, specialist military units of the French secret service performed intelligence-gathering exercises on behalf of African leaders in fulfilment of the defence agreements, a form of assistance which persists even if it is sparingly offered. While there were undoubtedly rivalries between the professional intelligence services and Foccart's more informal network, the web of inter-relationships which were created in the 1960s at least served further to interweave African and French interests.

Foccart's personal power was such that he was sometimes treated in Africa with the respect due a head of state. The closeness of his relations with African leaders was symbolized by the fact that throughout most of his tenure and with the full agreement of President de Gaulle, he retained a number of representatives of African states as advisers within his *secrétariat*.

These *chargés de mission* were nominated by African presidents to posts within the *secrétariat*, and even included representatives from states such as Dahomey which had not formally entered the French Community. In Foccart's view, this underscored the fact that de Gaulle was not obsessed with the precise form of juridical undertakings and could tolerate flexible arrangements with Africans as long as this helped to build strong relations.[5] As the individual who controlled all the information on Africa that was seen by de Gaulle, Foccart had a direct influence on policy-making, so much so that he has often been accused of drafting his own policy for Africa, making and unmaking governments throughout francophone Africa. The myths that surround Foccart's tenure of office, which ran throughout Pompidou's presidency as well as that of de Gaulle, are no doubt largely a collection of half-truths. In the 1960s and early 1970s there was a tendency to see in any African event the hand of Foccart, and while his influence was enormous, his historical importance lies less in the particular decisions he may have taken, than in what he represented: a permanent link between France and Africa. He constantly saw African presidents and ministers, both in Paris and in African capitals, and in this way reinforced the view that Africa had a special place in French foreign policy. His knowledge of political leaders and his wide connections were thought sufficiently valuable that between March 1986 and May 1988 he served as adviser to Jacques Chirac, who in appointing Foccart, wished to advertise his preference for a Gaullist approach to Franco–African relations.

Though in the 1960s de Gaulle could not have been aware of all of Foccart's decisions, there is no doubt that Foccart was the interpreter of de Gaulle's wishes, and it is unlikely that Foccart could have stayed in power for so long without his master's blessing. Even if there were rivalries between his office and the other French officials responsible for African affairs, he did consult more often than later myth has decreed. In any case, the relatively secret diplomacy of Foccart and his network engendered among the African leaders who benefited from the special relationship with France a sense of commonality of purpose. To the outsider, this had neo-colonial consequences on the ground, since the political futures of African leaders could still be dependent on decisions taken in Paris. Yet African leaders who remained attached to the French connection worked within the limits imposed by their nominal membership among the non-aligned group of nations to support French policy in international fora, and in this way implicitly supported the style of French diplomacy towards them.

In the early 1960s, the closeness of Franco–African relations affected the behaviour of these states at the United Nations, a place not close to President de Gaulle's heart, but an arena where French diplomacy was aided by the attitudes of francophone Black African states who, where possible supported, or did not oppose, certain French positions. The independent francophone Black African states after 1960 largely accepted the French argument that the Algerian problem was an internal matter and thus worked to convince others that it should not be taken up by the UN. In July 1961, after Tunisia had broken off diplomatic relations with France over a dispute concerning the French naval base at Bizerte, the francophone African states supported France's efforts to prevent the issue from being discussed at the UN. Though this attempt failed, (and eventually some states associated themselves with a resolution which reaffirmed Tunisia's sovereign rights), it reconfirmed a sub-Saharan African willingness to align with France even against a North African position. Again in October 1961, the francophone states refused to associate themselves with a resolution (to which Morocco and Tunisia attached importance), which proposed that Africa should be regarded as a 'denuclearized zone' and that France should be censured for conducting nuclear tests in the Sahara.[6]

In 1967, the CAR, Chad, Gabon, Ivory Coast, Madagascar, Niger, Senegal and Togo all abstained on a General Assembly resolution calling for independence for Djibouti. At the UN, much of this voting pattern was determined by close consultation among the francophone African states themselves and did not necessarily result from special French efforts to pressurize them. Indeed, from December 1960 onwards (for about a decade), the so-called 'Brazzaville Group' (Congo-Brazzaville, Cameroon, Ivory Coast, Dahomey, Gabon, Upper Volta, Madagascar, Niger, CAR, Senegal, Chad, Mauritania and Togo, which 'joined' the group in 1963), tended to co-ordinate their foreign policies at least as expressed in UN votes. During the early and mid-1960s, francophone African states tended to support French policy in a number of other fora, notably the IMF, where membership of the Franc Zone gave these states extra incentives to plead common cause with France.[7]

There was, however, no blind allegiance to France, no automatic genu-flection to French authority. Often in the 1960s France's voting pattern in the UN and other bodies was not followed by the 'Brazzaville Group'. In 1966 these states supported a National Assembly resolution revoking South Africa's mandate over Namibia (France with Great Britain had abstained), and in 1967, while France abstained, the Brazzaville Group supported a resolution calling for Great Britain to use all her means (including military force) to help bring order to Rhodesia.[8] But the importance of the close relations between France and francophone Black Africa at the UN lay less in the way they cast their votes in particular instances than in their essentially friendly attitude towards France which helped to strengthen

France's prestige at the UN even at times when, on specific issues, France found herself relatively isolated. French arms sales to South Africa were not so strongly condemned at the UN as were the South African policies of Great Britain and the United States. The Ivory Coast and Gabon even questioned at the UN the efficacy of the various UN 'threats' to South Africa and called for the initiation of a dialogue with South Africa. While the anglophone states at the UN (particularly Zambia) were strongly critical of France's arms sales policy, their efforts tended to focus on British policy. For some time, France benefited from the fact that Houphouet-Boigny felt that retention of contacts with South Africa was important, and this helped to weaken the strength of francophone African criticism of France's arms sales policy. It was only in the late 1970s that staunch French friends in Africa began to join the large group of protesters who could not accept France's continued aid to South Africa.[9]

The determining characteristic of de Gaulle's foreign policy towards Black Africa, which helped to maintain among the new African leaders a certain respect for France, was above all its intensity. Foccart is said to have received an average of eight senior African officials or ministers a day during his tenure. Both through Foccart's contacts and the regal policy pursued by de Gaulle himself, never more evident than on his well-organized trips to Black Africa, French diplomacy in and towards Black Africa was remarkably *attentive* and this helped to cultivate the loyalty of essential elites. This diplomacy was entirely driven by the need to ensure that French prestige on the continent remained high. Policies towards individual African states were developed always with this ultimate aim in mind, which often overrode economic calculations and the special interests of French commerce. French diplomacy in Africa, as elsewhere, was concerned with images of French power. General de Gaulle considered that 'France's rank depends on the honour of her flag and not on increases in her GNP.'[10] In Africa, the economic consequences of a particular policy decision were rarely a major feature of decision-making in the Gaullist years.

This emphasis on 'rank', and the geopolitical consequences that flowed from this priority, was evident in all the most dramatic choices of the Gaullist period. The military interventions in Chad were driven entirely by de Gaulle's personal sense (which Foccart encouraged) that France's reputation among other Black African states was at stake, as well as by the view that other fragile states close to Chad might collapse. The support of the Biafran secessionist movement flowed in part from similar considerations: neighbouring small francophone states would be saved from a too powerful Nigeria if it were broken up. The interests of French companies who wanted to establish and build on commercial ties with Nigeria were ignored, and it was only when the francophone states themselves showed that they supported Nigerian unity that de Gaulle's plans were abandoned. Only in the mid-1970s was there a substantial increase in economic exchanges between the two countries, and only in the 1980s did these economic exchanges become truly major. The visceral policy which de Gaulle inspired, and Foccart managed, towards Guinea was driven by a desire to punish a state that had opted out of the French system. Here too, there were French industrialists who regretted the diplomatic *cordon sanitaire* with which France surrounded Guinea whose rich mineral resources some industrialists felt warranted a more pragmatic policy.[11] Though some French companies like Pechiney, UTA, and French Cables and Radio operated in Guinea, a more complete penetration of French industry was hampered by the total lack of official contact between the two countries and de Gaulle's personal vendetta. Again, only in the mid-1970s was a process begun for the 'normalization' of Franco–Guinean relations, and even this fell short of re-establishment of formal diplomatic relations, which only took place after Sékou Touré's death in 1984.[12]

The substance of Gaullist foreign policy towards particular African states and the style of official French activity in Africa was therefore conditioned by de Gaulle's personal interpretations of how French prestige could best be advanced. Despite the fact that he undoubtedly saw French co-operation policy as an extension of the *mission civilisatrice*, he was reluctant to see French policy towards Black Africa lost in a wide cultural project. Hence his coolness to the idea of *francophonie*, initially advanced by African states as a better way to manage relations between those states who shared the French language. For *francophonie*, if it were turned into a political institution, would have deprived France of the dominant position she held within the *France–Afrique* system which de Gaulle's personalized policy towards Black Africa was intended to advance. The reasons it was proposed by African states and the reception the idea was to have in Gaullist France are instructive. It is clear that de Gaulle wished his diplomacy in Africa to operate through bilateral structures, even if the aim was the sustenance of a homogeneous bloc close to France.

Given the different place of the Maghreb states in French African diplomacy and the special place of Senegal in the history of French cultural assimilation it is significant that the proposal for a *Commonwealth à la française* came from President Bourguiba of Tunisia, on a trip he made to Senegal in November 1965. Bourguiba's proposal for 'a new association of French-speaking countries in Africa' was warmly received by President Senghor, and was formerly taken up in a 1966 meeting of OCAM, whose own creation had been partly linked to the fear felt by francophone African states that they would find themselves dominated by the English-speaking states at OAU meetings.[13] Senghor clearly hoped that a *francophonie* structure would serve to link the French-speaking Maghreb states, not members of OCAM, into a larger French-speaking entity. Tunisia favoured this, though Morocco and Algeria prized Arab solidarity more than they desired new links with France. At the 1966 OCAM meeting, a document was drafted, and later presented to de Gaulle, which laid out the structure of the new organization. Three concentric circles were defined which were meant to describe the relative roles and intensity of relations between the member states. The first, clearly tightest, circle would include France, the former territories of French West and Equatorial Africa (including Mali, but Guinea was not specifically mentioned), Madagascar, and if they so desired, Haiti and the three former Belgian colonies of Burundi, Rwanda and Congo. These states would consult on financial and cultural questions. The second circle would add Lebanon, the Maghreb and Indochina, and its members would manage their relations closely with the first circle, participating in regular meetings of heads of state, finance ministers and officials responsible for education and cultural policy. The third circle would comprise all other states using the French language such as Belgium, Canada, Switzerland and Luxembourg. Links with these countries would be primarily cultural.[14]

While Bourguiba, Senghor and Hamani Diori of Niger were particularly keen about the *francophonie* structure, other francophone states were more circumspect. The French government of de Gaulle never endorsed it, clearly because a *Commonwealth à la française*, like the British model which some of the francophone African states had in mind, would only reduce the role of the principal member. The inclusion, even in the outer circle, of other developed Western states must have represented, in de Gaulle's eyes, a potential threat to French manoeuvrability, even an assault on French independence of action towards the former Black African colonies. The nature of Gaullist diplomacy in Africa simply would not admit of such a multilateralization of francophone relationships. Senghor and Bourguiba were initially motivated precisely by the desire to widen francophone African links, and were concerned by the possibility that a post-Gaullist France might abandon a tradition of economic aid in Africa. De Gaulle's indifference to the *francophonie* concept effectively stalled this African attempt to diversify external contacts, but Pompidou's arrival to power did allow a certain widening of African diplomatic manoeuvre.

While Pompidou retained the services of Jacques Foccart, and consequently his individualistic and specialized approach to dealings with Black Africa, his own inclination was to place relations with Black Africa in the wider context of France's relations with all of Africa. As the previous chapters have shown, Pompidou's policy was Gaullist in that military and economic aid retained an important bilateral aspect, but as indicated by the leitmotif that had guided his election campaign, *continuité et ouverture*, Pompidou also felt that it was necessary to deepen links with others in Africa. His would be a policy which would refocus French interests on the Mediterranean, and while France's relations with the Maghreb counties would still correspond to a different diplomatic 'logic' and be dealt with in different diplomatic 'structures', Pompidou's rhetorical policy would pay greater homage to the need to develop a more global approach to French relations with Africa. In the eyes of the influential journalist at *Le Monde*, Jacques Fauvet, France's world role would still have to be defined in the Pompidou era largely through her relations with Africa. Writing in 1970 he argued that Pompidou's France:

has gone back to her natural position and dimensions. She knows that she can compete neither with Asia nor with the two Americas. She counted in the world only ephemerally, by virtue of the importance accorded to her thanks to the prestige of General de Gaulle. The same France now realizes that, if Europe ever does come into being, it will be neither the French nor the Franco–German Europe that the General had hoped for. Whether or not Great Britain joins it, it will certainly be more German than truly European. What then is left for France except the Mediterranean and those African countries to the south of it.

There friendly links have survived colonization and ... decolonization. There we can concentrate part of our limited financial and military, especially naval, resources. In this area it is perhaps less difficult to achieve a policy of independence vis-a-vis the blocs.[15]

In fact, there was no dramatic increase in French influence in the Mediterranean during the Pompidou period, but he did attempt to fashion a more comprehensive policy for the Maghreb. In Black Africa, as we have seen, his policy was influenced by the need to react satisfactorily to the African demands for revisions in the co-operation agreements. Difficulties in his dealings with some of the North African countries and his need to avoid an atmosphere of crisis in Black African relations especially after the reforms of 1973 made Pompidou receptive to (if still not enthusiastic about), some multilateralization of French diplomacy in Africa and particularly to the idea of summit meetings at which the nature of France's African policy would be discussed.

An early indicator of France's new concentration on the Arab world, was the sale of 112 *Mirage* aircraft to Libya in December 1969. Libya was a major oil exporter to France and agreed to pay hard currency for French arms. The delivery of these aircraft, and later of *Alouette* and *Super Frelon* helicopters as well as *Crotale* air defence missiles to the new regime of Colonel Gadaffi, who had come to power after the overthrow of King Idriss, helped to offset France's very large oil bill. But it also had a wider political purpose, as French officials hoped that Libya could be drawn into closer collaboration with Algeria, Morocco and Tunisia and hence also into a French sphere of interest along the Mediterranean. While North African dreams of a Greater Maghreb have since been revived and may be in the process of realization, it has been an elusive political project and not one from which France could benefit automatically or which she could manipulate in her own interest. Nevertheless, the Pompidou government in the early 1970s considered that a more united North Africa could be insulated from superpower pressures and made more amenable to French influence.[16] This in general would also help to keep other African states protected from outside pressures. By 1972 this ambitious strategy was proving to be costly, as Libya began to help the rebels in Chad against the Chadian government which France supported. Libya was also offering aid to *Polisario* guerrillas in Morocco. In 1973, against the terms of the initial arms sales, Libya transferred some *Mirage* planes to Egypt, which were then used in the Yom Kippur war. Not for the first time, France discovered that her attempts to curry favour with Libya only upset a more carefully developed policy towards both North and Black Africa.[17]

Pompidou's pursuit of a Mediterranean strategy also encountered difficulties with Algeria. In 1970 the Algerians challenged the terms of the 1965 oil agreement with France by which France agreed to buy Algerian oil for fifteen years at a fixed price and to provide finance for the exploitation of oil. In July 1970, Algeria unilaterally decided to raise the rate of taxes paid by French oil companies from 50 per cent to 80 per cent and set the reference price for oil at $2.85 a barrel up from the $2.08 stipulated in 1965. In February 1971 Algeria announced the nationalization of all French pipeline facilities and natural gas fields and the appropriation of 51 per cent ownership of the producer companies.[18] In April, the price of oil was again raised to $3.60 a barrel, prompting Prime Minister Chaban Delmas to remark that the era of *coopération exemplaire* with Algeria had drawn to a close.[19] By the late autumn, an agreement was reached between the French oil company Elf-Erap and the Algerian Sonatrach which helped to smooth over the disputes of the previous months. The difficulties with Algeria, just as the awkward policy pursued towards Libya, confirmed that a Mediterranean policy would remain elusive. Only in Black Africa, could France find the right touch to maintain good relations with almost effortless superiority.

In his first trip as president to francophone Black Africa in February 1971, Pompidou sought to emphasize the themes of European aid to Africa which would mark his approach to African affairs. While he laid considerable stress on the special role of France, he also pointed out repeatedly that this was part of a general European policy. Surprisingly, perhaps, he did not seem to mind that some francophone states were finding other aid partners. In Mauritania, he argued that France did not wish to monopolize co-operation policy, and for this reason France was not concerned by Mauritania's decision to accept aid from the People's Republic of China. In Cameroon he argued that to be the only donor of aid would be to prolong the colonial experience. But in Gabon, one of the most important states in francophone Africa, whose loyalty to France was always especially valued, he took a more sentimental (but also pragmatic) line, arguing that relations between France and Africa were founded on: 'geography, history and a certain conception of human relations ... which were profitable to the countries with whom we co-operate but also represented for France a certain number of advantages.'[20] By 1972, soon after this major trip, Pompidou and the Ministry of Co-operation were forced to begin dealing with the various requests for revision of the co-operation agreements with Black African states. New post-colonial pacts had to be negotiated and signed. The need to revise bilateral relations with each of the francophone countries who had co-operation agreements with France made it difficult for Pompidou to establish a dynamic policy for Africa. He responded to African demands, but was unable to develop new initiatives. Yet the successful renegotiation of the agreements, and the atmosphere thus created of 'equality and respect for sovereign rights', made it easier for the Africans themselves to help France lay the foundations of a more sweeping Africa policy. Perceived again as an enlightened, reforming power by the Black Africans, France was able to garner new promises of continued loyalty from francophone Africa.

When the process was over near the end of 1973, Hamani Diori of Niger, who had been the first francophone African leader to ask for a revision of the terms of the agreements linking his country to France, called for a summit meeting of the French and selected African heads of state. In May 1973, the OCAM had met in Mauritius, but its attempt to define a new role for itself had failed. Francophone African states wished to have another forum in which to discuss common problems.[21] No purely African forum was suitable, so the African states turned to France. The initial French reaction to the proposed summit was restrained, as Pompidou was not keen to be accused of resurrecting colonial structures, and he may well have also been suspicious about the ends to which such a summit could be put. But the African states insisted, for they wanted to develop a more organized way to deal with Franco–African issues. Many of the important leaders felt that for two or three years French–Black African relations had suffered from a certain inertia, interrupted only by the specific bilateral renegotiations of the co-operation agreements. President Senghor of Senegal publicly lamented, not without some bitterness, the passing of the era of 'grand designs'.[22] Senghor was not alone among francophone African leaders. Others also wished France to reaffirm more openly her *mission historique*. After some African urging, therefore, the first summit meeting of the French and African heads of state took place in Paris in November 1973 and included ten francophone African states plus France.

In his opening speech to the conference Diori went to some lengths to assure his French host that despite the recent renegotiations, Franco–African relations had a solid future: 'I can affirm that the large majority of the states which remain grouped within the Franc Zone are resolved to retain and reinforce the solidarity of the francophone ensemble by giving it a new basis.'[23] Pompidou could not easily demur from such an assertion, and while his policy towards Black Africa had always paid homage to the strength of bilateral relations, his own vision had always been of a greater collaboration between all Europeans, with all of Africa. Having concentrated some effort in opening up French markets in anglophone countries, and having lobbied within the European Community for a more generous European aid policy to Africa, it was clear that his own view of Franco-African relations was affected by a reinterpretation of the *Eurafrique* myth. In his address to the summit meeting Pompidou argued that:

The completely informal structure of our meeting proves, if this was necessary, that our common goodwill is in the service of co-operation and peace. I consider personally that the fact that we find ourselves here, Frenchmen and Africans, in the present circumstances, is encouraging. We should find ourselves here again, tomorrow, animated by the same spirit of understanding and dialogue, between Europeans and Africans, to hear, before it is too late, the voice of wisdom and of community of interests of our two continents.[24]

This slight preference for the Eurafrican thesis showed that the Pompidou diplomatic style in Africa, while largely in the Gaullist tradition, was still a variant on it. De Gaulle would never have invoked the need for European co-operation in Africa in quite the same way. There was also some modest progress in *francophonie* during Pompidou's tenure of office. In February 1969 delegates from over thirty countries had met to recommend to their countries that such a body be created, and in the first year of Pompidou's presidency some of the institutions of *francophonie*, the most important of which was the *Agence de Coopération Culturelle et Technique* (ACCT), began to fund cultural projects. But Pompidou, like de Gaulle, also felt uneasy about the *francophonie* structures and its wide membership. It was never considered seriously as a potential political instrument. In terms of the management of the Franco–African relationship, the Franco–African summit meeting would prove much more central. In fact, the most striking legacy Pompidou was to leave for his successor was this nascent institution, requested by the Africans themselves, which Valéry Giscard d'Estaing used skilfully to put France's relations with Africa at the centre of his ambitious overseas policy.

Giscard and the Franco-African Summits

When Giscard came to power he sought to give a broad dimension to French foreign policy, so broad that commentators were to dub it a policy of *mondialisme*, whose aim was *conciliation tous azimuts*.[25] His declaratory policy would emphasize the politics of dialogue, raise images of intercontinental unity and hold out promises of new international orders which France would design and then coax into existence. In Africa, he developed new personal contacts, not always wisely, but also built on existing institutions to give his African policy a structure and even a sense of ceremony. But to begin to carry this out he needed to ensure his own freedom of manoeuvre. To distinguish himself from his predecessors, he eliminated the general secretariat for African and Malagasy Affairs at the Elysée and dispensed with the services of Jacques Foccart.

He retained René Journiac, Foccart's former deputy, as his African adviser, but quickly set about dismantling at least part of Foccart's network. In Giscard's view France's African policy had been controlled for too long by devoted Gaullists or servants of Foccart. In his first five years in office Giscard got rid of over fifty diplomats who were considered too partisan. This included the removal of two Gaullist 'proconsuls' whose nicknames reflected the specific personal power they were thought to wield in the countries to which they were posted: Ambassador Jacques Raphaël-Leygues (*l'Ivorien*) and Ambassador Robert Delauney (*le Gabonais*).[26]

Like his predecessors, Giscard considered that France's African policy only really concerned Black Africa. In a speech delivered in January 1981 his first foreign minister declared this as a matter of fact:

what we call in France African policy, is our relations with the African countries south of the Sahara. The countries of the Maghreb, Morocco, Algeria, Tunisia, Libya, do not enter into this framework, anymore than does Egypt, because these belong to what in Paris we call Mediterranean policy, in which other considerations enter.[27]

Rather like Pompidou, but unlike de Gaulle, Giscard hoped that France's African policy and her Mediterranean policy could at least be made complementary, even if each necessarily proceeded from different premises. Again like Pompidou, he would find this a difficult trick to manage. But in pursuing his African policy Giscard made attempts, though exclusively through the rhetoric that began to dominate his speeches, to create linkages between France's policy towards the Arab world and her relationships with the states of Black Africa.

More than either of his predecessors, Giscard also tried, with more success, to build links with non-francophone states. The focus of this new effort was the ex-Belgian colonies and lusophone Africa, which gained independence from Portugal soon after Giscard took power. While de Gaulle had moved quickly in 1964 to establish good links with the ex-Belgian Congo, the thrust of France's African diplomacy had always been focused on certain key states in francophone Africa. At the Franco–African summit which took place in Bangui in March 1975, there were ministerial delegations from Zaire, Burundi and Rwanda. This was the last of the conferences to bear the title of '*Conférence des chefs d'États d'Afrique francophone*', for during the conference Giscard expressed the hope that at future conferences, new states of 'latin expression', with whom there were 'particular affinities', could also attend. In 1976, three lusophone states, Guinea-Bissau, Cap Vert, Sao Tomé et Principe, took part in the Franco–African summit in Paris, and from then on the numbers of states attending this new 'institution' of African international relations would grow.

The 1975 (and the 1976) summit meeting concentrated on economic issues. In Bangui, Giscard noted that the Lomé accord concluded between the European Community and the African, Caribbean and Pacific countries associated with the EEC, and which guaranteed these states a fixed level of income for their primary products, exemplified the 'New International Economic Order' for which his government would strive. He called for the establishment of a *Fonds de solidarité Africaine*. He also argued that in the future:

The Mediterranean states and the states of the Middle East, who are major oil producers, should now be in a position to give very low interest loans for development projects ... This aid that major oil producers can now provide to the

Third World should not incite Western states and particularly the Europeans, to relax their efforts of co-operation. It would not be a replacement of aid, it would be an addition of aid.[28]

This remark gave an indication of some of the grand designs which Giscard would later draft for African consideration. In April 1975 he visited Algeria, the first French head of state to do so, for neither de Gaulle, nor Pompidou, felt it diplomatically or politically possible to set foot in independent Algeria. During his meeting with Boumedienne Giscard went beyond the immediate bilateral problems between the two countries to discuss broad political policy options for Algeria and France, who according to the Algerian leader were 'condemned by history and by geography to collaborate.'[29] For the first but not the last time in his presidency, Giscard evoked the possibility of a greater Euro–Arab and Euro–Arab–African concert of powers. In May 1975, Giscard visited Morocco and in November, Tunisia, and these trips to the principal Maghreb states, seen in the context of Giscard's wider African policy were an indication that he might try to bridge the long-standing gaps between France's Mediterranean and African policies.

But managing France's relations even within the Maghreb would prove difficult, as was indicated by the fact that in 1975 Morocco and Algeria each asked France to support it against the other as the conflict in the Western Sahara began to take shape. Giscard's leanings towards Morocco on this issue, and the resultant quarrel with the Algerian president Boumedienne, undermined the *rapprochement* between France and Algeria many hoped would follow the French president's visit.[30] Still, after the 1976 Paris summit (where Giscard again concentrated on technical development issues related to the stabilization of commodity prices), the tenor of Giscard's diplomacy towards Africa was the importance of building a broad political relationship between Europe and Africa.

At the Franco–African summit in Dakar in 1977 (attended by twenty-one states), Giscard drew attention to the unstable situation in southern Africa, and argued that the external rivalries which weighed so heavily on the continent meant that the only way forward was 'a path which reserved Africa for the Africans'. In a major speech in Dakar, Giscard then drew on old themes borrowed from France's imperial past and not used in political discourse since the 1950s:

If we want to preserve our identity, we should try to avoid, we Europeans and you Africans, being enveloped in an environment created by the superpowers, and succumbing to a dependence on them. We should unite our destinies, in order to create a median way necessary to the blossoming of our peoples and our cultures: the median way, for the median continents of Europe and Africa.[31]

Numerous African leaders underscored the importance, given the new crises that were affecting African stability, of reaching a Eurafrican understanding that had a political content of consequence. Houphouet-Boigny, in an interview he gave after the summit added a practical consideration to the more sentimental, vague and allusive references which were brought out during the summit itself: 'If by some aberration, by *insouciance*, Europe let a foreign influence develop on our continent, there would be a risk that over time Europe's supply of primary materials would be dramatically compromised.'[32] References by most of the francophone African leaders to 'foreign influences' did not mean that the French military presence would be called into question: France belonged in Africa, the Cubans and particularly the Soviets, were 'foreigners'. But this perspective was not uniformly shared by all states, for while the more conservative African states hoped that Soviet adventurism in Africa could be treated as a separate item on the summit agenda, Benin (with a nominally marxist-leninist government), and all the lusophone states, wished to keep it out of the conference so that the meeting would not degenerate into an anti-Soviet rally.[33]

These differences between the growing number of states which attended the summits made it necessary to relegate purely political questions to discussions on the margins of the summit, or as Giscard himself put it in his opening address to the summit in Nice in 1980, it was wiser to 'raise more specifically political issues during meals'.[34] At the 1978 summit in Paris, for example, the Senegalese and Ivorian delegations, who wished to discuss security issues, still felt it necessary to fly their trial balloon of a *Pacte Eurafricain de solidarité* outside the summit's formal sessions.[35] By 1979, at the Kigali summit (which included twenty-four delegations, including some anglophone states), economic issues dressed up in grand designs for intercontinental solidarity had returned to centre stage.

This summit followed discussions which had taken place within the European Community about the promotion of a Euro–Arab dialogue, and Giscard, who wished France to have a central role in these inter-regional relations, felt that these discussions could be joined to the evolving Afro–Arab interchanges. Senghor and Bourguiba had long been supporters of greater co-operation between African and Arab states, and had argued that Arab capital, already available to Africans through the *Banque Arabe pour le développement economique en Afrique* (BADEA), might be combined with European technological assistance to further the development of Africa.[35] In his opening address at Kigali, Giscard invited his audience to consider the interrelationships between the European, Arab and African worlds:

this dialogue which has begun in the Franco–African family, can serve as an example and be extended to other parts of the world, and in particular the countries of Europe and of the Arab world. France, which was, with its African friends, the originator of these regular meetings, considers that we should be at the forefront of those countries whose existence ... is more and more mixed with the life of the African continent.

What are, in effect, the broad developments which we see in today's world? They are, outside the provisional solidarities created by fear or by riches, the permanent solidarities of geography, history and culture. These are a given for Europe, for Africa, and for the whole of the Arab world. In fact these three groupings have links between themselves which are closer and more strong than with any other part of the world.

Our preoccupation is that there should be an understanding of these permanent solidarities, which will as a result be better affirmed and made concrete, for we live in a time when large groups appear and organize themselves on the continental level.

It is necessary, for the equilibrium of tomorrow's world, that the group of West European, African and Middle Eastern states reflect on the ways of more closely linking their destinies.[36]

This call for a *trilogue* between Europe, Africa and the Arab worlds was a favourite idea of Giscard's but did not resonate either with his close collaborators or with leaders of some of the states to which the idea was directed. In a major speech on African policy in December 1979, the Foreign Minister, Jean-François Poncet, did not mention the concept, and concentrated instead on the importance of clinging to the Franco–African relationship, noting that 'it is in large measure through its association with Africa, that France has a vocation for a world role.'[37] The Gulf states expressed little interest in being ensnared by what they perceived as a French-led Eurafrican project.[38] The Gaullists who were out of power found the idea unattractive. Jacques Chirac dismissed *trilogue* and Giscard's various plans for new international economic orders as mere *bavardages*.[39] At the 1980 summit in Nice, Giscard lowered his sights, and noted merely that *trilogue* was an *état d'esprit*, a 'basic idea contributing to the organization of international relations', which could evolve from Franco–African relations, but which would take a long time to develop.[40]

Giscard's diplomacy in Africa was hyperactive. Punctuated by numerous military interventions, his presidency was evidence of the extraordinary fascination that African policy could hold for the French leadership. The last military operation ordered by Giscard was to depose the leader of one of the

African states that Giscard had brought into the first circle of Franco–African activity. Emperor Bokassa of Central Africa had become an embarrassment. News that he had killed a hundred schoolchildren because they had not bought uniforms from the Emperor's clothing factory led Giscard to reinstate David Dacko as leader of a new Central African Republic. Later revelations that Bokassa had made a gift of diamonds to the French president sparked a major domestic debate on the nature of Giscard's imperial presidency, and was a proximate cause of his election defeat to François Mitterrand. The style of Giscard's declaratory diplomacy, in which he mixed the old myths of *France–Afrique* and *Eurafrique* with the new one of *trilogue*, left even those African interlocutors of his who had longed for a return to the 'era of grand designs' gasping for breath. Giscard gave considerable priority to France's African policy, and sought to put it in a wider context of international relations; to situate it as an important instance of the North–South dialogue. His reference to the links between Europe and Africa were always made in this wider 'humanistic' spirit. As Jean-François Poncet once remarked 'It is absurd to talk of Giscard d'Estaing as a colonialist... He is the complete twentieth-century man who wants to use European wealth to help Africa into the twentieth century. He regards Africa as an extension of Europe, and wants to help African leaders who have the same conception.'[41] But Giscard's ambitious programme to transform the Gaullist policy of 'co-operation' into a Franco–African project for world order could not be sustained, given the heterogeneity of interests and the variety of perspectives to be found within the Franco–African family whose membership Giscard had actually tried to expand. In the more complex African world of the 1980s, it had become difficult to carry out France's African policy as part of a doctrine of international affairs. The need to avoid a *doctrinaire* approach to Africa, and to adopt more pragmatic attitudes, became obvious during the Mitterrand presidency.

Mitterrand's Approach to Africa

The first few months of Mitterrand's presidency were affected by the perceived need to distinguish the policy of the 'new parliamentary majority' from that of the Giscardian and Gaullist *ancien régime*, while reassuring African leaders that there would be no abandonment of France's traditional interests in Africa. He also wanted to show that there was a break from the past and that new channels were available for Franco–African co-operation. Further into the Mitterrand presidency, the need became that of transforming a 'socialist' policy for Africa into a new *politique africaine de la France.* Just as Mitterrand emphasized his wish to be President of 'all Frenchmen' so he wished to ensure that his external policy be seen as a national and not sectarian or party policy. The result of these various aims was that Mitterrand's discourse towards Africa had a different inflexion from that of his predecessors but was not revolutionary. If it was not a perfect continuation of past policy, there was still more continuity than rupture. The President's assertion in August 1981 that 'neither in substance nor in style can there be any common denominator with the failed policy of the *ancien régime*,' proved to be a considerable exaggeration.[42]

The creation of France's African policy still lay largely in the hands of the President who also kept a group of African advisers at the Elysée. Guy Penne led the team of advisers for much of the first *septennat*, and he collaborated quite effectively with Jean Ausseil, the director of the African and Malagasy department of the Quai d'Orsay. The President's son, Jean Christophe Mitterrand, a former *Agence France Presse* correspondent in Africa, also worked within the Elysée on African policy. The execution of particular missions *vis-à-vis* Africa was, however, spread around a number of different ministers and even party officials, more often, or at least more obviously, than had been the case in the past. To take a few examples from the early 1980s, it is noteworthy that the attempts to achieve a diplomatic understanding with the revolutionary leader of Burkina Faso, Thomas Sankara, in the summer of 1983 was largely managed by Jacques Huntzinger, a major figure in the Socialist Party, and the Minister of Co-operation Christian Nucci; the negotiation between Paris and Tripoli was in the hands of the Minister of Foreign Affairs, Claude Cheysson, with help from one of Mitterrand's closest friends, Roland Dumas, who was also charged with mending fences with Gabon when bilateral relations briefly fell into disrepair. Dumas in some respects broke with precedent in that he often travelled to Africa without representatives of the Elysée or the Ministry of Co-operation.[43] The President still controlled the main lines of France's African policy, but he relied on a wide array of personal emissaries to manage particular bilateral relations. Rarely did he intervene himself in the more delicate situations. But his familiarity with Africa as a former Minister of Overseas France and as a close associate of Houphouet-Boigny from the 1950s, made it easier for him to dispel some of the early concerns about the socialists' Africa policy.

Nevertheless, the first Mitterrand government took pleasure in being able to play host in Paris in November 1981 to thirty-four African states, including heads of state from marxist-leninist Benin and Congo and observers from several other states not normally associated with France's African policy, such as Egypt, Kenya, Angola, Ghana, Tanzania, Sudan and

Zimbabwe. The presence of delegations from Mauritania, Morocco and Tunisia (the latter two as observers), meant that problems relating to the Western Sahara dispute could also be addressed on the margins. During Giscard's presidency the attendance at the Franco–African summit meetings had increased each year; by the middle of Mitterrand's tenure, three-quarters of the membership of the OAU felt it right to attend.

Initially, the Mitterrand camp welcomed this overt show of approval of France's African role, and the heterogeneity of the participants and observers reflected in part the co-operation policy pursued by Jean Pierre Cot who wanted the French role in Africa to expand well beyond the traditional *chasse gardée*. As we have seen, not all francophone states were pleased with this expansion, and in the context of the summit meetings many openly regretted it, especially when the numbers of states attending hovered at around forty in the mid-1980s. In the 1983 summit at Vittel Mitterrand made a gesture to the francophone countries by offering a dinner for them the day before the summit. By 1985 it had become necessary to hold nearly a whole day's meeting of francophone states from which the ex-British, Portuguese, Italian and Spanish colonies were excluded, before the full plenary session opening the annual summit meeting took place.[44] The large number of states attending also made Mitterrand insist, in what became a ritual part of his opening statements to the Franco–African summits, that this 'institution' of French–African relations was not intended to replace the OAU, or become an 'OAU *bis*'. So great was the attraction of the summit meeting that many commentators began to observe that it was becoming an easier meeting place for African leaders than the official pan-African organization.

But managing the diverse group was also a difficult task. Even within the enlarged francophone African clan of states who now began to attend, there were important divisions which France had to take into account. In the middle 1980s the summits concentrated largely, but by no means exclusively, on the sensitive question of Chad. In 1984, after the failed Franco–Libyan mutual withdrawal agreement, dissatisfaction among African states was such that both conservative and radical states stayed away. The leaders of the Ivory Coast, Togo and Niger were absent, in part because they were concerned about French commitment to the security of Black Africa, while Benin, Burkina Faso and Guinea were perhaps still worried by a French policy that they viewed as being neo-colonial. Despite these notable absences, there were still thirty-seven states represented.[45] This ensured that a wide variety of subjects were treated, including debt, security questions and relations with the European Community. Much was made by the French government of the fact that these summits were now occasions to discuss any international issue of common interest. The presence of anglophone and lusophone states from southern Africa meant that the question of southern Africa figured more often in discussions at the summit meetings.

France's policy of arms sales to South Africa had been severely attacked in the late 1970s. Giscard's Foreign Minister Louis de Guiringaud had to cut short an official visit to Tanzania in August 1977 when he was greeted on arrival by demonstrators protesting against continued arms sales. Soon after all contracts were cancelled though South Africa was still producing *Mirage* 111s and F1s as well as some ground armour and machine-guns under licence from the French.[46] Well into Mitterrand's tenure of office, in 1983, Black African states were accusing France of supplying spare parts for aircraft and helicopters as well as some technical assistance to South Africa for licensed production.[47] At the 1985 Franco–African summit, the South African issue again featured, but principally because of a trip that President Abdou Diouf of Senegal had recently made to many of the front-line states. Just before the summit took place, the Mitterrand government had announced that it would take several diplomatic measures (withdrawal of the French ambassador and some economic sanctions) to show its hostility towards Pretoria. In 1985 the French government provided helicopters to the Angolan government. There was more public condemnation of South Africa's raids against her neighbours with which France began to trade more energetically (by 1985 France had become Botswana's third largest trading partner), and Mitterrand's cabinet officials, particularly the Prime Minister Laurent Fabius, who took part in a demonstration in front of the South African Embassy in Paris, began to take more overtly anti-apartheid lines.

Taken together, these various decisions and gestures still amounted (despite the criticism they drew from the conservative opposition) to essentially symbolic opposition to the South African regime with whom France still maintained important commercial links.[48] Nevertheless, it was sufficient to preserve a liberal reputation for France in sub-Saharan Africa. No Franco–African summit meeting in the first Mitterrand *septennat* saw the sort of condemnation of policy that Mrs Thatcher's government regularly suffered in the context of Commonwealth meetings. This was partly because of the relatively more muted voice of the anglophone states in the Franco–African meetings, but also because of a unique benefit of the doubt that France was able to cultivate in Africa about her relations with South Africa. A strong rhetorical anti-apartheid policy seemed enough to insulate the French government from bitter criticism.

The harmony of French relations with francophone Africa, disturbed by some of the 'empty chair' policies pursued even by France's closest allies at the summit meetings, also suffered setbacks owing to bilateral problems. In

1985, Burkina's president, Thomas Sankara, accused the French of supplying arms to Mali with whom Burkina had long had a border dispute which led to the brief Christmas war in 1985. French military aid to Mali had in fact been quite limited, and Paris officials regretted the complaints, especially given that earlier in the year the French had provided a good deal of food aid to Burkina, transporting food from ports in Lomé and Abidjan. Relations with Burkina became more relaxed in early 1986 once the war with Mali had been brought to an end. French relations with Gabon twice required artful diplomacy to set right. In 1983 President Bongo complained about the publication in France of a book by the investigative journalist Pierre Péan (*Affaires Africaines*) which strongly criticized Bongo's use of power and the nature of his relations with France. References to the inability in a democracy to exert total control over the press failed to appease, and it was only after Libreville obtained a promise in March 1984 (never seriously meant) that France would give consideration to the building of a nuclear power plant in Gabon, that President Bongo's anger was calmed. In 1985 Jean Christophe Mitterrand was appointed to the board of Comilog, a French–American–Gabonese company mining the manganese deposits near Franceville. But relations soured again when the Gabonese opposition group Morena formed a so-called government in exile in Paris. Though the French government claimed not to attach importance to this, Bongo remained displeased until a visit by Roland Dumas on the twenty-fifth anniversary of Gabon's independence. In the same year, France banned a press conference in Paris by a Togolese opposition group, which may have made it easier later in the year to have Togo nominated as the host of the 1986 summit. Also in 1985, the publication in France of a book about the close advisers to President Kolingba of the Central African Republic caused some strain in bilateral relations.[49] These events give an indication of the sensitivity of francophone Black African leaders to criticism, but also of the extent to which the French government was sometimes willing to go in order to ensure a congenial atmosphere between France and key African countries. The *attentiveness* of France to Africa which so characterized the early Gaullist period may have changed in form, in substance, but not in intensity. These examples also show that France's African partners are quick to jump on any French statement, act of commission or omission, which might be interpreted as against their interests. This sometimes forces the French leadership to stoop, not so much to conquer, as to appease old friends.

Mitterrand's appreciation of the broad forum for the expression of his views on foreign policy and for building stronger relations with France's closer allies, nurtured by his affection for the Franco–African summits despite the difficult conditions in which some of them were held, was also demonstrated by his decision to revive the *francophonie* concept. After six months of preparatory work, forty francophone states (from Europe, North America, the Middle East, Asia and Africa) met in Paris in February 1986 (one month before legislative elections in France) and discussed technical and cultural questions as well as broad issues of world politics.[50] At the following conference in Canada in September 1987, the announcement by the Canadian government that it was willing to write off some of the debt owed to it by African governments caused some embarrassment to France as the government insisted that this would set an unwelcome precedent. By June 1988, Mitterrand had come round to the view that for the poorest African countries some debt write-off might be appropriate.[51] The early decision to hold the 1989 *francophonie* conference in Dakar confirmed a willingness to accept the *Commonwealth à la française* idea originally treated sceptically by de Gaulle. But the primacy of the Franco–African summit as the main vehicle for dealing with the broad issues between France and Africa remained unquestioned.

Paradoxically, perhaps, the period of government *cohabitation*, in which François Mitterrand and Jacques Chirac shared power and both asserted themselves in foreign policy proved easy to manage in respect of France's African policy. This was in large measure because of the broad agreement that existed on the substance of policy. But given that the primary management problem that the Mitterrand administration had faced in its first five years in office was steering a course that satisfied both conservative and radical states (or which at least did not consistently offend one group), this basic problem was naturally eased by *cohabitation*. African leaders tended to choose the interlocutor in Paris with whom they felt most comfortable, and while this by no means followed a strict left/right divide it did mean that there was less opportunity for strident diplomatic protest by African states unhappy with France. Since responsibility was at least partly divided, this no doubt also muted any criticism there may have been. But the enduring reality is that the management of France's relations with Africa will become more difficult as, over time, these states, even if belatedly, begin to assert their individuality, and undertake a more diversified approach to their international relations.

Diplomatic Challenge of a Dissolving Bloc

The long-term aim of France's African policy has always been to so order relations with African states that France (while retaining an important position in Europe) could pretend to extra-continental influence of continental dimensions. That aim is under challenge both because of the difficulty of France's traditional state structures in dealing with the increased interdependence of African international relations and because of the inevitable tendency of African states to begin to demand more of France for their continued loyalty. In the 1985 Franco–African summit in Paris, François Mitterrand held fast to the traditional ideology of French state power in Africa:

Faced by the multiple problems which we must confront, wisdom advises us, without denying differences or disputes, to act in concert. And I wish to insist on the double solidarity which commands our future: solidarity between African states; solidarity between Africa and France, between Africa and Europe.[52]

But this form of political discourse, so successful for over a century of French activity in Africa, is vulnerable to the more dynamic nature of international exchanges within Black Africa and between Black Africa and North Africa. In principle this poses no automatic challenge to France, and indeed President Giscard d'Estaing attempted to sweep these emerging interrelationships under the French mantle constituted by the *trilogue* idea. But this did not appeal to either Arab or African states (and least, arguably, to the Afro–Arab states of the Maghreb). African interrelationships are no longer easily malleable by French influence or diplomatic entreaty. Despite the tendency to regional organization in both francophone West and Central Africa, the increasingly individualistic policies of francophone African states, their desire to make a national mark in African and sometimes wider international affairs, make it more difficult to speak usefully of a francophone bloc. Ultimately, it is therefore the Franco–African economic institutions (and especially the Franc Zone), as well the military links which tie Black Africa to France, which help French leaders in maintaining the special relationship. The innovation of the Franco–African summit, however, even if it becomes more difficult to manage for the reasons alluded to, gives France a forum to show that she is still relevant to African affairs. Its continuance will be an important sign that African membership in the Franc Zone and bilateral military links are not only based on need but also on historical ties that African states wish to take into the future. The challenge to French diplomacy in the years leading to the twenty-first century will be to keep the political advantages the French state will still perceive as necessary in Africa even as African states begin to shape their relationship with France more forcefully.

But the trend towards 'normalization' of the Franco–African relationship has already begun to establish itself. If it is not for tomorrow, the time for a final, fuller decolonization of Franco–African relations may be short; the clock has been set ticking. France cannot afford to sustain even these very poor states perpetually, and these states will look more assertively elsewhere for the extra assistance that is needed. Most francophone African states which are close to France will remain so, but they will want a less exclusive relationship. In the early 1970s most of these states requested a renegotiation of their relations with France and demanded that the more restrictve clauses of the co-operation agreements be removed, and that a greater 'africanization' of African economic institutions take place. It was only after this request was made, for example, that the two regional banks of West and Central Africa established their headquarters, which were formerly in Paris, in their present African homes of Dakar and Yaoundé. Even if there is no wholesale renegotiation of the co-operation agreements, individual African states are likely to demand further reforms in their relations with France, and it will be increasingly difficult for France to apply the logic of 'bloc politics' to her relations with francophone Africa.

France's diplomacy in Africa will aim to accommodate this evolutionary change, but if the language of French diplomacy will continue to emphasize a special relationship, African states will make more pragmatic calculations about the value of the French connection. Many may decide to stay close to France, but the heterogeneity of francophone African states, and their more dynamic policies both within and outside the African continent, will necessarily have the effect over time of dissolving the *France–Afrique* myth. France will experience more difficulty in keeping up its aid to a widening group of beneficiaries, and because this group is if anything growing poorer, the demand for French assistance will become tremendously greater than its available supply. For these states to survive, other European states may have to become more actively involved, and it is for this reason that one hears some French officials wonder whether the *Eurafrique* myth might still have some life in it.

Conclusion

The ambitious attempt by the French state to ensure that French power could be wielded in Africa, and particularly in Black Africa, has helped to shape the French identity in world affairs. National ambition and national identity have never, at least at the level of rhetoric, been so closely aligned as when French statesmen have spoken about, and used power in Africa. To be a power of the first rank, France had to have an external repository of French culture and activity. This was a nineteenth-century imperialist rallying cry. In the years leading to the twenty-first century, this view, if somewhat muted in its expression, is still part of the set of official assumptions about France's role in the world. The fact that French influence is now only awkwardly maintained in some sectors of the Middle East, of little import in South-east Asia, and under test at some of the remaining outposts of the French Empire in the Pacific, only reinforces an official predilection to cultivate enduring ties with Africa. French grandeur is considered bolstered by this external activity, and the nature of the African challenge is still such that the modest resources of France can have a noticeable impact. The old areas covered by France's imperial mantle still engage French political interest, but it is only in Africa where that mantle, changed in form, has relevance to current affairs. Louis de Guirangaud, as Foreign Minister, put these points forcefully in 1981:

France's African policy is without doubt one of the most original aspects of her external policy... Outside of Europe and the Mediterranean approaches, that is outside the countries of the Maghreb and the Levant, there is no region of the world with which France has such close or as diverse links, no other where she possesses such precise interests, no other where she possesses comparable means of action... I would add that Africa south of the Sahara is an *ensemble* which is 'to the measure' of France: neither the population mass, nor the size of the economic problems are out of proportion with the means which France can devote to a prolonged action outside of her own frontiers, whether this means co-operation experts, financial aid, or the military resources which can be brought to bear through the defence agreements.[1]

That a Western foreign minister could make these remarks in the early 1980s about a collection of ex-colonies attests to the uniqueness of France's post-colonial experience in Black Africa. No other European and no American in charge of foreign policy could afford to be at once so blasé and proud of his country's relations with a group of states in the developing world. This special relationship France has established in Black Africa has been all the more carefully maintained because it is seen as a distinguishing feature in international relations, and this helps to make France herself appear a special actor in international affairs. The intensity with which France has acted in Africa is both an expression of modesty and of pride. Modesty, insofar as there is a deep understanding that no other area of the world offers so congenial an environment for the perpetuation of French influence. Pride because, in dealing with African states, even three decades after juridical independence has been granted to them, France still uses language, even if guarded, which derives from her imperial past.

This language is itself an aspect of power. French leaders are diligent in their efforts to provide economic, military, and effectively cultural assistance to francophone African states. They do so for a variety of reasons related to the general welfare of these states, but the motivation behind such assistance is the same as it was in the imperial age: to give sustenance to otherwise abstract notions of French *rayonnement* beyond the 'hexagon' formed by metropolitan France. The broader geopolitical consequences of this successful offer and acceptance of French post-imperial aid remain difficult to measure, but in their own appreciation of French power in which the concepts of prestige and reputation are as important as tangible assessments of economic and military strength, French leaders draw considerably on the African experience. French power in general is thus in part defined by its extra-continental application. When the defence of French international stature is called for, the special role in Africa is invariably an element of France's public presentation. That presentation often takes on a virtually aesthetic – some might say artful – form, in that it relies heavily on idioms of French political influence and cultural strength abroad.

What is extraordinary about the French imperial and post-imperial experience is that the idioms of French power have been tailored to suit the structure of French influence. If in the 1890s the French state aim was encapsulated in the idea of a universal *mission civilisatrice*, a century later, French leaders still cling to a partial and unrealizable notion of *France–Afrique*, which if it defines a lost aspiration more than an immediate aim, has not yet been entirely rejected by the Africans themselves. The myth of the *France–Afrique* bloc may soon dissolve, and the nature of French activity be more widely denounced, but the fact will remain that France, better than any other ex-imperial power has been able to maintain, long after decolonization, tremendously close, even affectionate relations, with at least a portion of her former Empire. While other European great powers still exercise influence in some of their ex-colonies, none has been able to *order* its activity so efficiently as to make the sum of extra-European influence thus exercised greater than its parts.

From a political-diplomatic perspective, the continuance of what has become virtually a Franco–African partnership, if not actual alliance, has been possible because of the commanding role played by African leaders themselves in drafting the form of the post-colonial French-African contract. From the beginning, close relations between France and Black Africa have evolved through a collaborative effort. The policy of assimilation enunciated by French colonialists in the nineteenth century was never truly put into practice. In any case it would have taken centuries to develop a deep sense of common culture between Frenchmen and Africans, and whatever the idealistic notions of some colonial propagandists, the establishment of a vast Eurafrican state would never have received the approval of the French metropolitan population. This fact came out during the heated debates on the French Union in 1946. Yet the African *évolués* played a role in developing the oratory of French colonial expansion and approved of the eventual goal of assimilation. The attachment to the *mère patrie* demonstrated by Black Africans in 1914, and the later participation of African leaders in the French government, offered proof of an assimilationist desire of the elite. What is surprising is less that after decolonization certain links persisted, than that between 1946 and 1960 there was pressure from these leaders, who were so close to achieving the form of assimilation mixed with respect for their own native cultures which they desired, for a new relationship with France.

Clearly the British decolonizations of 1947, Ghana's independence in 1957, the Indochinese and the Algerian wars created international circumstances which made it appear right for francophone Black African leaders to put their relations with France on a more modern footing.[2] But decolonization meant neither a return to pre-imperial days nor a complete break with the immediate past. In any case, a complete break with France would have been difficult. Despite being led by well-educated and charismatic leaders most of the French colonies in Black Africa were strikingly weak. Throughout the 1950s, France had still been able to control local elections and processes, and in the absence of any attempt to encourage representative local government, old authoritarian structures were used to mitigate some of the early effects of nascent nationalism.[3] After the 1960 wave of independence in Black Africa, which the French saw was impossible to resist, control was still possible because the important Black African leaders had been long-time associates of French politicians, and themselves needed to further their collaboration with French leaders in order to harvest the fruits of French assistance which would help to maintain them in power.

Since much of the language that had accompanied France's imperial design threw up images of power held in common – *France–Afrique* or *Eurafrique* – these images could survive the process of decolonization. They could even be more efficiently exploited by French statesmen who wished to preserve French status in Africa by warning Black Africans of the dangers of too revolutionary a change in Franco–African relations. As in imperial times, collaboration between metropolitan and overseas leaders became a basic condition of continuing French power. The fact that these personal relationships, so strong between de Gaulle and the major African leaders, and carried forward in the governments of all of de Gaulle's successors, were supported by structures of the French state created to manage French power in Africa, meant that there was a bond between France and Africa not easily weakened by the vagaries of local African politics, or by the other priorities given to France's foreign policy. Georges Pompidou did not shy away from proclaiming before the French National Assembly in 1964 that 'at the end of the day, and in its essence, the policy of co-operation is but the extension of the policy of European expansion in the nineteenth century, which was characterized by the creation or the expansion of vast colonial empires.'[4] French power in Africa, possessed of its own ideology and rhetoric, has thus been perpetuated with the collaboration of African leaders, whose personal aspirations for power have been in part fulfilled by their links with the French leadership and whose political requirements have been partly catered for by the institutions of French aid, whose activities penetrate into every part of francophone Black African administrations. A combination of shared ideology, mutual seduction and French bureaucratic weight has helped to maintain the closeness of French–African relations.

For most of the post-colonial period, French military, economic or diplomatic activity in Black Africa has been relatively invulnerable to whatever local or international criticism might be mustered against it. A tradition of post-colonial activity has served to breed its own justification, and against the charge of neo-colonialism which might be levelled against France can be raised the defence that French activity has largely taken place with the demonstrable support of African governments, who have more often complained of the absence or weakness of particular forms of French aid than of the nature of French policy in Africa as a whole. The limitations of French influence in Black Africa since 1960 have been more a function of a natural declining capacity to deploy military force at will and with a complete assurance that it could not face strong opposition; of a rise in the gross economic cost to France of running the Franc Zone, supporting growing African debt and financing African state structures; and of a more complex international environment in Africa which makes it more difficult both to treat Black Africa as a bloc and to treat it separately from other parts of the continent.

These different restrictions on French power have not diminished French interest in remaining a key factor in African affairs. Jean Pierre Cot, whose reformist credentials as a socialist Minister of Co-operation were strong, wrote soon after leaving office that 'France maintains a universal discourse, but applies it in Africa to give it fullest effect.'[5] Africa still being 'to the measure' of French power, virtually the whole of the French *classe politique* consider that French status requires that efforts be made to meet the new challenges posed by Africa. Thus, military modernizations in France are undertaken very much with her external commitments in mind and improvements in transport capacity and light armaments are conceived to ensure that French military power remains adequate to offer protection for Black Africa. Similarly, in the economic crisis that has seized francophone African states, France has given structural adjustment support and direct financial aid to heavily burdened treasuries over and above the regular technical assistance offered through the co-operation agreements. Efforts are therefore made to show that France can offer emergency support as well as a regular rhythm of military and economic assistance. The degree of help of this kind which can be given will be limited by economic constraints; it may soon be that only the favoured states within the French orbit in Africa (Senegal, Ivory Coast, Gabon, Cameroon, Togo, Central African Republic, Chad, Djibouti and one or two others depending on particular circumstances) will be assured of full and consistent French assistance.

But the effectiveness of France's African strategy as a whole, as opposed to a capability to assist individual African allies, will be increasingly dependent on whether French leaders can develop a view of Africa which transcends old imperial categories. Algeria, which was formerly considered an integral part of France, and Tunisia and Morocco, both former protectorates, have been dealt with since decolonization in the context of France's vague 'Mediterranean policy'. Distinct from France's African policy, policy towards the Maghreb states has followed a different logic, determined largely by the more difficult process of decolonization which took place in North Africa. Pompidou sought to make his 'Mediterranean policy' compatible with France's 'African vocation', while Giscard tried to combine these normally separate lines of policy within the *trilogue* rubric. Yet these attempts never produced a French strategy which could fully take into account the sometimes awkward, occasionally useful links being established between the Maghreb and Black Africa which necessarily would affect French power there. In the 1970s, it was only within the network of *francophonie*, which in any case was devoid of any political-economic significance, and which never met at summit level, that the Maghreb was treated by France together with the other African states. By the late 1980s there was a clear recognition that this artificial separation had to stop. Two Maghreb countries began to attend, as full members, the Franco–African summit meetings, and it was decided to hold the 1988 summit in Morocco, the first time that a Maghreb country would play host to a summit which had in its origins been the near exclusive club of francophone Black African states. It is a noteworthy symbol of the extraordinary division in the French official mind between North Africa and sub-Saharan Black Africa, that the ex-Belgian colonies and the ex-Portuguese colonies in Africa entered the Franco–African summit earlier and with greater ease, than did the Maghreb states, for whom the concepts of *Eurafrique* and *France–Afrique* had first been invented in the previous century. While Algeria has always, as a matter of policy, stayed away from these meetings – precisely because it sees them as unwelcome reminders of the past – it remains the case that Algeria's sometimes ambitious foreign policy can have implications for sub-Saharan African states close to France.

As the tremendous pain of France's experience of decolonization in North Africa begins slowly to ease, it will be necessary, if France still wishes to remain a power of consequence in Black Africa, to grapple somehow with the fact that what happens in North Africa can profoundly affect the stability of sub-Saharan Africa. Morocco already demonstrated her relevance to Black African stability, and to the French role there, when she assisted France during the Shaba interventions in the late 1970s. Hassan's armed forces have sometimes contributed to the presidential guards of Black African states and thus played a not insignificant role in providing external support to African leaders. In the 1980s, Morocco's shifting attitude towards Gadaffi's Libya affected the adventurism and self-confidence displayed by Libya in Black Africa. For a brief period following the 1984 Treaty of Oudja between the two countries, Libya stopped supplying arms to *Polisario*, and Morocco in return muted her criticism of Libyan policy in Chad. The Western Sahara conflict itself, which has so divided Morocco and Algeria, also has affected Mauritania's neutrality, resulting in a brief French intervention in the late 1970s. Now Mauritania is a member of the ANAD, and her security is a matter of concern to the other members, all Black African states close to France. Tunisia has for long had to maintain a carefully ambiguous policy towards Libya and has suffered from her neighbour as much as many Black African states. Given their own problems of a religious nature, Black African states have watched with interest Tunisia's handling of domestic Islamic fundamentalism. These three Maghreb countries Morocco, Algeria and Tunisia, may well also begin to engage themselves more actively in Black Africa, and the interdependence between these regions thus intensified may well affect France's power as much as the generational change in the francophone Black African leadership, and the activities of rival extra-continental powers.

If this is true in the Maghreb it may also be the case for southern Africa, another 'strategic' area in Africa to which French leaders have paid only minimal attention. The fact that Zaire, and then the lusophone states of southern Africa, Mozambique and Angola, have come to receive French aid has not yet required France to adopt a more ostentatious stand against apartheid, but France's attitudes towards the regime in South Africa are certain to come under closer scrutiny the more France chooses to engage herself in the region. The problems of South Africa are not easily susceptible to the benign influence of outside Western powers. As the United States discovered, a 'constructive' policy towards South Africa is difficult both to fashion and to implement. In the Maghreb too, the development of a 'balanced' policy is made awkward by the sometimes diametrically opposed viewpoints of the Maghreb countries. France has perhaps been wise to keep a relatively low profile in these other regions of Africa. Failed attempts to 'solve' problems in these areas could well have been disastrous for her reputation in Africa. Yet for how long will France be able to treat francophone Black Africa as a bloc immune from the political, economic and diplomatic developments in other parts of the continent? The paradox of the future of French power in Black Africa is that the problems confronted by these states are becoming ones which will increasingly stretch French military, economic and even diplomatic resources, and yet to ensure that France can wield that power which she possesses in Black Africa with efficacy, it may become necessary for France to deploy more energies, even if primarily diplomatic, in other parts of Africa where the solutions to existing problems may be even more elusive.

So far as relations with Black Africa are concerned, these will in any case have to evolve as a function of the natural tensions in what is still a remarkable relationship. I have pointed to some very broad ways in which the 'specificity' of France's Black African policy might come under stress. Yet that policy is still not easily broken. No other Western country can claim, as does France with justification, to have created an alliance with a group of developing countries in the Third World. This partnership which straddles the 'North–South' divide in international politics is unique, though it will be subject to many of the problems that occur within alliances in which there is one very strong partner. France will continue to see direct action in Black Africa as an expression of both national interest and national status, though there may sometimes be domestic doubts whether such action is affordable. Francophone Black African states will accept a sometimes pervasive French presence insofar as their economies and national stability still require it. The example of Guinea remains instructive to other small, weak, African states of the dangers of an overly ideological approach to international connections. Both the French and the Africans have interests in changing the balance of responsibilities for African stability. This will be difficult for both sides. France would like a *mondialiste* policy without losing the benefits of a sphere of influence; the African states want to be independent of France while retaining the advantages of their close association with her.

These partly compatible but still different priorities will mean that negotiation will ritually take place between France and her Black African partners on how to manage a relationship both sides want to endure. The mechanism of the Franco–African summit meeting, itself a testimony to France's status on the continent, since so many states wish to attend it, will give French presidents the opportunity to design a policy on a grand, and near continental scale. Its implementation will increasingly require France to develop policies and projects carefully tailored to the needs of particular states. The growth of regional organizations in West and Central Africa, whose formation has owed much to francophone African leaders, will give these states a greater sense that they are managing their own affairs. It will also help African states to cross the frontiers between them created by their colonial pasts. But ultimately, most francophone African states will feel that, in times of crisis, their salvation comes through France. That perception, especially when overtly revealed by African leaders, will be a source of prestige for France, just as the initial acquisition of colonies enhanced French status.

The capacity of a major Western power to capture the ear of various states of the developing world is probably rightly considered a 'strategic' advantage in the current international system. Whether, as some French politicians have hoped, French–African relations will be considered as one of the 'ordering principles' of international relations may be open to question, but these relations have certainly established themselves as a permanent, and relatively structured feature of the international system. France's leaders will therefore persist in deploying images of power in Africa, referring to new concepts of how the French–African link is special, while at the same time carefully adjusting the practice of French power in Africa to contend with shifting perceptions and needs. The new relationships which African states wish to establish with each other, the intractability of African economic problems, the cynicism which sometimes accompanies requests for French military assistance, the unpredictability with which some of these states might reject French help of any kind, and the ambitions of other powers on the African continent, will make the efficient practice of French power and influence tremendously difficult. But the African connection is still considered a source of status. Black Africa is the only place where the modesty of French resources permits an ambitious policy. The idea of French power in Africa having survived decolonization, French leaders will still want to impose French influence and power where it can be deployed with grace and effectiveness.

Yet the francophone Black Africans will be, more than ever before, in control of that influence. This factor will be the most important in determining whether France will be able to hang on to its special relationships in Africa. Should the sub-Saharan states decide that the modified form of decolonization they have negotiated with France requires more drastic change, they will be able to usher in a new phase of decolonization which is more complete and more like that undergone by other states in Africa. It may be that three decades of residual links with the former imperial power have sapped any revolutionary zeal amongst the francophone Black Africans. It is more likely that they will seek to normalize their relations with France. This will be an evolutionary process. If it occurs, it would still permit a degree of French assistance and friendly relations. But since the ultimate, declared, aim of French aid to Black Africa is to provide Black Africans with the means to defend their independence, it would not be surprising if a new generation of African leaders decided near the end of the twentieth century that further collaboration with France's post-imperial vision of Africa was no longer in their interest. In that event, French power in Africa would be affected. More strikingly, France's image of herself in world politics would have to be reconfigured and the idea of French power generally reconceived.

Notes

Introduction

1 *The Cambridge Modern History*, (planned by Lord Acton), ed. Sir A.W. Ward, Sir G.W. Prothero and Sir Stanley Leathes, KCB, vol. 12: *The Latest Age*, Cambridge, at the University Press, 1934, p. 813.
2 Miles Kahler, *Decolonization in Britain and France: The Domestic Consequences of International Relations*, Princeton University Press, New Jersey, 1984, p. 77.
3 Christopher Andrew, 'La Colonisation Française en Afrique: Aspects politiques', in Centre des Hautes Études sur l'Afrique et l'Asie Modernes, *L'Afrique Noire Depuis la Conférence de Berlin*, Paris, 1985, p. 119.
4 Kahler, *Decolonization*, p. 75.
5 Paul Clay Sorum, *Intellectuals and Decolonization in France*, University of North Carolina Press, Chapel Hill, 1977, p. 205.
6 Edward A. Kolodziej, *French International Policy Under De Gaulle and Pompidou: The Politics of Grandeur*, Cornell University Press, New York, 1974, p. 583.
7 Peter Jay, 'Regionalism and Geopolitics', in *Foreign Affairs*, 58, no. 3, *America and the World 1979*, 1980, p. 485.
8 Ibid., p. 486.
9 Ibid., p. 495.
10 Dorothy Pickles, *The Government and Politics of France*, Methuen and Co., Ltd, London, 1972, vol. 2, p. 308.

Chapter 1   The Nature of French Power and its African Dimension

1 Raymond Aron, *Peace and War: A Theory of International Relations*, tr. Richard Howard and Annette Baker Fox, Weidenfeld and Nicolson, London, 1966, p. 47.
2 Theodore Zeldin, *France 1848–1945: Intellect and Pride*, Oxford University Press, 1980, p. 6.
3 These distinctions are nicely drawn by Neville Waites in 'French Foreign Policy: External Influences on the Quest for Independence', *Review of International Studies*, 9, no. 4, October 1983, pp. 260–3.
4 Bertrand Russell, *Power: A New Social Analysis*, George Allen and Unwin, London, 1939, p. 9.
5 Daniel Halevy, *Essay on the Acceleration of History*, Librairie Fayard, Paris, 1961, pp. 105–6.
6 Cited in Ernst Robert Curtius, *The Civilisation of France: An Introduction*, George Allen and Unwin Ltd, London, 1932, p. 31.

7   Curtius, *Civilisation*, p. 33.
8   Speech in Assemblée Nationale, *Journal Officiel*, July 1885.
9   Winfried Baumgart, *Imperialism: The Idea and the Reality of British and French Colonial Expansion, 1880–1914*, Oxford University Press, 1982, p. 72.
10   E. H. Carr, *Great Britain as a Mediterranean Power*, Cust Foundation Lecture, University College, Nottingham, 1937, p. 10, cited in Martin Wight, *Power Politics*, (ed. Hedley Bull and Carsten Holbraad), Leicester University Press, 1978, p. 98.
11   Harold Nicolson, *The Meaning of Prestige*, Rede Lecture, Cambridge University Press, 1937, p. 30.
12   Ibid., p. 15.
13   Maurice Couve de Murville, *Une Politique Étrangère 1958–1969*, Plon, Paris, 1971, pp. 431–2. See analysis in Philip G. Cerny, *The Politics of Grandeur: Ideological Aspects of de Gaulle's Foreign Policy*, Cambridge University Press, 1980, pp. 33–4.
14   Charles de Gaulle, tr. Jonathan Griffin and Richard Howard, *The Complete War Memoirs of Charles de Gaulle*, Simon and Schuster, New York, 1964, p. 3.
15   Curtius, *Civilisation*, p. 49.
16   Général Béthouart, 'Union Française et l'Afrique du Nord', *La Revue des Deux Mondes*, Jan.–Feb. 1955, p. 199.
17   Ibid., p. 206.
18   François Valentin, 'L'Impératif Algérien', *La Revue des Deux Mondes*, Nov.–Dec. 1959, p. 247.
19   Charles Hernu, 'Répondre aux défis d'un monde dangereux', *Défense Nationale*, Dec. 1981, p. 9.
20   John Kenneth Galbraith, *The Anatomy of Power*, Corgi Books, London, 1985, p. 53.
21   Cerny, *The Politics of Grandeur*, p. 65.
22   See the analysis in ibid., p. 4.
23   Christopher M. Andrew, and A. S. Kanya-Forstner, *France Overseas: The Great War and the Climax of French Imperial Expansion*, Thames and Hudson, London, 1981, p. 13.
24   D. Bruce Marshall, *The French Colonial Myth and Constitution-Making in the Fourth Republic*, Yale University Press, 1973, p. 13.
25   Alexis de Tocqueville, 'Travail sur l'Algérie (octobre 1841)', *Oeuvres Complètes* (sous la direction de J.P. Mayer), tome III, *Ecrits et Discours Politiques*, Gallimard, Paris, 1962, pp. 213-14.
26   Alexis de Tocqueville, 'Rapport à la Chambre des Députés, au nom de la commission chargé d'examiner le projet de loi relatif au crédits extraordinaires demandés pour l'Algérie (24 May 1847)', *Oeuvres Complètes* (publiés par Madame de Tocqueville), tome IX, *Etudes Economiques, Politiques et Littéraires*, 2nd edn, Calmann Levy, Paris, 1878, p. 168.
27   François Mitterrand, *Présence et Abandon*, Tribune Libre, Paris, 1957, p. 237.
28   Raymond Aron, in an interview with Jean-Jacques Brochier recorded in *Magazine Littéraire*, Sept. 1983, p. 28.
29   Wight, *Power Politics*, p. 98.
30   Ministère des Affaires Etrangères, France, Conférence de Presse, Sommet des Chefs d'états de France et Afrique, Oct. 1983.
31   Martin Staniland, 'Francophone Africa: The Enduring French Connection', in Gerald J. Bender (ed.) *International Affairs in Africa*, The Annals of the American Academy of Political and Social Science, Jan. 1987, p. 62.
32   Ronald E. Robinson, 'Introduction' in Henri Brunschwig, *French Colonialism, 1871–1914: Myths and Realities*, New York, Frederick A. Praeger, 1964, p. ix.
33   Kahler, *Decolonization*, p. 384.

Chapter 2 The Imperial Instinct

1 See Alistair Horne, *A Savage War of Peace; Algeria 1954–1962*, Macmillan Papermac, rev. edn, London, 1987, p. 29; Douglas Porch, *The Conquest of Morocco: A Savage Colonial War*, Macmillan Papermac, London, 1987, p. 5; and Pierre Montagnon, *La France Coloniale: La Gloire de L'Empire*, Pygmalion, Gerard Watelet, Paris, 1988, p. 102.
2 *The Cambridge Modern History*, vol. 12, p. 813.
3 There are numerous examples of anti-colonial writing, some of which are reviewed below, but the idea that colonies were a drain on French power was nicely covered in Yves Guyot, *Lettres sur la Politique Coloniale*, Paris, 1885, especially at p. 285.
4 Raoul Girardet, *L'Idée coloniale en France de 1871 à 1962*, La Table Ronde, 1972, Le Livre de Poche, Collection Pluriel 1979, Paris, p. 34.
5 Raymond Aron, 'Imperialism and Colonialism', Seventeenth Montague Burton Lecture on International Relations, The University of Leeds, 1959.
6 Pierre Guillen, *L'Expansion: 1881–1898*, Collection, 'Politique Etrangère de la France', Imprimerie Nationale, Paris, 1984, p. 80.
7 Ibid., p. 71.
8 Pierre Biarnes, *Les Français en Afrique Noire de Richelieu à Mitterrand: 350 ans de présence française au sud du Sahara*, Armand Colin, Paris, 1987, p. 194.
9 This summary of the debates about a colonial army is adapted from Pierre Guillen, *L'Expansion*, pp. 79–81.
10 For a splendid and detailed description of these various forces see Anthony Clayton, *France, Soldiers and Africa*, Brassey's, London, 1988.
11 A. S. Kanya-Forstner, *The Conquest of the Western Sudan: A Study in French Military Imperialism*, Cambridge University Press, 1969, p. 12.
12 Guillen, *L'Expansion*, p. 83.
13 Ibid., p. 86.
14 Baumgart, *Imperialism*, p. 74.
15 Guillen, *L'Expansion*, pp. 88–92.
16 Ibid., p. 33.
17 Kanya-Forstner, *The Conquest of the Western Sudan*, p. 8.
18 Cited in ibid., p. 8.
19 Cited in ibid., p. 14.
20 Ibid., p. 263.
21 Henri Brunschwig, 'Anglophobia and French African Policy', in P. Gifford and Wm R. Louis, *France and Britain in Africa*, Yale University Press, 1971, p. 23.
22 Andrew and Kanya-Forstner, *France Overseas*, p. 12.
23 Christopher M. Andrew, 'French Attitudes to Empire', unpublished paper presented to the British Committee on the Theory of International Politics, Sept. 1980, p. 1.
24 Cited in Girardet, *L'Idée coloniale*, pp. 68 and 75.
25 Dorothy Shipley White, *Black Africa and De Gaulle: From the French Empire to Independence*, Pennsylvania State University Press, 1979, p. 27.
26 Guillen, *L'Expansion*, p. 106.
27 Paul Leroy-Beaulieu, *De la Colonisation chez les peuples modernes*, Guillaumin, Paris, 1874, pp. 605–6 quoted in Girardet, *L'Idée coloniale*, p. 55.
28 Cited in Charles-Robert Ageron, *France Coloniale ou Parti Colonial*, Paris, Presses Universitaires de France, 1978, p. 75.
29 Guillen, *L'Expansion*, p. 104.
30 Baumgart, *Imperialism*, p. 24.
31 Ibid., pp. 28–9.

32   Ministère de la Marine et des Colonies, *Sénégal et Niger: La France dans l'Afrique Occidentale 1879–1883*, Paris, Challamel Ainé Editeur, Librairie Coloniale, 1884, p. 189.

33   Charles-Robert Ageron, 'Gambetta et la reprise de l'expansion coloniale', *Revue française d'histoire d'outre-mer*, 59, no. 215, 1972, p. 191.

34   Louis Vignon, *Expansion de la France*, Libraire Guillaumin et Cie., Paris, 1891, p. 360.

35   Girardet, *L'Idée coloniale*, p. 78.

36   Ageron, 'Gambetta...', pp. 197–9.

37   Both cited in Pierre Montagnon, *La France Coloniale*, p. 242.

38   Cited in Guillen, *L'Expansion*, p. 101

39   Ibid., p. 135.

40   Gabriel Charmes in *Journal des Débats*, 10 September 1882, quoted by Charles-Robert Ageron, *France Coloniale*, pp. 76–7.

41   Alfred Rambaud, preface to J. R. Seeley, *L'Expansion de l'Angleterre*, Paris, 1885, cited by Ageron, ibid., p. 77.

42   Cited in Biarnes, *Les Français en Afrique Noire*, p. 219.

43   Cited in Girardet, *L'Idée coloniale*, p. 93.

44   Cited in Biarnes, *Les Français en Afrique Noire*, p. 222.

45   Andrew and Kanya-Forstner, *France Overseas*, p. 11.

46   Christopher M. Andrew and A. S. Kanya-Forstner, 'The French Colonial Party: Its Composition, Aims and Influence', *The Historical Journal*, 14, no. 1, 1971, p. 113.

47   Christopher M. Andrew and A. S. Kanya-Forstner, 'French Business and the French Colonialists', *The Historical Journal*, 19, no. 4, 1976, p. 991.

48   Ibid., p. 992.

49   Guillen, *L'Expansion*, p. 388.

50   Cited in Andrew and Kanya-Forstner, 'The French Colonial Party', p. 125.

51   Joseph Chailley-Bert, *Dix années de politique coloniale*, Librairie Armand Colin, Paris, 1902, p. 11.

52   Ageron, *France Coloniale*, p. 195.

53   Guillen, *L'Expansion*, p. 109.

54   Ageron, *France Coloniale*, p. 195.

55   R. F. Betts, *Assimilation and Association*, Columbia University Press, 1961, p. 8.

56   Horne, *A Savage War of Peace*, p. 53.

57   R. F. Betts, *Uncertain Dimensions: Western Overseas Empires in the Twentieth Century*, University of Minnesota Press, Minneapolis, 1985, p. 68.

58   Marc Michel, 'Un Mythe: la "Force Noire" avant 1914', *Relations Internationales*, no. 2, 1974, p. 83.

59   Marc Michel, 'Colonisation et Défense Nationale: Le Général Mangin et la Force Noire', *Guerres Mondiales et Conflits Contemporains*, 145, Jan. 1987, p. 31.

60   Ibid., p. 32.

61   Andrew and Kanya-Forstner, *France Overseas*, p. 134.

62   Ibid., pp. 134–5.

63   Ibid., p. 138. For general information on the 'force noire' see Marc Michel, *L'Appel à l'Afrique. Contributions et réactions à l'effort de guerre en AOF, 1914–1919*, Publications de la Sorbonne, Paris, 1982.

64   Charles John Balesi, *From Adversaries to Comrades-in-Arms: West Africans and the French Military 1885–1914*, Crossroads Press, Massachusetts, 1979, p. 2.

Chapter 3   The *France–Afrique* and *Eurafrique* Ideas

1   Marc Michel, 'Un mythe', p. 90.
2   Andrew and Kanya-Forstner, *France Overseas*, p. 237.
3   Wm Roger Louis, 'The Berlin Conference', in P. Gifford and Wm Roger Lewis, *France and Britain in Africa*, Yale, 1971, pp. 200–16 *passim.*
4   Ibid., p. 217.
5   Charles-Robert Ageron, 'L'Idée de l'Eurafrique et le débat colonial franco–allemand de l'entre deux guerres', *Revue d'Histoire Moderne et Contemporaine*, 22, July-Sept. 1975, p. 446.
6   Christopher M. Andrew and A. S. Kanya-Forstner, 'France and the Disposition of Germany's African Colonies, 1914–1922', Ecole des Hautes Etudes en Sciences Sociales, *Etudes Africaines: Offertes à Henri Brunschwig*, Paris, 1982, p. 209.
7   Ibid., p. 211.
8   E. D. Morel, *Africa and the Peace of Europe*, National Labour Press Ltd, London, 1917, p. 70.
9   Ibid., p. 109.
10 Ageron, 'Eurafrique', p. 449.
11 Ibid., p. 448.
12 Ibid., p. 445.
13 Ibid., p. 457.
14 Jean Bouvier, René Girault and Jacques Thobie, *L'Impérialisme à la française 1914–1960*, Editions La Découverte, Paris, 1986, p. 229.
15 Girardet, *L'Idée coloniale*, p. 185.
16 Gouverneur Général Olivier, 'Philosophie de L'Exposition Coloniale', in *Revue des Deux Mondes*, 15 Nov. 1931, p. 293.
17 Albert Sarraut, *Grandeurs et Servitudes Coloniales*, Editions du Sagittaire, Paris, 1931, p. 221.
18 Ibid. p. 239.
19 Andrew and Kanya-Forstner, *France Overseas*, p. 249.
20 Girardet, *L'Idée coloniale*, p. 186.
21 Ibid., p. 187.
22 Octave Homberg, *La France des Cinq Parties du Monde*, Paris, Plon, 1927, quoted in Girardet, *L'Idée coloniale*, pp. 433–4.
23 Ageron, 'Eurafrique', p. 457.
24 W. W. Schmokel, *Dream of Empire: German Colonialism 1919–1945*, Yale University Press, 1964, p. 57.
25 Max Liniger-Goumez, *L'Eurafrique, Utopie ou Réalité: les Métamorphoses d'une Idée*, Editions CLE, Yaoundé, 1972, p. 47.
26 Ageron, *France Coloniale*, p. 260.
27 Christine Levisse-Touze, 'La Préparation Économique, Industrielle et Militaire de l'Afrique du Nord à la Veille de la Guerre', in *Revue d'histoire de la deuxième guerre mondiale et des conflits contemporains*, no. 142, 1986, p.1.
28 Ibid., p. 11–12.
29 Charles-Robert Ageron, 'La Perception de la Puissance Française en 1938–1939: Le Mythe Impérial', in René Girault and Robert Frank (eds) *La Puissance en Europe 1938–1940*, Publications de la Sorbonne, Paris, 1984, p. 230.
30 Ibid., pp. 232, 233.
31 Andrew and Kanya-Forstner, *France Overseas*, p. 250.
32 Ageron, 'La Perception', p. 236.

33   Serge Bernstein, 'La Perception de la puissance par le parti radical socialiste', in *Revue d'histoire moderne et contemporaine*, July–Sept. 1984, p. 633.

34   Girardet, *L'Idée coloniale*, p. 189

35   Ageron, 'Eurafrique', p. 474.

36   Liniger-Goumez, *L'Eurafrique*, p. 32.

37   Christopher M. Andrew, 'France: Adjustment to Change', unpublished paper presented to the British Committee on the Theory of International Politics, Sept. 1980, p. 3.

38   Andrew and Kanya-Forstner, *France Overseas*, p. 250.

39   Charles-Robert Ageron, 'La Survivance d'un Mythe: La Puissance par l'Empire Coloniale 1944–1947', *Revue française d'histoire d'outre-mer*, 72, no. 269, 1985, p. 388.

40   Ibid., p. 391.

41   A review of these policies is contained in Marc Michel, 'La Coopération inter-coloniale en Afrique noire, 1942–1950: un néocolonialisme éclairé?', *Relations Internationales*, no. 34, Summer 1983.

42   Pierre Nord, *L'Eurafrique Notre Dernière Chance*, Paris, 1955, pp. 1–11.

43   Raymond Cartier, *Paris Match*, 14 November 1953, quoted in Paul Clay Sorum, *Intellectuals and Decolonization in France*, p. 201.

44   Charles Richet, 'L'oeuvre de la France en Afrique du Nord', *Revue des Deux Mondes*, 15 Jan. 1954, p. 219.

45   Horne, *A Savage War of Peace*, Macmillan Papermac, London, 1987, p. 108.

46   Jacques Soustelle, in *Journal Officiel* of Mar. 1956, p. 787; see also Tony Smith, 'The French Colonial Consensus and People's War', 1946–1958,' *Journal of Contemporary History* , Oct. 1974, p. 235.

47   M. F. Lenormand, 'L'Eurafrique devant l'Armement Soviétique', *Eurafrique-Alger*, Jan. 1955, p. 73.

48   Général O. Meynier, 'Vers la Réalisation de l'Eurafrique', *Eurafrique-Alger*, Jan. 1955, p. 7.

49   John Steele, 'The Possibilities in Europe–Africa', *The European*, Sept. 1955, pp. 18, 21.

50   See generally J. M. Lattre, 'Sahara, Clé de Voutre de l'Ensemble Eurafricain Français', *Politique Etrangère*, no. 4, 1957.

51   L. S. Senghor, Centre Militaire d'Informations et Documentation Outre-Mer, Document no. 465A, 1953.

52   Ibid., p. 8.

53   L. S. Senghor, *Liberté*, Sevil, Paris, 1977, vol. 2, p. 91.

54   Ibid., p. 148.

55   D. Bruce Marshall, *The French Colonial Myth*, pp. 204–5.

56   White, *Black Africa and de Gaulle*, 1979, p. 209.

57   René Pleven, in 'Conférence de l'Assemblée Parlementaire Européenne avec les Parlements des Etats Africains et de Madagascar', 19–24 June 1961, Maison de l'Europe, Strasbourg, *Compte Rendu in extenso des Séances*, p. 22.

Chapter 4   Decolonization and the Assertion of Power in Black Africa

1   M. F. Walter, in Siriex-Hertrich, *L'Empire au combat*, Office français d'édition, 1945, p. 143, quoted in Alain Ruscio, *La Décolonisation tragique 1945–1962*, Messidor/Editions sociales, Paris, 1987, pp. 25–6.

2   Marc Michel, 'Y a-t-il eu Impréparation de la France à la Décolonisation?', in Institut d'Histoire des Relations Internationales Contemporains, *Enjeux et Puis-*

sances: Pour une histoire des relations internationales au XXième siecle: Mélanges én l'Honneur de Jean Baptiste Duroselle, Publications de la Sorbonne, Paris, 1986, p. 183.

3 J. P. Duroselle, 'Opinion, attitude, mentalité, mythes, idéologie: essai de clarification', *Relations internationales*, no. 2, Nov. 1974, p. 11.

4 For a full description of the struggle for independence by Syria and Lebanon see, for example, Naomi Joy Weinberger, *Syrian Intervention in Lebanon: The 1975–76 Civil War*, Oxford University Press, 1986, pp. 57–9.

5 H. Laurentie, 'Recent Developments in French Colonial Policy', in *Colonial Administration by European Powers*, Papers presented at the Royal Institute for International Affairs, London, 1947, p. 7.

6 This summary history is drawn in part from Pierre Biarnes, *Les Français en Afrique Noire*, pp. 281, 283–4.

7 The best summary of the origins of the Brazzaville Conference is in Martin Shipway, 'The Brazzaville Conference 1944: Colonial and Imperial Planning in a Wartime Strategy', M.Phil. thesis, Oxford, 1986.

8 Pierre Biarnes, *Les Français en Afrique Noire*, p. 285.

9 White, *Black Africa and de Gaulle*, p. 115.

10 Cited in Shipway, The Brazzaville Conference, p. 99.

11 *La conférence africaine française*, Editions du Baobab-Brazzaville, Documentation Française, p. 28, cited in Robert Bourgi, *Le général de Gaulle et l'Afrique noire 1940–1969*, Librairie Générale de droit et de jurisprudence, Paris, 1980, p. 116.

12 Cited in Bourgi, *Le général de Gaulle*, p. 117.

13 This is also the view expressed in White, *Black Africa and de Gaulle*, p. 121.

14 This is cited in Charles de Gaulle, *Discours et Messages pendant la Guerre, juin 1940–janvier 1945*, Paris, 1946, p. 35, reprinted by Plon, 1970, p. 35. See for further discussion, *inter alia*, Ruscio, *La Décolonisation*, p. 28.

15 See Bourgi, *Le général de Gaulle*, pp. 119–23 for a summary of the conference's proposals.

16 Cited in Wm Roger Louis, *Imperialism at Bay: The United States and the Decolonisation of the British Empire, 1941–1945*, Oxford University Press, New York, 1978, pp. 45–6.

17 Laurentie, 'Recent Developments', p. 12.

18 Jean Rémy Ayoumé, 'Occidentalisme et africanisme', *Renaissances*, nos 3–4, 1944, p. 263, cited by Henri Brunschwig, 'The Decolonisation of French Black Africa', in Prosser Gifford and Wm Roger Louis, *The Transfer of Power in Africa: Decolonisation 1940–1960*, Yale University Press, 1982, p. 219.

19 A full analysis of some of these distinctions is contained in Marshall, *The French Colonial Myth*, pp. 295–6.

20 Laurentie, 'Recent Developments', p. 15

21 Cited in Marshall, *The French Colonial Myth*, pp. 296–7.

22 Cited in Girardet, *L'Idée coloniale*, p. 287.

23 R. Clement-Cuzin, 'Eléments d'une Politique Outre-Mer', *La Revue des Deux Mondes*, Nov.–Dec. 1954, p. 505.

24 This summary is based on Tony Smith, *The Pattern of Imperialism: The United States, Great Britain, and the Late-Industrialising World since 1815*, Cambridge University Press, 1981, pp. 113–17 and Yves Person, 'French West Africa and Decolonisation' in Gifford and Louis, *The Transfer of Power*, pp. 150–1.

25 Statement by de la Tournelle (Political Director, Quai d'Orsay) to George McGhee, Assistant Secretary of State, *Foreign Relations of the United States 1950*, vol. 5, p. 1561, Memorandum of Conversation, Paris, 25 September 1950, cited by John

Hargreaves in 'Decolonisation: French and British Styles', p. 12, paper presented to Round Table: Francophone Africa since Independence, St Antony's College, Maison Française Oxford, 29–30 April 1988.

26   See Smith, *The Pattern of Imperialism* , p. 118.

27   Person, 'French West Africa', p. 154–5.

28   Cited in Jacques Marseilles, *Empire colonial et capitalisme français: Histoire d'un divorce*, Albin Michel, Paris, 1984, p. 350.

29   Cited in Ruscio, *La Décolonisation*, p. 213.

30   Biarnes, *Les Français en Afrique Noire*, p. 340.

31   Person, 'French West Africa', p. 162.

32   Cited in Zan Semi-Bi, 'Il y a trente ans . . . l'accélération du processus de décolonisation en Afrique noire francophone', *Le Mois en Afrique*, Feb.-Mar. 1987, p. 9.

33   Ibid., p. 9.

34   Edward Mortimer, *France and the Africans: 1944–1960*, Faber and Faber, London, 1969, p. 260.

35   White, *Black Africa and de Gaulle*, p. 184.

36   Mortimer, *France and the Africans*, p. 276.

37   Bourgi, *Le général de Gaulle*, p. 351.

38   Ibid., p. 352.

39   Mortimer, *France and the Africans*, pp. 311–12.

40   Bourgi, *Le général de Gaulle*, p. 343.

41   White, *Black Africa and de Gaulle*, p. 200.

42   Bourgi, *Le général de Gaulle*, p. 344.

43   George Chaffard, *Les Carnets Secrets de la Décolonisation*, Calmann-Levy, 2 vols, Paris, 1965, 1967, vol. 2, p. 197.

44   Bourgi, *Le général de Gaulle*, p. 345.

45   *Le Monde*, 16 September 1958.

46   *Abidjan-Matin*, 25 August 1958, cited in Zan Semi-Bi, 'Il y a trente ans', p. 25.

47   Yves Guéna, *Historique de la Communauté*, Fayard, Paris, 1962, pp. 74–5.

48   White, *Black Africa and de Gaulle*, quoting the French journalist Philippe Decraene, p. 212.

49   Cited in Charles-Robert Ageron, *France Coloniale*, p. 295

50   See Alfred Grosser, *La politique extérieure de la Vieme République*, Seuil, Paris, 1965, p. 74, and Moshe Amni-Oz, *Les Interventions Extra-militaires des Forces Armées Nationales dans les Etats d'Afrique Noire Francophone*, Doctoral Thesis, University of Paris, 1978, p. 41.

51   Albert Bourgi, *La Politique Française de Coopération en Afrique: Le Cas de Sénégal*, Librairie Général de droit et de jurisprudence, Paris, 1979, p. 2.

52   Ibid., pp. 11–12.

53   Cited in Marcel Merle, 'La politique Africaine dans la politique Etrangère Générale de la France', in Institut Charles de Gaulle, Centre d'Etudes d'Afrique Noire, *La Politique Africaine du Général de Gaulle 1958–1969*, Editions A. Pédone, Paris, 1980, p. 150.

54   *Journal Officiel*, Assemblée Nationale, Débats, 29 December 1959. Part of this statement was not exactly true, since Algeria had been included in the NATO treaty area. This ceased to be so only on 16 January 1963 when the NATO Council took note of the declaration of the French representative who recalled that by the vote on self-determination on 1 July 1962 the Algerian people had pronounced in favour of independence and thus the Algerian departments, listed in the treaty, no longer existed as such.

55   Merle, 'La politique Africaine', pp. 159–60.

Chapter 5 French Military Power and Black Africa

1 Jacques Fremaux and André Martel, 'French Defence Policy 1947–1949', in Olav Riste (ed.), *Western Security: The Formative Years*, Norwegian University Press, Oslo, 1985, p. 93.

2 Cited by Christopher Coker in *NATO, the Warsaw Pact and Africa*, London, Macmillan, 1985, p. 29.

3 For a general assessment of these problems see John Chipman (ed.), *NATO's Southern Allies: Internal and External Challenges*, London, Routledge, 1988.

4 Chef de Bataillon Laboureix, 'La France et la Constitution des Armées des Etats Indépendants d'Afrique Noire d'Expression Française', Paris, Centre Militaire d'Informations et Documentations Outre-Mer, Document of March 1963, pp. 5-6.

5 Chester Crocker, 'France's Changing Military Interests', *Africa Report*, June 1968, p. 20.

6 *Le Monde*, 9 March 1961 (no byline).

7 Maurice Ligot, 'La Coopération Militaire dans les Accords Passés entre la France et les Etats Africains et Malagache d'Expression Française', *Revue Juridique et Politique*, 17, 1963, p. 521.

8 The agreement is dated 17 August 1960.

9 General Revol, 'Communauté et Stratégie Mondiale', Paris, Centre Militaire d'Informations et Documentations Outre-Mer, Document 6279, 1961.

10 Jacques Guillemin, 'L'Importance des Bases dans la Politique Militaire de la France en Afrique Noire Francophone et Madagascar', *Revue française d'études politiques africaines*, Aug.-Sept. 1981, p. 38.

11 Geoffrey Gower, *African Dances*, London, Faber, 1935, p. 131, quoted in Clayton, *France, Soldiers and Africa*, p. 379.

12 Guillemin, 'L'Importance des Bases', note 10, p. 31.

13 Chef d'Escadron Leprêtre, 'L'Assistance Militaire Technique', in *Revue Militaire d'Information*, Jan. 1963, no. 341, p. 59.

14 Guillemin, 'L'Importance des Bases', p. 38.

15 Ligot, 'La Coopération Militaire', p. 518.

16 Anonymous, 'La Force d'Intervention et le remaniement du dispositif Français en Afrique Noire et Madagascar', *Frères d'Armes*, no. 2, April 1963.

17 Jacques Guillemin, 'Les Campagnes Militaires Françaises de la Décolonisation en Afrique Sub-Saharienne', *Le mois en Afrique*, June 1982, pp. 131, 135.

18 *Le Monde*, 10 October 1964 (no byline).

19 Quoted in A. Mabileau and P. Quantin, 'L'Afrique Noire dans la Pensée Politique du Général de Gaulle', in Institut Charles de Gaulle et Centre d'Etude d'Afrique Noire, *La Politique Africaine du Général de Gaulle, 1958–1969*, Editions A. Pédone, Paris, 1980, p. 60.

20 *New York Herald Tribune* (European Edition), 6 January 1966 (no byline).

21 *Le Monde*, 8 January 1966 (no byline).

22 Edward Kolodziej, *Making and Marketing Arms: The French Experience and its Implications for the International System*, Princeton University Press, New Jersey, 1987, pp. 380–1.

23 Michel Debré, 'La France et sa Défense', *Revue de Défense Nationale*, Jan. 1972, p. 15.

24 See 'La Coopération Militaire Franco-Africaine', *Europe-France Outre-Mer*, Apr.–May, 1977.

25 Bernard Fessard de Foucault, 'Indépendances Nationales et Coopération Africaines', *Etudes*, April 1974, p. 556.
26 Kolodziej, *Making and Marketing Arms*, p. 374.
27 Dominique Möisi and Pierre Lellouche, 'French Policy in Africa: A Lonely Battle Against Destabilisation', *International Security*, Spring 1979, p. 121.
28 Jacques Guillemin, 'L'Intervention Extérieure dans la Politique Militaire de la France en Afrique Noire Francophone et Madagascar', *Revue française d'études politiques africaines*, July 1981, p. 2.
29 See generally, P. Mangold, 'Shaba I and Shaba II', *Survival*, May–June 1979, and Bruce Palmer 'US Security Interests and Africa South of the Sahara', *AEI Defence Review*, 12, no. 6, 1978.
30 *Journal Officiel*, Assemblée Nationale, 19 December 1979, p. 12323.
31 Cited in Pascal Chaigneau, 'Afrique: de l'affectif au rationnel', in Francois Joyaux and Patrick Wajsman, *Pour une nouvelle politique étrangère*, Hachette, collection Pluriel, Paris, 1986, p. 340.
32 See generally, John Chipman, 'Mitterrand's Afrika Politik: Wiederbelebung der Dritten-Kraft', *Europa Archiv*, June 1984.
33 'Le parti socialiste et l'Afrique sub-Saharienne', Paris 1981, published in *Le mois en Afrique*, no. 185–6.
34 *Projet socialiste pour la France des années 80*, Club Socialiste du Livre, Paris, 1980 p. 359.
35 'Loi no. 83–606 du 8 Juillet 1983 Portant Approbation de la Programmation Militaire pour les Années 1984–1988', published in *Journal Officiel*, 9 July 1983, Assemblée Nationale, pp. 2114–21.
36 Critias, 'Entre l'Europe et l'Outre-Mer', *Le Monde*, 25 Oct. 1983.
37 See Jacques Isnard, 'La Force d'Action Rapide Française pourra Intervenir en Europe', *Le Monde*, 20–21 Nov. 1983 and more generally, Dominique David, 'La Force d'Action Rapide en Europe: Le Dire des Armes', *Défense Nationale*, June 1984.
38 See G. Moutard, 'La Programmation Militaire 1984–88 et la Réorganisation de l'Armée de Terre,' *L'Ancre d'Or Bazeilles*, Jan.–Feb. 1984.
39 Patrice Buffotot, 'La FAR et le 3ième Cercle', in *Cirpes, Paix et Conflits*, nouvelle série, no. 6, 1984.
40 See *Le Monde*, 18 Feb. 1984 (no byline).
41 See 'Avis Presenté au Nom de la Commission de la Défense Nationale et des Forces Armées sur le Projet de Loi de Finances pour 1984', Tome 1, by M. le député Jacques Huygues des Etages, Annexe no. 1738 du P.V. de la Séance du 6 Octobre, *Assemblée Nationale* , p. 52.
42 Rapport de Luc Tinseau, deputé, Annexe no. 1485 du P.V. de la Séance du 11 Mai 1983, *Assemblée Nationale*, 'Résumé des Travaux de la Commission de Défense et Conclusions', p. 68.
43 Gérard Turbe, 'France's rapid deployment forces', in *International Defense Review*, 20, no. 8, 1987, p. 1026.
44 See Anonymous, 'Le C.O.T.A.M.', *Frères d'Armes*, no. 129, July-Aug., 1984.
45 See Antoine Sanguinetti, 'Aspects Maritimes et Aériens de l'Intervention Extérieure', in *Cirpes, Paix et Conflits*, pp. 5–6.
46 Tinseau, 'Résumé des Travaux', p. 63.
47 See John Chipman, 'France, Libya and Chad', Note of the Month, *The World Today*, Oct. 1983.
48 See *Le Monde*, 16 Nov. 1988.
49 See General Lacaze, 'La Politique de Défense de la France', *L'Armement*, no. 79, Mar. 1984.

50 Lt.-Col. Paul Vallin, 'La Logistique', in 'Les Forces d'Action Rapide: Dossier du Mois', *Armees d'Aujourd'hui*, no. 83, Sept. 1983.

51 A number of Quai d'Orsay departments are assigned to work on these problems with the *Bureau des Transports Maritimes, Aériens et de Surface* (BTMAS) of the French Armed Forces.

52 Moshe Amni-Oz, 'La formation des cadres militaires africains lors de la mise sur pied des armées nationales', *Revue française d'études politiques africaines*, 133, 1977, p. 89.

53 Robin Luckham, 'French Militarism in Africa', *Review of African Political Economy*, 24, 1982, pp. 56–8.

54 Anonymous, 'Moanda 87', in *Frères d'Armes*, Nov.–Dec. 1987.

55 Anonymous, 'Katcha et Mayumba 83', in *Frères d'Armes*, Sept.-Oct. 1983.

56 Jacques Guillemin, 'Coopération et Intervention, la politique militaire de la France en Afrique noire francophone et madagascar', Doctoral Thesis, University of Nice, Jan. 1979, p. 125.

57 During a long peace-keeping mission or intervention, as in Lebanon, or Chad, such rotation takes place as a matter of course, and over time a great many troops may be involved.

58 Guillemin, 'Coopération et Intervention', thesis, p. 125.

59 The N'Diambour exercise involved 5,000 French soldiers from the FAR and those stationed in Dakar.

60 Anonymous, 'Bandama '84 exercise bilateral franco-ivorien', *Frères d'Armes* , May–June 1984, p. 22.

61 The Ivory Coast, though one of France's closest allies in the African continent, decided in 1984 to repatriate 1,000 French advisers over a two-year period, a decision taken largely for financial reasons and which would represent a saving of 200 million francs per year after all were withdrawn. See *Le Monde* , 20 Mar. 1984.

62 Francois Charollais and Jean de Ribes, *Le défi de l'outre-mer: l'action extérieure dans la défense de la France*, Fondation pour les études de défense nationales, cahier no. 26, Paris, 1983 p. 13.

63 See *Le Monde*, 16 Nov. 1988.

64 See *Jeune Afrique*, 27 Apr. 1988.

65 Charollais and de Ribes, *Le défi de l'outre-mer*, p. 86.

66 See *Strategic Survey 1983–1984*, London, IISS, 1983, p. 108.

67 Charollais and de Ribes, *Le défi de l'outre-mer*, p. 173.

68 See I. Wiliam Zartman, 'Africa and the West: The French Connection', in Bruce E. Arlinghaus (ed.), *African Security Issues: Sovereignty, Stability and Solidarity*, Westview Special Studies on Africa, Epping, Essex, Bowker Publishing Co., 1984, p. 41.

69 See Robin Luckham, 'French Militarism in Africa', in *Review of African Political Economy*, 24, 1982, p. 70.

70 See generally, Libération Afrique, 'Les Particules de Giscard: l'Uranium Africain', in Tricontinental, *La France Contre l'Afrique*, Maspero, Paris, 1981.

71 The price paid for strategic materials from Africa varies greatly. On the one hand France has sometimes paid as much as 25% above the market price for gas she has acquired from Algeria, and has chosen to buy uranium from Niger at a particularly beneficial price, often one-third above the market value, when that country was in financial trouble. These facts help support France's claim that she gives 'meaning' to the North–South dialogue. Yet the opposite can also happen: Elf-Aquitaine has sometimes paid as little as $7 a barrel of petrol in Gabon when the world price was closer to $34.

72 Charollais and de Ribes, *Le défi de l'outre-mer*, pp. 180-1.

73   Marie Mendras, 'La Stratégie oblique en afrique sub-saharienne', in GERSS, *L'URSS et le Tiers-Monde: Une Stratégie Oblique*, Cahiers de la Fondation pour les Études de Défense Nationale, no. 32, Paris, 1984, pp. 263–9.

Chapter 6   France and Regional Stability in Africa

1   Robert Cornevin, 'Treize Coups d'Etat Africains en trois ans', *Projet*, May 1966, no. 5 Jean-Pierre Pabanel, *Les Coups d'Etat Militaires en Afrique Noire*, Editions l'Harmattan, Paris, 1984.

2   Christian Coulon, *Les musulmans et le pouvoir en afrique noire*, Karthala, Paris, 1983, p. 81.

3   K. Mathews, 'The Organisation of African Unity', in Domenico Mazzeo (ed.), *African Regional Organizations*, Cambridge University Press, 1984, p. 67.

4   Colin Legum, 'The OAU After Twenty Years: An Asset in Jeopardy', *International Herald Tribune*, 26 May 1983.

5   See *Guardian* (London), 30 June 1984.

6   Mathews, 'The Organisation of Africa Unity', p. 67.

7   *Afrique Défense*, 'L'Afrique et sa Défense: Pactes et Accords', April 1984.

8   Alex Rondos, 'Chad: Conflict, Intervention and the OAU', in Nosakhare O. Obasake (ed.), *African Regional Security and the OAU's Role in the Next Decade*, International Peace Academy, Report no. 19, New York, 1984, p. 64.

9   Neil MacFarlane, 'Africa's Decaying Security System and the Rise of Interventionism', *International Security*, Spring 1984.

10   See William Gutteridge, 'The Future of the OAU After Twenty Years', *ISSU and Strategic Review*, August 1983, pp. 16–17.

11   ECOWAS states are Cape Verde, Benin, Ivory Coast, Gambia, Ghana, Guinea, Guinea Bissau, Burkina Faso, Liberia, Mali, Mauritania, Niger, Nigeria, Senegal, Sierra Leone and Togo. All these states except the Cape Verde Islands, Guinea Bissau and Mali signed the agreement.

12   *Défense et Diplomatie*, VI, 4 May 1981, no. 18.

13   See Articles 6, 16, 17, 19 of 'Protocol Relating to Mutual Assistance on Defence', in *Official Journal of the Economic Community of West African States* (ECOWAS), vol. 3, June 1981.

14   Member states: Ivory Coast, Burkina Faso, Mali, Mauritania, Niger and Senegal. Togo is a signatory of the ANAD, and Benin is an observer state.

15   The text of the protocol is published in *African Defense Journal*, May 1983.

16   The member states of ANAD adopted the general definition of aggression used by the UN Charter, though certain heads of state, such as Sankara of Burkina Faso, argued that a definition which made reference to the problem of subversion would be more appropriate.

17   *Marchés Tropicaux et Méditerranéens*, 4 Nov. 1983, p. 2610.

18   'The ANAD Non-Aggression and Defence Assistance Agreement: Serving Peace, the People and the Economy', *African Defense Journal*, Dec. 1983.

19   For details of these various agreements see *Journal Officiel de la République du Sénégal*, 20 Feb. 1988, and 13 Feb. 1988.

20   The words are those of Ivory Coast President, Houphouet-Boigny.

21   See Philippe Decraene, 'Barthelemy Boganda, ou du Projet d'Etat Unitaire Centrafricaine à celui d'Etats-Unis d'Afrique latine', in *Relations Internationales*, 34, Summer 1983, pp. 215–26.

22   *West Africa*, 28 Mar. 1988, p. 552.

Chapter 7   French Economic Power and Black Africa

1 Jacques Marseille, *Empire colonial et capitalisme français: Histoire d'un divorce*, Albin Michel, Paris, 1984, p. 356.
2 This is Jacques Marseille's thesis in the book cited above. Basing his argument on very extensive evidence, he argues that while the interests of the state and French 'capitalism' were close in the prewar period they eventually diverged, until on the eve of decolonization, these interests were essentially 'divorced'.
3 *Plan de modernisation des territoires d'outre-mer*, Présidence du Conseil, 1946, p. 16, cited in Marseille, *Empire colonial*, p. 274.
4 Ibid., p. 365.
5 See remarks reported of Raymond Triboulet in Institut Charles de Gaulle and Institut du Droit de la Paix et du Développement, *De Gaulle et le Tiers Monde*, Editions A. Pédone, Paris, 1984, p. 240.
6 Franck Magnard and Nicolas Tenzer, *La crise africaine: quelle politique de coopération pour la France*, Presses Universitaires de France, Paris, 1988, p. 24.
7 Ibid., pp. 20, 21.
8 Jean-Marcel Jeanneney, *Rapport sur la politique de coopération avec les pays en voie de développement*, Documentation Française, Paris, 1964, pp. 43–4.
9 Ibid., p. 45.
10 See Brigitte Nouaille-Degorce, 'Les Structures et les Moyens de la Politique de Coopération avec les états Africains et Malgache au sud du Sahara de 1958–1969', in Institut Politique de Bordeaux, Centre d'Etudes d'Afrique Noire, *La Politique Africaine de Général de Gaulle 1958–1969*, Editions A. Pédone, Paris, 1981, pp. 96–9.
11 R. C. Robarts, *French Development Assistance, A Study in Policy and Administration*, Sage Publications, London, 1974, p. 71.
12 Jean Poirier and Jean Touscoz, 'Aid and Cooperation: French Official Attitudes as seen in the Jeanneney, Gorse, and Abelin Reports', in W. H. Morris-Jones and Georges Fischer (eds) *Decolonisation and After: The British and French Experience*, Frank Cass, London, 1980, p. 227.
13 Philippe Decraene, 'Le voyage de M. Pompidou en Afrique Noire', *Revue Française d'études politiques africaine*, March 1971, p. 84.
14 Paul Carriere, 'Les Problèmes qui pose à la France dans ses rapports avec les Etats africains et malgache associés et les territoires d'outre-mer l'élargissement des communautés européens', *Rapport au Conseil Economique et Sociale, Journal Officiel*, C.E.S., 22 Feb. 1974, pp. 315–86.
15 *Le Monde*, 31 Mar.–1 Apr. 1974, cited in Albert Bourgi, *La Politique Française de Coopération en Afrique: Le Cas du Sénégal*, Librairie Générale de droit et de jurisprudence, Paris, 1979, p. 137.
16 Pierre Abelin, *Rapport sur la Politique Française de Coopération*, La Documentation Française, Paris, 1975, p. 8.
17 *Le Monde*, 30 Sept. 1974.
18 Abelin, *Rapport sur la Politique*, p. 66.
19 'Le parti socialiste et l'Afrique sub-Saharienne', *Le mois en Afrique*, no. 186–187, 1981, p. 30.
20 Ibid., p. 37.
21 Jean Pierre Cot, *A l'épreuve du pouvoir: le tiers-mondisme, pour quoi faire?*, Editions du Seuil, Paris, 1984, pp. 121–3.

22 'La nouvelle politique de coopération du R.P.R.', *Le mois en Afrique*, 243–244, 1986, p. 3.

23 *Marchés Tropicaux et Méditerranéens*, 14 Oct. 1988, p. 2703.

24 This feature of interdependence is often criticized on the grounds that French politicians might use links existing through the Ministry of Co-operation to impose pressure on African states to accept French positions in international fora, e.g. pressure putatively exerted on African states in 1987 to support the French line on independence to New Caledonia in the UN. See Alain Ruellan, 'Continuités et ruptures des politiques de coopération', *Le Monde Diplomatique*, Jan. 1988, pp. 12–13.

25 This historical information is taken from the 1987 brochure of the *Caisse Centrale de Coopération Economique*.

26 Guy Martin, 'The Franc Zone, underdevelopment and dependency in Francophone Africa', *Third World Quarterly*, Jan. 1986, p. 207.

27 While Algeria, Tunisia and Morocco have their own currencies and their own central banks they retain special drawing accounts at the *Banque de France* which provide them with short-term, limited, monetary assistance. See Martin, ibid., p. 217.

28 Bernard Vinay, 'La zone franc aujourd'hui', *Marchés Tropicaux et Méditerranéens*, 28 Nov. 1986, p. 2979.

29 Mayotte and the French overseas departments and territories are also members, but this part of the study refers only to those states who use the CFA franc.

30 See Vinay, 'La zone franc aujourd'hui', p. 2980.

31 This summary of the old and newer arguments is taken from Marie-France L'Heriteau, 'La Zone Franc dans une perspective d'Ajustement et de Croissance', Document de Travail, Division des Etudes Générales, *Caisse Centrale de Coopération Economique*, May 1987, p. 2.

32 See Vinay, 'La zone franc aujourd'hui', p. 2983.

33 One of the basic rules of the Franc Zone's operations account mechanisms is that the total amount of foreign exhange other than French francs deposited in each central bank's operations account should not exceed 35 per cent of their net foreign reserves (excluding IMF gold tranche and Special Drawing Rights), which in effect means that 65 per cent of the African central banks' foreign reserves must be denominated in French francs. See Martin, *The Franc Zone*, p. 211.

34 Some of these arguments can be found in L'Heriteau, 'La Zone Franc', pp. 12–16.

35 Ibid., p. 17.

36 Cited in François Kouadio, 'La Zone Franc est-elle une zone de démonétisation?', *Le mois en Afrique*, 245–246, June–July 1986, p. 106.

37 See generally Jean Coussy, 'La Zone Franc au Cours des Trois Derniers Décennies (1960–1988)', paper presented to Round Table: Francophone Africa since Independence, St. Antony's College, Maison Française Oxford, April 1988.

38 The most comprehensive and exhaustive comparison between the economies of the Franc Zone and non-Franc Zone states is to be found in Patrick and Sylvanie Guillaumont (eds), *Stratégies de développement comparées: Zone franc et hors Zone franc*, Economica, Paris, 1988. See especially pp. 128–30 for the conclusions cited above.

39 Ibid., 37, p.28.

40 Vinay, 'La zone franc aujourd'hui', p. 2984.

41 Coussy, 'La Zone Franc', note 37, p. 20.

42 These proposals can be found elaborated in Albert Ondo Ossa and Alice Tshibuabua Lapiquonne, 'Faut-il réformer la Zone franc?', *Le mois en Afrique*, no. 215–216, Dec. 1984 and Philippe Hugon, 'Les Modèles et les Performances Économiques des Pays

d'Afrique Francophone', paper presented to Oxford Round Table, April 1988 (as note 34). Summaries of the two systems discussed are taken from the excellent paper by Hugon, pp. 19–22.

43 See for example, Jean-Marc Kalflèche, 'Un Dysfonctionnement mortel', in *Géopolitique Africaine*, no. 8, Apr.–May 1988, p. 21.

44 See Philippe Hugon, 'La politique française de coopération et la crise financière des pays d'Afrique sub-saharienne', *Mondes en Développement*, 14, no. 53, 1986, pp. 35–68.

45 The OCAM was dissolved in 1985.

46 Lynn Krieger Mytelka, 'Competition, conflict and decline in the Union Douanière et Economique de l'Afrique Centrale (UDEAC)', in Domenico Mazzeo, *African Regional Organizations*, Cambridge University Press, 1984, p. 132.

47 Daniel Bach, 'Régionalismes Francophones ou Régionalisme Franco–Africain', paper presented to Oxford Round Table (as note 34), p. 6.

48 Ibid., p. 8.

49 See Hugon, 'La politique française', p. 10.

50 Mytelka, 'Competition, conflict and decline', p. 139

51 *Africa Research Bulletin*, Economic Series, 31 Jan. 1988.

52 *Africa Research Bulletin*, Economic Series, 31 Mar. 1988.

53 Magnard and Tenzer, *La crise africaine*, p. 231.

Chapter 8 The Diplomacy of French Power in Black Africa

1 See Guy de Lusignan, *French Speaking Africa Since Independence*, Pall Mall Press, London, 1969, p. 372 and Edward M. Corbett, *The French Presence in Black Africa*, Black Orpheus Press, Washington DC, 1972, p. 66.

2 Marie-Claude Smouts, 'Bilateral Relations and World Diplomacy: Franco-African relations on trial at the UN', in Morris-Jones and Fischer, (eds) *Decolonisation and After*, p. 349.

3 Cited in ibid., p. 362.

4 Samy Cohen, *Les conseillers du Président: de Charles de Gaulle à Valéry Giscard d'Estaing*, Presses Universitaires de France, Paris, 1980, p. 156.

5 See the statement by Jacques Foccart in Institut Charles de Gaulle and Centre d'Etudes d'Afrique Noire, *La Politique africaine du Général de Gaulle: 1958–1969*, Editions A. Pédone, Paris, 1984, p. 401.

6 Smouts, 'Bilateral Relations', pp. 351–2.

7 Jacques Soubeyrol, 'La Politique Africaine du Général de Gaulle et le Système des Nations Unies', in Institut Charles de Gaulle and Centre d'Etudes d'Afrique Noire, pp. 174–5.

8 Ibid., p. 178.

9 Kolodziej, *Making and Marketing Arms*, p. 369.

10 Cited in Daniel Bach, 'Le Général de Gaulle et la Guerre Civile au Nigéria', in Institut Charles de Gaulle and Centre d'Etudes d'Afrique Noire, p. 345.

11 Ibid.

12 See Marie Claude Smouts, 'La Normalisation des Rapports Franco–Guinéens: Analyse d'Une Médiation', *Revue Française de Science Politique*, 31, 1981, p. 580.

13 Pierre Alexandre, 'Francophonie: The French and Africa', *Journal of Contemporary History*, 4, no. 1, Jan. 1969, p. 120.

14 S. K. Panter-Brick, 'La Francophonie with special reference to educational links and language problems', in Morris-Jones and Fischer (eds), *Decolonisation and After*, p. 339.

15 Jacques Fauvet, 'Une Politique Méditerranéene', *Le Monde*, 24 Jan. 1970.

16 Kolodziej, *Making and Marketing Arms*, p. 358.

17 Ibid., p. 359.

18 Robert Mortimer, 'Algeria and the Politics of International Economic Reform', *Orbis*, Fall 1977.

19 Joseph Limagne, 'France-Algérie: La Fin des Relations Privilégiés', *Revue Française d'Etudes Politiques Africaines*, May 1971.

20 Philippe Decraene, 'Le Voyage de M. Pompidou'.

21 Emeka Nwokedi, 'Franco-African Summits: a new Instrument for France's African strategy?', *The World Today*, 38, no. 12, 1982.

22 Jean-Luc Dagut, 'Les Sommets Franco-Africains: Un Instrument de la Présence Française en Afrique', Centre d'Etude d'Afrique Noire, *Année Africaine 1980*, Editions A. Pédone, Paris, 1981, p. 304.

23 Quoted in ibid., p. 304.

24 Georges Pompidou, *Entretien et Discours: 1968–1974*, vol. 2, Plon, Paris, 1975, p. 221.

25 Charles Zorgibe, 'La diplomatie Giscardien ou les contradictions du "mondialisme"', *Le Monde Diplomatique*, Mar. 1978.

26 Cohen, *Les conseillers du Président*, p. 164.

27 Louis de Guiringaud, 'La Politique Africaine de la France', *Politique Etrangère*, no. 2, June 1982, p. 441.

28 See 'Conférence Franco-Africaine de Bangui', Allocution prononcée par M. Valéry Giscard d'Estaing, a la séance d'ouverture, Bangui, 7 March 1975, *Documents d'Actualité Internationale*, no. 18, 1975.

29 Anonymous, 'Algérie-France: Quatorze ans après', *Revue française d'études politiques africaines*, Apr. 1975, p. 9.

30 Paul Balta, 'French Policy in North Africa', *Middle East Journal*, Spring 1986, p. 242.

31 Cited in J. L. Dagut, 'L'Afrique, La France et Le Monde dans le discours Giscardien', *Politique Africaine*, 5, February 1982.

32 J. E. Peter, 'La sécurité a été la 1ère préoccupation des pays africains a 4ième sommet franco–africain de Dakar', *Afrique Industrie Infrastructures*, no. 140, 15 May 1977, p. 23.

33 Dagut, 'L'Afrique, La France', p. 311.

34 Ibid.

35 *L'Echo de l'Afrique*, Paris, 23 May 1979.

36 Conférence Franco–Africaine (Kigali 21–22 May 1979), Déclaration du président Valéry Giscard D'Estaing, *Documents d'Actualité Internationale*, no. 28, 1979, p. 545.

37 *Journal Officiel*, Assemblée Nationale, 19 Dec. 1979, p. 12318.

38 J. P. Gomane, 'Les Limites de Trilogue', *Le Monde*, 23–24 Mar. 1980.

39 Anonymous, 'Quelques Commentaires sur la Politique Française en Afrique', *Marchés Tropicaux et Méditerranéens*, 26 Sept. 1980.

40 *Note d'Actualité*, 13 May 1980, French Embassy, London.

41 Cited in James O. Goldsborough, 'Dateline Paris: Africa's Policemen', *Foreign Policy*, Winter 1978–1979, p. 180.

42 Cited in Jean-François Bayart, *La Politique africaine de François Mitterrand*, Editions Karthala, Paris, 1984, p. 21.

43 Ibid., p. 100.

44 Claude Wauthier, 'France's Year in Africa: New Emphasis', in *African Contemporary Record 1985–1986*, African Publishing Co., London, 1987, p. A216.

45 Claude Wauthier, 'France's Year in Africa: President Mitterrand's Policies Come under Challenge', *African Contemporary Record, 1984–1985*, African Publishing House, London, 1986, p. A173.
46 Kolodziej, *Making and Marketing Arms*, p. 370.
47 Ibid., p. 371.
48 Wauthier, 'New Emphasis', p. A223.
49 These bilateral strains are nicely summarized in both the Wauthier articles cited above.
50 See generally, Jacques Leprette, 'D'Un Sommet à l'Autre de l'Espace Francophone', *Défense Nationale*, Dec. 1987.
51 Edward Cody, 'France to Cut a Third of Debt Owed by the Poorest Nations', *International Herald Tribune*, 9 June 1988.
52 François Mitterrand, *Reflexions sur la politique extérieure de la France: Introduction à vingt-cinq discours*, Fayard, Paris, 1986.

Conclusion

1 Louis de Guirangaud, 'La Politique Africaine ', pp. 441, 442, 443.
2 Henri Brunschwig, 'De l'Assimilation à la Décolonisation', in Institut d'Histoire du Temps Présent, *Les Chemins de la Décolonisation de l'Empire Colonial Français*, Editions du Centre National de la Recherche Scientifique, Paris, 1986, p. 52.
3 John D. Hargreaves, *Decolonization In Africa*, Longman, Essex, 1988, p. 143.
4 Cited in Marcel Amondji, *Félix Houphouet et le Côte d'Ivoire*, Karthala, Paris, 1984, p. 222.
5 Cited by Jean-Marc Kalflèche, 'France: pour redonner souffle à la coopération', *Géopolitique Africaine*, March 1986, p. 8.

Select Bibliography

This is a selection of some of the more important books relevant to this study. The reader is referred to the footnotes for a comprehensive list of references.

Ageron, Charles-Robert, *France Coloniale ou Parti Colonial*, Presses Universitaires de France, Paris, 1978.

Amondji, Marcel, *Félix Houphouet et la Côte d'Ivoire: l'Envers d'Une légende*, Editions Karthala, Paris, 1984.

Andrew, Christopher M., and Kanya-Forstner, A.S., France Overseas : *The Great War and the Climax of French Imperial Expansion*, Thames and Hudson, London, 1981.

Aron, Raymond, *Peace and War: A Theory of International Relations*, Richard Howard and Annette Baker Fox, Weidenfield and Nicolson, London, 1966.

Balesi, Charles John, *From Adversaries to Comrades-in-Arms: West Africans and the French Military 1885–1914*, Crossroads Press, Massachusetts, 1979.

Baumgart, Winfried, *Imperialism: The Idea and Reality of British and French Colonial Expansion, 1880–1914*, Oxford University Press, 1982.

Bayart, Jean-François, *La Politique Africaine de François Mitterrand*, Karthala, Paris, 1984.

Benoit, Jean-Paul, *Indispensable Afrique*, Berger-Levrault, Paris, 1986.

Betts, R.F., *Assimilation and Association*, Columbia University Press, 1961.

Betts, R.F., *Uncertain Dimensions: Western Overseas Empires in the Twentieth Century*, University of Minnesota Press, Minneapolis, 1985.

Biarnes, Pierre, *Les Français en Afrique Noire De Richelieu à Mitterrand: 350 ans de présence française au sud du Sahara*, Armand Colin, Paris, 1987.

Bourgi, Albert, *La Politique française de Cooperation en Afrique: Le cas de Sénégal*, Librairie générale de droit et de jurisprudence, Paris, 1979.

Bourgi, Robert, *Le Général de Gaulle et l'Afrique Noire 1940–1969*, Librairie générale de droit et de jurisprudence, Paris, 1980.

Bouvier, Jean, Girault, René Thobie, Jacques, *L'Impérialisme à la Française, 1914–1960*, Editions La Découverte, Paris, 1986.

Brunschwig, Henri, *Mythes et Realités de l'impérialisme colonial français, 1871–1914*, Armand Colin, Paris, 1960.

Buijtenhuijs, Robert, *Le Frolinat et les Révoltes Populaires du Tchad, 1965–1976*, Mouton, Paris 1978.

Bury, J.P.T., *Gambetta's Final Years: The Era of Difficulties 1882–1887*, Longman, 1982.

Centre des Hautes Etudes sur l'Afrique et l'Asie Modernes, *L'Afrique Noire Depuis La Conférence de Berlin*, Paris, 1985.

Cerny, Philip G., *The Politics of Grandeur : Ideological Aspects of de Gaulle's Foreign Policy*, Cambridge University Press, 1980.

Chaffard, Georges, *Les Carnets Secrets de la Décolonisation*, two vols, Calmann-Levy, Paris, 1965, 1967.

Chaigneau, Pascal, *La Politique militaire de la France en Afrique*, Centre des Hautes Etudes de l'Afrique Moderne, Paris, 1984.

Chailley-Bert, Joseph, *Dix annees de politique coloniale*, Armand Colin, Paris, 1902.

Charollais, Francois de Ribes, Jean, *Le défi de l'outre-mer: l'action extérieure dans la défense de la France*, Fondation pour les Etudes de Défense Nationale, cahier no. 26, Paris, 1983.

Clayton, Antony, *France, Soldiers and Africa*, Brassey's, London, 1988.

Cohen, Samy, *Les conseillers du Président: de Charles de Gaulle à Valéry Giscard d'Estaing*, Presses Universitaires de France, Paris, 1980.

Comte, Gilbert, *L'Empire Triomphant 1871/1936*, vol. 1, *Afrique occidentale et equatoriale*, Denoel, Paris, 1988.

Corbett, Edward M, *The French Presence in Black Africa*, Black Orpheus Press, Washington DC, 1972.

Cot, Jean Pierre, *A l'épreuve du pouvoir. Le tiers-mondisme pour quoi faire?*, Le Seuil, Paris, 1984.

Coulon, Christian, *Les musulmans et le pouvoir en afrique noire*, Karthala, Paris, 1983.

Couve de Murville, Maurice, *Une Politique Etrangère 1958–1969*, Plon, Paris, 1971.

Curtius, Ernst Robert, *The Civilization of France: An Introduction*, George Allen and Unwin Ltd, London, 1932.

Deffie, Auguste, *Un Plan de Fédération Europafricaine*, Editions Felix Monaho, Rabat, 1954.

Duroselle, J.B. and Meyriat, S., *Politiques Nationales envers Les Jeunes Etats*, Cahiers de la Fondation Nationale des Sciences Politiques, Paris, 1964.

Ecole des Hautes Etudes en Sciences Sociales, *Etudes Africaines: offertes à Henri Brunschwig*, Paris, 1982.

Fidel, Camille, *La Paix Coloniale Française*, Librairie Recueil Sirey, Paris, 1918.

Freud, Claude, *Quelle Coopération? Un bilan de l'aide au développement*, Karthala, Paris, 1988.

Ganiage, Jean, *L'Expansion coloniale de la France sous la Troisième Republique 1871–1914*, Payot, Paris, 1986.

Germain, Commandant Prosper, *La France Africaine*, Plon, Paris, 1907.

GERSS, *L'URSS et le Tiers Monde: Une Stratégie Oblique*, Fondation pour les etudes de Défense Nationale, Paris, 1984.

Gifford, P. and Roger-Louis Wm, *France and Britain in Africa*, Yale University Press, 1971.

Gifford, P. and Roger-Louis Wm, *The Transfer of Power in Africa: Decolonisation 1940–1960*, Yale University Press, 1973.

Girardet, Raoul, *L'idée coloniale en France de 1871–1962* La Table Ronde, 1972, Le livre de Poche, Collection 'Pluriel' Paris, 1979.

Girault, René and Frank, Robert, (eds) *La Puissance en Europe 1938–1940*, Publications de la Sorbonne, Paris, 1984.

Gonidec, P.F., *L'Evolution des territoires d'outre-mer depuis 1946*, Paris, Editions Montchrestien, 1958.

Gonidec, P.F., *Droit d'outre-mer*, Paris, 1960.

Grimal, Henri, *La Décolonisation, 1919–1963*, Armand Colin, Paris, 1967.

Grosser, Alfred, *La politique extérieure de la Vième République*, Editions J. Moulin, Seuil, Paris, 1965.

Guéna, Yves, *Historique de la Communauté*, Fayard, Paris, 1962.

Guillaumont, Patrick and Sylviane (eds) *Stratégies de développement comparées: Zone franc et hors Zone franc*, Economica, Paris, 1988.

Guillen, Pierre, *L'Expansion 1881–1898*, Collection 'Politique Etrangere de la France', Imprimerie Nationale, Paris, 1984.

Guyot, Yves, *Lettres sur la politique coloniale*, Paris, 1885.

Hardy, Georges, *Histoire sociale de la colonisation française*, Larose-Paris, Paris, 1953.

Hargreaves, John D., *West Africa Partitioned*, vol. 1, *The Loaded Pause: 1885–1889*, Macmillan, London, 1974.

Hargreaves, John D., *Decolonization in Africa*, Longman, Essex, 1988.

Horne, Alistair, *A Savage War of Peace: Algeria 1954–1962*, Macmillan Papermac, rev edn, London, 1987.

Institut Charles de Gaulle, and Centre d'Etudes d'Afrique Noire, *La Politique africaine du Général de Gaulle: 1958–1969*, Editions A. Pédone, Paris, 1980.

Institut Charles de Gaulle, and Institut du Droit de la Paix et du Développement, *De Gaulle et le Tiers Monde*, Editions A. Pédone, Paris, 1984.

Institut d'Histoire des relations internationales au XXième siècle, *Mélanges en l'Honneur de Jean Baptiste Duroselle*, Publications de la Sorbonne, Paris, 1986.

Institut d'Histoire du Temps Présent, *Les chemins de la décolonisation de l'Empire français*, Editions du Centre National de la Recherche Scientifique, Paris, 1986.

Joyaux, Francois, and Wajsman, Patrick, *Pour Une Nouvelle Politique Etrangère*, Collection Pluriel, Hachette, Paris, 1986.

Kahler, Miles, *Decolonization in Britain and France: The Domestic Consequences of International Relations*, Princeton University Press, 1984.

Kanya-Forstner, A.S., *The Conquest of the Western Sudan: A Study in French Military Imperialism*, Cambridge University Press, 1969.

Kolodziej, Edward, *French International Policy under de Gaulle and Pompidou, The Politics of Grandeur*, Cornell University Press, 1974.

Kolodziej, Edward, *Making and Marketing Arms: The French Experience and Its Implications for the International System*, Princeton University Press, 1987.

Liniger-Gormez, Max, *L'Eurafrique, utopie ou realité, les Métamorphoses d'une idée*, Editions CLE, Yaoundé, 1972.

Luchaire, François, *Droit d'Outre-Mer*, Presses Universitaires de France, Collection Themis, Paris, 1959.

Lusignan, Guy de, *French Speaking Africa Since Independence*, Pall Mall Press, London, 1969.

Magnard, Franck, and Tenzer, Nicolas, *La crise africaine: quelle politique de coopération pour la France?*, Presses Universitaires de France, Paris, 1988.

Marseille, Jacques, *Empire coloniale et capitalisme francais: Histoire d'un divorce*, Albin Michel, Paris, 1984.

Marseille, Jacques, *L'Age d'Or de la France Coloniale*, Albin Michel, Paris, 1986.

Marshall, D. Bruce, *The French Colonial Myth and Constitution Making in the Fourth Republic*, Yale University Press, 1973.

Martin, Michel Louis, *Warriors to Managers: The French Military Establishment since 1945*, The University of North Carolina Press, Chapel Hill, 1981.

Mazzeo, Domenico, *African Regional Organisations*, Cambridge University Press, 1984.

Michel, Marc, *L'Appel à l'Afrique: Contributions et réactions a l'effort de guerre en AOF, 1914–1919*, Publications de la Sorbonne, Paris, 1982.

Mitterrand, François, *Présence Française et Abandon*, Tribune Libre 12, Paris, 1957.

Mitterrand, François, *Reflexions sur la politique extérieure de la France: Introduction à vingt-cinq discours*, Fayard, Paris, 1986.

Morris-Jones, W.H., and Fischer, Georges (eds), *Decolonisation and After: The British and French Experience*, Frank Cass, London, 1980.

Mortimer, Edward, *France and the Africans*, Faber and Faber, London, 1969.

Neurisse, Andre, *Le Franc C.F.A.*, Librairie Générale de droit et de jurisprudence, Paris, 1987.

Obasake, Nosakhare O., *African Regional Security and the OAU's Role in the Next Decade*, International Peace Academy, Report no. 19, New York, 1984.

Onwuka, R.I., and Sesay, A.(eds) *The Future of Regionalism in Africa*, Macmillan, London, 1985.

Pabanel, Jean Pierre, *Les coups d'états militaires en Afrique noire*, Editions Harmattan, Paris, 1984.

Porch, Douglas, *The Conquest of Morocco: A Savage Colonial War*, Macmillan Papermac, London, 1987.

Ruehl, Lothar, *La Politique Militaire de la Cinquième République*, Fondation Nationale de Sciences Politique, Paris, 1976.

Roger-Louis, Wm, *Imperialism at Bay: The United States and the Decolonisation of the British Empire 1941–1945*, Oxford University Press, New York, 1978.

Ruscio, Alain, *La Décolonisation Tragique: Une histoire de la décolonisation française, 1945–1962*, Messidor, Editions Sociales, Paris, 1987.

Sarrault, Albert, *Grandeur et Servitudes Coloniales*, Editions du Sagittaire, Paris, 1931.

Senghor, Leopold S., *Liberté*, vol. 2, Sevil, Paris, 1977.

Schmokel, W.W., *Dream of Empire : German Colonialism, 1919–1945*, Yale University Press, 1964.

Smith, Tony, *The French Stake in Algeria 1945–1962*, Cornell University Press, 1978.

Smith, Tony, *The Pattern of Imperialism: The United States, Great Britain, and the late industrialising world since 1815*, Cambridge University Press, 1981.

Sorum, Paul Clay, *Intellectuals and Decolonization in France*, University of North Carolina Press, Chapel Hill, 1977.

Spillmann, Georges, *De L'Empire a L'Hexagon: Colonisation et Décolonisation*, Librairie Academique Perrin, Paris, 1981.

Tricontinental, *La France Contre l'Afrique*, Maspero, Paris, 1981.

Twitchett Cosgrove, Carol, *Europe and Africa : from association to partnership*, Saxon House, London, 1978.

Vignon, Louis, *L'Expansion de la France*, Librairie Guillaumin et Cie., Paris, 1891.

Vinay, Bernard, *Zone Franc et Coopération Monetaire*, Ministère de la Coopération, Paris, 1980.

Ward, Sir A.W., Prothero, Sir G.W. and Leathes, Sir Stanley, (eds) *The Cambridge Modern History*, vol. 12, *The Latest Age*, Cambridge, at the University Press, 1934.

Wight, Martin, *Power Politics*, (ed by Hedley Bull and Carsten Holbraad) Leicester University Press, 1978.

White, Dorothy Shipley, *Black Africa and de Gaulle: From the French Empire to Independence*, Pennsylvania State University Press, 1979.

Zeldin, Theodore, *France 1848-1945: Intellect and Pride*, Oxford University Press, 1980.

Index